This book introduces the heartbeat of an African theological agenda developed around the critical question: "What does salvation means for us?" It reads the Bible with an African hermeneutic that is distinctly different from a Western one as it deals with the continent's colonial heritage, African Traditional Religion, and various challenges facing Africa. It opposes the prosperity cult, ethnocentrism, political manipulation, and the ever-present self-centered spectrum of excesses. What does salvation mean where there is poverty, war, refugees, gross injustice, famine, and HIV/AIDS? African theologians understand the interconnectedness of life and the futility of a sacred-secular split. The consensus of the book is that salvation is holistic, it addresses life and afterlife issues. Experiencing salvation is about following Jesus Christ in the power of the Holy Spirit in enacting the kingdom of God. For the church to be true to following Christ, its focus should be on justice, mercy and humbly helping where it hurts. In doing so, suffering is unavoidable.

H. Jurgens Hendriks, PhD
Emeritus Professor Practical Theology and Missiology,
Network for African Congregational Theology Advisor,
Faculty of Theology, Stellenbosch University, South Africa

As Christianity continues to settle and take shape in the lives of many African Christians, there is need to relook at some classical teachings on major doctrinal issues and how these are conceived within the African Christian faith. The ASET volumes are doing just that. This volume, *Salvation in African Christianity*, is extremely relevant to the African Christian because salvation, in African ontology, is intricately tied to death and the African ancestor – an African reality that often clashes with the accepted biblical teaching on the matter.

In response to the question "What must I do to be saved?," the distinguished contributors to this book have provided compelling answers to not only this question but most of the critical issues around salvation through the eyes and ears of the African Christian. They have provided a biblically grounded intellectual piece that is encouraging, readable, and extremely practical using excellent case studies of African communities. The volume compels us to change our views about African scholarship as we deepen our faith and practice. Consequently, this piece will help lay people, theology and Bible students, and prospective foreign missionaries to Africa to understand and appreciate the role of African theologies in global theological discourse.

John Kpaleh Jusu, PhD
Africa International University, Kenya
Theological Education Consultant, United World Mission

Salvation is a central theme in both Christian teachings and in African Christianity. This volume addresses salvation in African Christianity by seasoned and emerging African theologians from an evangelical perspective. The topics discussed in this volume are relevant, biblically grounded, and well articulated by African scholars who are engaging with some of the critical issues facing African Christianity. The depth of the discussions, insights, and issues, addressed from a contextual perspective makes the volume an important contribution not only to African Christian theology but also to the global conversations on salvation and to global Christianity. I strongly recommend this volume to all who desire to know and learn more about Christian theology emerging from the Majority World.

James Nkansah-Obrempong, PhD
Professor of Theology and Ethics,
Dean, NEGST, African International University, Kenya

Africa Society of Evangelical Theology Series

We live with the reality that in these days that the center of Christianity has moved to the Global South and Africa is a key player in that movement. This makes the study of African Christianity and African realities important – even more so when it is being done by Africans themselves and in their own context. The Africa Society of Evangelical Theology (ASET) was created to encourage research and sustained theological reflection on key issues facing Africa by and for African Christians and those working within African contexts. The volumes in this series constitute the best papers presented at the annual conferences of ASET and together they seek to fill this important gap in the literature of Christianity.

TITLES IN THIS SERIES

Christianity and Suffering: African Perspectives
2017 | 9781783683604

African Contextual Realities
2018 | 9781783684731

Governance and Christian Higher Education in the African Context
2019 | 9781783685455

God and Creation
2019 | 9781783687565

Forgiveness, Peacemaking, and Reconciliation
2020 | 9781839730535

Who Do You Say I Am? Christology in Africa
2021 | 9781839735325

The Holy Spirit in African Christianity
2022 | 9781839736469

For more information about the Africa Society of Evangelical Theology, see the Society's Facebook page at:
facebook.com/AfricaSocietyOfEvangelicalTheology
or contact ASET at: asetsecretary@gmail.com

ASET
SERIES

Salvation in
African Christianity

Salvation in African Christianity

General Editors

**Rodney L. Reed
and
David K. Ngaruiya**

© 2023 Africa Society of Evangelical Theology (ASET)

Published 2023 by Langham Global Library
An imprint of Langham Publishing
www.langhampublishing.org

Langham Publishing and its imprints are a ministry of Langham Partnership

Langham Partnership
PO Box 296, Carlisle, Cumbria, CA3 9WZ, UK
www.langham.org

ISBNs:
978-1-83973-918-7 Print
978-1-83973-929-3 ePub
978-1-83973-930-9 PDF

David K. Ngariuya and Rodney L. Reed hereby asserts their moral right to be identified as the Author of the General Editor's part in the Work in accordance with sections 77 and 78 of the Copyright, Designs and Patents Act 1988.

All rights reserved. No part of this publication may be reproduced, stored in a retrieval system or transmitted, in any form or by any means, electronic, mechanical, photocopying, recording or otherwise, without the prior written permission of the publisher or the Copyright Licensing Agency.

Requests to reuse content from Langham Publishing are processed through PLSclear. Please visit www.plsclear.com to complete your request.

All Scripture quotations, unless otherwise indicated, are taken from the Holy Bible, New International Version®, NIV®. Copyright ©1973, 1978, 1984, 2011 by Biblica, Inc.™ Used by permission of Zondervan.

Scripture quotations marked ESV are from The Holy Bible, English Standard Version® (ESV®), copyright © 2001 by Crossway, a publishing ministry of Good News Publishers. Used by permission. All rights reserved.

Scripture quotations marked NKJV are from the Holy Bible, New King James Version (NKJV). Copyright © 1982 by Thomas Nelson, Inc. Used by permission. All rights reserved.

Scripture quotations marked NLT are taken from the Holy Bible, New Living Translation, copyright © 1996, 2004, 2007, 2013, 2015 by Tyndale House Foundation. Used by permission of Tyndale House Publishers, Inc., Carol Stream, Illinois 60188. All rights reserved.

British Library Cataloguing-in-Publication Data
A catalogue record for this book is available from the British Library

ISBN: 978-1-83973-918-7

Cover & Book Design: projectluz.com

Langham Partnership actively supports theological dialogue and an author's right to publish but does not necessarily endorse the views and opinions set forth here or in works referenced within this publication, nor can we guarantee technical and grammatical correctness. Langham Partnership does not accept any responsibility or liability to persons or property as a consequence of the reading, use or interpretation of its published content.

Contents

	Preface	xiii
	Acknowledgments	xv
1	Jeremiah 29:11: Rightly Applying an Old Testament "Salvation" Text	1
	Jamie Viands	
2	Concepts of Repentance and Sanctification in African Perspectives	21
	An Assessment of Biblical and African Understandings of Salvation in African Christianity	
	Daniel M. Mwailu	
3	Salvation – Prosperity or Poverty? An Assessment of African Pentecostal Christianity	39
	Mica Onserio Moenga	
4	"Jesus Is My Personal Savior"	57
	Engaging Evangelical Themes of Individual Salvation in African Communal Contexts	
	Kyama Mugambi	
5	Household Conversions in Acts and Their Significance for House-to-House Evangelism in Africa	73
	Isaac Ampong	
6	A Pauline Theology of Justification and Its Implications for Ecclesiology in Kenya amid Ethnic Divisions	93
	An Exegesis of Galatians 2:11–21	
	Danson Ottawa Wafula and Edwin Mwangi Macharia	
7	Past, Present, and Future	111
	Paul's View of Salvation in the Thessalonian Correspondence	
	Gift Mtukwa	
8	How Can Women Be Saved?	133
	A Reinterpretation of 1 Timothy 2:15 Within a Nigerian Context	
	Moses Iliya Ogidis	

9   Understanding the Soteriological Conceptualization of the Early
    Church Fathers 155
       An Exploration of the Legacy of Athanasius and Its Relevance to
       African Christianity
       Henry Marcus Garba

10 The Sacrifice of Christ in African Perspective 181
       A Contribution to the Atonement Debate
       Samuel K. Bussey

11 Critical Analysis of the Doctrine of Adoption through the Honor
    and Shame Paradigm 207
       An African Perspective
       Kenosi Molato

12 A Balanced Approach to Understanding the Concept of Salvation
    in Contemporary African Christianity 225
       Joseph Mavulu

13 An Exploration of Understanding Seven Dimensions of Salvation
    in African Christianity... 241
       David K. Ngaruiya

14 Holism in Salvation 273
       Philemon Ongole

15 The Logical Implications of Trinitarian Exclusivism............. 293
       Joseph B. Onyango Okello

16 Emerging Soteriological Issues in African Christianity in the Light
    of Resurgent African Cultures 307
       The Practice of Ancestral Debts
       Kamau Thairu

17 Finding New "Alphabets" for Proclaiming Salvific Faith in Africa.... 325
       Julius Kithinji and Pauline K. Mwaura

18 Salvation and the Problem of Negative Ethnicity and Schism in
    the Church in Kenya 341
       Toward an *Ubuntu* Salvation Theology
       Rev. Jackline Makena Mutuma and Rev. Dr. John M. Kiboi

19 An All-Embracing, Contextual, Challenging, Now and Not Yet
    Salvation for Ugandan Rural Communities 357
       Timothy J. Monger

20 An Exploration of Pentecostal Theology and Praxis of
    Salvation in Kenya 381
        Kevin Muriithi Ndereba

Contributors 401

Subject Index 407

Scripture Index 411

Preface

"What must I do to be saved?" That question, raised in the book of Acts by the jailer in Philippi, is a question for the ages. Wherever the gospel of Jesus Christ has been, is, or will be preached, this question must be answered in some form. Standing behind (or perhaps in the foreground of) this question is an entire set of other questions: What does it mean to be saved? What is the nature and extent of salvation? Salvation from what? Salvation for what? What role does the death of Christ play in our salvation? Is salvation for this life or the next? Is salvation something of a purely spiritual nature or does it have physical/material consequences as well? Who will be saved and who will not? Does God determine who will be saved or do we? What, if any, are the conditions for salvation? Can salvation be lost? Does salvation apply to humans only or does the entire cosmos participate in it? These questions demand answers.

Just as questions such as those above have been asked down through the ages, so too have answers been given, and those answers have reflected the rich variety of human culture and experience. The study of theology, more specifically *soteriology*, attempts to answer them in a consistent and rational manner. The growth of Christianity across the Global South and in particular in Africa makes listening to African voices on the subject of soteriology all the more important because the African experience of salvation in Jesus Christ will increasingly shape the entire world's understanding of it. One only need note that among the most vibrant worshipping congregations in some parts of Europe and America are those populated by immigrants from Africa!

So, how do Africans experience salvation in Christ? (Of course, that is a myopic way of putting the question because Africa is so diverse.) This volume responds to that question and indeed all of the great questions mentioned above that surround the Christian doctrine of soteriology. The largest set of chapters in this volume digs into what the Bible says about salvation. Various passages of Scripture are examined for their implications for salvation, conversion, poverty/prosperity, ethnicity, eschatology, and even fertility. This is followed by a collection of chapters addressing the topic of soteriology from historical, systematic, and philosophical perspectives. It begins by consulting one of the great North African fathers, Athanasius, and moves on to examine salvation through the lenses of the atonement, adoption, and wholeness/holism. These chapters continue with a look at seven dimensions of salvation in African Christianity and conclude with a Trinitarian look at the matter of exclusivism (who will and will not be saved?). The final collection of chapters in this volume focuses more on the practical implications of soteriology and its specific relation to African life and practices, including ancestral debts, negative ethnicity, rural community, and African Pentecostalism.

The chapters in this, the eighth volume in the ASET Series are discrete units. Therefore, the reader is welcome to check out the Table of Contents and find something of interest and start reading from there. While six countries are represented among the authors, these chapters were originally presented as papers at the eleventh annual conference of the Africa Society of Evangelical Theology at which scholars presented from twenty-five countries of service or origin. This alone speaks to the richness of God's salvation.

Welcome to the feast!

Rodney L. Reed, PhD
Editor, ASET Editorial Committee
Associate Professor,
Africa Nazarene University, Nairobi, Kenya

Acknowledgments

The chapters in this volume represent the best of the papers presented at the eleventh annual conference of the Africa Society of Evangelical Theology (ASET), which was held at Africa Nazarene University (ANU) in Nairobi, Kenya, on 4–5 March 2022. This conference took place in the midst of the COVID-19 pandemic which had a lasting global impact particularly in the use of technology. This was a hybrid conference where some ASET members gathered at Africa Nazarene University while others participated virtually. Despite the challenges of the pandemic, this eighth volume in the ASET Series contains a resilient international aroma, with contributions from scholars either originally from or now serving in Kenya, Nigeria, Ghana, the USA, Botswana, the UK, Uganda, and the Netherlands.

The Editorial Committee of ASET is very grateful to Africa Nazarene University for hosting the 2022 hybrid conference. We are also very thankful to the contributors of these papers who worked unwearyingly with the Editorial Committee to make some revisions to them. We appreciate and acknowledge the indispensable role of all our reviewers, in conference proposals as well as post-conference papers. Their role was instrumental in helping identify the best-quality papers presented at the conference. We also owe an enormous debt of gratitude to the team at Langham Publishing, and especially Mark Arnold, who have worked with ASET on this eighth volume. Our special thanks also to our spouses, Sarah Reed and Annie Ngaruiya, for their unwavering support. Finally, to my editorial partner, Rodney Reed: thank you so much for helping to bear the load.

David K. Ngaruiya, PhD
Chair, ASET Editorial Committee
Associate Professor,
International Leadership University, Nairobi, Kenya

1

Jeremiah 29:11: Rightly Applying an Old Testament "Salvation" Text

Jamie Viands

Lecturer, Biblical Studies Department, NEGST/Africa International University

Abstract

There are few verses in the Old Testament that are more loved and more frequently quoted than Jeremiah 29:11, no doubt due to the "hopeful future" it promises, a message of salvation for God's people. Many Christians in Africa today understand this verse as a promise of imminent improvements in the quality of their lives, supporting the "prosperity theology" that is pervasive in many churches. This chapter examines the text in its original context to demonstrate that even for the original audience the timing and nature of this future hope are different from what is commonly believed. It then compares the original old covenant context to our present new covenant context to explore how the concepts present in Jeremiah 29:11 ought to be faithfully applied today. It concludes that while God does have a hopeful future in store for his people, this hope lies beyond our present lives, and the nature of this hope is not primarily focused on comfort in life but rather fellowship with Christ and final sanctification and glorification in the new creation.

Key words: Jeremiah 29, hope, salvation, application, prosperity, false prophecy, exile, return

Introduction

Within the context of the new covenant, salvation is most commonly associated with forgiveness of sins, deliverance from God's eternal wrath and judgment, and eternal life (e.g. Acts 4:12; Eph 1:3–13; 1 Thess 5:9; Heb 5:9). However, within the Old Testament, salvation typically entails God's deliverance of his people from their current difficulties, dealing with temporal rather than eternal concerns. Prior to the coming of Christ, the greatest act of God's salvation in Israel's history was his rescue of his people from slavery in Egypt. The dramatic deliverance at the Red Sea is celebrated as "the salvation of the LORD" (וּשִׁי הְוָהי תֶע; Exod 14:13; cf. 14:30; 15:2). A similar emphasis is evident above all in the Psalms. The primary Hebrew root that denotes salvation, ישׁע, occurs in its various forms 136 times in the Psalter, usually in the context of either requesting or acknowledging salvation from present suffering (e.g. 3:8 [Eng 7]; 7:2 [1]; 18:3–4 [2–3]; 34:7 [6]).[1]

In the book of Jeremiah, in light of the looming Babylonian threat, the people are inclined to turn to other gods for salvation (Jer 2:27–28; 11:12) and fail to acknowledge that God alone can save (3:23; 4:14). Therefore, though he will save faithful Jeremiah (15:20; cf. 17:14), God will not save wicked Judah (8:20) but will instead hand them over to Babylon. Yet Jeremiah anticipates that God *will* save them in the future after their period of judgment is ended. This salvation entails a reunified nation prospering under a just Davidic king (23:5–6; 33:14–16), but first and foremost rescue from their Babylonian oppressors and return to the promised land (23:3–8; 30:10–11; 31:7–9; 46:27–28).[2]

One of the best-loved, most frequently quoted verses in the Old Testament, Jeremiah 29:11, occurs in the context of one of Jeremiah's salvation texts (29:10–14).[3] Clinging to the promise of a "hopeful future," many Christians in Africa understand this verse to be a guarantee of imminent improvements in the quality of their lives, supporting the "prosperity theology" that is pervasive in many churches. Jeremiah 29:11 is employed to provide assurance that students will pass their exams, that a lonely young man will soon find a spouse, that

---

1. See Robert L. Hubbard Jr., "ישׁע," in *New International Dictionary of Old Testament Theology and Exegesis*, ed. Willem A. VanGemeren, vol. 2 (Grand Rapids: Zondervan, 1997), 559–61.

2. The concept of salvation is more pervasive in the book than is reflected in this summary; we have confined our focus here to the use of explicit language of "salvation" based on the ישׁע root.

3. Although the root ישׁע ("save," "salvation") does not appear in 29:10–14, the concept of salvation is central to this text since it emphasizes return from exile, which, as noted, is the primary referent for "salvation" in the book of Jeremiah.

financial breakthrough is lurking right around the corner, or that God will soon heal a chronic bodily ailment.

But is this a valid use of this verse? Does it in fact provide such assurances? In order to answer these questions, we will first examine Jeremiah 29:11 in its original context. Then we will consider in what ways Jeremiah 29:11 does not apply to us today, as well as the ways in which it does, primarily based on a comparison of the original old covenant context with our present new covenant context. It is commonly assumed that Old Testament (OT) texts can be directly applied to New Testament (NT) believers, but this is not necessarily the case since the coming of Christ has brought about various changes and transformations in the way that God relates to his people. Thus, the aim of this chapter is not only to serve as a corrective for misuse of Jeremiah 29:11, but also to model sound application of OT texts.

Jeremiah's Letter to the Exiles (29:4–23)

In 605 and 597 BC the Babylonians under Nebuchadnezzar had already deported some of God's people to Babylon, especially those in the upper classes. The climactic destruction of Jerusalem and the temple, and the final wave of exile, was still to come in 586 BC. During this time (597–586) prophets were active both in Jerusalem and among the exilic community in Babylon, proclaiming salvation and prosperity rather than further judgment (see, e.g., 27:12–22). It is not difficult to imagine that these prophets would have gained a wide hearing since this was the message the people wanted to hear. Hananiah was a prime example of these prophets in Jerusalem, predicting that within two short years those who had been exiled would return (28:2–4, 11).[4] In response, Jeremiah denounced and proclaimed judgment against Hananiah since he had caused the people to "trust in a lie [שֶׁקֶר]" (28:15). Instead, much to the consternation of prophets, kings, and people, Jeremiah proclaimed that their situation would only get worse before it got better (e.g. 24:8–10; 25:8–14; 27:6–8).

---

4. It is likely that the message of Hananiah and others was rooted in a belief that Jerusalem and the temple were invincible due to God's presence and power, especially based on the events in 701 BC when God defeated Assyria in the days of Hezekiah (2 Kgs 18–19; see, e.g., William J. Dumbrell, *The Faith of Israel: A Theological Survey of the Old Testament*, 2nd ed. (Grand Rapids: Baker, 2002), 143.

In order to address this false teaching in faraway Babylon, he writes a letter to the elders and people there, now recorded for us in Jeremiah 29:4–23.[5] Verses 1–3 provide the details of the context of the letter, including its recipients (v. 1), approximate timing (v. 2),[6] and the "mailman" (v. 3). We then find the content of the letter itself, structured as follows:

- Command: Settle in to life in Babylon (4–7)
- Command: Don't listen to your prophets (8–9)
- Promise: I will restore you when you call on me (10–14)
- Coming judgment: Those who remain in Jerusalem (15–19)
- Coming judgment: Two false prophets in exile (20–23)

The introduction to the letter in verse 4 provides the fundamental theological lens both for the content of the whole letter and for the events it addresses: this is a message from God himself, and though Nebuchadnezzar has served as his instrument (see v. 1), God is the one who has sovereignly orchestrated the exile and banished his people to Babylon. He first commands the exiles to build houses, plant gardens, get married, and have families (vv. 5–6). These basic activities of human existence and flourishing are naturally pursued by people who are already settled where they wish to reside, but will be placed "on hold" by those who believe their current situation is quite temporary. By commanding these activities, the message is loud and clear: "Settle down; get comfortable; go on with 'normal life' as best you can, because *you are going to be there for quite some time.*" This message is reinforced in verse 7 as they are encouraged to pursue the welfare or "prosperity" (שָׁלוֹם) of Babylon, precisely because they will themselves benefit from this since it will be their home for now. They have been looking for and hoping in a near-term salvation, namely, deliverance from Babylon, oppression, and the difficulties associated with living in a foreign land, but this hope is futile. Since this is not

---

5. Jeremiah Unterman rightly notes that this material is carefully and perfectly situated within the larger book: "Chapter 29 has two interests – the favorable future of the Jehoiachin exiles and the false prophets in their midst. As such, it is situated between Jeremiah's confrontation with the false prophet Hananiah in ch. 28 and the redemption messages of the 'book of comfort' in chs. 30–31." *From Repentance to Redemption: Jeremiah's Thought in Transition*, JSOTSup 54 (Sheffield: JSOT, 1987), 83.

6. Given the details provided in v. 2, the letter is sent sometime after 597 and before 586, but cannot otherwise be dated precisely. Some suggest that the letter may coincide with a period of rebellion and unrest in Babylon in 595/594, as recorded in "The Babylonian Chronicle" (see J. A. Thompson, *The Book of Jeremiah*, NICOT (Grand Rapids: Eerdmans, 1979), 544; G. L. Keown et al., *Jeremiah 26–52*, WBC (Dallas: Nelson, 1995), 69. It is plausible to suggest that the false prophets would have encouraged rebellion and hope during such a time, but ultimately this date remains speculative.

God's plan, for now their best hope is to make the most of a decidedly less-than-ideal situation as they endure God's judgment.

The next section (introduced again with the divine speech formula) reinforces this message, but directly confronts the primary issue, which provides the rationale for why Jeremiah has written the letter: their "prophets" are misleading them (vv. 8–9): "Do not let your prophets and your diviners who are among you deceive you, and do not pay attention to your dreams that you are dreaming.[7] For it is a lie they are prophesying to you in my name. I did not send them, declares the LORD."[8]

Jeremiah is presenting the people with a choice to make between competing prophets with competing and contradictory messages. Should they heed the "prophets of hope" who claim to have a message of imminent salvation from the Lord, a message which clearly demands a certain kind of "faith" since humanly speaking it may seem unlikely that powerful Babylon would so soon be overcome so that they might return home? Or should they heed this lone "prophet of doom" who also claims to speak for God? If there was any doubt about who the true prophet of God was at the time, it would become evident as events unfolded over the next few years and the predictions of the "prophets of hope" did not transpire (cf. Deut 18:20–22; Jer 28:9).

But God's (and Jeremiah's) message for the people does not end here. God *does*, in fact, intend to save and restore his people, and bring them back to their own land (vv. 10–14). However, this is a distant hope. Only after seventy years of Babylonian domination[9] will God orchestrate their return (v. 10). This is beyond the lifetimes of all (or nearly all) of those receiving this letter, and the message would have been clear to them: you will not personally see

---

7. Some English translations employ third-person pronouns and read similar to the ESV, "do not listen to the dreams that they dream," since this seems to fit better in context (cf. NLT, NRSV). However, Hebrew manuscripts uniformly use second-person pronouns, literally, "do not listen to your dreams that you are dreaming" (וְאַל־תִּשְׁמְעוּ אֶל־חֲלֹמֹתֵיכֶם אֲשֶׁר אַתֶּם מַחְלְמִים). The second-person pronouns are best retained, likely implying that these "dreams" ultimately represent the hopes of the people themselves, which are encouraged and reinforced by the prophets. Perhaps the hiphil should be rendered causatively, leading to the NIV translation, "Do not listen to the dreams you encourage them to have."

8. This is my translation here and throughout, unless otherwise noted.

9. Scholars debate both whether this is to be understood as a literal or approximate number as well as when this period begins. The most likely understanding is that the period begins with the first "wave" of exile in 605 and ends with the fall of Babylon in 538, a period of sixty-seven years, easily rounded to seventy (see Keown et al., *Jeremiah 26–52*, 74–75, for a summary of positions).

the return. This lends further clarity to and justification for[10] the need for the people to continue to get married and have children: it is future generations, not they themselves, who will experience this restoration.

The rest of the letter returns to the theme of present judgment. First, Jeremiah describes the fate of those who have (so far) remained in Jerusalem (vv. 15–19). Most would naturally assume they were the ones who had been favored by God. On the contrary, they are like "bad figs" (v. 17; see 24:8–10) who will be judged (vv. 17–18) since they, like the exiles, have refused to listen to God through his true prophets (v. 19). Finally, he pronounces judgment upon two particular false prophets, Ahab and Zedekiah (vv. 20–23), who are among those who are telling "a lie" (שֶׁקֶר; cf. v. 9) in God's name.

We are not told how the exilic community as a whole reacted to Jeremiah's letter, but the rest of Jeremiah 29 records the response of yet another false prophet, Shemaiah. He writes to the people in Jerusalem and to the priestly leaders to denounce and complain about the message of Jeremiah that "your exile will be long" (v. 28), encouraging them to "rebuke" (v. 27) this "madman" Jeremiah (v. 26). In response, God instructs Jeremiah to write yet another letter to the exiles (vv. 29–32) proclaiming God's judgment against Shemaiah and his descendants (v. 32) because he had caused them to "trust in a lie" (וַיַּבְטַח אֶתְכֶם עַל־שָׁקֶר; v. 31).[11] Thus he further reinforces that there is no near-term salvation – only judgment for those who would dare to predict it!

God's Promise of Future Salvation (vv. 10–14)

Bearing this context in mind, we must look more closely at the message of future salvation and how verse 11 contributes to it.[12] At the heart of this hope is God's commitment to deliver them from Babylon and restore them to their own land:

---

10. Verses 10–14 are introduced with כִּי, which likely conveys that this section provides the grounds for the commands of vv. 4–9.

11. Given that this is the same phrase used of Hananiah in 28:15, Leslie C. Allen appropriately observes, "Shemaiah abroad was as reprobate as Hananiah at home." *Jeremiah*, OTL (Louisville: Westminster/John Knox, 2008), 322.

12. Many critical scholars contend that some or all of vv. 10–14 are a late Deuteronomic redaction (see Unterman, *From Repentance*, 62–63). See William L. Holladay, *Jeremiah*, vol. 2, Hermeneia (Minneapolis: Fortress, 1989), 132–33, for an example of a scholar who gives priority to the LXX translation and thus omits about half of the content of vv. 10–14 as original, including some of v. 11. We cannot delve into such complex issues here, but will assume Jeremiah's authorship and the priority of the Masoretic Text for our purposes.

Jeremiah 29:11: Rightly Applying an Old Testament "Salvation" Text

> For thus says the LORD: When seventy years are completed for Babylon, I will visit you and fulfill my good promise concerning you, namely, to bring you back to this place. Because I know the plans I have concerning you, declares the LORD, plans for welfare and not for disaster, plans to give you a hopeful future. (vv. 10–11)

When God's allotted period of punishment, characterized by Babylonian supremacy over Judah (cf. 25:11–12), comes to an end, he will act on their behalf once again. Whereas he had previously "visited" (פָּקַד) Judah through punishment,[13] bringing disaster (רָעָה; 4:6; 6:19; 11:11, 23; 18:11; 19:3; 21:10) upon them, now he will "visit" (אֶפְקֹד) Israel through salvation. His purpose is to fulfill his prior promise (דְּבָרַי הַטּוֹב; cf. 23:3–8; 24:4–7; 27:22; 33:14)[14] to orchestrate a "second exodus" event, bringing them back to Canaan.

Verse 11 then provides the reason for this reversal in God's attitude toward the people: his ultimate intention for – and fundamental disposition toward – them is goodness (cf. 31:3, 9, 20; 32:40–41).[15] These "plans" or "intentions" (הַמַּחֲשָׁבֹת) are expressed through quite general language. These are plans "for welfare" (מַחְשְׁבוֹת שָׁלוֹם): for the present the "welfare" (שָׁלוֹם) of the people depends upon the welfare of the city of their exile (v. 7), but in the future God himself will work for their welfare by delivering them from this city.[16] In other words, these are not plans for "disaster" (לְרָעָה).[17] Previously, this is precisely what God had planned against them if they continued to ignore the call to

---

13. פָּקַד occurs thirty-seven times in Jeremiah. The majority of these uses refer to how God will punish his own people (5:9, 29; 6:15; 9:9, 25; 11:22; 14:10; 21:14; 23:2, 34; 29:32; 30:20; 36:31; 44:13, 29), though in some cases it refers to his judgment of other nations (25:12; 27:8; 46:25; 49:8; 50:18, 31; 51:44, 47, 52). Apart from 29:10, only in 27:22 does he "visit" Judah in a salvific sense.

14. Keown et al., *Jeremiah 26–52*, 62, note that the expression "good word" "usually has a more legal-contractual sense in the OT and in other ancient Near Eastern sources," and could thus be translated "pledge."

15. See Walter Brueggemann, *A Commentary on Jeremiah: Exile and Homecoming* (Grand Rapids: Eerdmans, 1998), 258. Gerald H. Wilson translates the first phrase of the verse "I alone know the plans . . ." and suggests that this unusual expression is designed to emphasize God's freedom to act and reveal as he sees fit, over against the false prophets who wrongly claim to know these plans. "The Prayer of Daniel 9: Reflection on Jeremiah 29," *Journal for the Study of the Old Testament* 48 (1990): 95, 98.

16. Brueggemann notes that whereas "shalom" was a task for the exiles in v. 7, in v. 11 it is a gift from God (*Commentary on Jeremiah*, 259).

17. Since this is likely an allusion to God's past actions toward the people, it is better to translate this as "disaster" rather than the traditional "evil" to avoid the implication that God performs morally evil deeds. See NIV: "plans to prosper you and not to harm you."

repent (see 18:11; 26:3; 36:3),[18] but such designs are now a thing of the past. In other words, these are plans for "a hopeful future" (אַחֲרִית וְתִקְוָה).[19]

Given the logic of these verses, it is clear that these "plans for welfare" do not entail any and all manner of prosperity as defined by the people, but rather the specific promise as defined by God that he will restore the people to their land.[20] Notably, the only other place in the book where similar language of a "hopeful future" appears (וְיֵשׁ־תִּקְוָה לְאַחֲרִיתֵךְ; 31:17) likewise refers to their return to the land (31:16–17). In light of the content of Deuteronomy 30:1–10 (see vv. 5, 9), which may serve as Jeremiah's "source text," and restoration texts elsewhere in Jeremiah (e.g. 30:18–21; 31:4–14, 23–28), this return may further imply enjoyment of God's many blessings in the land, though this is not explicit here. Since God will then be favorably disposed toward his people, we might assume that a physical return is only the beginning of this goodness.[21]

The following verses expand on this future deliverance, but focus on God's renewed accessibility, emphasizing how the people will approach him (plain text) and how he will respond (italics):

> You will call to me
>   and come
> and pray to me
>   *and I will hear you.*
> You will search for me
>   *and you will find me*
> when you seek me with all your heart. (vv. 12–13)[22]

The five actions of the people, calling (וּקְרָאתֶם), coming (וַהֲלַכְתֶּם), praying (וְהִתְפַּלַּלְתֶּם), searching (וּבִקַּשְׁתֶּם), and seeking (תִדְרְשֻׁנִי), cannot be easily distinguished as separate activities, but together express a holistic and wholehearted (v. 13b) seeking after the Lord. Previously, when God had been determined to judge them, he refused to "hear" (שָׁמַע) them when they "called to" him (קְרָאָם; 11:14; see also 11:11). Thus not even Jeremiah himself was to

---

18. Note that each of these three texts employs the same language as 29:11 whereby God "planned" (חָשַׁב) "disaster" (רָעָה) against his people.

19. This expression is likely to be understood as hendiadys (see Prov 23:18; 24:14 where these are complementary terms). See, e.g., John Bright, *Jeremiah*, AB 21 (New York: Doubleday, 1965), 209; F. B. Huey Jr., *Jeremiah, Lamentations*, NAC (Nashville: Broadman, 1993), 254.

20. See Richard L. Schultz, *Out of Context: How to Avoid Misinterpreting the Bible* (Grand Rapids: Baker, 2012), 82.

21. See Christopher J. H. Wright, *The Message of Jeremiah*, BST (Nottingham: Inter-Varsity, 2014), 295.

22. Formatted here as separate clauses for the sake of analysis.

bother to pray for them (7:16; 11:14; 14:11). Previously, the people did not "search for" (מְבַקֵּשׁ) truth (5:1) or "seek" (דְרָשׁוּ) God (10:21). But in exile all of this will change: his people will[23] seek him, and when they call to him and pray to him he will once again be responsive.[24] Thus this promise adds to their present and future hope, reinforcing that even while they are still in exile God will not remain distant. "Their hope lies in God's willingness to be found, not in Israel's ability to search."[25]

Thus the most natural way to understand these verses, especially in light of verse 14, is that this search for God will take place prior to, and possibly as a prerequisite for, their return to the land.[26] Doubtless this is how Daniel understood this same text. Just after the fall of Babylon, at the completion of the seventy-year period, he realizes that the time for return has arrived according to Jeremiah 25:11 and 29:10–14 (Dan 9:1–2). In response, he "seeks [the LORD]

---

23. Each of the first six clauses begins with a *weqatal* verb. The verbs for which the people are the subject could be understood as contingent commands (i.e. "call . . . come. . . . pray . . . search . . . seek"), indicating that *if* they do these things, then God "will hear" them and they "will find" him (see LXX). Alternatively, these could be predictions, assurances that they *will* seek out God, resulting in God's favorable response (see ESV; NIV; KJV; John Calvin, *Commentaries on the Book of Jeremiah and the Lamentations*, vol. 3, trans. John Owen (Grand Rapids: Eerdmans, 1950), 434–35; Wright, *Message of Jeremiah*, 296). The latter understanding is preferable in light of the prior guarantee that he will restore them to the land (v. 10). Christopher Wright explains, "The movement of the people's heart to seek God is itself a gift of God's grace, even while it is at the same time the necessary condition in which they can receive his grace. God's grace gives what God demands" (*Message of Jeremiah*, 296).

24. Keown et al., *Jeremiah 26–52*, 76; Terence E. Fretheim, *Jeremiah*, SHBC (Macon: Smyth and Helwys, 2002), 403–5, 410. Many have suggested that vv. 12–13 envision the people's repentance (see, e.g., Unterman, *From Repentance*, 85–86; Brueggemann, *Commentary on Jeremiah*, 259; Calvin, *Jeremiah*, 434–35). This is quite possible, perhaps even likely, since these verbs do often occur in contexts where repentance is explicit (Deut 4:29–31; Hos 3:5; 5:15 – 6:1), and it is hard to envision "seeking God with all one's heart" without turning from sin. Nevertheless, it is noteworthy that the key term for repentance in both Deuteronomy and Jeremiah, שׁוּב, is not employed here. Perhaps this is deliberate since the main point appears to be God's renewed accessibility rather than Israel's repentance.

25. Wright, *Message of Jeremiah*, 296.

26. Unterman, *From Repentance*, 85; Tremper Longman III, *Jeremiah, Lamentations*, NIBC (Peabody: Hendrickson, 2008), 194; J. Andrew Dearman, *Jeremiah/Lamentations*, NIVAC (Grand Rapids: Zondervan, 2002), 262; Thompson, *Book of Jeremiah*, 547; Walter Brueggemann, *The Theology of the Book of Jeremiah* (Cambridge: Cambridge University Press, 2007), 119; Huey, *Jeremiah*, 254. The introductory *weqatal* verb of v. 12 (וּקְרָאתֶם) is thus understood to indicate expansion on the content introduced in v. 10 rather than as a temporal progression, as appears to be indicated by many English translations that begin v. 12 with "then" (e.g. ESV, NIV, KJV, NRSV).

by prayer" (לְבַקֵּשׁ תְּפִלָּה; Dan 9:3), confessing the sins of the people and pleading with God to fulfill his promise to restore them to the land (Dan 9:4–19).[27]

The final verse of the message of salvation (v. 14) does not introduce new ideas, but summarizes the content of verses 10–13:

> I will be found by you, declares the LORD, and I will restore your fortunes[28] and gather you from all the nations and from all the places where I had scattered you, declares the LORD, in order to bring you back to the place from which I sent you into exile.

The first clause of the verse ("I will be found by you") summarizes the primary point of verses 12–13, namely, God's renewed availability to the people.[29] After they "find" God,[30] he will bring them back to the land so that the message concludes in the same way as it began in verse 10, forming an inclusio around the text. Remarkably, even as God stresses his favorable disposition toward his people through salvation, he reminds them twice that he is the same God who had judged them for their sin: he had "scattered" them (8:3; 16:15; 23:3, 8; 24:9), but now he will "gather" them (23:3; 31:8; 32:37); he had "exiled" them, but now he will "bring them back."

Thus, at present the experience of the people is that God "will by no means clear the guilty" (Exod 34:7b), but Jeremiah grants them hope that God is also "merciful and gracious, slow to anger, and abounding in steadfast love and faithfulness, keeping steadfast love for a thousand generations, forgiving iniquity and transgression and sin" (Exod 34:6–7a). God is gracious to preserve

---

27. It is tempting to associate vv. 12–13 with the new covenant realities described in 31:31–34, based on God's gift of a new heart (24:7; cf. Deut 30:6). However, given that these promises are fulfilled centuries after the physical return at Christ's first advent, and since it would defy the logical flow of the text to divorce vv. 12–13 from the physical return from the land, it is best to view this pursuit of God as something apart from (though perhaps anticipating) these new covenant promises. Fretheim comments, "The seeking of the Lord in v. 13 assumes a time before the new heart and the new covenant is given, when seeking is no longer necessary" (*Jeremiah*, 411).

28. This common expression in Jeremiah (אֶת־שְׁבוּתְכֶם; 11, 8x in Jer 29–33) is often associated with return to the land (30:3; 31:23; 32:44; 33:11; cf. Deut 30:3), and may entail little more than this in this context (see John M. Bracke, "*Sûb sebût*: A Reappraisal," *Zeitschrift für die alttestamentliche Wissenschaft* 97 (1985): 237). See Bracke, 233–44, for a review of scholarship on this idiom and a defense of the translation "restore your fortunes, "denoting a reversal of judgment.

29. Although some argue that this clause belongs with the previous section and that the final clause of v. 13 is dependent upon it (e.g. Unterman, *From Repentance*, 62; Bright, *Jeremiah*, 205; Allen, *Jeremiah*, 320), v. 13 is nearly an exact quote from Deut 4:29, which indicates that the final clause of v. 13 is subordinate to the prior clause rather than to the following one.

30. The *weqatal* sequence (וְשַׁבְתִּי) likely indicates temporal progression.

them in exile, he is gracious to enable them to cry out to him once again, he is gracious to respond, and he is gracious to save and bring them back to their land. He has broken them down, but he will also build them up (Jer 1:10). Rather than despair that there will be no imminent deliverance, the exiles are to press on in faithfulness (29:5–9) and faith in these future promises (vv. 10–14).

Applying Jeremiah 29:11 for the New Testament Church

Jeremiah 29:11 is often used by Christians today as though it expresses a general principle that God plans all kinds of good for all kinds of people in all places and at all times. However, as explained above, the promise of a "hopeful future" pertains to a specific situation for God's people in Babylonian exile in the sixth century BC. Therefore, this promise does not *directly* apply to contemporary Christians since it is not addressed to them. This does not mean, though, that this portion of God's word is of no relevance for us. It remains "profitable" and applicable in various ways (see 2 Tim 3:16), but we must be careful in discerning precisely *how* the ideas found in Jeremiah 29:11 remain instructive today.

We will explore six different aspects of Jeremiah 29:11 to discern in what ways it does and does not apply today. Two principles will guide us in doing so: (1) The application of verse 11 must be consistent with what it teaches in its original literary and historical context. Thus our exposition above will be crucial to ensure that potential applications are not in tension or at odds with its original meaning. (2) We must explore how the ideas found in verse 11 are developed or transformed in light of the coming of Jesus Christ. Jeremiah 29 is situated within the context of the old covenant between God and the nation of Israel, but Christians today relate to God in the context of a new covenant mediated and enacted by Jesus Christ. Therefore, we must consider the entire teaching of the New Testament to determine how concepts found in verse 11 apply today. To use a simple analogy, a father may promise to give one of his children money, intended for payment of school fees. Another of his children may wish to "claim" this promise of money for him- or herself, to be used in some other fashion. But it would be inappropriate for that child to do so – *unless he or she can demonstrate that their father has made other statements indicating that the promise of money has broader application and that it includes this other child as well.*

With these two principles in mind, the following six statements summarize how Jeremiah 29:11 applies to Christians today.

God Has Indeed Promised Us a Hopeful Future, But It Is a Long-Term Hope, Beyond Our Lifetimes

It is common to cite Jeremiah 29:11 to assert that God has promised that breakthrough, deliverance, and prosperity are "right around the corner," perhaps coming within the next year or two. Ironically, this is precisely what the *false* prophets were proclaiming in the context of Jeremiah 29 (cf. 28:15–17). God's plans for welfare and restoration would indeed be implemented, but only after seventy years of judgment in exile. Jeremiah's message for the present was to accept and endure God's judgment upon his people, a crucial aspect of the original context that we hardly wish to apply today! Eric Bargerhuff rightly concludes, "If [Jer 29:11] could not be used as a promise for the immediate future of those who first heard it, then it should not be used for my immediate future either."[31]

When we consider the teaching of the NT, there is indeed a genuine sense in which everything that God plans for his people even now is good. Another oft-quoted verse, Romans 8:28, asserts just this: "We know that for those who love God all things work together for good."[32] However, this "good" does not entail health, wealth, and comfort, but rather conformity to the image of the Son (v. 29). In fact, God's present plans for the good of his people typically include suffering, difficulty, lack, and hardship (see Acts 14:22; Rom 8:16–23; 1 Pet 4:12–13) since these are some of the means that he uses to bring about the ultimate "good" of Christlikeness in us and the spread of his kingdom across the world (see Acts 8:1–4; Rom 5:3–5; Jas 1:2–4).[33] Perhaps this is not unlike how God had planned "welfare" for his people in exile (Jer 29:7), even if this was not necessarily the kind of welfare that the people had desired.[34] Present hardship for God's people is not the same experience as the judgment of the exile in the sixth century BC since Christ has absorbed God's judgment

---

31. Eric Bargerhuff, *The Most Misused Verses in the Bible* (Grand Rapids: Baker, 2012), 38.

32. All quotations of Scripture in this section of the chapter are from the English Standard Version.

33. Theodore Laetsch asserts, "His plans concerning his people are always thoughts of good, of blessing. Even if he is obliged to use the rod, it is the rod not of wrath, but the Father's rod of chastisement for their temporal and eternal welfare. There is not a single item of evil in his plans for his people, neither in their motive, nor in their conception, nor in their revelation, nor in their consummation." *Jeremiah* (St. Louis: Concordia, 1965), 234–35, cited in Philip Graham Ryken, *Jeremiah and Lamentations: From Sorrow to Hope*, PTW (Wheaton: Crossway, 2001), 426.

34. Ryken, *Jeremiah*, 425.

and wrath against our sin at the cross (Isa 53:4–6; Gal 3:13; 1 Pet 2:24).[35] Nor does it have the same purpose since God has good rather than punitive aims in it. But there is a similar "suffering now, glory later" pattern in both cases, a pattern that mirrors the path of Jesus himself (Luke 24:26; Phil 2:5–11; 1 Pet 1:10–11; 2:21).

If our hope is for a day when sickness, lack, suffering, conflict, and hardship will be past, God has made no such *promise* for our present experience, though of course he *can* and *may* bring relief from these things in his grace and in response to prayer. But the day will come when Christ will return to implement a final and holistic salvation that includes the removal of all suffering. This is the ultimate "hopeful future" that God has promised, which believers long for, and which best reflects the good plans of Jeremiah 29:11 in our day. In the meantime, God's people are "strangers" and "exiles" (Heb 11:13; 1 Pet 1:1; 2:11), just like the recipients of Jeremiah's letter, citizens of a land other than the one they currently reside in (see Phil 3:20; Heb 11:1–40). Jeremiah encouraged the exiles to go on with life as normal, preparing for and hoping in the distant future. In a similar way, Paul encourages believers to faithfully endure present trials and to consider them as a "light momentary affliction" that "is preparing for us an eternal weight of glory beyond all comparison" (2 Cor 4:17; cf. Rom 8:18). The NT writers consistently encourage followers of Christ to hope not in the present life but in the life to come (see Matt 6:19–21; 1 Cor 15:19; Col 3:1–2), "in the coming ages" when God will "show the immeasurable riches of his grace in kindness toward us in Christ Jesus" (Eph 2:7). We do cling to God's "good plans" for us, but they are distant plans.

God's Good Plans for Us Are Primarily Focused on Spiritual Realities, Not Material Things

In the context of Jeremiah 29:10–14, the promised "hopeful future" entailed the return of the exiles to the land of Canaan, which likely also implied restored prosperity and well-being in that land. Under the old covenant, God had promised to bless his people in a multitude of ways if they loved, feared, served, and obeyed him (Deut 10:12–13). There was a particular material, "earthy," and temporal nature to these blessings, all to be enjoyed in the promised land, as summarized in Deuteronomy 28:1–14. Although most contemporary Christians might not be interested in relocating (unless they are refugees), it

---

35. Believers are, however, subject to God's fatherly, loving discipline in their lives (Heb 12:4–11).

is tempting to apply Jeremiah 29:11 to one's life with the desire to experience these same kinds of blessings.

However, a significant shift has taken place in both the location and nature of blessings under the new covenant, which can be seen by comparing Deuteronomy 28:1–14 with an NT text focused on blessings such as Ephesians 1:3–14. Whereas under the old covenant blessing was experienced "in the land," for the Christian blessing is experienced "in Christ" (Eph 1:3, 7, 11, 13), no longer in a place but in a person. And whereas under the old covenant blessings were largely focused on physical realities, under the new covenant the believer experiences an abundance of "spiritual blessings" (Eph 1:3). In various ways the old covenant served as a "shadow" or foretaste that anticipated greater (and sometimes rather different) realities in Christ under the new covenant, many of which are developed in the book of Hebrews. The blessings God bestows upon his people are among these aspects of typology: the visible, tangible, temporal blessings experienced by Israel were designed to foreshadow the greater, eternal, spiritual blessings that believers enjoy today.[36]

Therefore, when Christians consider the nature of God's good plans for them, they should not envision a bountiful harvest, financial abundance, or a large and healthy family. As already noted, though these are indeed blessings from God, they are not promised to the Christian during the church age, and both Jesus and Paul discourage us from focusing on such things (e.g. Matt 6:25–34; Phil 4:11–13; 1 Tim 6:6–8). God's supreme desire for believers at present is not their comfort or happiness, but their holiness (1 Thess 4:3), "godliness with contentment" (1 Tim 6:6). Therefore, instead of temporal things, the believer ought to hope in blessings such as resurrection from the dead (1 Cor 15:42–57), deliverance from the coming wrath of God (Rom 5:9; 1 Thess 1:10), glorification (Rom 8:17, 30; Phil 3:20–21), intimate fellowship with the triune God (Rev 21:3), and reigning with Christ (Rev 5:10; 22:5), "an inheritance that is imperishable, undefiled, and unfading, kept in heaven for you" (1 Pet 1:4). God's "gathering" of Israel back to the promised land is eclipsed by his gathering of believers in Christ from every tongue, tribe, and nation to live eternally in a new heaven and a new earth (Rev 21:1).[37] In other words, our hope lies in salvation as defined in the NT rather than in salvation as typically described in the OT. Contemporary "prosperity" preaching encourages believers to hope in our land of exile and its paltry,

---

36. See Peter Y. Lee, "Jeremiah," in *A Biblical-Theological Introduction to the Old Testament*, ed. Miles V. VanPelt (Wheaton: Crossway, 2016), 297; Bargerhuff, *Most Misused Verses*, 38–40.

37. Calvin, *Jeremiah*, 439; Bargerhuff, 38–39.

inferior comforts. In contrast, the NT consistently encourages believers in Christ to hope in eternal life with Christ in a greater land, a new creation, a new Jerusalem (e.g. Heb 11:13–16; 12:18–24).

The Promise of a Hopeful Future Is Only for Those Who Call upon the Lord

God does not have good plans for everyone. This was clearly the case in Jeremiah's context (29:15–23), and it is clearly the case in the NT in that those who reject Christ will not experience "welfare" but rather the ultimate "disaster" (Jer 29:11) of eternity in hell (Matt 10:28; John 5:25–29; Rev 20:15). In Jeremiah 29:10–14 God's restoration of his people depended upon their calling out to him, and his commitment to be accessible, to listen, and to respond to them. But God graciously granted what he required, guaranteeing that his good designs for them could come to fruition.

In a similar manner, God's good plans in the new covenant era are reserved for his own people, for "those who love God" (Rom 8:28). The condition of "seeking God with all one's heart" (cf. Jer 29:13), namely, turning from sin in repentance and turning to Christ in faith, must be met to receive the blessings of salvation, including forgiveness, reconciliation with the Father, glorification, and citizenship in heaven (e.g. Mark 1:15; Luke 13:3; John 8:24; Acts 2:38; 16:31; Rom 10:9). In his first sermon in Jerusalem, Peter quotes from Joel 2:32 and uses language similar to Jeremiah 29:12–13 in proclaiming that "everyone who calls upon the name of the Lord shall be saved" (Acts 2:21). And as in Jeremiah 29:10–14, God graciously grants what he requires, granting his people repentance and faith (e.g. Acts 11:18; Eph 2:8; 2 Tim 2:25), thus guaranteeing that his good designs for them will indeed come to fruition. Accordingly, Bargerhuff suggests that the contemporary application of Jeremiah 29:11 is that "a future 'heavenly hope' exists for those who have placed their faith and trust in Christ alone for their salvation."[38]

If verse 11 is understood in context, those who interpret this as God's promise to them of a "hopeful future" ought to reflect on whether they have repented of their sins and embraced the gospel. If they have not, the content of Jeremiah 29:11 cannot be claimed in any sense at all.

---

38. Bargerhuff, 40.

These Are God's Plans for His Collective People, Not Our Own Individualistic Plans for Ourselves

Often Jeremiah 29:11 is applied as if it is a special, private promise that God has made to "me" as an individual. However, both of the references to "you" in verse 11 are plural, addressed to the corporate exilic community. Similarly, many appeal to Jeremiah 29:11 with a specific idea in mind of what these "good plans" are (and their timing), whether passing exams this year, finding a spouse in the imminent future, or achieving financial stability. It may not occur to them that these are not necessarily God's plans for them, but merely their own hopes and desires, based on "a lie." In the context of Jeremiah 29:10–14, though, these plans for welfare are not undefined, a blank check for the exiles to fill. Rather, God himself has defined this plan as restoration to the land of Israel.

Faithful application must maintain this same focus, searching God's word for the good plans that God has stated he has in mind for his new covenant people rather than claiming subjective "personal promises" that originate from within our own hearts, many of which may be motivated by sinful and selfish desires. To be sure, God also has good plans for us individually (see Rom 8:28), but maintaining the corporate, divinely directed focus of Jeremiah 29:11 points to the salvific realities already emphasized, such as God's good plans to sanctify and glorify his people, and to raise them to life to dwell eternally with him in a new creation.

With the encouragement of the false prophets, and likely bolstered by "faith" in God's power and prayer, the Babylonian exiles no doubt hoped that God's plan for them was that they might return imminently. Yet God's message for them was essentially, "It doesn't matter how much 'faith' you exercise or how much you pray, this is not my plan for you." Contemporary Christians ought to acknowledge that God's answer is often the same today. Yet this should not result in dismay since God's plans for his people are indeed good, better than those we can conceive for ourselves. While we struggle to look beyond our immediate circumstances, God works in our lives for the sake of his glory and our eternal good.

God's Good Plans Point to the Gracious Character of God That Believers Experience in Christ

Everything in Jeremiah 29:4–14 is grace, God's undeserved favor toward sinners who deserve nothing but judgment.[39] It is God's grace to preserve

---
39. See Ryken, *Jeremiah*, 424; Wright, *Message of Jeremiah*, 295–96.

them in Babylon so that they are able to build houses, plant gardens, and have families (vv. 5–6). It is God's grace that he hears their prayers for the city of their exile (v. 7). It is God's grace to warn them of the false prophets in their midst (vv. 8–9). It is God's grace to grant them hope of a future return to the land (vv. 10, 14). It is God's grace to guarantee and enable their search for him, and grace that he will respond (vv. 12–14a). It is owing entirely to God's grace and steadfast love toward his people that his plans for them are "plans for welfare . . . a hopeful future" (v. 11).

Thus, the letter of Jeremiah is among the many OT texts that anticipate and remind the Christian of the far greater measure of grace on display in the gospel: that "God shows his love for us in that while we were still sinners, Christ died for us" (Rom 5:8); that "God, being rich in mercy, because of the great love with which he loved us, even when we were dead in our trespasses, made us alive together with Christ – by grace you have been saved" (Eph 2:4–5); that "God . . . has blessed us in Christ with every spiritual blessing in the heavenly places" (Eph 1:3), including adoption (v. 5), redemption (v. 7), and forgiveness of sins (v. 7), all "to the praise of his glorious grace" (v. 6).

When the hopeful future of Jeremiah 29:11 is compared with the hopeful future of believers in Christ, it is surely appropriate to bask in the benefits of the grand, salvific plans that God has for his people because of the finished work of Christ. But even better is to turn one's attention from the gifts to the Giver, and respond to our gracious God with adoration, gratitude, worship, and love.

Jeremiah's Letter Serves As a Warning against Contemporary False Prophets of Imminent Prosperity

There are many disagreements in our day regarding the existence of prophets in the church and the nature of prophecy. But regardless of one's views on such matters, there should be little debate that false prophets abound just as much today as in Jeremiah's time, and that one must be on guard to identify and denounce them, as Jeremiah did. Scripture provides God's people with a number of criteria for identifying a false prophet (e.g. Deut 18:15–22; Matt 7:15–20; 2 Pet 2:1–22), but of greatest relevance here is that these prophets contradict the teaching of God's word by denying the seriousness of sin and the realities of suffering and God's judgment (cf. Deut 13:1–5; Jer 23:21–22). This was the case for the prophets in Jeremiah's day, who apparently had little regard for the sin of the people and proclaimed the messages of prosperity that they most wanted to hear, saying, "Peace, peace" (Jer 6:13–14; 8:10–11).

In a similar way, many so-called prophets in Africa today have little to say about God's present and future judgment on sin, but proclaim the messages of imminent prosperity that people want to hear.[40] In so doing, they also typically deny the expectation and divine designs for trials and suffering in the Christian life, as clearly taught in the NT. Any supposed prophet who denies these realities and only teaches prosperity can surely be identified as false. And as was the case for the prophets Jeremiah opposed, it should only be a matter of time before this can be verified for certain: when predictions of prosperity do not come about, all should know and conclude that "it is a lie that they are prophesying to you in my name" (Jer 29:9; cf. vv. 21, 23; Deut 18:15–22). Any true herald of God's plans of a "hopeful future" for his people will encourage the faithful to hope in the life to come and in Christ's return rather than in this life.

Conclusion

The Bible is full of verses where God announces salvific intentions for his people, both in the OT and in the NT. We might wonder, then, why Jeremiah 29:11 in particular is so well loved and has such great appeal. Perhaps it is because the language of the verse is very general, enabling people to conceive of God's good plans for them in whatever way they wish. But therein lies the danger, since verse 11 did not function this way in its original context, but pertained to a specific situation.

When we bear this in mind and consider verse 11 in light of the teaching of the NT, the following application emerges: *New covenant believers in Christ should hope in God's good plans to gather his redeemed, sanctified, and glorified people in a new creation where they will enjoy unhindered fellowship with God himself, and they should respond to the God who has graciously promised and guaranteed this "hopeful future" with gratitude, love, and worship.* Or, more simply, the message of Jeremiah 29:11 today is, "God has a plan for you, *in Christ*."[41] Such "plans for welfare" transcend God's plan to restore the exiles to their land, and are of far greater significance than the common ways in which Jeremiah 29:11 is understood to promise improvements in the quality of our

---

40. Lee notes, "The modern era of the church shares a disturbing similarity to the ministry of Jeremiah – both reject the call to repentance by divinely appointed preachers in favor of a false message of optimism that denies divine wrath" ("Jeremiah," 292).

41. Russell D. Moore, "Does Jeremiah 29:11 Apply to You?," The Gospel Coalition, 1 January 2018, accessed 8 April 2022, https://www.thegospelcoalition.org/article/jeremiah-2911-apply/; emphasis added.

lives at present. In addition to applying Jeremiah 29:11 rightly for themselves, God's people must be vigilant against "prophets of prosperity" who claim to speak for God but proclaim a message that contradicts the meaning of verse 11 in its original context as well as the teaching of the NT.

Indeed, believers must endeavor to cling to the good promises of God – but we must also be clear on what exactly those promises are in the new covenant era, including their nature and when they will be realized. Much like the hope that Jeremiah announced to the exiles, the "hopeful future" described in the NT may be a distant hope, but it is a genuine hope that demands faith and faithfulness in the present, a hope that is designed to overcome despair in the midst of hardship.

Bibliography

Allen, Leslie C. *Jeremiah*. Old Testament Library. Louisville: Westminster/John Knox, 2008.

Bargerhuff, Eric. *The Most Misused Verses in the Bible*. Grand Rapids: Baker, 2012.

Bracke, John M. "*Sûb sebût*: A Reappraisal," *Zeitschrift für die alttestamentliche Wissenschaft* 97 (1985): 233–44.

Bright, John. *Jeremiah*. Anchor Bible Commentary 21. New York: Doubleday, 1965.

Brueggemann, Walter. *A Commentary on Jeremiah: Exile and Homecoming*. Grand Rapids: Eerdmans, 1998.

———. *The Theology of the Book of Jeremiah*. Cambridge: Cambridge University Press, 2007.

Calvin, John. *Commentaries on the Book of Jeremiah and the Lamentations*. Vol. 3. Translated by John Owen. Grand Rapids: Eerdmans, 1950.

Dearman, J. Andrew. *Jeremiah/Lamentations*. NIV Application Commentary. Grand Rapids: Zondervan, 2002.

Dumbrell, William J. *The Faith of Israel: A Theological Survey of the Old Testament*. 2nd ed. Grand Rapids: Baker, 2002.

Fretheim, Terence E. *Jeremiah*. Smyth & Helwys Bible Commentary. Macon: Smyth and Helwys, 2002.

Holladay, William L. *Jeremiah*. Vol. 2. Hermeneia. Minneapolis: Fortress, 1989.

Hubbard, Robert L., Jr. "עשׁי." In *New International Dictionary of Old Testament Theology and Exegesis*, edited by Willem A. VanGemeren, 556–62. Vol. 2. Grand Rapids: Zondervan, 1997.

Huey, F. B., Jr. *Jeremiah, Lamentations*. New American Commentary. Nashville: Broadman, 1993.

Keown, G. L., P. J. Scalise, and T. G. Smothers. *Jeremiah 26–52*. Word Biblical Commentary. Dallas: Nelson, 1995.

Lee, Peter Y. "Jeremiah." In *A Biblical-Theological Introduction to the Old Testament*, edited by Miles V. VanPelt, 277–303. Wheaton: Crossway, 2016.

Longman, Tremper, III. *Jeremiah, Lamentations*. New International Biblical Commentary. Peabody: Hendrickson, 2008.

Lundbom, Jack R. *Jeremiah: A Study in Ancient Hebrew Rhetoric*. 2nd ed. Winona Lake: Eisenbrauns, 1997.

Moore, Russell D. "Does Jeremiah 29:11 Apply to You?" The Gospel Coalition. 1 January 2018. Accessed 8 April 2022. https://www.thegospelcoalition.org/article/jeremiah-2911-apply/.

Ryken, Philip Graham. *Jeremiah and Lamentations: From Sorrow to Hope*. Preach the Word. Wheaton: Crossway, 2001.

Schultz, Richard L. *Out of Context: How to Avoid Misinterpreting the Bible*. Grand Rapids: Baker, 2012.

Thompson, J. A. *The Book of Jeremiah*. New International Commentary on the Old Testament. Grand Rapids: Eerdmans, 1979.

Unterman, Jeremiah. *From Repentance to Redemption: Jeremiah's Thought in Transition*. Journal for the Study of the Old Testament Supplement Series 54. Sheffield: JSOT, 1987.

Wilson, Gerald H. "The Prayer of Daniel 9: Reflection on Jeremiah 29." *Journal for the Study of the Old Testament* 48 (1990): 91–99.

Wright, Christopher J. H. *The Message of Jeremiah*. The Bible Speaks Today. Nottingham: Inter-Varsity, 2014.

2

Concepts of Repentance and Sanctification in African Perspectives

An Assessment of Biblical and African Understandings of Salvation in African Christianity

Daniel M. Mwailu

Senior Lecturer in Theology and Biblical Studies at Africa Nazarene University since 2012 and a former Superintendent minister and lay preachers' tutor in the Methodist Church of Great Britain

Abstract

Integral to an understanding of salvation in biblical Christianity is repentance that leads to sanctification and new life in Christ. In most countries in Africa, there are high percentages of people who profess Christianity. Yet, there are also severe issues of integrity, corruption, impunity, graft, theft of public funds, and other ethical evils condemned by the Bible. The national media have also reported on sensational sex scandals involving pastors and other high-ranking church officials, including bishops. These issues and scandals imply a dissonance between profession and practice, creed and credulity. This leads to the conclusion that there may be a misunderstanding among African Christians about the meaning of repentance, sanctification, and salvation. Such dissonance contributes to the famous assertion that "African Christianity is a mile wide and an inch deep."[1] Troutman suggests that an African theology of Christian holiness will take the universal biblical core elements of holiness and articulate and describe them using African philosophical concepts and vocabulary.[2] This chapter explores how far this has taken place in African theologizing.

It critically examines and assesses the understanding of biblical concepts of salvation, repentance, and sanctification in African perspectives. It evaluates their African cultural dynamic equivalents to see if they carry the same meaning. The African understanding of the concepts of repentance and sanctification has influenced the type of Christianity practiced in Africa; as either syncretistic (phony) or genuine to the one catholic (universal) apostolic faith whose quintessential meaning is often known as the "ABC of the gospel": Accepting that one is a sinner (Rom 3:23); Believing in Jesus Christ as Lord and the only Savior from a life of sin (John 3); and Confessing (repenting of) sin (1 John 1:9) and becoming a new creature (2 Cor 5:17). In a biblical Christian understanding, the salvation experience creates new people who form a new community that exhibits a new life of love and holiness in Christian discipleship. Wherever the truth of the gospel has prevailed, this ABC of the gospel is in evidence. This chapter contends that the depth of the African understanding of repentance and sanctification informs an African understanding of salvation; a faulty understanding of repentance and sanctification leads to an unsound understanding of salvation. If the fruit of salvation is lacking, namely in repentance, sanctification, and holiness of life, it suggests a misunderstanding of the meaning of salvation in the Christian life. African concepts of salvation, repentance, and sanctification in light of both the biblical and African Traditional Religious understandings of these concepts shed light on the apparent dissonance in salvation between faith and practice in African Christianity.

Key words: salvation, soteriology, sin, sanctification, confession, repentance

---

1. See Ben Byerly, "Why African Christianity Is 'a Mile Wide and an Inch Deep,'" *Confluence: Ben Byerly's Muddy Mix* (blog), 11 Dec. 2008, accessed 24 Aug. 2021, https://benbyerly.wordpress.com/2008/12/11/why-african-christianity-is-a-mile-wide-and-an-inch-deep/.

2. Philip H. Troutman, "Towards an African Theology of Christian Holiness: A Journey from Israel to Africa," in *Africa Speaks: An Anthology of Africa Nazarene Theological Conference 2003*, ed. Linda Braaten (Florida, South Africa: Africa Nazarene Publications, 2004), 110.

Introduction

Certain concepts and statements cannot stand alone without creating a *petitio principii*. One example is the assertion that "Jesus is the answer": If Jesus is the answer, what is the question?[3] The concept of salvation similarly begs four principal questions: Salvation by whom? Salvation from what and how? Salvation into what or to become what? And what is the evidence of salvation? In this sense, salvation has four Siamese quadruplets: repentance, forgiveness, regeneration, and sanctification. This chapter contends that discussing the concept of salvation in African Christianity, therefore, entails a parallel discussion on repentance, forgiveness, regeneration, and sanctification. The concept of salvation in biblical Christianity is also pregnant with other concepts. "It is comprehended in a series of biblical concepts: election, calling, regeneration, conversion, justification, adoption, sanctification, and glorification."[4] However, an appraisal of the Siamese quadruplets of repentance, forgiveness, regeneration, and sanctification reveals that these are the central tenets of the concept of salvation in biblical Christianity. This echoes G. Brand's suggestion that the concept of salvation can "be the equivalent of reconciliation or sanctification or liberation."[5]

The Biblical Christian Understanding of the Concept of Salvation

The theme of salvation permeates the entire Bible. In biblical theology, the Old Testament presents God as the God of salvation whose all-consuming desire is for humankind to repent and be saved.[6] He is the ultimate Savior of the nation of Israel and humankind. The key Hebrew verb, *Yasha*, is translated in English as "to deliver – to save." The biblical idea of salvation depicts three aspects: rescue from danger, from harm, or from death. The cumulative teaching in Judeo-biblical Christianity crystallizes into two elements: salvation from sin and death; and renewal of the human heart or spiritual, moral purity. "God's salvation always renews the spirit of a person to lead a life that is morally pleasing to Him."[7]

---

3. See James J. Genova, *If Jesus Is the Answer, What Is the Question? Questions from God* (Bloomington: Westbow Press, 2016).
4. C. Horne, *The Doctrine of Salvation* (Chicago: Moody Bible Institute, 1991), ix.
5. G. Brand, *Speaking of a Fabulous Ghost* (New York: Peter Lang, 2002), 58.
6. See e.g. 2 Pet 3:9; Ezek 18:32; 1 Tim 2:3–4.
7. Trent C. Butler, Editor. Entry for "Salvation." *Holman Bible Dictionary*. https://www.studylight.org/dictionaries/eng/hbd/s/salvation.html. 1991.

A cursory reading of the Old Testament gives the impression that salvation or deliverance is a monopoly of the nation of Israel. Exodus gives the account of Israel's deliverance from slavery in Egypt, and a reminder of this event is presented in the book of Deuteronomy. Joshua chapters 9–14 document the extermination of the tribes in Canaan before the children of Israel's entry to occupy the promised land.

As the nation of Israel settled into a covenant community, its deliverance or salvation from disease and other threats depended on their obedience and observance of ritual sacrifices detailed in the book of Leviticus. Further reading of the poetic and prophetic literature in the Old Testament gives evidence of salvation from sin for individuals and other nations.[8] In the New Testament, salvation is centered on and realized through the person of Jesus Christ, the new Joshua who saves or delivers not only the nation of Israel but all humanity (Rom 3; 8–11). In Jesus Christ, salvation becomes universal for all who call on him, a notion also alluded to in the Old Testament.[9] Some scholars maintain that in the Old Testament salvation is legalistically earned, limited, and restricted to the nation of Israel. The same scholars would posit that salvation was earned through obedience and observance of religious rituals. Nevertheless, a comprehensive study of biblical theology shows that in both the Old and the New Testament, salvation is by grace and is a gift of God.

In the New Testament, Pauline theology emphasizes that salvation is imputed to and embraces all humanity. It is by grace and not earned. Rather than depending on religious ritual, it depends on having a relationship with God through faith in Jesus Christ (Eph 2:8–10). The Holy Spirit empowers it, rather than it being earned by good deeds. This relationship with God results in the New Testament community of faith, which constitutes the church. In the Old Testament, salvation required the nation of Israel or God's covenant community to turn from idols in repentance. In the New Testament, the concept involves a change of mind, remorse, a reversal of thought, and turning from self to God.

The ministry of John the Baptist, the harbinger of Jesus's ministry, was to bring the message of repentance. Thus, repentance is a precursor of salvation, conversion, or regeneration, and it is maintained by perpetual sanctification in the newness of life that characterizes those saved. Such are the dynamics of salvation in Judeo-biblical Christianity.

---

8. See e.g. Pss 13; 18; 51; Isa 2; Mic 4; Zech 8.
9. See e.g. Rev 22:17; Acts 2:21; Rom 10:13; John 1:11–12; 3:16; 7:37; Isa 55:1.

Suppose salvation were understood in these terms in Africa. It would mean that those countries in Africa that claim to have large proportions of Christians would see people transformed from a life of sin and engaged in living holy lives, serving and transforming their communities and consequently keeping at bay the scourge of the trinity of evil: corruption, graft, and impunity. Where this is not the case, this chapter poses the question: how is African Christianity consonant with Judeo-biblical Christianity with regard to the concept of salvation?

What Is the Traditional African Religious Understanding of Salvation?

One of the most in-depth studies to date on salvation in the African context is a book by Tokunboh Adeyemo.[10] An article summarizes the main argument of the book.[11] His overall assessment is that the "idea of salvation" in African Traditional Religion is "ritualistic and utilitarian,"[12] similar to that of Hinduism. He cites other scholars who have come to the same conclusion.[13] He identifies several different means of salvation in world religions: humanism, based on the pursuit of pleasure; asceticism, the withdrawal from the community; moralism, doing the right actions; mysticism, through philosophical speculation (yoga, meditation); and submission. Salvation by submission as a religious phenomenon emphasizes strict adherence to law and set religious rituals. It is essentially salvation by works and is found in Islam. In Islam, salvation is achieved through submission to Allah, the only true God, and the demands of *iman* – belief in the articles of faith and the observance of *din*, and the practice of religious duties, or the five pillars of the Islamic faith. From Adeyemo's analysis, it is evident that in the three main monotheistic religions – Judaism, Islam, and Christianity – salvation is achieved by submission. In Christianity, submissive compliance reached its crescendo in the Middle Ages. Roman Catholicism emphasized penance by paying indulgences and its dogma *Extra ecclesian nulla salus*: outside the church there is no salvation. That led to the religious revolt of the Reformation and the birth of Protestant Christianity. As

---

10. Tokunboh Adeyemo, *Salvation in African Tradition* (Nairobi: Evangel, 1979; rev. ed. 1997).

11. Tokunboh Adeyemo, "Ideas of Salvation," *Africa Journal of Evangelical Theology* 16, no. 1 (1997): 67–75.

12. Adeyemo, "Ideas of Salvation," 69.

13. For example, O. Imasogie, *African Traditional Religion* (Ibadan:University Press, 1982), 76.

discussed above, in the Judeo-biblical view salvation has two phases: the Old Testament phase implies salvation by the observance of religious rituals and sacrifices; New Testament Christianity emphasizes salvation by grace, God's unmerited favor, and the empowerment of the Holy Spirit. As practiced today on the vast African continent with its myriads of primal traditional religions, African Christianity amalgamates these two phases, leaning more toward that of the Old Testament.

In contextualizing the concept of salvation in Africa, one needs to be aware of the fact that "although soteriology or the doctrine of salvation has always occupied a central place in Christian theology, the shape of soteriology has changed many times as Christianity's centre of gravity shifted to a new cultural context."[14] Also, as a religious phenomenon, salvation is "the deliverance of humankind by religious means from sin or evil, the restoration of human beings to their true state, and the attainment of eternal blessedness."[15] This definition implies that most religions, such as Buddhism, Confucianism, Hinduism, Islam, and Christianity, espouse the concept of human deliverance from a bad state to a better state. But while the concept of salvation is common in the phenomenology of religions, achieving it differs. "The notion that people need to be saved implies that a defective condition is normally prevalent, and the major religions have differing views as to the root of the problem."[16] In Christian theology, salvation is discussed under the category of "soteriology," meaning "doctrine of salvation" or "the way of salvation," referring

> to the salvation of individuals, but it can also relate to the salvation of a group. The idea implies that human beings are in some unfortunate condition and may achieve an ultimately good state either by their efforts or through the intervention of some divine power. There is a common belief in a saviour God, who is concerned with the welfare of the human race.[17]

Regarding salvation in Africa, Ninian Smart states,

---

14. G. Brand, "Salvation in African Christian Theology: A Typology of Existing Approaches," *Exchange* 28, no. 3 (1999): 193–224.

15. Rosemary Goring, ed., "Salvation," in *The Wordsworth Dictionary of Beliefs and Religions* (Ware: Wordsworth, 1995), 455; cited by Adewale J. Adelakun, "A Theological Reflection on Mbiti's Conception of Salvation in African Christianity," *Nebula* 8, no. 1 (Dec. 2011), 25.

16. Ninian Smart, "Soteriology," in *The Encyclopaedia of Religion*, vol. 13, ed. Mircea Eliade (New York: Macmillan, 1987), 418.

17. Smart, "Soteriology," 418.

Classic small-scale religions, such as those in Africa, are typically more concerned with group welfare than with ultimate judgment about individuals. Nevertheless, the growth of modern individualism has highlighted the importance of thinking about how traditional patterns of soteriology might throw light on the symbols of judgment and ultimate meaning that remain vital in understanding the human condition.[18]

Mbiti, a doyen of African Traditional Religions and theology, pioneered a detailed study of African religious concepts of salvation. He argued for a holistic understanding of physical and spiritual salvation and criticized Western missionaries for "stressing the spiritual dimension to the neglect of the physical."[19] He argued that "the biblical message of salvation has landed on fertile soil in African societies . . . particularly so in the case of the biblical portrait of salvation which embraces several meanings that are readily applicable to the African world."[20] However, he does not elucidate what these meanings are. Mbiti nevertheless underscores the importance of deliverance from witchcraft, sorcery, and magic.[21] In the African worldview, witchcraft, sorcery, and magic are the quintessential trinity of evil from which people need salvation. The means of achieving salvation in most African societies seems to be punitive retribution, eliminating the perpetrator of witchcraft, sorcery, and magic. This implies a paucity of developed concepts of repentance, forgiveness, regeneration, and sanctification, leading one to ask whether repentance and forgiveness are substantive conceptual entities in traditional African thought forms.

I juxtapose this question with an experience I had counseling a British couple. A Muslim medical consultant from an Islamic country needed British citizenship and decided that the most straightforward way was to marry a British woman. He faked conversion to Christianity, told the woman he had converted to Christianity and started attending church. The woman believed that the man had genuinely converted to Christianity and married him. After the marriage, she assumed that serving a regular British diet with an English breakfast made of eggs, sausages, and bacon would be all right. After the man gained British citizenship, he divorced the woman because he had achieved

---

18. Smart, 423.
19. John S. Mbiti, *Bible and Theology in African Christianity* (Nairobi: Oxford University Press, 1986), 159.
20. Mbiti, *Bible and Theology*, 159.
21. Mbiti, 159.

his objective. In their married life, he had hidden from her that he already had a wife in his country of origin, and that he even had a child with her! As I counseled the couple, the man told the woman that she had offended him by serving him sausages and bacon, knowing that Muslims do not eat pork! In tears, the woman apologized, explaining that she thought he had become a Christian and that serving him pork would not be an offence. The man, however, remained unmoved. As I watched the woman sobbing her heart out in repentance and the man's hardened attitude, it made me wonder whether the two were operating from two different fields of conceptual discourse. The woman expected forgiveness for any offence she had caused, but the man believed in the heaviest punishment once an offence had been committed. I wondered whether the woman's intrinsic Christian belief in a God of grace, love, and forgiveness was contrary to the man's religion that possibly believed only in a God of punishment once an offence had been committed. As the man continued to harden his heart while the woman beseeched him for forgiveness, it made me wonder whether the concept of forgiveness resonated at all within the religion of Islam. I never resolved this conundrum because the marriage was dissolved and I did not pursue the question.

A further question is whether the traditional African religious conceptual framework has any established cultural dynamic equivalents for repentance, forgiveness, and sanctification to accommodate the concept of salvation found in Judeo-biblical Christianity in African Christianity. Turning back to our four central questions, what light do they throw on African Christianity?

Salvation by Whom?

The African "patristic fathers," in their pioneering and exhaustive works on African Traditional Religions,[22] have established the existence of a common belief in the supreme God among primal African peoples. God is transcendent and immanently involved in the affairs of individuals, and he punishes sin and any broken taboo. Idowu's findings are summarized by an African proverb from the Igbo people of West Africa: "An Igbo man believes that when he

---

22. E. Geoffrey Parrinder, *African Traditional Religion* (1st ed., London: London University Press, 1954; 2nd ed., London: SPCK, 1962, 1968; 3rd ed., London: Sheldon, 1974); *Religion in Africa* (New York: Praeger, 1969); E. Bolaji Idowu, *Olodumare: God in Yoruba Belief* (London: Longmans, 1962); *African Traditional Religion: A Definition* (Maryknoll: Orbis, 1973); J. S. Mbiti, *African Religions and Philosophy* (London: Heinemann, 1969); *Concepts of God in Africa* (London: SPCK, 1970).

sins, he makes the high-power frown."²³ The Yoruba people also have a saying: "You who steal in the cover of the night, know you assuredly that if the earthly king does not see you, the heavenly King (i.e. God) does."²⁴ The question as to whom sin is committed against is aptly summarized in the following assertion:

> Africans do not have a rigid distinction between an offence committed against a person or society and one committed against Deity or divinities and spirits. There is no sharp dividing line in this regard between the sacred and the secular such as is assumed by the Western world. God is regarded as the founder and guardian of morality. To disregard God, the divinities and the ancestral spirits is to commit sin.²⁵

According to Parrinder, "if a man breaks a taboo, he expects the supernatural penalty to follow. If lightning strikes a man or a house, he is judged at once to be an evildoer, without question, for he must have offended the gods."²⁶ This religious conceptual thought process makes it safe to posit that the supreme God who punishes must be the same who ultimately saves.

Salvation from What and How?

Mbiti examines the concepts of evil, ethics, and justice.²⁷ He acknowledges African peoples' "awareness of evil in the world and [how] in various ways they endeavour to fight it."²⁸ His appraisal affirms the duality of good and evil, observing that

> in nearly all African societies, it is thought that the spirits are either the origin of evil or agents of evil . . . an independent and external object which, however, cannot act on its own but must be employed by human or spiritual agents. . . . African peoples recognise social order and peace as essential and sacred.²⁹

---

23. Idowu, *Olodomare*, 148.
24. J. Omosade Awolalu, "Sin and Its Removal in African Traditional Religion," *Journal of the American Academy of Religion* 44, no. 2 (June 1976): 280.
25. Awolalu, "Sin and Its Removal," 279.
26. E. G. Parrinder, *West African Religion* (London: Epworth, 1949), 199.
27. Mbiti, *African Religions*, 204–5.
28. Mbiti, 204.
29. Mbiti, 204–5.

Mbiti goes on to comment that due to African communal living, any offence or evil committed by an individual "is an offence against the community and its consequences affect not only the thief but also the whole body of his relatives."[30] The community's customs and regulations are sacred; any breach is punishable by the corporate community, "and God may also inflict punishment and bring about justice."[31] He further surveys the acts considered sinful in African societies: adultery, among the Burundi; stealing, neglect of ageing parents, murder, and adultery, among the Bachwa; murder, theft, rape, and witchcraft, among the Gikuyu; and pride, among the Nuer. He points out that African people collectively believe that these evils are punishable by God.[32] Throughout his appraisal of the various traditional African societies' beliefs in evil, ethics, and justice, his survey indicates paucity or even a complete lack of discussion on the concepts of repentance, forgiveness, and sanctification as understood within the Judeo-biblical Christian view of salvation and which are intricately related. There are two facets, however, that emerge in his appraisal: first, what is considered evil that requires repentance leading to forgiveness; and second, "the sinner," or the subject from and to whom repentance, confession, and forgiveness are expected.

In African Traditional Religions, the concepts of repentance and forgiveness are expressed in purificatory rituals to appease the supreme being (God), the divinities, ancestors, or the community. The rituals involve physical activities such as "shaving, bathing in a flowing stream, anointing, fasting, rolling on the ground to indicate remorse or offering propitiatory sacrifices."[33] Physical and spiritual sin requires washing off or chasing away for the community.[34] Washing sins off in a flowing river cleanses the person because one cannot touch the same water twice, as rivers never flow upstream; therefore, the offence washes downstream and is gone forever. Repentance is symbolized by casting off old clothes and wearing white ones. It is also expressed by covering one's body and face with charcoal. In the last few decades a new phenomenon has emerged in African Christianity in the form of contextualized Pentecostalism related to the prosperity gospel.[35] The subject has generated much research,

---

30. Mbiti, 204–5.
31. Mbiti, 204–5.
32. E. Evans-Pritchard, *Nuer Religion II* (Oxford: Oxford University Press, 1956), 24, 189.
33. Awolalu, "Sin and Its Removal," 284.
34. Awolalu, 284.
35. See J. K. Asamoah-Gyadu, "'Christ Is the Answer': What Is the Question? A Ghana Airways Prayer Vigil and Its Implications for Religion, Evil and Public Space," *Journal of Religion in Africa* 35, Fasc. 1 (Feb. 2005): 93–117.

which suggests that in its attempt to contextualize Christianity in Africa, Pentecostalism has styled its preachers to take the place of the medicine men and other African traditional specialists in dealing with poverty, witchcraft, and sorcery, portraying these preachers as purveyors of powerful prayers and potent medicines for protection against evil and poverty. Contextualized Pentecostalism occupies center stage in African Christianity today.

Salvation into What or to Become What? What is the Evidence of Salvation?

The third and fourth principal questions belong together. The Judeo-biblical Christian concepts of sanctification, grace, and the empowering Holy Spirit seem to lack dynamic cultural equivalents in the written resources reviewed so far. Salvation in African Traditional Religions resembles more of the Old Testament than of the New Testament. It is based on doing and keeping rituals and cyclical punishment. It is characterized by a fear of punishment rather than love and is by good works and communal compliance. The chasm between the supreme being and humanity is unbreachable. Various African myths relate how God once lived close to humankind but withdrew because of their misdeeds. These myths boil down to the idea that "man did something contrary to the directions of God, and that humankind's misdemeanour contributed largely to disruption of the relation that hitherto existed between humans and God."[36] According to Mbiti, the misdemeanor "brought disadvantageous and tragic consequences to men. God left them alone, death came, and man lost happiness, peace and the free supply of food."[37] Most African Traditional Religions have resonances with the Old Testament priesthood communal cleansing; the traditional African priest assumes the role of representative of the community and performs symbolic acts of confession on behalf of the people. The Old Testament scapegoat concept also exists in a similar way. In some parts of Africa, people "bury" sins in the ground as a symbolic act of dealing with them.[38] There are concepts symbolizing the atonement which are comparable to those in the Old Testament, such as reparations and propitiatory sacrifices where "a violation of taboo results in death."[39]

---

36. Awolalu, "Sin and Its Removal," 282.
37. Mbiti, *African Religions*, 98.
38. Awolalu, "Sin and Its Removal," 285.
39. Awolalu, 287.

What Is Sin or Evil in African Traditional Societies?

Unlike Judeo-biblical Christianity, a religion based on a book, the Bible, African Traditional Religion is vibrant, pervasive, and embracing. It is communicated orally and "is largely written in the people's myths and folktales, in their songs and dances, in the liturgies and shrines and their proverbs and pithy sayings."[40] In his appraisal of sin in African Traditional Religions, Awolalu disagrees with Parratt's assertion that sin is not "comparable with the developed ethical conception of sin found in both the OT and the NT."[41] He instead argues that "Africans are as conscious of sin as the Jews of the OT."[42] However, he concedes that in African Traditional Religions, "it is not easy to draw the line between the merely ritual and the purely ethical, as they are often involved one in the other."[43] Although sin is both personal and corporate, the latter is more predominant.

> The Africans know about sin and evil, their confession and removal. The many taboos [the African] has to observe are not to be regarded as mechanical things that do not touch the heart, but that avoidance is a sacred law respected by the community. In breaking it, you offend a divine power.[44]

In his appraisal of Westermann, Awolalu concurs that "Africans tenaciously hold the belief that moral values are based upon the recognition of the divine will, and that sin in the community must be expelled if perfect peace is to be enjoyed."[45] Africans do not have a rigid distinction. To repeat words we quoted above, "to disregard God, the divinities and ancestral spirits is to commit sin."[46] According to Westermann, African society is characterized by the prevalence of the idea of the community. "Community, as conceived by Africans, is a creation of God, and it is a moral society."[47]

---

40. Awolalu, 282.

41. J. K. Parratt, "Religious Change in Yoruba Society," *Journal of Religion in Africa* 2, Fasc. 1 (1969): 118.

42. Awolalu, "Sin and Its Removal," 276.

43. Awolalu, citing Idowu, *Olodumare*, 148.

44. D. Westermann, *Africa and Christianity* (New York: Oxford University Press, 1937), 96–97; cited by Awolalu, 278.

45. Awolalu, 278.

46. Awolalu, 279.

47. D. Westermann, *The African Today and Tomorrow* (London: International African Institute, 1949), 65.

What Concepts of African Traditional Religions Affect an African Christian Understanding of Salvation?

"If Not Punished, It Is Not Evil"

Mbiti, citing earlier research by Evans-Pritchard,[48] refers to an innocuous observation that makes evil in African societies relative, acquiescing to modern relative morality and permissive ethics: "Evil lies not in the act itself but in the fact that God punishes the act . . . such is the logic according to the Nuer people . . . [and to] many other African peoples, something is evil because it is punished; it is not punished because it is evil."[49] In his summary of evil, ethics, and justice in African societies, he remarks,

> To sleep with someone else's wife is not considered "evil" if these two are not found out by the society which forbids it. . . . It is not the act itself which will be "wrong" as such, but the relationship involved in the act: if relationships are not hurt or damaged, and if there is no discovery of a breach of custom or regulations, then the act is not "evil" or "wicked" or "bad."[50]

Such beliefs raise crucial questions. First, if evil or sin is determined by societal stipulations, and getting away with it, if not found out, is acceptable, it is at variance with Judeo-biblical Christianity, where salvation means being born again and turning away from personal and societal evil. If African Christianity "acculturates" or contextualizes such an understanding, it becomes syncretistic and denies the gospel. It leads one to speculate whether such reasoning explains recent major sexual scandals among pastors and bishops in the African church. Second, this begs the question as to how deep-rooted these beliefs are in African Christianity. How far has this relative morality and these permissive ethics infiltrated African Christianity? How much has the biblical teaching of salvation influenced traditional concepts?

A Hierarchical Understanding of Evil

Mbiti highlights the role of hierarchy in understanding evil, in which "something is evil not because of its intrinsic nature, but by who does it to whom and which level of status."[51] This hierarchical view means that those who are higher in status cannot commit evil to those who are lesser or lower in rank.

---

48. Evans-Pritchard, *Nuer Religion II*, 24, 189.
49. Mbiti, *African Religions*, 207.
50. Mbiti, 213.
51. Mbiti, 208.

It also means that the higher one is in the hierarchy, the less one is attributed sin or mistakes. It is as if the higher one rises in society, the more "divine" one becomes. In most African cultures, there is a belief that God commits no evil, and kings and princes are viewed similarly. Making an apology is also treated according to hierarchy. The lower person must always apologize to the higher person; parents do not sin against their children.

Mbiti cites the Gikuyu, who perform the ritual of "vomiting the sin to cleanse a person from ritual evil."[52] However, he does not discuss whether the cleansed person is forgiven or simply averts punishment for the community. In African Traditional Religions, restitution and punishment are meted out by God in this life rather than in the distant eschatological final judgment, as borne out by the Burundi proverb, "God exercises vengeance in silence."[53]

According to Mbiti, "the essence of African morality is more 'societary' than 'spiritual'; it is a morality of 'conduct' rather than of being."[54] In various African communities, the people administer restitution and punishment by paying fines. In Mbiti's assessment of traditional African societies' ethics, morality, and judgment, he mentions only repentance in reversing curses.[55] The repentance in relation to curses is communal because the curse affects the cursed person and his or her relatives and community. The summative mantra of African morality is "I am because we are, and since we are, therefore I am."[56] This is similar to Jewish theology.

For most African people, nothing sorrowful happens by "accident" or "chance": it must be caused by some agent, either human or spiritual. As noted above, the hierarchy begins with God:

> God does not and cannot commit evil. . . . As a rule, a person of a lower rank, status or age commits an offence against another person or being of a higher rank or age. One may also offend a person of the same status. Never or rarely does a person or being of a higher status do what constitutes an offence against a person of a lower status. What is considered evil or offensive functions from a lower level to a higher level.[57]

---

52. Mbiti, 210.

53. Mbiti, 211; citing E. W. Smith, ed., *African Ideas of God* (London: Edinburgh House, 1961).

54. Mbiti, *African Religions*, 214.

55. Mbiti, 211.

56. Mbiti, 214.

57. Mbiti, 208.

The innocuous understanding of these African concepts parallels that of other tribal cultures. The classic case is Richardson's book about a Western missionary sharing the gospel with the Sawi people in Indonesia.[58] The tribal people hailed Judas Iscariot as a hero in the gospel story because their culture valued treachery. They did, however, have a concept of "peace child" that resonated with Jesus as God's peace child who guarantees God's eternal peace. This traditional concept brought a breakthrough in understanding salvation in Judeo-biblical Christian terms among the Sawi people. Similar concepts need to be researched and established concerning salvation in African Christianity.

Conclusion

What does the above-stated African Traditional Religious background regarding evil, ethics, and justice tell us about salvation in African Christianity? First, African Christianity must exercise vigilance in contextualization or acculturalization to avoid compromising personal aspects of salvation. As observed concerning morality and ethics, "African ontology is deeply anthropological."[59] It promotes relativism in understanding salvation in Judeo-biblical Christian terms because social ritual and taboo determine what is evil and what is not. Society becomes the arbiter of right and wrong, rather than the Bible.

Second, the acculturalization of traditional social ethics might be the source of the dissonance between professing Christianity and practice, creed and credulity. A hierarchical understanding of evil in traditional African thought forms encourages corruption and impunity. African Christianity must reject the beliefs that the higher one climbs in social status, the less accountable one becomes, and that the higher in rank in the community commit no evil to those lower in rank. Such notions are unbiblical and contrary to Judeo-biblical Christianity. Once beliefs are established as legal ethics, society enters a moral maze, ethical mayhem, and a miasma that results in a lack of moral absolutes. It paves the way for dictatorial rule in civil government and the church, as evidenced by the proliferation of self-appointed bishops in the new African instituted churches. If African Christianity does not address this authoritarian trend in church life, the church will go back to how it was in the Middle Ages, under the control of the Papacy that sparked the Reformation and the rise of

---

58. Don Richardson, *The Peace Child: An Unforgettable Story of Primitive Jungle Treachery in the 20th Century* (Ventura, CA: Regal, 1975).

59. Mbiti, *African Religions*, 215.

Protestantism with its emphasis on *sola scriptura*. Once this happens, salvation loses its primary meaning as emancipation and liberation from spiritual, social, and physical bondage as espoused by Jesus when he inaugurated his ministry (Luke 4:16–21).

Third, African Christianity must take seriously the challenge of the new phenomenon of contextualized Christianity in Africa in the form of the prosperity gospel. It is lopsided, skewed toward eradicating poverty and the procurement of prosperity, wealth, and physical well-being rather than spiritual formation and sanctification. We noted above that research has revealed that prosperity gospel preachers in Africa mimic medicine men in African Traditional Religions rather than revival evangelists in Judeo-biblical Christianity. Such preachers lack balanced biblical teaching and exegetical knowledge of the Scriptures. They have a narrow view of the church's catholicity as taught in the Bible. Commenting on Pentecostalism's contextualization of African Christianity, Ngong observes that "African neo-Pentecostal/charismatic Christianity draws from African Traditional religious thought."[60] While he agrees with other scholars regarding the worth and necessity of contextualization, he cautions regarding the danger of syncretism, stating that "such [an] uncritical approach undermines the difference within Christianity, thus collapsing Christianity into African Traditional Religion."[61]

African concepts of repentance and sanctification concerning salvation have not been thoroughly studied and developed by scholars and exponents of acculturalization in African Christianity. Although the concept of punishment is well documented, the concepts of forgiveness, grace, and sanctification are conspicuously lacking. These concepts form the core teaching of salvation. Therefore, African scholars need to carry out robust research on the concepts of repentance, forgiveness, regeneration, and sanctification as integral facets of salvation in African Christianity.

Bibliography

Achtemeier, Paul J. ed., *The HarperCollins Bible Dictionary,* York: HarperCollins Publishers, 1996.

Adelakun, Adewale J. "A Theological Reflection on Mbiti's Conception of Salvation in African Christianity." *Nebula* 8, no. 1 (Dec. 2011): 25–33.

---

60. David T. Ngong, "Salvation and Materialism in African Theology Studies," *World Christianity* 15, no. 1 (2009): 1–21.

61. Ngong, "Salvation and Materialism," 1.

Adeyemo, Tokunboh. *Salvation in African Tradition*. Nairobi: Evangel, 1979. Rev. ed. 1997.

———. "Ideas of Salvation." *Africa Journal of Evangelical Theology* 16, no. 1 (1997): 67–75.

Asamoah-Gyadu, J. K. "'Christ Is the Answer': What Is the Question? A Ghana Airways Prayer Vigil and Its Implications for Religion, Evil and Public Space." *Journal of Religion in Africa* 35, Fasc. 1 (Feb. 2005): 93–117.

Awolalu, J. Omosade. "Sin and Its Removal in African Traditional Religion." *Journal of the American Academy of Religion* 44, no. 2 (June 1976): 275–87.

Brand, G. "Salvation in African Christian Theology: A Typology of Existing Approaches." *Exchange* 28, no. 3 (1999): 193–224.

———. *Speaking of a Fabulous Ghost*. New York: Peter Lang, 2002.

Butler, Trent C., ed. "Salvation." https://www.studylight.org/dictionaries/eng/hbd/s/salvation.html.

Byerly, Ben. "Why African Christianity Is 'a Mile Wide and an Inch Deep.'" *Confluence: Ben Byerly's Muddy Mix* (blog), 11 December 2008. Accessed 24 August 2021. https://benbyerly.wordpress.com/2008/12/11/why-african-christianity-is-a-mile-wide-and-an-inch-deep/.

Easton, M. G. *Easton's Bible Dictionary*. New York: IBM Corp., 1993.

Evans-Pritchard, E. *Nuer Religion II*. Oxford: Oxford University Press, 1956.

Genova, James J. *If Jesus Is the Answer, What Is the Question? Questions from God*. Bloomington: Westbow Press, 2016.

Goring, Rosemary, ed. "Salvation." In *The Wordsworth Dictionary of Beliefs and Religions*. Ware: Wordsworth, 1995.

Horne, C. *The Doctrine of Salvation*. Chicago: Moody Bible Institute, 1991.

Idowu, E. Bolaji. *African Traditional Religion: A Definition*. Maryknoll: Orbis, 1973.

———. *Olodumare: God in Yoruba Belief*. London: Longmans, 1962.

Imasogie, O. *African Traditional Religion*. Ibadan: University Press, 1982.

Mbiti, J. S. *African Religions and Philosophy*. London: Heinemann, 1969.

———. *Bible and Theology in African Christianity*. Nairobi: Oxford University Press, 1986.

———. *Concepts of God in Africa*. London: SPCK, 1970.

Ngong, David T. "Salvation and Materialism in African Theology Studies." *World Christianity* 15, no. 1 (2009): 1–21.

Parratt, J. K. "Religious Change in Yoruba Society." *Journal of Religion in Africa* 2, Fasc. 1 (1969): 113–28.

Parrinder, E. Geoffrey. *African Traditional Religion*. 1st ed., London: London University Press, 1954; 2nd ed., London: SPCK, 1962, 1968; 3rd ed., London: Sheldon, 1974.

———. *Religion in Africa*. New York: Praeger, 1969.

———. *West African Religion*. 1st ed. London: Epworth, 1949.

Richardson, Don. *The Peace Child: An Unforgettable Story of Primitive Jungle Treachery in the 20th Century*. Ventura: Regal, 1975.

Smart, Ninian. "Soteriology." In *The Encyclopaedia of Religion*, vol. 13, edited by Mircea Eliade. New York: Macmillan, 1987, 418–23.

Smith E. W., ed. *African Ideas of God*. 2nd ed. London: Edinburgh House, 1961.

Troutman, Philip. H. "Towards an African Theology of Christian Holiness: A Journey from Israel to Africa." In *Africa Speaks: An Anthology of Africa Nazarene Theological Conference 2003*, edited by Linda Braaten, 107–11. Florida, South Africa: Africa Nazarene Publications, 2004.

Westermann, D. *Africa and Christianity*. New York: Oxford University Press, 1937.

———. *The African Today and Tomorrow*. London: International African Institute, 1949.

3

Salvation – Prosperity or Poverty? An Assessment of African Pentecostal Christianity

Mica Onserio Moenga
Pan Africa Christian University, Nairobi, Kenya

Abstract

Within the African Pentecostal church today there is endless debate regarding the doctrine of salvation. The crux of the problem lies in two critical terms: prosperity and poverty. The debate has gained in popularity with the growth of the prosperity gospel in the USA since the late nineteenth century. One school of thought emphasizes prosperity as a sure mark of true salvation, while another emphasizes poverty. The reality of this debate plays out in everyday life in African Pentecostal churches. It has left sincere adherents confused and unable to grasp what salvation really means. This study is an assessment of the doctrine of salvation within African Pentecostalism. It seeks to answer the fundamental question: Is salvation representative of prosperity or poverty, or both? Selected Scripture passages on salvation are analyzed exegetically for their correct interpretation and application, demonstrating that the problem emanates in particular from a misunderstanding of the doctrine of salvation as presented in the Bible. While prosperity and poverty do represent certain aspects of salvation, the extremes must be avoided when teaching on salvation. Thus it is hoped that the impasse in discussing salvation in the narrow senses of prosperity and poverty will be resolved.

Key words: African Christianity, African Pentecostalism, poverty, prosperity, salvation, wealth, health

Introduction

Within the sphere of African Pentecostal Christianity there remains a challenge in the presentation of the doctrine of salvation. The major impediment to understanding this doctrine lies in two terms: prosperity and poverty. One group within African Christianity emphasizes prosperity as a key characteristic of salvation, while another group views salvation as purely for the poor, hence poverty is a key precursor to salvation.

For instance, the prosperity ministries, as noted by Lindhardt, "emphasize material abundance with their rhetoric of victory, achievement, and success, and thus offer a version of Christianity that is focused on the here-and-now."[1] This has created a huge gulf between churches that emphasize holiness on the one hand and those that promote prosperity on the other. In this line of argument, churches that focus on holiness do not emphasize prosperity as a key evidence of salvation. Lindhardt observes that perhaps a more relevant distinction to make in contemporary Africa is between the (mostly urban) congregations that focus mainly on prosperity and the healing-focused churches of the poorer rural and urban areas.[2]

This study seeks to adjudicate between these two concepts, prosperity and poverty, and demonstrate their relationship to the doctrine of salvation. Golo observes that the majority of Africa's neo-Pentecostal/charismatic churches propagate prosperity preaching.[3] Such preaching is evidence of how they view the doctrine of salvation. According to the prosperity gospellers, as they are sometimes termed, right standing with God, earned through salvation, must yield or trigger the blessings of good health, prosperity, and wealth.[4] Thus, salvation is viewed from the perspective of physical manifestations of the well-being of a born-again Christian. However, this study proposes the need for a balanced approach to understanding the doctrine of salvation.

---

1. Martin Lindhardt, *Pentecostalism in Africa: Presence and Impact of Pneumatic Christianity in Postcolonial Societies* (Leiden: Brill, 2014), 9.
2. Lindhardt, *Pentecostalism in Africa*, 9.
3. Ben-Willie Kwaku Golo, "Africa's Poverty and Its Neo-Pentecostal 'Liberators': An Ecotheological Assessment of Africa's Prosperity Gospellers," *Pneuma* 35, no. 3 (Dec. 2013): 367.
4. Golo, "Africa's Poverty," 368.

This study engages biblical exegesis to present the doctrine of salvation. This involves an analysis of some select Bible passages critical to an understanding of the doctrine. The study encompasses three major themes. The first theme is a lexical study of the term "salvation" as it is used in both the Old and New Testaments. The second theme is to focus on specific texts that are problematic when it comes to understanding salvation. The third theme draws on the first two throughout the chapter to highlight the correct understanding of the doctrine of salvation for proper epistemological and pragmatical considerations by the church in Africa.

Clarification of Terms

Before we delve into the terminology of salvation, it is vital to clarify some of the terms that we will employ in this study. The term "Pentecostalism" and its sister term "charismatic" in general are hard to define. This has resulted in a revitalized interest in recent decades in studying them. However, these studies have only afforded to make the terms more complex for both scholars and laypeople, rather than simplifying them. Some scholars think that we should talk of "Pentecostalisms" rather than "Pentecostalism." For instance, Anderson et al. argue, "It is probably more correct to speak of pentecostalisms in the contemporary global context, though the singular form will continue to be used to describe these movements."[5] To correctly define "Pentecostalism," Anderson asserts, "If we are to do justice to this global movement, we must include its more recent expressions in the independent, Charismatic and neo-Charismatic movements."[6] It is evident that the terms "Pentecostalism" and "charismatic" describe aspects of Christianity that manifest themselves very differently from conservative Christianity.

Generally speaking, the term "Pentecostalism" describes a movement of Christianity that emphasizes the manifest presence of the Holy Spirit, with speaking in tongues understood as the initial evidence of this. Coleman notes, "Tongues were . . . an important indication of the reception of grace but also a form of subsequent empowerment."[7] In this study, we shall use the term "Pentecostalism" in the singular, not to exclude other shades of the

---

5. Allan Anderson et al., eds., *Studying Global Pentecostalism: Theories and Methods* (Berkeley: University of California Press, 2010), 15.
6. Anderson et al., *Studying Global Pentecostalism*, 16.
7. Simon Coleman, *The Globalisation of Charismatic Christianity: Spreading the Gospel of Prosperity* (Cambridge: Cambridge University Press, 2000), 21.

movement but rather to include them all. In addition, "Pentecostalism" is used synonymously with "charismatic."

Many aspects characterize African Pentecostalism. Brown observes the depiction of African worldviews in which disease and poverty are both understood as the work of Satan and his demonic hosts, while health and finances are envisioned as material blessings from God that tangibly express complete salvation.[8] On this basis, African Pentecostalism emphasizes material prosperity as a key characteristic of salvation. It cannot be denied that the gospel of health and wealth characterizes African Pentecostalism. This is evident in the kinds of sermons preached in many churches by television evangelists and preachers. This has become the standard way of preaching in today's churches in Africa.

Close to this is a second key aspect of African Pentecostalism that is noted by Brown (quoting Gifford), who understands the defining characteristic of African Pentecostalism to be a vision of "victorious" living that encompasses health while being even more concerned with the financial blessing needed for a successful life in the present world.[9] The Christian life is portrayed as that of a victor and winner in every circumstance in every sense – physical, economic, and spiritual. This being the case, illnesses are unnecessary intruders that must be fought with all ferocity, mainly through prayer. The same applies to both economic and spiritual stability.[10]

Such aspects of "prosperity" are commonly understood as relating to "salvation." The next term that relates to the doctrine of salvation and which will be used in this study is "poverty." "Poverty" here is used to imply a focus on the spiritual as opposed to the material. The term is not a celebration of poverty in a physical sense but the pursuit of holiness or spirituality as a key indicator of genuine salvation. It is a kind of poverty by choice, or Christ's poverty,[11] not poverty as a result of one's birth or socioeconomic oppression.[12] This kind of poverty was vividly demonstrated by Christ at his incarnation.[13] He willingly emptied himself of divine attributes and privileges for the sake of

---

8. Candy Gunther Brown, *Global Pentecostal and Charismatic Healing* (Oxford: Oxford University Press, 2011), 17.

9. Brown, *Pentecostal and Charismatic Healing*, 17–18.

10. The emphasis is drawn from 3 John 2: "Beloved, I pray that you may prosper in all things and be in health, just as your soul prospers" (NKJV).

11. Vincent J. Genovesi, "Christian Poverty: Sign of Faith and Redemptive Force," *The Way*, Supplement 32 (1977): 78.

12. This is congruent with Christ's advice to the rich young man in Matt 19:16–24.

13. See Phil 2:6–7.

humankind. Christians are therefore to imitate Christ in demonstrating their willingness to forgo certain privileges for his sake. Genovesi sees a connection between Christ's poverty and the introduction of a new law (of love) and new salvation (by grace and faith).[14]

We will now turn to consider the meaning of the doctrine of salvation.

Scholarly Concepts of Salvation and Prosperity

The doctrine of salvation has occupied a central place in scholarly discussions since the dawn of the twenty-first century. A brief survey of different views held by scholars is therefore necessary. John Hick, cited by Asamoah-Gyadu, uses the hybrid term "salvation/liberation" to describe "the transformation of our human situation from a state of alienation from the true structure of reality to a radically better state in harmony with reality."[15] This is an interesting concept. The key denominator here is the transformation of the human situation. As we will see, the aspect of transformation is critical in the discussion of the effects of salvation. In other words, the impact of salvation on an individual should be a clear manifestation of a changed lifestyle.

However, in Asamoah-Gyadu's consideration of this, the exact elements of transformation are missing. Asamoah-Gyadu notes that "in Charismatic ministries . . . salvation is something to be experienced. The key 'soteriological goals' therefore include the realization of 'transformation and empowerment,' 'healing and deliverance,' and prosperity and success in the lives of believers."[16] He observes that in many African Pentecostal churches salvation is inclined toward prosperity. Golo's analysis of prosperity preachers also reveals that the main emphasis is on "material prosperity and abundance to those who faithfully depend on God by virtue of their salvation wrought through Christ."[17] Van der Watt observes that the main emphasis of neo-Pentecostal churches is on all kinds of prosperity as the sure sign of God's favor and the only mark of genuine faith.[18] On this understanding, salvation is a means to eradicate poverty and bring meaningful transformation. The question arises as to whether salvation is meant to solve all human problems – political, socioeconomic, and spiritual

---

14. Genovesi, "Christian Poverty," 80.
15. J. Kwabena Asamoah-Gyadu, *African Charismatics: Current Developments within Independent Indigenous Pentecostalism in Ghana* (Leiden: Brill, 2004), 133.
16. Asamoah-Gyadu, *African Charismatics*, 133.
17. Golo, "Africa's Poverty," 368.
18. Gideon van der Watt, "'. . . But the Poor Opted for the Evangelicals!' Evangelicals, Poverty and Prosperity," *Acta Theologica* 32, Supplement 16 (2 Jan. 2012): 45.

in the here and now. If so, to what extent – wholly or partially? These and many other questions often arise in discussing soteriological matters. Even Jesus's disciples were at one point concerned about the material benefits of following him.[19]

Another model suggested by proponents of prosperity is the holistic frame. According to Barnes, "a holistic frame attempts to consider the many dynamics believed to perpetuate poverty. Most importantly, it stems from the spiritual premise that after salvation, godly living can result in economic and non-economic benefits."[20] This model is prevalent in many black megachurches. While it is true that certain benefits do accompany salvation, attaching prosperity to salvation in a rigid manner does not fully present the biblical doctrine of salvation. The holistic model condemns poverty to the core, arguing that poverty distorts God's image in humankind. In addition, poverty is viewed as a problem of one's mindset, which must undergo a paradigm shift. Such transformation of the mind can happen only after one receives salvation.[21] However, it is simplistic to argue that salvation offers an escape from poverty.

This study does not delve into the famous historical debate of the Arminian or Calvinist views of salvation. The focus is on the basic meaning of salvation and how it relates to the concepts of poverty and prosperity. In this case, salvation can be defined as the "deliverance from the power and effects of sin."[22] This kind of salvation is centered on the person and work of Christ.[23] The means of attaining salvation is by grace and through faith in the finished work of Christ on the cross.[24] Further discussion of the meaning of salvation follows in the lexical survey below.

The Concept of Salvation in the Old Testament Canon

To talk of salvation in the Old Testament (OT) may sound theologically inconsistent since God's people, Israel, specifically belonged to God. How could they be in need of salvation? Yet the nation of Israel kept shifting the goalposts

---

19. See Matt 19:27.

20. Sandra L. Barnes, *Live Long and Prosper: How Black Megachurches Address HIV/AIDS and Poverty in the Age of Prosperity Theology* (New York: Fordham University Press, 2012), 149.

21. Barnes, *Live Long*, 148.

22. "Salvation," Merriam-Webster online, accessed 15 August 2022, https://www.merriam-webster.com/dictionary/salvation.

23. Corneliu C. Simut, *The Doctrine of Salvation in the Sermons of Richard Hooker* (Berlin: De Gruyter, 2005), 45.

24. See Eph 2:8; Acts 16:30–31; 4:12; Rom 10:9–10.

as far as their relationship with God was concerned. The book of Judges in particular sheds light on Israel's unfaithfulness and the many times God handed them over to their enemies because of their apostasy. So from time to time they needed God's salvation. Salvation would be enjoyed only as long as they remained within covenantal parameters. For instance, Deuteronomy 28 sets out the grounds on which the nation of Israel would experience the benefits of salvation and the consequences of breaching the covenant.

Lopez has noted that the word "salvation" in the OT comes from the verbal stem "save," *yāŝa*. It originally meant "to be roomy, broad," which is the opposite of the concepts of "oppression" or "narrowness."[25] In this context, "salvation" meant deliverance from oppression due to captivity or imprisonment. On many occasions, the nation of Israel fell into the hands of their enemies due to their infidelity in breaching their covenant with God. Psalm 107 recounts salvation history noting the numerous times when the nation of Israel cried out to God for salvation.

In the *New Bible Dictionary*, the basic meaning of "salvation" is given as to "bring into a spacious environment" (see Pss 18:36; 66:12), but it carries from the beginning the metaphorical sense of "freedom from limitation" and the means to that, namely, deliverance from factors which constrain and confine. It can be seen as deliverance from disease (Isa 38:9, 20), from trouble (Jer 30:7), or from enemies (2 Sam 3:18; Ps 44:7).[26]

The Hebrew word translated "salvation" is יְשׁוּעָה (*yeshuah*). According to Strong's Concordance, the term means deliverance, rescue, salvation, safety, and welfare.[27] Derivatively, the term has a broader sense in meaning which is attested in many lexical tools. For instance, the discussion in the *New Dictionary of Biblical Theology* states that in biblical usage, "salvation" is a comprehensive term denoting all benefits, physical or spiritual, that are graciously bestowed on humans by God.[28] From the lexical meaning, it is clear that salvation is holistic. Any attempts to emphasize one aspect above others are likely to create a logical quagmire in understanding the term's usage. Consequently, the term

---

25. René A. Lopez, "Old Testament Salvation – From What?," *Journal of the Grace Evangelical Society* (Autumn 2003): 50.

26. G. Walters and B. A. Milne, "Salvation" in *New Bible Dictionary*, edited by D. R. W. Wood and I. Howard Marshall, 3rd ed. (Leicester: Inter-Varsity Press, 1996), 1046–47.

27. James Strong, *The New Strong's Exhaustive Concordance of the Bible* (Nashville: T. Nelson Publishers, 1990), 61.

28. M. J. Harris, "Salvation" in *New Dictionary of Biblical Theology*, edited by T. Desmond Alexander and Brian S. Rosner, IVP Reference Collection (Leicester: Inter-Varsity Press, 2000), 762.

"salvation" does not mean the entire range of meanings discussed above in every context in which it occurs. To avoid misuse and misunderstanding it is necessary to consider the context in which the term is used. The following passage from the Old Testament demonstrates this.

The term "salvation" first occurs in Genesis 49:18, which reads לִישׁוּעָתְךָ קִוִּיתִי יְהוָה. In translation, this reads, "I have waited for your salvation, Yahweh." But what does the word "salvation" mean in this context? Ignoring the context will be detrimental to our understanding of the term.

First of all, the words were spoken by Jacob while in Egypt. The opening verse of the chapter indicates that the pronouncement was prophetic: "And Jacob called his sons and said, 'Gather together, *that I may tell you what shall befall you in the last days*'" (Gen 49:1 NKJV; emphasis added). The patriarch might have been anticipating his descendants' "salvation" from the foreign country. As the biblical narrative unfolds, the Israelites were delivered from the hand of Pharaoh the king of Egypt. The kind of deliverance here was emancipation from the oppression inflicted on the Israelites by the king. The immediate context of the verse also shows that the salvation anticipated by the patriarch was from danger. It is after he has described the dangerous characteristic of Dan as a "serpent by the way" that Jacob makes his pronouncement "I have waited for your salvation." Therefore, salvation in this context is also deliverance from danger or harm.

In many instances in the Old Testament, this is the sense in which the term is used: salvation from an enemy, disease, or danger. There is no doubt that the biblical sense of salvation was holistic, summed up in the Hebrew term *šālôm* (peace), which means personal wholeness and well-being in every sphere.

In many references to salvation, God is the author of salvation. For instance, one of the climactic acts of God's deliverance of his people was the exodus event (see below). Moses understood this very well when he told the Israelites, "Stand still, and see the salvation of the LORD" (Exod 14:13 NKJV). Therefore, God is the Savior of humankind. The discussion in the *New Bible Dictionary* affirms this, saying, "The words 'God' and 'saviour' are virtually identical terms in the OT."[29]

In the OT, God used various means (personal or impersonal) to achieve salvation for his people. For instance, in the case of the Israelites in their wilderness journeys, God used the pillar of cloud and the wind at the Red Sea (e.g. Exod 14:19–21). On other occasions, God used people such as Gideon (Judg 6–8) and Esther (Esth 4–7). Despite the means God chooses to use,

---

29. G. Walters and B. A. Milne, "Salvation," 1047.

ultimately it is God and God alone who brings salvation. He declares in Isaiah, "I, even, I, am the LORD, and apart from me there is no savior" (Isa 43:11).

We now turn to consider the use of the term "salvation" in the New Testament (NT).

The Concept of Salvation in the New Testament

The Greek equivalent of the Hebrew *yĕša* is the noun *sōtēria*, a derivative of the Greek verb *sōzō* ("to save"). It is also from the Greek verb *sōzō* that we get *sōtēr* ("savior"); *sōtērios* ("bringing salvation"); and the compound verbs *anasōzō* ("to rescue") and *diasōzō* ("to preserve").[30] This analysis shows that the NT usage of the term "salvation" is consistent with the OT usage. However, it is worth noting the emphasis given in NT usage. The *New Bible Dictionary* states that "the religious usage of a moral/spiritual deliverance becomes almost wholly dominant as far as the idea of salvation is concerned. Non-religious usage is virtually confined to saving from acute danger to life (Acts 27:20, 31; Mk. 15:30; Heb. 5:7)."[31]

In the Synoptic Gospels, for instance, Jesus announces his mission of bringing salvation to the lost (Luke 19:9). It is important to understand the kind of salvation Jesus is announcing here to Zacchaeus. Zacchaeus is said to have been a tax collector. In the first century AD world, tax collectors were detested because of their use of force and extortion. Zacchaeus himself confesses the likelihood of his having stolen from people: "Then Zacchaeus stood and said to the Lord, 'Look, Lord, I give half of my goods to the poor; and *if I have taken anything from anyone by false accusation, I restore fourfold*'" (Luke 19:8 NKJV; emphasis added). The salvation Jesus announced to Zacchaeus was that of imparting pardon. In other words, salvation is associated with the forgiveness of sins. This does not imply that the other senses of "salvation" that we have already seen in both Testaments are not applicable. It means that the primary emphasis of the word, and its strict sense especially in the New Testament, is that of forgiveness of sins. Van der Watt argues, "The focal point in Matthew's history of salvation is illustrated by the episodes where the words αφεσις (forgiveness) and σωζω (I save) occur. Absolution supposes forgiveness."[32] However, the term αφιημι ("I forgive") has a wider meaning

---

30. Alexander and Rosner, *New Dictionary of Biblical Theology*, 762.
31. Wood and Marshall, *New Bible Dictionary*, 1047.
32. Jan G. van der Watt, *Salvation in the New Testament: Perspectives on Soteriology* (Leiden: Brill, 2005), 15.

beyond simply forgiveness, as van der Watt indicates: "In the New Testament, the term αφιημι is used to refer to the remission of monetary debt (Matt 18:27, 32), to being freed from captivity (Lk 14:18), and to absolution from sin (Matt 6:14–15; Mk 2:5–10; 3:28; Lk 7:47–50)."[33]

Besides this, salvation involves a change of conduct. It has been argued that "salvation calls for a contrite heart, childlike, receptive helplessness, and the renunciation of all for Christ – conditions it is impossible for man unaided to fulfil."[34] Salvation implies a life of total surrender to Christ and total dependence on him. In this sense, "salvation" is an all-inclusive term that includes deliverance or rescue from danger and, more specifically, from sin and the world which pose such dangers to humanity.

Textual Analysis: Selected OT Passages

We now turn to a textual analysis of selected passages of Scripture to shed further light on the sense of "salvation" in contemporary biblical hermeneutics and application. This will provide a check to the misinterpretation and misapplication of the concept. In order to provide balance, passages from both the OT and the NT are considered.

Salvation as Spiritual Restoration: Analysis of Psalm 51

The book of Psalms contains numerous occurrences of the word "salvation." It is not practical to analyze all the sections where it occurs; thus, for the purpose of this study, we restrict ourselves to Psalm 51. The context of the psalm is that David had committed adultery with Bathsheba, Uriah's wife (1 Sam 11). David was an individual in the OT who enjoyed close fellowship with God. The Bible calls him "a man after [God's] own heart" (1 Sam 13:14; Acts 13:22). The first time this phrase was used was when the prophet Samuel went to anoint David as king over Israel and described the man who would replace King Saul in office. The replacement of King Saul was necessitated by Saul's act of assuming the office of a priest and deciding to offer a sacrifice instead of waiting for the prophet Samuel. From that time on, as indicated in 1 Samuel 13:14 by the use of an adverb of time, *'attāh* ("now"), God had rejected Saul and sought out for himself a man after his own heart. Auld explains, "The basic sense of *'attāh* is temporal, 'now' or 'at this time.' But it is often used rhetorically, and even

---

33. Van der Watt, *Salvation in the New Testament*, 15.
34. Wood and Marshall, *New Bible Dictionary*, 1047.

logically, as 'now' and 'then' are in English, to introduce the main point of an argument."[35] This is to say that Saul never cared about his relationship with God, but David did.

God's choice of David does not imply that David was perfect. In fact, David's life was full of flaws; yet he was quick to repent and seek God's forgiveness. In the current chapter (Ps 51), David, upon realizing the sin he has committed, seeks God's forgiveness. David knew what it meant to lose fellowship with God. It was equivalent to losing his salvation. Verse 12a reads, "Restore to me the joy of your salvation." What was at stake was the likelihood of David's losing the joy of his salvation. The verb "restore" is in the hiphil imperfect, third-person feminine singular. The hiphil stem is generally used to express causative action in the active voice. In this case, salvation is an act of God and not a human being. Indeed, salvation belongs to God, as the psalmist indicates in Psalm 3:8. Salvation here was all to do with the restoration of a relationship that was on the verge of breaking down. Sin threatens our fellowship with God. David felt a desperation in his spirit that he had never felt before, and he pleaded with God to restore the joy of salvation.

True salvation brings joy, as attested in many passages (Ps 95:1–2; Luke 2:10–11; 15:7; Gal 5:22–23). In Galatians 5, it is intriguing to note that joy is the fruit of the Holy Spirit. This is what David sought to have restored in his life. In response to the prosperity gospel, then, we note that it is simplistic to emphasize material well-being at the expense of the spiritual. David desperately wanted a restored relationship with God, not even his kingdom, which might be given to another, just as was the case with King Saul. David knew that what was at stake was his relationship with God. Hence, he sought forgiveness and mercy from God to restore the relationship (v. 14).

It is theologically correct to argue that salvation is about outward well-being. We have seen that, while salvation is a broader term covering many aspects of life (physical and spiritual), the main emphasis throughout the Bible is on the spiritual, which manifests in the physical. It is therefore necessary to keep this balance. Indeed, David emphasizes the spiritual aspect of salvation when he prays, "Create in me a clean heart, O God, and renew a steadfast spirit within me" (51:10 NKJV). David here asks God to do what he alone can do, *bara* (בְּרָא, imperative of בָּרָא, "to create"). The choice of verb here is interesting. Why the verb "create" and not *asah* (עָשָׂה, "to make or do")?

---

35. A. Graeme Auld, *I & II Samuel: A Commentary* (Louisville: Westminster John Knox, 2012), 142.

The verb בָּרָא ("to create") has always been associated with creating out of nothing, *ex nihilo*. While this is the primary sense in which the verb "create" is used, sometimes the two verbs "to create" or "to make" are used interchangeably in Genesis. For instance, we are told that God created the first male and female humans (Gen 5:2). But we know from Genesis 2:7 that God formed, יָצַה, Adam from the dust of the earth, and in Genesis 2:22 we are told that God fashioned, בָּנָה, Eve from the rib of Adam.

The kind of creation David was seeking has been explained in different ways by scholars. Ibn Ezra argues,

> Being that David earlier said that he was brought forth in iniquity (v. 5), that is, that the lust which is implanted in human heart brought him to sin, he now prayed to God and asked him to help him overcome the impulse so that he would not commit a similar sin again.[36]

Given all this, we can conclude that the intention of the verb "create" was to communicate empowerment and transformation at the same time: empowerment in the sense that David needed supernatural enabling to overcome sin, while at the same time he needed a transformation of his heart. This way, David would continue to enjoy fellowship with God, which is critical to salvation.

Salvation as Deliverance from a Physical Danger: The Exodus Event

The exodus event stands as one of the major salvific events accomplished by God in the history of the Israelites. As we noted earlier, the aspect of salvation emphasized is deliverance from oppression by Pharaoh and the Egyptians. The Israelites were in bondage in Egypt for about 430 years. The suffering they experienced is recounted in Exodus 1. God responded by sending Moses to deliver them from their slavery and oppression (Exod 3). Moses typifies Jesus Christ, the Messiah – that is, Israel's savior – in many ways. Deuteronomy 18:15 foretells of Jesus as a prophet like Moses. There are numerous points of convergence between the two. Both of them are associated with the word of God. Moses is portrayed as the lawgiver, while Jesus is presented as the law-interpreter (Matt 5). In her monograph, Dharamraj asserts, "While Moses remains a prophet without equal, hope that the prophetic line would yield

---

36. Abraham Ibn Ezra, *Commentary: On the Second Book of Psalms*, trans. H. Norman Strickman (Boston: Academic Studies Press, 2009), 63.

another of Moses' fibre rests on the Lord's promise through Moses, made in response to Israel's request for a mediation of the divine word to the people (Deut 18:15–22)."[37]

The fact that Moses was particularly involved in the deliverance of the Israelites from slavery in Egypt also presents him in parallel to Jesus, the savior of Israel (Matt 1:21; Luke 2:10–12). The two figures represent different aspects of salvation. Moses is primarily to bring deliverance in the physical sense, with spiritual implications (Exod 20:2–3). We noted earlier that the exodus event was mentioned as a preamble to the covenant (Exod 20:2; Deut 5:6). The Israelites were to respond in gratitude for God's act of deliverance and remain loyal to him. The benefits of salvation would be enjoyed as long as the Israelites remained faithful to God (Deut 28).

The idea of understanding salvation as deliverance from physical danger, that is, from enemies and sickness among other things, is attested in many other OT passages as well. For instance, David composed and sang many psalms depicting this aspect of salvation. In Psalm 18, David praises Yahweh for delivering him from his enemies. In his lifetime, David encountered many enemies, including King Saul who sought his life. In all these instances, David experienced God's deliverance. David therefore calls God his "salvation."[38] God's deliverance of his people was intended to foster covenantal relationship.

Having analyzed the usage of the term "salvation" in the OT, it is evident that what is propagated by the majority of African Pentecostal churches is not consistent with the teachings of the OT. The emphasis on prosperity as proof of salvation is not the focus. The OT instead has an emphasis on relationships and behavioral change. It is paradoxical that the Christian movement is the largest in the Global South while its influence is least felt. This is because of the rise of many social evils in Africa that are characteristic of the continent, such as socioeconomic oppression, injustice, and corruption. It is therefore vital that African Pentecostal churches reflect biblical views in their understanding of salvation.

---

37. Havilah Dharamraj, *A Prophet Like Moses? A Narrative-Theological Reading of the Elijah Cycle* (Milton Keynes: Authentic Media, 2011), 1.

38. See Ps 18:2.

Textual Analysis: Selected NT Passages
Jesus's Ministry

The emphasis on salvation in the New Testament again touches on the realms of both the spiritual and the physical. The dawn of salvation is connected with the coming of Jesus Christ. In Matthew, argues van der Watt, "Jesus, as the Davidic Messiah, has a particular connotation because God's salvation is attached to the name Jesus."[39] The four canonical Gospels indicate that the primary purpose of Jesus's coming was to save his people Israel and the Gentiles from their sins (Matt 1:23; Mark 1:15; Luke 19:10; John 1:29). The concept of holistic salvation is emphasized by the Gospel writers. Luke 4:18–19 elaborates on Jesus's mission on earth. Besides coming to preach the good news of the gospel, Jesus also came to liberate people holistically. The use of infinitives in the two verses points to Jesus's purpose in coming to the world. The first infinitive is εὐαγγλισασθα, "to preach the gospel." The gospel here is directed to the poor. This raises the question as to whether the gospel is for the poor. It is necessary to investigate what Luke had in mind. Carroll argues, "The poor include those who are held captive, the blind, and those who are oppressed (an illustrative list, not comprehensive), and the gospel news concerns their liberation and restoration of sight."[40] This brings out the holistic aspect of the gospel. Further, Carroll asserts that the gospel Jesus proclaimed points to an era of salvation in which social, economic, and cultic dimensions of communal life will be radically reshaped.[41] Therefore, "the poor" here refers to "the afflicted and oppressed" but not those who believe they do not need repentance. It is also important to note that Luke uses the accusative noun ἄφεσιν (an inflection of ἄφεσις, "release") to demonstrate the intended purpose of Jesus's ministry. Carroll makes a detailed observation of the usage:

> Elsewhere, Luke often uses *aphesis* with the meaning of "forgiveness," indicating a release from sin (e.g. 1:77; 3:2; 24:47). In the ensuing narrative, however, the realities of sin (requiring "release" in the sense of gracious forgiveness), indebtedness (requiring "release" in the sense of debt relief), and oppression by demonic powers (requiring "release" in the sense of liberation) overlap.[42]

---

39. Jan G. van der Watt, *Salvation in the New Testament*, 11.
40. John T. Carroll, *Luke: A Commentary* (Louisville: Presbyterian Publishing, 2012), 112.
41. Carroll, *Luke*, 112.
42. Carroll, 111.

In considering Carroll's statement, it is clear that Jesus's ministry was intended to bring total liberation to people. It is important to maintain this kind of understanding of salvation. However, it should also be noted that, just like the kingdom of God which is expressed in two senses, "the already" and the "not yet," ultimate salvation is eschatological as well. This is where the prosperity gospel gets it wrong in its argument that total salvation is for the here and now. If this were the case, then the kingdom of God would have been established long before Jesus came to announce the gospel. All that Jesus did was to inaugurate the kingdom of God, which, like "a mustard seed," will grow steadily until its culmination at his second advent.

Pauline Soteriology

In Paul's soteriology he emphasizes the transformation of the life of the believer. Phrases the apostle Paul commonly uses to describe salvation include "new creation," "passing from death to life," and "new birth." For instance, drawing from the allegory of Sarah and Hagar in Galatians 4:29, he clarifies the difference between the two sons of these two women, that is, the one born κατὰ πνεῦμα ("according to the spirit," Isaac) and the one born κατὰ σάρκα ("according to the flesh," Ishmael). Hubbard, in his monograph *New Creation in Paul's Letters and Thought*, argues, "He [Paul] reads his perception of Christian experience into the Genesis narrative and defines it as new birth by the spirit."[43] According to this statement, Paul's thought is that salvation is a matter of experiencing the new birth. It is not an imaginary occurrence in the life of a believer but one that can be experienced. Paul's understanding of salvation encompasses a threefold process: identification with the cross of Christ, empowerment, and transformation – as Hubbard demonstrates: "Rom. 6:1–11 stresses ritual suffering (death, burial, and crucifixion with Christ), empowerment ("so that we might walk in newness of life," v. 4), and transformation ("alive to God," v. 11)."[44]

For the purposes of this study, we will look at 2 Corinthians 5:16–17. Matera asserts that "these verses draw out the consequence of Paul's statement in verses 14–15 that Christ died for all, and all died with him."[45] Paul's understanding

---

43. Moyer V. Hubbard, *New Creation in Paul's Letters and Thought* (Cambridge: Cambridge University Press, 2002), 87.
44. Hubbard, *New Creation*, 103.
45. Frank J. Matera, *II Corinthians: A Commentary* (Louisville: Westminster John Knox, 2013), 135.

is that Christ's death has led to a radical transformation of a believer's life (2 Cor 5:17). Paul writes that he no longer views anyone from a merely human point of view; if someone is in Christ, that person is a new creation.[46] This fact is important, especially when considering the view of many prosperity gospel preachers who emphasize material acquisition as a mark of salvation. That is a merely human view; it does not reflect a proper understanding of the doctrine of salvation. Both verses 16 and 17 begin with the conjunction ωστε, "so." This means that the ideas of both verses are drawn from the previous verses, 14–15, which state that Christ's love was manifested in his saving death for all.[47] Consequently, it is Christ's love that controls and directs Paul's convictions, not human, worldly views as before. Even though verse 16 expresses the fact negatively while verse 17 does so positively, they both testify to the same truth: that Christ's death has radically altered Paul's perception of the human person.[48]

Verse 17 expresses the effect of Christ's death positively: "Therefore, if anyone is in Christ, he is a new creation" (v. 17a NKJV). Paul's phrase "new creation" here is an import from Isaiah 65:17. Swindoll elaborates beautifully on the phrase:

> Paul applies this imagery to the redeemed believer, indicating the stunning, radical, dramatic transformation that God designed to take place when a believer says, "I do" to Jesus Christ. When Christ invades a life, He performs a miraculous act of re-creation, analogous to the extreme overhaul of creation itself that He will perform at the second coming. He brings into being something new.[49]

Swindoll's explanation best explains the reality of salvation. Paul's thought of salvation is a transformation of the human character. It is a creation of a new nature, the divine nature. This is the emphasis that Paul gives throughout his letters.

---

46. Matera, *II Corinthians*, 135.
47. Matera, 135.
48. Matera, 137.
49. Charles R. Swindoll, *Insights on 1 and 2 Corinthians* (Carol Stream: Tyndale House, 2017), 366.

Conclusion

As we have demonstrated throughout this study, the doctrine of salvation has suffered misinterpretation through the ages of Christendom. The debate is usually over which emphasis best describes salvation: prosperity or poverty. However, both ideas fall short in presenting a full understanding of the doctrine of salvation. We have also argued that the term "salvation" has a broader sense of meaning. Salvation is holistic, involving physical, spiritual, and social dimensions. Therefore, it is important to consider all three dimensions when presenting the doctrine of salvation.

We conclude that salvation is a transformation of the inner person that affects those three realms. Most prosperity gospel preachers understand salvation as working from the outside in. Salvation should, however, instead be understood as working in the reverse order – that is, from the inside out.

Bibliography

Alexander, T. Desmond, and Brian S. Rosner, eds. *New Dictionary of Biblical Theology*. IVP Reference Collection. Leicester: Inter-Varsity Press, 2000.

Anderson, Allan, et al., eds. *Studying Global Pentecostalism: Theories and Methods*. Berkeley: University of California Press, 2010.

Asamoah-Gyadu, J. Kwabena. *African Charismatics: Current Developments within Independent Indigenous Pentecostalism in Ghana*. Leiden: Brill, 2004.

Auld, A. Graeme. *I & II Samuel: A Commentary*. Louisville: Westminster John Knox, 2012.

Barnes, Sandra L. *Live Long and Prosper: How Black Megachurches Address HIV/AIDS and Poverty in the Age of Prosperity Theology*. New York: Fordham University Press, 2012.

Brown, Candy Gunther. *Global Pentecostal and Charismatic Healing* (Oxford: Oxford University Press, 2011).

Carroll, John T. *Luke: A Commentary*. Louisville: Presbyterian Publishing, 2012.

Coleman, Simon. *The Globalisation of Charismatic Christianity: Spreading the Gospel of Prosperity*. Cambridge: Cambridge University Press, 2000.

Dharamraj, Havilah. *A Prophet Like Moses? A Narrative-Theological Reading of the Elijah Cycle*. Milton Keynes: Authentic Media, 2011.

Genovesi, Vincent J. "Christian Poverty: Sign of Faith and Redemptive Force." *The Way*, Supplement 32 (1977), 78–82.

Golo, Ben-Willie Kwaku. "Africa's Poverty and Its Neo-Pentecostal 'Liberators': An Ecotheological Assessment of Africa's Prosperity Gospellers." *Pneuma* 35, no. 3 (Dec. 2013): 366–84. https://doi.org/10.1163/15700747-12341366.

Harris, M. J. "Salvation." in *New Dictionary of Biblical Theology*, edited by Desmond Alexander and Brian S. Rosner, IVP Reference Collection. Leicester: Inter-Varsity Press, 2000, 762.

Hubbard, Moyer V. *New Creation in Paul's Letters and Thought*. Cambridge: Cambridge University Press, 2002.

Ibn Ezra, Abraham. *Commentary: On the Second Book of Psalms*. Translated by H. Norman Strickman. Boston: Academic Studies Press, 2009.

Lindhardt, Martin. *Pentecostalism in Africa: Presence and Impact of Pneumatic Christianity in Postcolonial Societies*. Leiden: Brill, 2014.

Lopez, René A. "Old Testament Salvation – From What?" *Journal of the Grace Evangelical Society* (Autumn 2003): 49–64.

Matera, Frank J. *II Corinthians: A Commentary*. Louisville: Westminster John Knox, 2013.

"Salvation." Merriam-Webster online. Accessed 15 August 2022. https://www.merriam-webster.com/dictionary/salvation.

Simut, Corneliu C. *The Doctrine of Salvation in the Sermons of Richard Hooker*. Berlin: De Gruyter, 2005.

Swindoll, Charles R. *Insights on 1 and 2 Corinthians*. Carol Stream: Tyndale House, 2017.

van der Watt, Gideon. "'. . . But the Poor Opted for the Evangelicals!' Evangelicals, Poverty and Prosperity." *Acta Theologica* 32, Supplement 16 (2 Jan. 2012): 35–53. https://doi.org/10.4314/actat.v32i1S.3.

van der Watt, Jan G. *Salvation in the New Testament: Perspectives on Soteriology*. Leiden: Brill, 2005.

Walters, G., and B. A. Milne. "Salvation" in *New Bible Dictionary*, edited by D. R. W. Wood and I. Howard Marshall, 3rd ed. Leicester: Inter-Varsity Press, 1996: 1046–47.

4

"Jesus Is My Personal Savior"

Engaging Evangelical Themes of Individual Salvation in African Communal Contexts[1]

Kyama Mugambi
Researcher, Centre for World Christianity

Abstract

"Personal salvation" is a common evangelical framing of the conversion experience among evangelical Christians. Though personal experience is an important biblically supported aspect of conversion in evangelical theology, this chapter examines the role of communality as a crucial dimension for consideration. Soteriological themes that emerge from communal lived faith engage in discourse with prevalent evangelical perspectives. The chapter employs biblical textual analysis of concepts emerging from research in churches in a communal context. We find that communal contexts highlight dimensions of soteriology which are biblical and grounded in the local lived Christian experience. Communal themes regarding salvation from oral Christian communities critique and enlarge the prevailing evangelical soteriological perspectives. The issues raised provide fruitful avenues for theological reflection that broaden the overall theological discourse.

---

1. The research for this paper has benefited from the Engaging African Realities grant from the Nagel Institute. The author is the principal investigator for the research project titled, "Alternative Kinship Structures within Emerging African Ecclesiologies."

Key words: salvation, individual salvation, communality, conversion, context, worldview, evangelical soteriology

Introduction

Evangelical theology has historically prioritized individualistic interpretations of salvation. The self-descriptive phrase "Jesus is my personal savior," commonly used during introductions among evangelical Christians in East Africa, illustrates the widely accepted personalized perspective and private quality of salvation in their lives.[2] A "personal salvation" implies a soteriology predicated on an individualized conversion experience. The influential Puritan-era text *The Pilgrim's Progress* typified this approach to Christian faith among early evangelicals.[3] The text gained popularity among evangelical missionaries as an allegory of a Christian's life.[4] In the first volume of *The Pilgrim's Progress*, Christian, the protagonist, leaves his family behind and embarks on a journey which, after many setbacks, leads him to the Celestial City.[5] The allegory presents conversion and discipleship as a lonely endeavor undertaken at great cost in the absence of other members of one's community. Modern evangelical materials about conversion continue to advance this perspective. I submit that "personal salvation" is, in part, a Christian framing of conversion emerging from a particular intellectual, cultural, and historical context. I further illustrate how this approach may be enriched through a dialogue and critical engagement with biblical perspectives coming from within indigenous communal worldviews.

The individualistic approach to conversion gained currency among African Christians from their contact with Western missionaries through preaching and

---

2. For an early example of this see John Gatu's biographical account in John G. Gatu, "Jesus Christ the 'Truthful Mirror': My Finding Jesus Christ in the Ministry of the East African Revival Movement," in *The East African Revival: History and Legacies*, eds. Kevin Ward and Emma Wild-Wood (Kampala: Fountain, 2010), 49, 51. This position is articulated in a widely circulated evangelistic tract in the English-speaking Global North: Bill Bright, *Have You Heard of the Four Spiritual Laws?* (Peachtree City: Campus Crusade for Christ, 2007).

3. John Bunyan, *The Pilgrim's Progress from This World to That Which Is to Come, Delivered under the Similitude of a Dream* (London, 1678).

4. Isabel Rivers, "*The Pilgrim's Progress* in the Evangelical Revival," in *The Oxford Handbook of John Bunyan*, eds. Michael Davies and W. R. Owens, Oxford Handbooks Online (2018), 537–54, https://doi.org/10.1093/oxfordhb/9780199581306.013.36.

5. The second book features Christian's wife Christiana and his sons undertaking the same journey without their father. The book ends with Christian's sons staying behind after Christiana and others enter the Celestial City.

discipleship.⁶ Early converts engraved into their narratives this personalized quality of Christian conversion, hence popularizing the self-introductory expression "I am born again; Jesus is my personal savior."⁷ This privatized formula of self-identity transmitted orally survives in present iterations of indigenous Christian movements that have evangelical roots.⁸ Materials used for evangelism and discipleship further reinforce this notion.⁹

Beyond the local church, many Protestant theological schools promote the position as presented in the Western evangelical literature their libraries rely on. I argue that communal contexts may highlight dimensions of soteriology which are also biblically sound but grounded in a non-Western Christian experience. Additionally, communal perspectives can provide useful critiques on existing discourse, while offering insights into the broad reach of the concept of salvation.

Soteriology in the Biblical Context

We define salvation here as the divine rescue Christ brings from sin and evil (Rom 10:13).¹⁰ Salvation necessarily includes the reconciliation between God and God's people (2 Cor 5:11–21).¹¹ Within the evangelical perspective, salvation highlights the redemptive role Jesus played through his passion and eventual death on the cross. Hundreds of years of Protestant theological debate

---

6. To this end Derek Peterson argues that translating *The Pilgrim's Progress* was viewed by missionaries as an urgent task for early East African Christians. The first Swahili edition of the book appeared before the Swahili Old Testament, five years after the completion of the New Testament in 1888. This pattern was also followed with several other significant languages. While the point is made about the missionaries' urgency in translating the book, that the early African Christians had a real say in the decision to translate *The Pilgrim's Progress* is a matter of conjecture. See Derek R. Peterson, *Ethnic Patriotism and the East African Revival: A History of Dissent, c.1935–1972* (New York: Cambridge University Press, 2014), 37–40.

7. See for example Gatu, "Finding Jesus Christ"; Hannah W. Kinoti, "Christology in the East African Revival," in *Jesus in African Christianity: Experimentation and Diversity in African Christology*, eds. J. N. K. Mugambi and Laurenti Magesa (Nairobi: Acton, 1998), 54–59.

8. I make this observation in my book, where I propose that this formula of individualized faith is a core feature in oral narratives carried beyond the East African Revival to modern Pentecostal and evangelical movements in Kenya. See Kyama M. Mugambi, *A Spirit of Revitalization: Urban Pentecostalism in Kenya* (Waco: Baylor University Press, 2020), 55–56.

9. See for example Bright, *Four Spiritual Laws*; Nicky Gumbel, *The Alpha Course Manual* (London: Holy Trinity Brompton, 1999); Rick Warren, *The Purpose Driven Life: What on Earth Am I Here For?*, 2nd ed. (Grand Rapids: Zondervan, 2002).

10. Biblical references and quotations used in this chapter are from the NIV.

11. The terms "born again" and "committed believer" are often used by evangelical Christians to refer to the concept of salvation as we address it in this chapter.

on the nature of salvation (especially since the Reformation) have focused on the themes of atonement, justification, and sanctification. The finer points of these concepts remain the subject of sustained debate, responsible for the proliferation of different denominational positions. These are beyond the scope of this chapter.

The Scriptures present a personal God restoring a fractured relationship with his creation (John 3:16–17). As a practical outworking of this initiative, Christ's invitation is decidedly personal and invokes an individual response (Rev 3:20). The resulting transformation encompasses the individual as an outworking of God's grace, which meets with the individual's faith (Eph 2:1–10).[12] Evangelical perspectives, while varied, attempt to provide a comprehensive framework for understanding this dimension of salvation.[13] We here take prima facie the general Protestant view, that salvation is by grace through faith. The specific mechanism by which grace and faith play out in salvation lies outside the purview of this discussion. Our focus is the interface between the individual and the community specifically with regard to salvation, rather than the select contested modalities that animate the debate.

Contemporary discourse focuses on the outcome of salvation for the individual. However, a biblical approach accepts the idea that salvation encompasses not just the individual but also his or her community and all creation.[14] Salvation is the product of God's grace at work through the death of Christ (Rom 3:23–24). As a result of God's love expressed in God's grace, Christ's death occurred for those who believe, and in their stead. This grace functions through faith alone, without depending on human effort.[15] Such faith is the gift of God at work empowered by the Holy Spirit.[16] Thus, evangelical soteriology privileges the divine work done from the perspective of God's own initiative.

---

12. The passage illustrates the important interplay between the individual and the community that is the central point of this chapter's argument.

13. Eastern Orthodox and Roman Catholic positions are less adamant on the individualistic dimension.

14. For a short discussion on this see N. T. Wright's summary in *Justification: God's Plan and Paul's Vision* (Downers Grove: InterVarsity, 2009), 10–11.

15. The precise interpretation of the role of faith is a major point of discussion among Protestants, and a key point of departure from Roman Catholic doctrine.

16. The pneumatic dimension of salvation is often overlooked in mainline Protestant discourse. Pentecostal-charismatic Christianity by definition is an attempt to recover, and in many cases privilege, this aspect. See again Wright, *Justification*, 10.

Conversion as Central to Salvation

The starting point of the salvific process is a life-changing encounter with God.[17] The encounter initiates a deep-rooted shift away from a self-oriented existence to a God-directed life. From an evangelical perspective, it is this conversion that marks the beginning of Christian life. The actual mechanism of this conversion remains a mystery, but its genesis and results are clear.

Conversion centers on God's love expressed in his only begotten Son Jesus (John 3:16–17; Rom 5:8). Conversion is a response to these truth claims of the gospel. When they are presented to, and received by, the individual, the Holy Spirit initiates movement toward conversion (Rom 10:8–15). Conversion is therefore an active process of the believer responding to God's overtures in his word (Rev 3:20). Contact with, and response to, God's revelation of himself through his word is a key part of the process.

Turning to the triune God implies turning away from sin and self (Gal 2:20). The result of such conversion is, or should be, transformation (Gal 5:16–25). While positions vary as to whether one can fall back, evangelicals generally agree that this conversion marks the beginning of a turning away from self and toward God.

The inextricable linkage of the salvific process to the personal conversion experience in evangelicalism has historically left little room for communal dimensions of understanding salvation. In particular, common evangelical perspectives limit community participation in the conversion process to proclaiming the gospel and incorporation into a new community.[18] In this perspective, community exists for the purpose of bringing in believers and effectively nurturing their individual spirituality.[19] The American evangelist and founder of Campus Crusade for Christ, Bill Bright, used the following analogy: "Several logs burn brightly together, but put one aside on the cold hearth and the fire goes out. So it is with your relationship with other Christians."[20]

Increased emphasis by post-Enlightenment Protestants on individual faith diminished the role of the community as an aspect in the conversion process. Catholic and Eastern Orthodox expressions, for their part, emphasized community participation in conversion through ritual and tradition.

---

17. Stanley J. Grenz, *Theology for the Community of God* (Grand Rapids: Eerdmans, 2000), 405.
18. Grenz, *Community of God*, 423–27.
19. Heb 10:24–25 is commonly used as a proof text for this.
20. See Bright, *Four Spiritual Laws*, 15.

Involvement in the sacraments – for example, among Catholics – entrenched the community's role in the salvific process.[21] In the same way, the sacrament of (infant) baptism presupposes a family community whose role includes presenting the child for the rite in the context of the wider participant church community.[22]

Among Protestants, and especially evangelicals, the sacraments have taken on a symbolic role that is important but incidental to the salvific process. Such understandings of salvation emerging from the Reformation era became entrenched in the emerging catechisms.[23] The Protestant movements that produced evangelicalism built on this approach to further develop the theme of personal salvation.[24] The holiness movement, for example, drew from this foundational Protestant theology and the early revivals to accentuate the individual's conversion as the critical entry point to the faith.

For evangelical Christians, individual conversion thus became the single most important event to entering, as it were, the salvific process. Through this prism, evangelical missionaries and televangelists viewed dissociation from familial structures as a necessary consequence of conversion.[25] Missionaries and evangelists made few references to the construction of a new kinship in Christ. They emphasized leaving one's birth family and ethnic communal practices as a requisite for effective conversion. The new birth necessitated a new family. While this is not the only factor, that dissociation from the community was a contributor to the poor response to earlier missionary work

---

21. The Catholic understanding of the sacraments is that they are necessary for salvation.

22. Among Catholics the Christian faith of the parents is a factor in the inclusion of their children into the community of faith. There is no express requirement for a conversion event in a child if he or she is part of a Catholic family. The faith of the community is integral to the children's conversion and growth. See *Catechism of the Catholic Church* (Vatican: Librera Editrice Vaticana, 1994), 1250–53.

23. For example, the Heidelberg Catechism, dating from 1563, teaches conversion as a reflective personal journey involving a dying to self, a deep sense of repentance, and a rebirth in joy. The community does not play a central role in this process. See Zacharius Ursinus, *The Heidelberg Catechism* (Altenmünster: Jazzybee Verlag, 2012), 88–90.

24. See for example the Anglican Catechism in The Church of England, *The Book of Common Prayer* (London: Oxford University Press, 1928), 581.

25. Sometimes this dissociation is seen as a precursor to conversion. Common texts quoted are Matt 19:29 and Mark 10:29–31, passages which speak about prioritizing one's relationship with Jesus beyond earthly families. See further discussion on this below.

in East Africa.²⁶ Such a missionary approach to religion without kinship involvement did not fit within the early indigenes' plausibility structures.²⁷

Conversion, Context, and Worldview

Converts interpret religious concepts through the lenses of their lived experience. The prevailing religious and cosmological context provides the categories with which people come to terms with their new religious reality.²⁸ Salvation as a personal endeavor devoid of community participation originates from a post-Enlightenment and increasingly individualist context. That is not to say the communal aspects are entirely absent. As we will see, Christianity has communalism built into the very fabric of its existence from its inception in the New Testament. However, forms of evangelicalism prioritize the individual perspective in ways that may affect engagement with the gospel in communal societies.

Epistemologies of communal society favor oral approaches and not literary ones.²⁹ Such communities prioritize the spoken word through which they receive, store, and communicate knowledge. Furthermore, the nature of communication in these oral communities is high-context. Communication in these cultures depends to a large measure on the context within which something is spoken.³⁰ Fundamental components of the lived context are the people within it and their relationships with the communicator. This necessarily has implications for how members of the community communicate and understand concepts such as those found in religion.

Within these communities, members interact with the concept of Christian salvation and interpret it orally from a communal perspective. Soteriology

---

26. I devote more time to examining this issue of kinship and conversion in early initiatives in African Christianity in Mugambi, *Spirit of Revitalization*, 44–48.

27. This was an important contributor to the rise of Early African initiatives in Christianity.

28. For more on this see Andrew F. Walls, *Crossing Cultural Frontiers: Studies in the History of World Christianity*, ed. Mark R. Gornik (Maryknoll: Orbis, 2017), 38.

29. See Paul G. Hiebert, *Transforming Worldviews: An Anthropological Understanding of How People Change* (Grand Rapids: Baker Academic, 2008), 116.

30. This concept provides understanding for how communication functions in oral, relational cultures. High-context cultures rely on cues from the environmental context to give meaning to pieces of communication. These are usually oral, relational cultures. Such communication may be shaped by relationships between speakers, their immediate surroundings, the prevailing community lore, and so on. Low-context cultures derive less material from the surrounding context in order to communicate clearly and draw meaning. They tend to be literary and less relational. The concept was first articulated in Edward Twitchell Hall, *The Silent Language* (New York: Anchor, 1959).

within such an oral, highly communal culture can thus be properly appreciated only if it fits within their communality. Subsequently, soteriology appreciated from a communal context may highlight other dimensions which may enrich discourse.[31]

Communality and Soteriology

Soteriology and communality are intricately connected in Scripture, though certain Christian expressions do not adequately acknowledge the connection. As we have noted, evangelical engagement with soteriology starts from the individual's conversion experience. Conversion is, in this sense, a decision from the individual's heart that works out into the community.[32] Evangelical authors would argue that the journey of faith is, at its core, a personal pursuit of a relationship with God.[33] Their discipleship materials on conversion and subsequently living the Christian life focus on personal responsibility for the process. The convert should forsake his or her family or clan as part of the individualized pursuit of Christ.[34]

The result is an internal endeavor whose ramifications should progressively move outward into the Christian community. Christian community, as described within that evangelical thought, refers to the gathered body of people who have made this personal decision.[35] Discipleship, governance, leadership, and other aspects vital to this community have at their core this commitment to an individualized faith.

---

31. Emic theological exploration of soteriology from within the communal environment is a developing area in Africa. This is because of the relatively small number of theologians engaging in this field. The few who are available work within existing evangelical frameworks. It is for this reason that these reflections are necessary.

32. This is different from the Catholic position, for example, which as we have seen gives a more prominent role to ritual, liturgy, and tradition in the salvific process.

33. C. S. Lewis, *Mere Christianity* (Grand Rapids: Zondervan, 2001); J. I. Packer, *Knowing God* (Downers Grove: InterVarsity, 2021); Philip Yancey, *The Jesus I Never Knew* (Grand Rapids: Zondervan, 2008); Bright, *Four Spiritual Laws*.

34. Family in communal contexts often goes beyond the nuclear family to include the extended family. Luke 14:26 is often used as a proof text to advocate converts' abandonment of their families, and self-denial as a necessary consequence of their transformation in Christianity. This passage was used with effect for early African converts, many of whom had to leave their families in their conversion journey.

35. The emphasis on community in this evangelical perspective comes after conversion, not before or alongside. See Grenz, *Community of God*, 438–40.

Proof texts for this individualized perspective are found in the New Testament.[36] English renditions of passages in the New Testament do not differentiate between the plural or singular "you."[37] Interpretations of passages calling people to follow almost always refer, in evangelical literature, to the individual. Biblical instructions in the Gospels and Epistles refer to the individual, even where community is implied (as with the Matt 4:19 example). The resultant effect within evangelical circles is the construction of a faith paradigm lived on the individual plane. However, a closer look at both the language and the context of the New Testament reveals that salvation goes beyond the individual.

The call to follow Jesus is also a communal call. Evangelical churches in communal contexts have begun exploring the possibilities of the critical role an individual's community plays in his or her conversion and discipleship.[38] The recruitment of two sets of brothers among the disciples, for example, is a direct reference to family and community in the call to Christian faith (Matt 4:18–22; John 1:35–42; Luke 5:1–11; Mark 1:19–20). That all the Gospels highlight these relatives among the disciples is evidence of the vital role of communality in the call into the family of God. The call to be disciples also included workmates. In this way, Jesus demonstrated that families and colleagues can be involved in the call to follow Christ. Several examples of Christian communality in the New Testament have found expression in church life. These instances illustrate different aspects of the relational nature of soteriology.

Familial Companionship after Conversion

Several examples in the New Testament show how consenting family members were welcome companions in the journey to conversion. Peter's mother-in-law entertained Jesus and his followers and became a part of the gospel narrative (Luke 4:38–40). Later in the New Testament, Paul makes reference to Peter's believing wife (1 Cor 9:5). In Acts, the accompanying role of family is evident when, for example, Cornelius and his entire household participate in a conversion event. Other converts shared in the life of the church along

---

36. Consider the aforementioned Luke 14:26. The Matt 4:19 invitation "Come, follow me," though addressed to a group of individuals, is often understood to refer to an individual call.

37. Consider for example the Greek *hymas* in Matt 4:19, which in all common English translations is rendered "you," but is a second-person plural pronoun.

38. We explore this shortly.

with their households.[39] There is no perceptible segregation between believing family members and non-believers within the households mentioned. We see this concept accommodated in the discipleship initiatives of churches such as Christ Is the Answer Ministries (CITAM), a Pentecostal denomination in Kenya.

At CITAM, conversion of the individual is the first step in that person's journey of faith. The goal of the faith journey of believers is to enhance their faith and encounter God as they live their lives in their communities.[40] In this church, discipleship for individuals involves a commitment to their church communities and service using their skills and gifts. The resulting growth in faith finds expression in community. CITAM considers the accompanying role of the community essential for a comprehensive discipleship. Four of their five levels of discipleship are based on different configurations of the community: the small group, the local assembly, affinity groups, and the entire wider church community.[41] Discipleship involves the active participation at each of these levels in the conversion and growth of the individual.

Community Evangelism

Paul argues that a convert's familial participation in community may result in conversion (1 Cor 7:16).[42] Proximity to a believer's lived faith provides contact that may lead a non-believer to accept the Christian faith. Thus, not only does the community participate in discipleship, but the individual also has a positive effect on the non-believing community. Conversely, complete isolation from one's community is counterproductive to the evangelistic cause. Paul suggests, for example, that abandoning family responsibilities may constitute a gross violation of Christian virtues (1 Tim 5:8). Evangelism in the Christian context is thus both a communal exercise and an individual one.

---

39. See Acts 11:14. The same is true of the conversion of the households of Lydia (Acts 16:15), the jailer (Acts 16:33), Crispus (Acts 18:8), and Stephanus (1 Cor 16:15). Passing reference is also made to the believing households of Aristobulus and Narcissus (Rom 16:10–11), Caesar (Phil 4:22) and Onesiphorus (2 Tim 1:16; 4:19).

40. CITAM, *Enter: The Call to Know, Laying the Foundations – The Safari* (Nairobi: CITAM CED, 2014), 4.

41. CITAM, *Enter*, 4.

42. A similar point is made by Peter; see 1 Pet 3:1–2.

Churches like CITAM and Mavuno encourage their members to convene small groups in their homes and neighborhoods.[43] These groups provide continuous contact points for the individual's family and the surrounding communities. They induct their neighbors and families into their activities, in part for companionship, but also for evangelistic purposes.

Christian Community as Family

Paul's second letter to Timothy presents a family legacy of faith beginning with Timothy's grandmother (2 Tim 1:2–3, 5). Elsewhere Paul fondly refers to the Philippian community as a source of his joy and pride. He sees the churches and the broader community of faith as one family headed by Christ and stewarded by leaders. In referring to this broader community, Paul uses the language of adoption into the family of God (Eph 1:5; 2:19). Conversion thus marks the moment of induction into the new family within which believers grow in their faith. From then on they grow in relationship with Christ within God's family (Eph 4:15).

Churches in communal contexts enact this adoption into Christian family through constant self-identification as a family. In Jubilee Christian Church in Nairobi, for example, the senior pastor and his wife, Allan and Kathy Kiuna, present themselves as the spiritual parents of the community. They then cast their church community as a family of which the members are part. The founding pastors present their relationship as a marriage with two dimensions. Their own marriage and children constitute a physical family.[44] Their marriage is also the foundational spiritual unit of their church family which they lead. The Kiunas regularly refer to their marriage with the hope of inspiring their congregants. In this regard, as with other charismatic-Pentecostal churches, conversion implies adoption into a spiritual family where members are "spiritual" equivalents of physical family members.[45]

---

43. Mavuno Church is a Pentecostal charismatic church in Nairobi. See also CITAM, *Enter*; Muriithi Wanjau, *Mizizi* (Nairobi: Fearless, 2007).

44. See Kathy Kiuna and Allan Kiuna, *Marriage Works: So Why Is It Falling Apart?* (Nairobi: Jubilee, 2012).

45. We do not have the space here to explore a full critique of this model, with its strengths and failings. Suffice it to say that the model offers useful insights into how important the spiritual family is within the context. Kinship family models can be seen in other Christian communities such as student Christian unions and various affinity groups. Popular affinity groups include gender-specific gatherings such as Daughters of Zion and Men of Valor, both found at Jubilee Christian Church and at Kenyatta University Christian Union.

Communality Critiquing Individualist Soteriology

The above examples enrich the existing evangelical church's perspectives on Christian communality. They also open up the discussion about the theological and missiological challenges of the one-dimensional individualistic view of soteriology. The first challenge that becomes evident is that a personal soteriology does not adequately represent the scriptural position. A thorough analysis of the New Testament reveals a profound level of communality that is lost in individualist interpretations. Evangelical experiences from communal perspectives may point to the need for a recovery of the communal dimension of soteriology.

An individualist understanding of salvation is potentially limiting because it may minimize the role of community in the important function of discipleship. The examples above demonstrate the ways in which emerging models of discipleship necessarily involve community. If we define discipleship as the socialization of an individual into his or her faith, then the engagement of community becomes apparent. CITAM's model is one example of how community has been vitally connected with the process of discipleship.

Neighborhood-based discipleship groups provide avenues for nonbelievers to come into contact with a lived Christian faith. Without the groups, evangelism within communal cultures will also be less effective. As shown, the call to follow Jesus may also be carried out within family and other close relationships. New Testament narratives highlight the important place of the family and household in the believer's lived faith.

Salvation in the context of a lived community implies the transmission of abundant life not just eschatologically, but also within this present life. The outcomes of God's work in the individual should overflow beyond the family and neighborhood into the community at large. Old Testament narratives exemplify this in the lives of the patriarchs. Abraham and Joseph's stories demonstrate tangible consequences in their world as a result of their obedience to God. This societal perspective of salvation is not negated but carried over into the New Testament. Evaluated this way, salvation does have concrete dimensions whose effects reach outward to the various levels of community.

Individual and Communal Perspectives in Dialogue
Conversion As Intellectual Assent versus Conversion As Belonging

Individualized perceptions of salvation place the epistemology of salvation within a person's own internal reflection. The individual receives the facts of faith from Scripture, then makes a decision for or against, based on his or her evaluation of the truth claims of these facts. The basis of this decision is intellectual and, to some extent, an emotional assent to these facts of the faith. One oft-quoted example of this thought progression is in Romans 10. Here Paul makes the case that one cannot make a faith decision unless one has received the word from one who has been "sent." The only way one can evangelize is after having received missional instructions.

Communal evangelical models illustrate that conversion may also be the result of a well-considered evaluation of community. Communities that embody shared belief in Christ become catalysts for conversion. Acts 2:42–47 provides an ideal vision of a community living out their faith in ways that draw others into it. Such a community attracts a variety of people to live out their Christian faith together, as a family. The result is a conversion of the society as well as of the individuals within it who witness this societal change.

The benefits of the communal dimensions of conversion emerge in several stories in the book of Acts. The case of Cornelius's household in Acts 10 portrays conversion as a considered community decision initiated by the head of the home. The sense of belonging within the family became an aid to the conversion event in this Gentile's household. The communality of the faith in Cornelius's household became an opportunity for additional conversions, baptisms, and displays of the miraculous.

Eschatological Function versus Concrete Faith

The concept of personal salvation emphasizes individual piety. Individuals live out their lives separate from the world as they await their final destiny in heaven. Personal salvation becomes the means by which the individual endures the travails of this earthly life. The quest for personal purity – being uncontaminated by the world – often supersedes the call to mingle and bring about transformation. Subsequently, the pure "await their crown" at the end of time when Christ will return.

The oral, communal communities examined above appreciate this eschatological perspective but they also value the concrete dimensions of their faith lived in the present world. To them, salvation is not just a means to a heavenly end, but also an important expression of God's love for a broken world. The communal Christian's connection with his or her family puts that person constantly in touch with the dysfunction of the world and its need for redemption. Communal cultures may therefore restore a balanced perspective by drawing attention to the tangible results of a lived faith.

Personal Discipleship versus Communal Discipleship

Individualized salvation lends itself to individualist discipleship modes. These include one-on-one activities and devotional books whereby the convert charts his or her own path. The safeguards for doctrinal integrity here are largely literary. The individual depends on the manual as the ultimate guide to his or her discipleship journey.

Oral, communal communities are at once prejudiced against through such a perspective. This is because their epistemology depends on interpersonal relations and the oral narrative – the story. Where they have been developed, communal understandings of salvation invite a shared model of discipleship. Here converts walk with each other as they make meaning of their salvation. Guided by their indigenous literary sources, the narrative provides a medium for effective communication.

Conclusion

We have argued that an engagement with soteriological themes from a communal perspective enriches the prevalent perspectives drawn from non-communal contexts. I have emphasized the contrasts between individual perspectives and communal ones. In practice, the differences are more nuanced, and the starkness of the contrast differs depending on a wide range of factors. However, the questions raised and potential perspectives opened up can provide fruitful avenues for theological reflection that broadens the overall theological landscape. Communal salvation models from relational Christian communities critique and enlarge the prevailing soteriological models from the dominant widely accepted individualistic views. Soteriological issues as addressed by evangelical communal communities can therefore nuance the existing theological discourse.

Bibliography

Bright, Bill. *Have You Heard of the Four Spiritual Laws?* Peachtree City: Campus Crusade for Christ, 2007.

Bunyan, John. *The Pilgrim's Progress from This World to That Which Is to Come, Delivered under the Similitude of a Dream.* London, 1678.

Catechism of the Catholic Church. Vatican: Librera Editrice Vaticana, 1994.

The Church of England. *The Book of Common Prayer.* London: Oxford University Press, 1928.

CITAM. *Enter: The Call to Know, Laying the Foundations – The Safari*. Nairobi: CITAM CED, 2014.

Gatu, John G. "Jesus Christ the 'Truthful Mirror': My Finding Jesus Christ in the Ministry of the East African Revival Movement." In *The East African Revival: History and Legacies*, edited by Kevin Ward and Emma Wild-Wood, 47–59. Kampala: Fountain, 2010.

Grenz, Stanley J. *Theology for the Community of God*. Grand Rapids: Eerdmans, 2000.

Gumbel, Nicky. *The Alpha Course Manual*. London: Holy Trinity Brompton, 1999.

Hall, Edward Twitchell. *The Silent Language*. New York: Anchor, 1959.

Hiebert, Paul G. *Transforming Worldviews: An Anthropological Understanding of How People Change*. Grand Rapids: Baker Academic, 2008.

Kinoti, Hannah W. "Christology in the East African Revival." In *Jesus in African Christianity: Experimentation and Diversity in African Christology*, edited by J. N. K. Mugambi and Laurenti Magesa, 54–59. Nairobi: Acton, 1998.

Kiuna, Kathy, and Allan Kiuna. *Marriage Works: So Why Is It Falling Apart?* Nairobi: Jubilee, 2012.

Lewis, C. S. *Mere Christianity*. Grand Rapids: Zondervan, 2001.

Mugambi, Kyama M. *A Spirit of Revitalization: Urban Pentecostalism in Kenya*. Waco: Baylor University Press, 2020.

Packer, J. I. *Knowing God*. Downers Grove: InterVarsity, 2021.

Peterson, Derek R. *Ethnic Patriotism and the East African Revival: A History of Dissent, c.1935–1972*. New York: Cambridge University Press, 2014.

Rivers, Isabel. "*The Pilgrim's Progress* in the Evangelical Revival." In *The Oxford Handbook of John Bunyan*, edited by Michael Davies and W. R. Owens, 537–54. Oxford Handbooks Online, 2018. https://doi.org/10.1093/oxfordhb/9780199581306.013.36.

Ursinus, Zacharius. *The Heidelberg Catechism*. Altenmünster: Jazzybee Verlag, 2012.

Walls, Andrew F. *Crossing Cultural Frontiers: Studies in the History of World Christianity*. Edited by Mark R. Gornik. Maryknoll: Orbis, 2017.

Wanjau, Muriithi. *Mizizi*. Nairobi: Fearless, 2007.

Warren, Rick. *The Purpose Driven Life: What on Earth Am I Here For?* 2nd ed. Grand Rapids: Zondervan, 2002.

Wright, N. T. *Justification: God's Plan and Paul's Vision*. Downers Grove: InterVarsity, 2009.

Yancey, Philip. *The Jesus I Never Knew*. Grand Rapids: Zondervan, 2008.

5

Household Conversions in Acts and Their Significance for House-to-House Evangelism in Africa

Isaac Ampong

Pastor for Youth and Families, St. Paul's Anglican Church, Tervuren, Belgium

Abstract

In the book of Acts, Luke presents four accounts of household conversion where the salvation of the head of the household leads to the salvation of the other members of the household. These narratives can be found in the stories of Cornelius (Acts 10:1 – 11:18), Lydia (16:11–15), the Philippian jailer (16:25–34), and Crispus (18:8). Indeed, Paul and Silas's statement in Acts 16:31, "Believe in the Lord Jesus, and you will be saved – you and your household," expresses Paul's confidence that the jailer's salvation will extend to his household, which indeed actually happened. In spite of this, it is also certain that the other members of the household are not saved by the faith of the head of the household, as each member of the household must personally believe in Jesus Christ to be saved. However, while their faith and salvation are unquestioned, the narratives do also suggest that the other household members follow the head's religious conviction. Each will personally commit to the beliefs of the head. This study will explore how personal faith works in such household salvation. It will also explore how such dynamics can aid in missions and evangelism in Africa. Lastly, using Lydia as an example, this study will note that women, who often serve as household heads in the African context, can use their leadership to draw other members of their households to a personal relationship with Jesus Christ.

Key words: Acts of the Apostles, conversion, household, house-to-house evangelism, Cornelius, Lydia, Philippian jailer, Crispus

Introduction

In December 2011, at the end of the first semester of my final year at university in Ghana, I joined other university students from southern Ghana to embark on evangelism in Buipe, a village in northern Ghana. The primary method of evangelism was to visit homes and share the gospel with household members. One of the experiences that has stayed with me to this day is a conversation I had with a woman. After I had presented the gospel to her and asked if she was willing to place her trust in Jesus Christ, she replied that I should talk with her husband first. If her husband decided to convert to Christianity, she would follow. If he did not accept, then she also would not accept Christianity. Unfortunately, the husband was not home at the time so we could not talk with him. However, this particular phenomenon got me thinking about the nature of conversion and salvation. This chapter will largely draw from those musings.

In this chapter, I argue that in the household conversions in Acts, the conversion of the head of the household functions as a catalyst for the conversion of other members of the household. I will also argue that the Greco-Roman culture shares some similar values with African culture and, as such, Christians can employ similar strategies for household conversions.

The Nature of Conversion and Its Emphasis in Luke–Acts

From the beginning, Luke is clear about his purpose in writing his two-volume work Luke–Acts.[1] He states that he intends to provide "an orderly account" (καθεξῆς) for Theophilus and any other reader with the purpose that they might come to know with certainty the things they have been taught

---

1. I take the view that the Gospel According to Luke and the Acts of the Apostles are a unified two-volume work authored by Luke. For a brief discussion on the unity of Luke–Acts and responses to those who hold other views, see Darrell L. Bock, *A Theology of Luke and Acts: God's Promised Program, Realized for All Nations*, Biblical Theology of the New Testament (Grand Rapids: Zondervan, 2012), 55–61.

(κατηχήθης) (Luke 1:1–4).[2] Luke is a masterful theologian whose two-volume work dives deep into many theological topics: theology proper, Christology, soteriology, ecclesiology, eschatology, ethics, discipleship, and so on.[3] With regards to salvation, David Peterson notes, "The terminology [of salvation] is more frequently used by Luke than by any other Gospel writer, and with a wider application."[4] Even on the topic of salvation, Luke leaves no aspect of it undiscussed.[5] However, the interest of this chapter centers on just one aspect of the topic of salvation, namely, "conversion," and more specifically, household conversions.

In the study of religious conversions, William James's work *Varieties of Religious Experience*, though published many years ago (1902), still receives interest in academic circles. His definition of conversion has become a classic and continues to appear in discussions. He argued:

> To be converted, to be regenerated, to receive grace, to experience religion, to gain an assurance, are so many phrases which denote the process, gradual or sudden, by which a self hitherto divided, and consciously wrong inferior and unhappy, becomes unified and consciously right superior and happy, in consequence of its firmer hold upon religious realities.[6]

Not too long after, another landmark work was published by Arthur Nock, *Conversion*, in which he defined conversion as "the reorientation of the soul of an individual, his deliberate turning from indifference or from an earlier form of piety to another, a turning which implies a consciousness that a great change is involved, that the old was wrong and the new is right."[7] While some biblical scholars have rejected these psychological analyses of what conversion

---

2. David A. DeSilva, *An Introduction to the New Testament: Contexts, Methods and Ministry Formation*, 2nd ed. (Downers Grove: InterVarsity, 2018), 270–71.

3. For an extensive survey of some theological themes in Luke–Acts, see Bock, *Theology of Luke and Acts*.

4. David Peterson, *The Acts of the Apostles*, The Pillar New Testament Commentary (Grand Rapids: Eerdmans, 2009), 65.

5. For a discussion of the different aspects of salvation in Luke–Acts, see I. Howard Marshall, *Luke: Historian and Theologian*, 3rd ed. (Carlisle: Paternoster, 2006), 188–215; Bock, *Theology of Luke and Acts*, 239–78.

6. William James, *The Varieties of Religious Experience: A Study in Human Nature*, Oxford World's Classics (1902; repr., Oxford: Oxford University Press, 2012), 150.

7. Arthur Darby Nock, *Conversion: The Old and the New in Religion from Alexander the Great to Augustine of Hippo* (London: Oxford University Press, 1933), 7.

is, others, such as Joel Green, find them helpful in understanding what the Scriptures say about conversion.[8]

In the New Testament, conversion, repentance, penitence, and faith are strongly connected.[9] I. Howard Marshall describes them as "the human side of receiving salvation."[10] "Repentance" and "conversion" are often used interchangeably. This is due to the fact that the Greek word μετανοέω (and its cognates) can mean both conversion and repentance. Yet, we must distinguish these terms. Matthew Michael rightly helps in this regard as he points out that conversion is a process with two main aspects: repentance from sin and exercising of faith in Christ Jesus.[11]

Repentance and conversion are among the biggest themes in Luke–Acts. The theme of conversion occurs more in Luke's Gospel than in the Gospels of Matthew and Mark combined.[12] David Matson notes that conversion narratives occupy the second-largest formal grouping in Acts.[13] Thomas Finn also notes that "conversion is the major theme in Luke's second volume, the Acts of the Apostles."[14] For Charles Talbert, "conversion is a central focus of Acts, maybe *the* central focus" (emphasis original),[15] and Guy Nave also notes that Acts is "full of conversion stories."[16]

---

8. For example, Joel Green asserts that "there is no actual turning to God that does not involve human psychological processes." See Joel B. Green, *Conversion in Luke–Acts: Divine Action, Human Cognition, and the People of God* (Grand Rapids: Baker Academic, 2015), 10. See especially pp. 4–17 for a helpful discussion and criticism of the psychological aspects of conversion and how they can be integrated into the study of biblical conversion.

9. Fritz Laubach, Jürgen Essen Goetzmann, and Ulrich Becker, "Conversion, Penitence, Repentance, Proselyte," in *New International Dictionary of New Testament Theology*, ed. Colin Brown, 4 vols. (Grand Rapids: Zondervan, 1975–78), 1:353–61.

10. Marshall, *Luke*, 192.

11. Matthew Michael, *Christian Theology and African Traditions* (Eugene: Wipf & Stock, 2013), 178. For the same point, see also Marshall, *Luke*, 194; Millard J. Erickson, *Christian Theology*, 3rd ed. (Grand Rapids: Baker Academic, 2013), 865.

12. Ronald D. Witherup, *Conversion in the New Testament* (Collegeville: Liturgical, 1994), 44.

13. David Lertis Matson, *Household Conversion Narratives in Acts: Pattern and Interpretation*, Journal for the Study of the New Testament 123 (Sheffield: Sheffield Academic, 1996), 11.

14. Thomas Macy Finn, *From Death to Rebirth: Ritual and Conversion in Antiquity* (New York: Paulist, 1997), 27.

15. Charles H. Talbert, "Conversion in the Acts of the Apostles: Ancient Auditors' Perceptions," in *Reading Luke–Acts in Its Mediterranean Milieu* (Leiden: Brill, 2003), 135.

16. Guy Nave, "Conversion," in *New Interpreter's Dictionary of the Bible*, ed. Katharine Doob Sakenfeld, 5 vols. (Nashville: Abingdon, 2006–9), 1:729.

Household Conversions in Acts

Luke records four household conversions in Acts: the conversions of Cornelius and his household (Acts 10:1 – 11:18), Lydia and her household (16:11–15), the Philippian jailer and his household (16:25–34), and Crispus and his household (18:8). I will discuss each of these in turn. However, since the account of the Philippian jailer and his household's conversion clearly brings out many of the issues involved in household conversions, this account will be discussed first, and then the other accounts will be discussed in the order in which Luke presents them.

The Conversion of the Philippian Jailer and His Household (Acts 16:25–34)

In Acts 16:19–24, Luke tells of Paul and Silas's arrest for exorcising the slave girl with a spirit of divination (πνεῦμα πύθωνα). However, the main charge given for their arrest by the owners of the slave girl was that Paul and Silas, being Jews, were advocating for the people of Philippi to observe certain customs which were not lawful for them to observe as a Roman colony. Having been flogged, Paul and Silas were put in a highly secure prison and fastened in the stocks.

In verse 25, Paul and Silas prayed and sang hymns to God. Then an earthquake opened the prison doors and loosened the prisoners' chains. When the jailer, who was commissioned to keep Paul and Silas secured in the prison, found out what had happened, he attempted to kill himself. At that point, Paul and Silas called out to him, telling him that all the prisoners were still there. The jailer then asked, "What must I do [literally, "What is necessary for me to do"] to be saved?"

Commentators are divided over what the jailer meant by "be saved." Was he referring to his physical safety, or did he have an idea of Christian salvation in mind?[17] I. Howard Marshall notes that since the prisoners were still present and all right, the question was not borne out of the fear of being punished by his superiors. The most probable option is that the jailer, who probably had heard of Paul and Silas proclaiming God, recognized that everything that had

---

17. For scholarly works which argue that the jailer was asking a question about his physical safety, see Charles H. Talbert, *Reading Acts: A Literary and Theological Commentary on the Acts of the Apostles*, rev. ed., Reading the New Testament (Macon: Smyth & Helwys, 2005), 147; Ben Witherington III, *The Acts of the Apostles: A Socio-Rhetorical Commentary* (Grand Rapids: Eerdmans, 1998), 498; Bruce J. Malina and John J. Pilch, *Social-Science Commentary on the Book of Acts* (Minneapolis: Fortress, 2008), 119.

happened was of divine origin. Therefore, the jailer asks how he can escape the wrath of the God Paul and Silas proclaimed.[18]

Whatever the jailer meant, Paul and Silas took advantage of the situation to share the gospel with him. Their response was, "Believe in the Lord Jesus, and you will be saved – you and your household" (v. 31). This succinct response is "the shortest version" of the gospel.[19] As brief as it is, it captures all that is necessary for the salvation of the jailer. In 4:11–12, Peter makes it clear that in Jesus, and in him alone, can one find salvation, and the only means to appropriate this salvation is by faith (Rom 10:9).

Nevertheless, there is something startling about Paul and Silas's words to the jailer. They stated that not only would the jailer be saved, but his household as well. This is a staggering statement. Does it in any way mean that the jailer's household could also be saved on the basis of his faith in Jesus Christ? The syntax in the Greek allows for this interpretation, as Barclay Newman and Eugene Nida state in their book to aid translators:

> The relationship between the jailer's belief in the Lord Jesus and the salvation of his family is not clear. Did Paul say that the jailer's belief was sufficient both for him and for his family, or did Paul tell the jailer that if he believed he would be saved, and if his family believed they also would be saved? The first of these alternatives more naturally suits the meaning of the Greek.[20]

It is important to recognize that this is not the only way the Greek can be interpreted. As important as syntax is, it is not the only thing that should be considered in interpreting a passage in the Scriptures. Furthermore, the entire New Testament stresses that each person must personally place his or her faith in Jesus Christ (Mark 16:16; John 3:36; Eph 2:8). Because of these numerous New Testament affirmations of the need for a personal trust in Jesus, several commentators on this verse react against a possible misinterpretation by stressing what Paul and Silas are *not* saying. For example, David Williams says,

---

18. I. Howard Marshall, *Acts: An Introduction and Commentary*, Tyndale New Testament Commentaries (Downers Grove: IVP Academic, 2008), 289. Other scholarly works that take this position include Eckhard J. Schnabel, *Acts*, Zondervan Exegetical Commentary on the New Testament (Grand Rapids: Zondervan, 2012), s.v. 16:30; Craig S. Keener, *Acts: An Exegetical Commentary* (Grand Rapids: Baker Academic, 2014), 3:2510; L. Scott Kellum, *Acts*, Exegetical Guide to the Greek New Testament (Nashville: B&H Academic, 2020), s.v. 16:30.

19. Hans Conzelmann, *Acts of the Apostles: A Commentary*, trans. James Limburg, A. Thomas Kraabel, and Donald H. Juel, Hermeneia (Philadelphia: Fortress, 1987), 133.

20. Barclay M. Newman and Eugene A. Nida, *A Translator's Handbook on the Acts of the Apostles* (New York: United Bible Societies, 1972), 322.

"This should not be taken to mean that his [the jailer's] faith was sufficient for their [the jailer's household's] salvation also. They too would have to believe."[21] Marshall comments with similar words and thoughts: "The jailer's own faith does not cover them [the household]."[22] Richard Lenski does the same: "The jailor's believing will certainly not save his wife, children, etc. As he must believe in his person, so must each member of his house in his or her person."[23]

These commentators take other extreme positions in which they let other passages overshadow Paul and Silas's bold statement to the jailer. I think it is necessary to assert Paul and Silas's startling claim and, at the same time, stress what they do not mean. C. K. Barrett's comment gets closer to this: "The conversion of the head of the household carries with it the members of the household."[24] William Larkin also tries to emphasize both when he states: "Personal salvation for the head of the household has spiritual implications for the rest of the members. It does not mean automatic salvation for all household members."[25] John Chrysostom states that the possibility of his family's salvation was among the reasons for the jailer's conversion: "For this above all, wins men: that one's house also should be saved."[26] Craig Keener also states, "The text is hardly an unconditional guarantee for the conversion of family members. . . . Rather, in context, it implies the expectation (again based on the normal cultural pattern) that other members will be saved because they also will believe."[27] I believe the rhetoric of the text suggests more than an expectation.

---

21. David John Williams, *Acts*, New International Biblical Commentary (Peabody: Hendrickson, 1990), 290.

22. Marshall, *Acts*, 290.

23. R. C. H. Lenski, *The Interpretation of the Acts of the Apostles* (Minneapolis: Augsburg, 1944), 681.

24. C. K. Barrett, *The Acts of the Apostles*, International Critical Commentary (London: T&T Clark, 1998), 2:798.

25. William J. Larkin Jr., *Acts*, IVP New Testament Commentary (Downers Grove: InterVarsity, 1995), 242. In another place, Larkin states, "This was not automatic salvation but a gracious promise that God intended that as household members heard the word of the Lord, they would believe (16:32, 34) and become part of God's people." See William J. Larkin Jr., "Acts," in *Luke and Acts*, ed. Philip Wesley Comfort, Cornerstone Bible Commentary (Carol Stream: Tyndale House, 2005), 535.

26. John Chrysostom, *Homilies on the Acts of the Apostles* 36, in vol. 11 of the *Nicene and Post-Nicene Fathers*, Series 1, ed. Philip Schaff, 14 vols. (Grand Rapids: Eerdmans, 1956), 225.

27. Keener, *Acts*, 3:2510.

I think Paul and Silas expressed a *confident* expectation that the household of the jailer's family would also be saved.[28]

The Conversion of Cornelius and His Household (Acts 10:1 – 11:18)

The previous section on the conversion of the Philippian jailer and his household has raised the problem of how the jailer's faith in Jesus Christ could lead to the salvation of members of his household. My initial proposal for this problem is that Paul and Silas had a confident expectation that if the jailer placed his faith in Jesus, that action would lead not only to his salvation but also to the salvation of all his household.

The conversion of Cornelius and his household poses a similar problem, for the promised salvation was not only for Cornelius but for his entire household (Acts 11:14). To undergird this discussion, it is important to note that the significance of the conversion of Cornelius and his household in the narrative of Acts cannot be overemphasized.[29] Luke is careful to stress that the conversion of Cornelius and his household was part of a divine scheme.[30] In Acts 10:1–2, Luke describes Cornelius as a centurion, a generous and prayerful man, and – critical for this discussion – a devout man (εὐσεβὴς) who feared God with all his household (φοβούμενος τὸν θεὸν σὺν παντὶ τῷ οἴκῳ αὐτου). These descriptions, as well as the fact that Cornelius was not circumcised (11:3), suggest that he was a God-fearer.[31] Acts 10:2 also points out that Cornelius performed his pious acts alongside his household. This indicates that even before his conversion, Cornelius not only adopted godly values in managing his household, but he

---

28. Even though the subject of the verb σωθήσῃ is singular, it does not mean the salvation applies only to the jailer, for two subjects joined by καὶ often take a singular verb. See A. T. Robertson, *A Grammar of the Greek New Testament in the Light of Historical Research*, 4th ed. (London: Hodder & Stoughton, 1923), 402; Friedrich Blass, Albert Debrunner, and Robert W. Funk, *A Greek Grammar of the New Testament and Other Early Christian Literature* (Chicago: University of Chicago Press, 1961), §135.

29. Barrett states, "The importance of the story [Cornelius' story] for Luke and for Luke's book is . . . unmistakable." See Barrett, *Acts of the Apostles*, 491.

30. David R. Bauer, *The Book of Acts as Story: A Narrative-Critical Study* (Grand Rapids: Baker Academic, 2021), 152.

31. The God-fearers, often described as οἱ σεβόμενοι τὸν θεόν and οἱ φοβούμενοι τὸν θεόν (13:16, 26, 43, 50; 16:14; 17:4, 17; 18:7), were Gentiles who had not converted to Judaism but had embraced certain aspects of the Jewish religion. See Joseph A. Fitzmyer, *The Acts of the Apostles: A New Translation with Introduction and Commentary*, Anchor Bible (New Haven: Yale University Press, 2010), 449–50.

also involved them in pious acts.[32] This therefore foreshadows how Cornelius would carry his household along in his salvation.

In Acts 10:24, Luke narrates that Cornelius gathered his relatives (συγγενεῖς) and his closest friends (ἀναγκαίους φίλους) as they waited to hear Peter. Up to this point in the narrative, Luke does not state why Cornelius brought his relatives and intimate friends. However, Acts 11:14 says that when the angel appeared to Cornelius, he told Cornelius that Peter would bring him a message by which he and his whole household would be saved. As such, 11:14 fills in some gaps in 10:24.[33] Cornelius brought his relatives and close friends because he knew the message Peter was going to deliver was not for him alone.

Commenting on Acts 11:14, Kellum notes that "and your whole house" is not a promise of household salvation, but to show that the message Peter is going to deliver is not for the head of the household (Cornelius) alone, but for the entire household.[34] The verse seems to indicate that whatever was promised to Cornelius was also promised to the rest of the household.[35] Perhaps Kellum is implying that there was no promise of salvation even for Cornelius. But that does not fit the narrative. The purpose of the meeting with Peter was for Cornelius's household to hear the gospel, and the purpose of their hearing the gospel was their salvation.[36] Cornelius had been *promised* by the angel of God that salvation would come to his household through the message Peter would bring to them.[37] This promise, perhaps, is among the key factors that account for Cornelius's expedient response to what he heard from the angel. Thus, Mikeal Parsons is right to assert that "the significance of the entire event

---

32. Barrett, *Acts of the Apostles*, 501; Richard I. Pervo, *Acts: A Commentary*, Hermeneia (Minneapolis: Fortress, 2009), 268.

33. Luke Timothy Johnson argues that Acts 11:14 is read back into 10:5, 22, 33. See Luke Timothy Johnson, *The Acts of the Apostles*, Sacra Pagina (Collegeville: Liturgical, 1992), 198. James Dunn also describes 11:14 as an example of storyteller's license which reflects the outcome of Peter's preaching. See James D. G. Dunn, *The Acts of the Apostles* (Grand Rapids: Eerdmans, 2016), 150. However, these two observations are not necessary to explain the slight variation in Acts 11:14. Keener points out that its omission is an example of Luke's abbreviation technique. See Craig S. Keener, *Acts: An Exegetical Commentary* (Grand Rapids: Baker Academic, 2012), 2:1825. Another way to read this is to treat it as a "functional redundancy" in which Luke keeps back the information but releases it later to achieve a higher literary effect. See Larkin, "Acts," 481.

34. Kellum, *Acts*, 136.

35. As in 16:31, the singular verb does not mean the salvation is promised only to Cornelius. Clearly, Cornelius and his household are the subject of σωθήσῃ. See footnote 28 above.

36. Kellum rightly notes that the prepositional phrase ἐν οἷς indicates the purpose of the message (ῥήματα) as salvation. See Kellum, *Acts*, 136.

37. Richard Pervo also explicitly notes that the message from the angel was a promise. See Pervo, *Acts*, 287.

has been boiled down to the salvation of a Gentile household."[38] This salvation, described with a divine passive, σωθήσῃ, suggests that the salvation of Cornelius and his household will be accomplished by God.[39]

The Conversion of Lydia and Her Household (Acts 16:11–15)

In Acts 16:9–10, Paul receives a vision in which a man calls out to him to come to Macedonia. Intriguingly, the first convert in Macedonia is a woman (16:13–15).[40] This woman, by the name of Lydia, traded in purple clothes (πορφυρόπωλις) and was a worshipper of God (σεβομένη τὸν θεόν).[41] The phrase σεβομένη τὸν θεόν suggests that Lydia was a God-fearer, which might explain why she would go to the place of prayer.[42] The fact that she had a house at which she could host Paul, his friends (16:15), and other believers (16:40) suggests she was quite well-to-do and also a person of importance in the community.[43]

Luke mentions that Paul met her and other women at a place of prayer (προσευχὴν), which was most likely a synagogue.[44] Luke also attributes her conversion to a divine initiative when he states that it was the Lord who opened her heart (διήνοιξεν τὴν καρδίαν) for her to pay attention to what Paul was saying (16:14). In Acts, Luke tends to highlight the divine initiative and stress its role in conversions (2:21, 39–40; 4:12; 9:3–6; 10:3–6, 44; 11:15–18; 13:48; 14:27; 15:8–11; 18:27; 19:6; 20:24; 21:19; 22:6–10; 26:13–15).[45] The next action in the narrative is intriguing. Luke does not state that the divine role which led to Lydia's conversion also applied to the other members of Lydia's household. However, at her baptism, her household are baptized alongside her (16:15). Luke does not explicitly state at what point her household were converted or even what led to their conversion. Their conversion is known to us because

---

38. Mikeal Carl Parsons, *Acts*, Paideia Commentaries on the New Testament (Grand Rapids: Baker Academic, 2008), 161.

39. Schnabel, *Acts*, 510.

40. Bauer, *Book of Acts*, 198.

41. Witherington notes that even though the Greek could mean "the Lydian woman," reading "Lydia" as the proper name of the woman makes best sense of the Greek. See Witherington, *Acts of the Apostles*, 491.

42. Schnabel, *Acts*, 681.

43. Witherington, *Acts of the Apostles*, 492; Schnabel, *Acts*, s.v. 16:14.

44. Bernadette J. Brooten, *Women Leaders in the Ancient Synagogue: Inscriptional Evidence and Background Issues* (Providence: Brown Judaic Studies, 2020), 139–40.

45. Talbert, *Reading Acts*, 141.

of the mention of their baptism. Lydia then uses her new status as a believer (πιστὴν)⁴⁶ to demand that Paul and his colleagues stay in her house (16:15).⁴⁷ While Lydia may have needed to compel Paul and his companions to stay (v. 15), at the end of the narrative they went without any such compulsion to Lydia's house to strengthen the church that had begun there (16:40).

The question to explore in this section is, what led to the conversion of Lydia's household? In answering this, we first note that Lydia was the head of the household, signified by the phrase "her household" (ὁ οἶκος αὐτῆς). Lydia being a female head of the household suggests that she was either a widow or divorced.⁴⁸ Also, since the other members of the household were not at the place of prayer, it suggests that their conversion occurred after Lydia's conversion. The head of the household converting first and the other members of the household converting later strongly suggests that the conversion of the other members of the household was influenced by the conversion of the head of the household, as was also the case for Cornelius and the Philippian jailer.⁴⁹

The Conversion of Crispus and His Household (Acts 18:8)

Luke presents the conversion of Crispus and his household as the last household conversion in Acts. This account is preceded by Paul experiencing face-to-face opposition (ἀντιτασσομένων) and reviling (βλασφημούντων) as he reasoned (διελέγετο) and tried to persuade (ἔπειθέν)⁵⁰ both Jews and Greeks (Acts 18:4, 6) in the city of Corinth. However, when Paul could not take it any longer, Luke narrates that he decided: "From henceforth, I will go to the Gentiles" (v. 6, authors translation). Obviously, this statement does not mean that he was not previously ministering to the Gentiles (cf. v. 4), nor does it mean he will no longer minister to Jews. It rather means that Paul's ministry in Corinth would

---

46. The accusative adjective πιστὴν in this verse (16:15) can function as a substantival predicate, with the translation "believer." See Martin M. Culy and Mikeal Carl Parsons, *Acts: A Handbook on the Greek Text* (Waco: Baylor University Press, 2003), 313; Barrett, *Acts of the Apostles*, 783–84. The NIV and the CSB are among the English versions that adopt this translation.

47. For the significance of Lydia's hospitality in the narrative, see Matson, *Household Conversion*, 147–49.

48. Schnabel, *Acts*, 680; Witherington, *Acts of the Apostles*, 493.

49. Witherington, *The Acts of the Apostles*, 493 n. 102.

50. The imperfect tense here suggests an ongoing discussion and therefore is best translated as "tried to persuade." See Darrell L. Bock, *Acts*, Baker Exegetical Commentary on the New Testament (Grand Rapids: Baker Academic, 2007), 578.

focus on Gentiles.[51] Paul moved his teaching location from the synagogue to a nearby house of a worshipper of God by the name of Titius Justus (v. 7).

In verse 8, Luke narrates that the ministry of Paul in the synagogue was successful. Not only did the president (ἀρχισυνάγωγος)[52] of the synagogue convert, but his whole household also believed in the Lord. Several other Corinthians who heard Paul's message became believers and were baptized.

Apart from describing him as the president of the synagogue, Luke does not tell us much more about who Crispus was. But in his first letter to the Corinthians, Paul mentions Crispus as one of two people he himself baptized (1 Cor 1:14), and it is likely that he is referring to the same person.[53] Jerome Murphy-O'Connor states that the title "president" "was an honorific title awarded by a community in gratitude for a donation to their place of prayer," which implied that Crispus was a man of means and probably a non-Jew.[54]

It is possible that the members of the household heard Paul's message and were converted apart from Crispus. However, the mention of "with all of his household" (σὺν ὅλῳ τῷ οἴκῳ αὐτοῦ) suggests that the whole household were converted on account of the head of the household.

Forced Conversion or Genuine Conversion?

Beneath much of the pushback against the idea of household conversion lies the suspicion that conversion of a household would not be genuine but rather forced. In other words, a group conversion is portrayed as a phenomenon that undermines or even contradicts personally trusting in Jesus. Scot McKnight notes that some people wrongly assume that group conversion is "a form of social control."[55] However, as will be demonstrated below, group conversions, such as household conversions, do not necessarily have to involve compulsion and coercion but can also exhibit all the essential qualities of a true conversion,

---

51. Schnabel, *Acts*, 759; Bock, *Acts*, 579.

52. Frederick W. Danker, Walter Bauer, William F. Arndt, and F. Wilbur Gingrich, *Greek-English Lexicon of the New Testament and Other Early Christian Literature*, 3rd ed. (Chicago: University of Chicago Press, 2000), s.v. "ἀρχισυνάγωγος."

53. Gordon D. Fee, *The First Epistle to the Corinthians*, New International Commentary on the New Testament (Grand Rapids: Eerdmans, 1987), 62.

54. Jerome Murphy-O'Connor, *Paul: A Critical Life* (Oxford: Oxford University Press, 1998), 267.

55. Scot McKnight, *Turning to Jesus: The Sociology of Conversion in the Gospels* (Louisville: Westminster John Knox, 2002), 51.

such as repentance and genuine faith in Jesus. They also are typical in societies that exhibit collectivism.

Ancient Households and Family Religion

In a typical Roman *familia*,[56] the household consisted of three generations all living together under one roof. The head of the family, the *paterfamilias*, usually lived with his children as well as his children's children. Within a household were uncles, cousins, nieces, and so on, as well as slaves.[57] As the head, the *paterfamilias* exercised authority over various aspects in the family, including the other members of the household. But as Francis Lyall notes, he was not only the head but also the heart of the household, as he was the central figure in the family.[58] He was the chief, the lord, the master, and the leader. Sometimes, family members who became more successful would leave their father's house, but they would still depend economically and legally on the *paterfamilias* for "no Roman who was subject to the authority of a father could do business in his own name or take possession of any good, unless the said father chose to emancipate him."[59] There was not a age cap at which, once a member of the family reached it, he or she became independent of the father's authority. In fact, according to Roman law, it was still possible even for an old man to be still under the authority of his father.[60]

Another essential aspect of the Roman *familia* was that decision-making did not involve a democratic process. The Roman law gave absolute authority to the father. However, this did not necessarily mean that the *paterfamilias* was a dictator. Though he had the right to take final decisions for the *familia*, he also had the moral duty to listen to the other members of the *familia* and to understand how they felt concerning his decisions.[61]

---

56. Because all the households studied in this chapter are Roman households, this section will deal mostly with the nature of Roman households. Of the key people considered here, Lydia is perhaps the only one who might be of Greek background, yet still it is more likely that she was Romanized while living in a Roman colony. See Richard S. Ascough, *Lydia: Paul's Cosmopolitan Hostess* (Collegeville: Liturgical, 2009), 27.

57. Florence Dupont, *Daily Life in Ancient Rome*, trans. Christopher Woodall (Oxford: Basil Blackwell, 1992), 103–4.

58. Francis Lyall, *Slaves, Citizens, Sons: Legal Metaphors in the Epistles* (Grand Rapids: Academie Books, 1984), 120.

59. Dupont, *Daily Life*, 104.

60. Lyall, *Slaves, Citizens, Sons*, 121.

61. Lyall, 121–22.

Lyall notes that what gave the *paterfamilias* the right of authority over the other family members was his role as a priest in the family, which included his representing the whole family before the family gods.[62] Indeed, the household was "a center of worship" and every person who belonged to the *familia* took part in the cult worship.[63]

Another group of people in Roman households were the slaves, and these slaves were also under the authority of the *paterfamilias*. Indeed, an aspect of Roman law, known as *dominica potestas*, made the slave-masters owners of them. Even though there were laws to protect slaves, these laws were "capable of avoidance."[64] On the other hand, not all slaves had harsh experiences. Some masters were kind to their slaves, and some even gave them capital with which to trade.[65]

This brief survey demonstrates that it was not a strange phenomenon for other members of a household to follow the head when he (the head) accepted a new religion. As a priest of the family cult, he also had the religious authority to guide the other members of the household in true worship. This survey also shows that the other members of the household were not compelled (with threats and pressure) to follow the *paterfamilias* in his conversion. It was the norm of the culture of the day.

In all the household conversion accounts except that of Crispus's household, Luke does not explicitly state that the other members of the household placed their faith in Jesus. However, it can be inferred that the other members of the household did place their trust in Jesus individually. Paul and the rest of the New Testament are clear that a person's trust in Jesus does not cover other people, even if they belong to the same household. Each person must believe in Jesus individually. This is similar to baptism. No one is baptized for another person. The head of the household's baptism did not cover the other members of his household, which implies that his faith in Jesus did not cover the other members of his household either. In another household conversion account in the Gospel of John, the Evangelist specified that the head of the household and the other members of the household all believed in Jesus (καὶ ἐπίστευσεν αὐτὸς καὶ ἡ οἰκία αὐτοῦ ὅλη; John 4:53). The account of the conversion of

---

62. Lyall, 84. See Lyall, 120, for his role of representing the family before the gods.

63. Carolyn Osiek and David L. Balch, *Families in the New Testament World: Households and House Churches*, The Family, Religion, and Culture (Louisville: Westminster John Knox, 1997), 82–83.

64. Lyall, *Slaves, Citizens, Sons*, 124–25.

65. Lyall, 125.

Crispus's household also explicitly states that all the other members of the household believed in the Lord along with Crispus. As such, we can infer that all members of a household converted personally and individually placed their trust in Jesus. The evidence of their personal faith in Jesus was their baptism.

The Catalyst of a Conversion

The theology of many Christian traditions affirms that God is the ultimate cause of conversion. There is some debate as to how he initiates it, whether by irresistible grace (also called effectual calling) or prevenient grace. The main point, however, is that, since all humans are dead in their sins (cf. Eph 2:5), they cannot turn to God on their own without some divine agency. On the other hand, the divine action that initiates conversion is usually carried forth with a catalyst. "Catalyst" in this context refers to the means which draws people to Christ and makes them accept him as Savior and Lord. In Acts, preaching (2:37–38; 4:3; 10:44; 11:19–21) and miracles (4:33; 9:32–34, 36–43; 14:3) seem to be the major catalysts for conversion.[66] Apart from these dominant catalysts, there are other minor ones, such as a crisis point. An example of this is the Philippian jailer who, not knowing what to do, cried out to Paul and Silas, asking them what he must do to be saved (Acts 16:31). As such, miracles and preaching are not the *only* catalysts for conversion. In the conversion narratives, the dominant catalyst for the household conversion is the conversion of the *paterfamilias*. In this sense, the conversion of the *paterfamilias* functions similarly to how miracles function in other conversions. In the same way that miracles make the gospel message believable to those who will accept it, so the conversion of the head of the household makes turning to God seem a good decision for the other members of the household.

Household Conversion and House-To-House Evangelism in Africa

This section of the chapter deals with how household conversions, as described above, can enrich the theology of salvation in Africa. At the outset, it must be noted that there is a large diversity among the cultures in Africa, and therefore the description that follows will not fit every single culture there is on the continent. On the flip side, there is also a need to talk about Africa as a whole, and this calls for macro-description.

---

66. Talbert, "Conversion," 143–44.

It is not uncommon to find several generations living together in a traditional African household.[67] Generally, while this trend is changing in many African cities due to factors such as urbanization and migration, there are still many households where grandparents live with their children and their children's children. There are two primary ways in which this happens: (1) either a married couple have brought their parents over to live with them and their children so that the grandparents can be taken care of; or (2) the couple did not leave their parents' house when they married and had children.

In addition to grandparents, it is not uncommon to have other members of the extended family in a household. These other members could be cousins, uncles, nieces, and so on. The father typically plays the role of the head of these households. These sociological elements within African society indicate some similarities with the ancient Greco-Roman world in the sense that both are typically patriarchal and collectivistic societies. In these collectivistic cultures, loyalty to the family is stressed and taken to be more important than personal interests. There is also a high level of respect for elders and those in authority.[68]

With these similarities in cultures, we should welcome some of the strategies of Paul in his missionary activities. A popular method of evangelism in many African countries is house-to-house evangelism, whereby people move from house to house and share the gospel with the households inside. A strategic method for house-to-house evangelism would be to identify the head of the household and have an extensive dialogue with him. Evangelistic actions, such as praying for new converts and inviting them to church, must include the household heads because of the power and authority they have over the other members of their households. If the evangelistic efforts to the head of the household are successful, it might lead to the conversion of the whole family. Also, the conversion of the head of the household makes the practice of the Christian faith in the home easier for the other converts in the family. There are several benefits to having the whole family actively participating in Christian faith: (1) Christ becomes the center and ultimate head of the family, and that redefines all other relationships among the members in the household. (2) Members of the family can challenge and encourage each other in the faith. (3) It is easier to raise up children in the fear of God.

Lydia and her household's conversion also carries great significance in the African context. Just like Lydia, many African women have been forced to

---

67. Molefi Kete Asante, "Family," in *Encyclopedia of African Religion*, ed. Molefi Kete Asante and Ama Mazama (Thousand Oaks: SAGE, 2009), 258.

68. Ascough, *Lydia*, 9–12.

take up the role of head of their families due to divorce or the deaths of their husbands. In that sense, it is wrong to presuppose that all heads of households in Africa are male. But just as happened with Lydia, the conversion of the female head of the household can also serve as a catalyst for the conversion of the other members of the family.

Conclusion

This chapter has drawn attention to the fact that Luke has a special interest in narrating conversion stories in his two-volume work. Part of this interest is his narration of household conversions. I have argued in this chapter that an important catalyst for household conversion is the conversion of the head of the household. This catalyst functions similarly to how miracles function in many individual conversion narratives. However, the function of this catalyst is not unique to the Greco-Roman world, which was a patriarchal and collectivistic culture. Since the typical African culture shares similar values of patriarchy and collectivism, I suggest that we can take some of Paul's strategies to the African context, and, if God permits, that this might lead to full household conversions.

Bibliography

Asante, Molefi Kete. "Family." In *Encyclopedia of African Religion*, edited by Molefi Kete Asante and Ama Mazama, 258–59. Thousand Oaks: SAGE, 2009.

Ascough, Richard S. *Lydia: Paul's Cosmopolitan Hostess*. Collegeville: Liturgical, 2009.

Barrett, C. K. *The Acts of the Apostles*. International Critical Commentary. London: T&T Clark, 1998.

Bauer, David R. *The Book of Acts as Story: A Narrative-Critical Study*. Grand Rapids: Baker Academic, 2021.

Blass, Friedrich, Albert Debrunner, and Robert W. Funk. *A Greek Grammar of the New Testament and Other Early Christian Literature*. Chicago: University of Chicago Press, 1961.

Bock, Darrell L. *Acts*. Baker Exegetical Commentary on the New Testament. Grand Rapids: Baker Academic, 2007.

———. *A Theology of Luke and Acts: God's Promised Program, Realized for All Nations*. Biblical Theology of the New Testament. Grand Rapids: Zondervan, 2012.

Brooten, Bernadette J. *Women Leaders in the Ancient Synagogue: Inscriptional Evidence and Background Issues*. Providence: Brown Judaic Studies, 2020.

Chrysostom, John. *Homilies on the Acts of the Apostles 36*. Vol. 11 of the *Nicene and Post-Nicene Fathers*, Series 1. Edited by Philip Schaff. 14 vols. Grand Rapids: Eerdmans, 1956.

Conzelmann, Hans. *Acts of the Apostles: A Commentary*. Translated by James Limburg, A. Thomas Kraabel, and Donald H. Juel. Hermeneia. Philadelphia: Fortress, 1987.

Culy, Martin M., and Mikeal Carl Parsons. *Acts: A Handbook on the Greek Text*. Waco: Baylor University Press, 2003.

Danker, Frederick W., Walter Bauer, William F. Arndt, and F. Wilbur Gingrich. *Greek-English Lexicon of the New Testament and Other Early Christian Literature*. 3rd ed. Chicago: University of Chicago Press, 2000.

DeSilva, David A. *An Introduction to the New Testament: Contexts, Methods and Ministry Formation*. 2nd ed. Downers Grove: InterVarsity, 2018.

Dunn, James D. G. *The Acts of the Apostles*. Grand Rapids: Eerdmans, 2016.

Dupont, Florence. *Daily Life in Ancient Rome*. Translated by Christopher Woodall. Oxford: Basil Blackwell, 1992.

Erickson, Millard J. *Christian Theology*. 3rd ed. Grand Rapids: Baker Academic, 2013.

Fee, Gordon D. *The First Epistle to the Corinthians*. New International Commentary on the New Testament. Grand Rapids: Eerdmans, 1987.

Finn, Thomas Macy. *From Death to Rebirth: Ritual and Conversion in Antiquity*. New York: Paulist, 1997.

Fitzmyer, Joseph A. *The Acts of the Apostles: A New Translation with Introduction and Commentary*. Anchor Bible. New Haven: Yale University Press, 2010.

Green, Joel B. *Conversion in Luke–Acts: Divine Action, Human Cognition, and the People of God*. Grand Rapids: Baker Academic, 2015.

James, William. *The Varieties of Religious Experience: A Study in Human Nature*. Oxford World's Classics. 1902. Reprint, Oxford: Oxford University Press, 2012.

Johnson, Luke Timothy. *The Acts of the Apostles*. Sacra Pagina. Collegeville: Liturgical, 1992.

Keener, Craig S. *Acts: An Exegetical Commentary*. Grand Rapids: Baker Academic, 2012.

———. *Acts: An Exegetical Commentary*. Grand Rapids: Baker Academic, 2014.

Kellum, L. Scott. *Acts*. Exegetical Guide to the Greek New Testament. Nashville: B&H Academic, 2020.

Larkin, William J., Jr. *Acts*. IVP New Testament Commentary. Downers Grove: InterVarsity, 1995.

———. "Acts." In *Luke and Acts*, edited by Philip Wesley Comfort, 349–668. Cornerstone Bible Commentary. Carol Stream: Tyndale House, 2005.

Laubach, Fritz, Jürgen Essen Goetzmann, and Ulrich Becker. "Conversion, Penitence, Repentance, Proselyte." In *New International Dictionary of New Testament Theology*, edited by Colin Brown, 1:353–61. 4 vols. Grand Rapids: Zondervan, 1975–78.

Lenski, R. C. H. *The Interpretation of the Acts of the Apostles*. Minneapolis: Augsburg, 1944.

Lyall, Francis. *Slaves, Citizens, Sons: Legal Metaphors in the Epistles*. Grand Rapids: Academie Books, 1984.

Malina, Bruce J., and John J. Pilch. *Social-Science Commentary on the Book of Acts*. Minneapolis: Fortress, 2008.

Marshall, I. Howard. *Acts: An Introduction and Commentary*. Tyndale New Testament Commentaries. Downers Grove: IVP Academic, 2008.

———. *Luke: Historian and Theologian*. 3rd ed. Carlisle: Paternoster, 2006.

Matson, David Lertis. *Household Conversion Narratives in Acts: Pattern and Interpretation*. Journal for the Study of the New Testament 123. Sheffield: Sheffield Academic, 1996.

McKnight, Scot. *Turning to Jesus: The Sociology of Conversion in the Gospels*. Louisville: Westminster John Knox, 2002.

Michael, Matthew. *Christian Theology and African Traditions*. Eugene: Wipf & Stock, 2013.

Murphy-O'Connor, Jerome. *Paul: A Critical Life*. Oxford: Oxford University Press, 1998.

Nave, Guy. "Conversion." In *New Interpreter's Dictionary of the Bible*, edited by Katharine Doob Sakenfeld, 1:729. 5 vols. Nashville: Abingdon, 2006–9.

Newman, Barclay M., and Eugene A. Nida. *A Translator's Handbook on the Acts of the Apostles*. New York: United Bible Societies, 1972.

Nock, Arthur Darby. *Conversion: The Old and the New in Religion from Alexander the Great to Augustine of Hippo*. London: Oxford University Press, 1933.

Osiek, Carolyn, and David L. Balch. *Families in the New Testament World: Households and House Churches*. 1st ed. The Family, Religion, and Culture. Louisville: Westminster John Knox, 1997.

Parsons, Mikeal Carl. *Acts*. Paideia Commentaries on the New Testament. Grand Rapids: Baker Academic, 2008.

Pervo, Richard I. *Acts: A Commentary*. Hermeneia. Minneapolis: Fortress, 2009.

Peterson, David. *The Acts of the Apostles*. The Pillar New Testament Commentary. Grand Rapids: Eerdmans, 2009.

Robertson, A. T. *A Grammar of the Greek New Testament in the Light of Historical Research*. 4th ed. London: Hodder & Stoughton, 1923.

Schnabel, Eckhard J. *Acts*. Zondervan Exegetical Commentary on the New Testament. Grand Rapid: Zondervan, 2012.

Talbert, Charles H. "Conversion in the Acts of the Apostles: Ancient Auditors' Perceptions." In *Reading Luke–Acts in Its Mediterranean Milieu*, 135–48. Leiden: Brill, 2003.

———. *Reading Acts: A Literary and Theological Commentary on the Acts of the Apostles*. Rev. ed. Reading the New Testament. Macon: Smyth & Helwys, 2005.

Williams, David John. *Acts*. New International Biblical Commentary. Peabody: Hendrickson, 1990.

Witherington, Ben, III. *The Acts of the Apostles: A Socio-Rhetorical Commentary*. Grand Rapids: Eerdmans, 1998.

Witherup, Ronald D. *Conversion in the New Testament*. Collegeville: Liturgical, 1994.

6

A Pauline Theology of Justification and Its Implications for Ecclesiology in Kenya amid Ethnic Divisions

An Exegesis of Galatians 2:11–21

Danson Ottawa Wafula
National Coordinator for Africa Center for Apologetics Research (ACFAR), Kenya

and

Edwin Mwangi Macharia
National Government Administrative Officer
MDiv Candidate at Africa International University

Abstract

This chapter will focus on an exegesis of Galatians 2:11–21 with an assessment of the Pauline theology of justification. Paul's polemic to the Galatians is focused on correcting a major theological misunderstanding as to how Gentiles are justified. The argument in Galatians 2:15–21 is about justification through faith in Christ. The recollection of the conflict with Peter serves as an ending to his apostolic apology and as a beginning to handling a theological misunderstanding in the Galatian church. This chapter thus seeks to explore the perspective of justification in this text and to see how it applies to Christians within the African context, which is faced with ethnic divisions, syncretism, and the proliferation of false teaching.

Key words: justification, works of the law, faith in Christ, union with Christ

Introduction

The church in Africa is in need of a robust theological reflection on the issues it faces, namely the proliferation of false teaching, divisions over ethnicity, and syncretism. Paul's letter to the Galatian church is useful in exploring how the doctrine of justification can help to solve these challenges. In Galatians 2, Paul demonstrates how the doctrine of justification is to be applied in a dynamic context for both Jews and Gentiles.

Paul comes to this section of his letter after he has labored to defend the fidelity of the gospel he preaches in the first chapter and the first section of the second chapter. Key to his defense is the source of his message, who is Jesus Christ whom God revealed to Paul.[1] Paul emphasizes that the message he preached was not merely taught to him by the apostles; he in fact learned it independently after the encounter with Christ.[2] However, he does not appeal to his own authority to establish the truth of the gospel he preached. In Galatians 2:1 Paul notes that after fourteen years he went to see the leaders in Jerusalem with the main intention that they might know what he was preaching and that it was the true gospel (2:7–8). The realization that the gospel preached by Paul was the same as that preached by Peter and the other apostles caused them to extend the right hand of fellowship to Paul. The apostles mentioned are those who were highly regarded: James, Cephas (Peter), and John. This was the second validation of the gospel preached by Paul. Thus his message had its source in the risen Christ and was affirmed by his close associates as being true.

The main challenge Paul is dealing with in Galatians 2 is circumcision and whether it is mandatory for the believer (Gal 2:3–6). There was pressure for Titus to be circumcised, yet he refused to oblige. Paul states that the reason why he did not cave in to the pressure was so that the gospel would be preserved for the sake of the Galatians (διαμείνῃ πρὸς ὑμᾶς).

---

1. Gal 1:12–17. Here Paul claims that God made his Son appear to him. The term ἀποκαλύψεως brings to mind the narrative in Acts 9 where Jesus reveals himself to Paul on the road to Damascus. Paul therefore had a physical encounter with the risen Christ just as the other apostles had. It is the risen Lord who is the source of his message.

2. See Gal 1:17.

The circumcision camp brought a different gospel by distorting the gospel of Christ.[3] The distortion was around the matter of circumcision. Paul indicates it as a point of contention right from chapter 1. It is notable that in 2:9 he distinguishes the Gentiles from the circumcised and in 2:7 he refers to the Gentiles as the "uncircumcised." This characterization is not inconsequential, but rather seeks to highlight the importance of the issue brought about by this one act of removing male foreskins.

The advocates of circumcision were not simply raising a social and ethnic matter, but were attacking the truth and identity of the gospel and distorting it. To address this, therefore, Paul does not launch into a social-ethnic response, but instead delves into the doctrine of justification. The solution to the glaring social-ethnic divide was not a social-ethnic moral prescription but a theology of justification which Paul introduces, clarifies, and also models.

The Setting for the Polemic (2:11–14)

This section starts with two conjunctions following each other, Ὅτε δὲ. The two play critical roles in the placement of the events of the entire pericope of 2:11–21. Ὅτε is a temporal conjunction. It serves to point to a certain time when a particular action happened. This is qualified by the following statement ἦλθεν Κηφᾶς εἰς Ἀντιόχειαν (Cephas came to Antioch). This refers to a certain time that would have been well known to the audience, and hence reference to it places the events described as happening afterwards. δὲ (But) is the conjunction that follows. This conjunction serves to introduce a transition from Paul's message regarding his faithfulness to the gospel to how he (Paul) processes the application of the good news in the lives of believers.

However, the conjunctive particle δὲ serves not simply to point to a transition but also to make clear that the transition must be interpreted in light of the previous section. Therefore, the δὲ here serves as a contrastive particle. Cephas (Peter), who is the subject of the phrase Ὅτε δὲ ἦλθεν Κηφᾶς εἰς Ἀντιόχειαν, is the same character mentioned as having been entrusted with the gospel to the circumcised.[4] He is also one of the apostles who gave Paul

---

3. Gal 1:7–9. There seem to have been people who were introducing other matters into the gospel. In v. 7, Paul says that such people aim to distort the gospel of Jesus Christ. For Paul to call this distortion (no matter how small) "another gospel" shows how significant its impact was.

4. Gal 2:7. In Acts 9:26–30, we do not have a description of what transpired within the meeting. However, we are certain that the apostles accepted Paul, for we see him being able to go in and out among them preaching the gospel of Christ.

the right hand of fellowship.[5] This same Cephas, who knows the truth of the gospel, now stands "condemned" by the very gospel he proclaims, leading Paul to oppose him.

Paul proceeds to explain why Peter already stood condemned. He cites Peter's fear of the circumcision party that made him withdraw from eating with the Gentiles. This was indeed strange given that, before the circumcision party arrived, Peter was comfortable sharing a table with the Gentiles. Also, by extending the right hand of fellowship to Paul, the same Peter had affirmed that the gospel he was entrusted with for the Jews was the same gospel Paul was entrusted with for the Gentiles. These two things made Peter's withdrawal absurd. Paul employs the rhetorical technique of comparison (2:7–8) in his bid to contrast Peter's refusal to comply with the decree of the Jerusalem Council with Paul's defense of it.[6] The word ἀντέστην has the idea of resisting or withstanding, from the words αντι and ἵστημι, meaning to "stand against."

Verse 12 is introduced by the conjunction γὰρ and helps to establish why Paul opposed Peter and pronounced him condemned. De Boer notes that pious Jews were not in the habit of engaging in fellowship involving meals with Gentiles (Acts 10:28; 11:3).[7] Peter's vision in Acts 10 "had taught him the worthlessness of these narrow traditions."[8] He had no scruples about living a ἐθνῶν (gentile) lifestyle. In this instance, however, he drew back and separated himself from the Gentiles as he overrode his own convictions. These words describe a cautious, timid withdrawal. Then Paul explains how he noted that the conduct of Peter and the other Jewish brothers was not in step with the truth of the gospel, and he narrates how he reacted to it. He expands on what he had earlier summarized (2:11) as his opposing Peter to his face, delving into the heart of the matter.

Peter's actions had made others follow him in his hypocrisy. Yet the matter was not as superficial as simply refusing to eat with Gentiles. Deeply etched in this tension is the division between those advocating for circumcision and those who, like Paul, did not see it as a necessity for faith. Peter, through his retreating in fear, would strengthen the circumcision party and, in effect, undermine the core issues of the gospel, as Paul will later enumerate in 2:15–21.

---

5. Gal 2:9.

6. C. S. Keener, *The IVP Bible Background Commentary: New Testament* (Downers Grove: InterVarsity, 1993).

7. M. C. de Boer. "Paul's Use and Interpretation of a Justification Tradition in Galatians 2:15–22." *Journal for the Study of the New Testament* 28, no. 2 (2005): 189–216.

8. J. B. Lightfoot, *The Epistle of St. Paul to the Galatians*, Zondervan Commentary (Grand Rapids: Zondervan, 1997), 112.

This section ends with Paul mentioning that even his close ally and companion Barnabas was led astray by this hypocrisy.

In verses 13 and 14, the fact that other Jews joined Peter in his hypocrisy is the simplest explanation for why the reproof was made in public. Peter was not only condemned, but he was also called a hypocrite: he was acting contrary to his convictions and, more importantly, to the truths of the gospel. Ngewa notes, "The word 'hypocrisy' carries with it the idea of playing a part on a stage. When used metaphorically, it means 'outward show by someone who is pretending to be something they are not.'"[9] In 2:14a, Paul's emphatic analysis of Peter's action is that Peter was not acting in line with the truth of the gospel. According to Lightfoot, "the word ὀρθοποδοῦσιν [in line with] appears not to occur elsewhere, except in later ecclesiastical writers, where its use may be traced to this passage. It has the idea of the direction to be observed, not necessarily the goal to be obtained."[10]

The truth of the gospel is a key theme in this chapter, especially in the first three sections of the discourse. The theme of the truth of the gospel has a bearing on the issue of contention in Jerusalem (2:1–10), Antioch (2:11–14) and Galatia. Any form of teaching that seeks to impose obligations beyond faith in Christ is to be condemned. It is far from the true gospel. It is to believe in another gospel which is no gospel at all (1:6–7). The question in verse 14, as to why Peter would force Gentiles to live as Jews if he as a Jew lived like a Gentile, seems strange at face value, especially when we think that the contention is simply around the matter of circumcision. Yet this issue is clearly seen to be in opposition to the truth of the gospel. Hence the matter runs deeper than mere circumcision.

Circumcision as Understood by the Jews

The matter raised by the so-called circumcision party was the question of how Gentiles might become acceptable before God. The separation practiced by these Judaizers was rooted in the Torah. In Genesis 17:1–14, we see the inauguration of circumcision among the nation of Israel. God instructs Abraham that all male children must be circumcised. Even a foreigner among them must be circumcised in order to enjoy fellowship with the people of God. Circumcision was a sign of the covenant between the Lord and the children of

---

9. S. M. Ngewa, *Galatians* (Nairobi: HippoBooks, 2010).
10. J. B. Lightfoot, *The Epistle of St. Paul to the Galatians*, Zondervan Commentary (Grand Rapids: Zondervan, 1997), 113.

Abraham (17:11–13). All those who are not circumcised are to be cut off from the community, for they have broken the covenant (17:14). Following the thread of circumcision, we observe that there is a constant difference in treatment and presumed privilege between the circumcised and the uncircumcised. Thus, for the Jewish party to try to push the agenda of circumcision was a deliberate move to say that this practice should be maintained and was mandatory for salvation. No one who was uncircumcised deserved fellowship. Such a person would face the consequences of Genesis 17:14.

Just before crossing into the promised land, Joshua circumcises all the men (Josh 5:4–8). This act preceding the capture of the promised land is significant as it illustrated the centrality of circumcision as a sign of the covenant people. To dwell in God's land, they had to be his people. More weight is given to the matter of circumcision in Exodus 12, which gives guidelines on who is to partake of the Passover, a crucial ceremony that in future would remind them of God's great deliverance. Key among these guidelines is that any foreigners must be circumcised before fellowshipping with God's people (Exod 12:44–49). Furthermore, circumcision is mentioned in several places as the distinguishing factor between God's people and the unbelieving Gentiles.[11]

In Acts 11, Peter is confronted by the other apostles for eating with the uncircumcised. He moves to defend his actions by narrating the story of the conversion of Cornelius. The response to the events was a glorification of God and an acceptance that God had granted repentance to the Gentiles. Yet these Gentiles had not been circumcised. Peter was also present at the council referred to in Galatians 2:1–5, which is the council recorded in Acts 15, where, being a member of this consortium and, in fact, a major contributor, Peter recounted his experience with Cornelius.[12]

The mention of where the conflict occurred and the question posed in Galatians 2:14 are designed to help readers see the double standards Peter was applying in his actions. The obvious answer to Paul's question is therefore that there are no grounds to force such a practice on the Gentiles – an answer

---

11. In Judg 14:3, Samson is asked whether there is no suitable woman among his people that he should go to look among the Philistines who are qualified by the word "uncircumcised." In 1 Sam 17:26, David asks why an "uncircumcised" Philistine is threatening God's people. Saul loathes the thought of being killed by an "uncircumcised" person (1 Chr 10:4), for it would be demeaning for a king appointed by God to die in the hands of a godless unbeliever.

12. In Acts 15:7–9, Peter notes clearly that God granted the Spirit to the Gentiles just as he had done to the apostles, and he cleansed their hearts by faith without any prerequisite of circumcision. We see that Peter knows that only faith is essential for the cleansing of the heart and repentance. It is logical to deduce that these events took place before the Antioch meeting, for it was after the deliberations of Acts 15:1–21 that Paul and Barnabas were sent to Antioch.

that the circumcision party, Peter, and everyone with them knew since a clear direction on the issue had been given in Acts 15. With this background, we then see that the idea of ἔργων νόμου ("works of the law") in 2:16 has strict reference to this notion of things that must be done to make one acceptable as a believer (to be justified and included in the family of God). These works are, as such, related to ritual cleanliness.

Our Justification: Paul's Polemic (2:15–16)

In verses 15–16 Paul notes that those who are Jews have come to Christ for justification. He appeals to the knowledge that they (Paul, Peter, and the others) have concerning the matter of being declared righteous. Righteousness in this context is not simply a matter of what state one is in but the standing that one has with God. A favorable standing and inclusion among the people of God, that is, eligibility for fellowship with God and his people, is the result of one's being justified.[13]

Verse 15 has a mildly concessive function in relation to verse 16, which here is signaled by "yet" (ESV). Douglas Moo paraphrases the sense in the following manner: "Although we Jews, in contrast to the Gentiles, would seem to have an inherent right to justification, even we have turned our backs on the law of Moses and have embraced faith in Christ as the means of justification."[14]

"Jews *by birth*" (φύσει) is a dative of respect which means that their status is determined by birth in the manner of ancestral inheritance. This is contrasted with the fact that they were not ἐξ ἐθνῶν ἁμαρτωλοί, literally, "sinners from among the Gentiles." ἐξ here denotes origin.[15] ἁμαρτωλοί is used here to denote the state of Gentiles who, according to Ephesians 2:12, were "excluded from citizenship in Israel and foreigners to the covenants of the promise, without hope and without God in the world."

The expression "sinners from among the Gentiles" was a term mostly used by Jews given the context. Now that Paul, Peter, Barnabas, and other Jews by birth had believed in Christ through faith, the demarcation that existed between them and Gentiles was removed. There was no longer any distinction

---

13. T. R. Schreiner, "Justification: The Saving Righteousness of God in Christ," *Journal of the Evangelical Theological Society* 54, no. 1 (2011): 25–26.

14. D. J. Moo, *Galatians*, Baker Exegetical Commentary on the New Testament (Grand Rapids: Baker Academic, 2013), 65.

15. Moo, *Galatians*, 153.

between Jew and Gentile, whether in respect to sin (Rom 3:22–23) or in respect to God's justifying grace (Rom 10:12).

This is the first time Paul makes an explicit mention of the term "justification." He makes a contrast between ἔργων νόμου ("works of the law") and πίστις Ἰησου Χριστου ("faith of Christ" or "faith in Christ"). The statement "we also have believed in Christ Jesus, in order to be justified by faith in Christ and not by works of the law" (ESV) forms the central thesis of the verse. This is enveloped by two fundamental theological assertions that give it weight, namely: "yet we know that a person is not justified by works of the law but through faith in Jesus Christ," and "because by works of the law no one will be justified" (ESV).[16] According to Moo, "none of the key parties, Paul, Peter, the agitators or the Galatians, were questioning the need for Christ's faith for justification."[17] What was in dispute was the necessity of works of the law (circumcision) for acceptance into the fellowship (the body of Christ). This acceptance into the fellowship is entirely dependent on our standing before God, namely justification. Therefore, if people do not share the same faith in Christ that grants justification, they cannot enjoy fellowship, for they are naturally alienated.

The Relationship between πιστεως χριστου and ἐξ ἔργων νόμου

This chapter's focus in verse 16 is the substantive relationship between these two phrases in connection with the issue of justification.[18] The contrast between these two phrases is seen by focusing on the words ἔργα and πιστις.[19] According to Luther and Calvin, Paul was "enunciating a critical distinction between human doing and human believing when it came to justification."[20] This focus is, however, contested, and contemporary scholarship is more concerned with ἔργα νόμου, "works of the law."[21]

---

16. See Moo, 157.
17. Moo, 157.
18. M. C. de Boer, "Paul's Use and Interpretation of a Justification Tradition in Galatians 2:15–21," *Journal for the Study of the New Testament* 28, no. 2 (2005): 196.
19. Moo, *Galatians*, 158.
20. Moo, 158.
21. Moo, 158.

πιστεως χριστου: "Faith in Christ" or "Faith of Christ"

The phrase πίστεως Ἰησοῦ Χριστοῦ in verse 16a is common in Pauline writing. A similar expression is found in verses 16c and 20, and in Romans 3:22, 26 and Philippians 3:9.

A question we must deal with in this phrase is the nature of the genitive πίστεως Ἰησοῦ Χριστοῦ. Scholars take two main positions on this issue. An objective genitive would be translated as "faith in Jesus Christ," indicating that Christ is the object of the believer's faith. In the subjective genitive, Jesus Christ is the subject who has the faith. De Boer highlights the main arguments in favor of each of the two positions as follows:

The Case for the Objective Genitive (Human Faith in Christ)

First, the phrase πίστεως Ἰησοῦ Χριστοῦ is parallel to the phrase ἐπιστεύσαμεν εἰς, "we came to believe in Christ Jesus," in 16b, supporting the meaning of faith in Jesus Christ. Second, there is similar parallelism between the noun πίστις and its cognate verb πιστεοῦ that occurs in 3:6–7. Third, if ἔργων νόμου is taken to denote human activity, then πίστεως Χριστοῦ must refer to human activity. Fourth, in Pauline literature there is no point where Christ appears as the subject of the cognate verb πίστεου.[22]

The Case for the Subjective Genitive (Jesus Christ's Own Faithfulness/Faith)

First, in Galatians 3:22 Paul refers to πίστεως Χριστὸν Ἰησοῦν in the same way as he does in 2:16a. In 3:23–25, Paul speaks of πίστεως in a personified sense pointing to Christ (3:24). Faith in this section is something that belongs to or defines Christ himself. Second, if Paul had wanted to say "faith in Christ," he would have used the expression found in Colossians 2:5, πίστεως εἰς Χριστὸν, corresponding to the verbal structure πίστεωεν εἰς, "to believe in" (Gal 2:16b). Third, in Romans 1:5 Paul describes faith as obedience in the phrase ὑπακοῆς πίστεως, meaning the obedience which is faith. In Romans 5:19, Paul refers to the ὑπακοῆς of Christ, which can then be described as the πίστεως of Christ.[23]

In line with de Boer's case for the objective genitive, a grammatical evaluation of the text leads to the translation of πιστεως χριστου as "faith in Christ." The writers of this chapter will therefore make a case for the objective genitive reading.

First, the logical flow of the text points to the fact that Paul is seeking to contrast ἐξ ἔργων νόμου with πιστεως χριστου. Advocates of the subjective

---

22. de Boer, "Justification Tradition," 205.
23. de Boer, 205.

genitive position argue that there is no other place in the writings of Paul where an objective lacks εἰς. Yet we must be open enough to accommodate the grammatical freedom of the writer to use words as he sees fit in any occasion of his writing.

The Function of ἐὰν μὴ

Second, we must interact with the function of ἐὰν μὴ, which occurs in verse 16a in the phrase. It is not the purpose of this chapter to analyze it in detail, but it cannot go undiscussed. Some scholars have seen ἐὰν μὴ as exceptive of the entire statement. The implication would then be that works are also needed in justification. However, justification happens only when faith is present.[24] Other scholars consider ἐὰν μὴ as adversative. This sets the works of the law in antithesis to faith in Christ, implying that one is not justified by the works of the law but *only* through faith in Christ.

The first view receives backing from N. T. Wright, who notes that there is a need to consider the self-understanding of the Jews as a factor in understanding the concept of justification.[25] He claims that the Jews never saw their actions as detached from their belief in God. Their identity was perceived to be interwoven with their works – that is, the observation of the law and keeping all the rituals – and ultimately with their faith. Hence, Wright argues that one could not divorce works from the faith they held firm. Works were not simply a result of justification but also a source of justification. The correlation between these two meant that people would see that the justification that seemed to emanate from works was effected only by faith in God.

The second school of thought, which is the traditional Protestant view, observes that ἐὰν μὴ is being used to make a contrast between "works of the law" and "faith in Christ." In the context of the text at hand, we propose that this view holds up better in the face of the evidence. First, we see that Paul mentions that there was pressure for Titus to be circumcised, yet they did not give in (2:4–5). Paul notes that this was essential so that the purity of the gospel could be preserved. The fact that Paul and Titus are not condemned for not

---

24. For further details, see J. D. G. Dunn, "The New Perspective on Paul," *Bulletin of the John Rylands Library of Manchester* 65, no. 2 (1983): 112; repr. in J. D. G. Dunn, *Jesus, Paul, and the Law: Studies in Mark and Galatians* (Louisville: Westminster John Knox, 1990), 195. N. T. Wright has also taken such an outlook on the matter of justification and has developed it on the basis of Dunn's work.

25. N. T. Wright, *Justification: God's Plan and Paul's Vision* (Downers Grove: IVP Academic, 2009).

yielding to the observance of circumcision serves as part of the support for the argument that these works achieve nothing in the justification of the believer.

In addition, one must ask: If "works of the law" played a role in justification, why then did Paul confront Peter after his separation from the Gentiles? We must also note that in 2:21, Paul seems to restate the same thing as stated in 2:16, noting that if righteousness came by the law, then Christ died for nothing. This reinforces the fact that there is nothing that can be added to faith in Christ in order for one to be justified. If such were done, then one would be nullifying the grace of God. Therefore, Paul aims to set the record straight for the Galatians, making it clear that there are no other means of justification apart from Christ.

Paul Addresses a Rebuttal from the False Teachers (2:17–18)

Continuing his discussion, Paul addresses a potential rebuttal from the false teachers in Galatia. In verse 17 he poses another question, asking whether Christ is a servant of sin, to which he answers μὴ γένοιτο. This is an emphatic rejection of the idea. His question stems from the hypothetical scenario that they have been found to be sinners by interacting with the Gentiles as they had done before. According to Jacobus, "Paul does this by means of a syllogistic statement in which the right premise is presented, and then from this right premise a false conclusion is drawn, which reduces Peter's position to the extremity of folly."[26]

Keener observes that Paul questions whether it is really a sin to eat with uncircumcised people:

> Peter's own conviction is obvious because Peter, though he is a Jew, acts like a gentile (as did Paul, 4:12; 1 Cor 9:21) in eating with gentiles. Yet Peter now expects gentiles to follow Jewish practices to be able to eat with Jews (2:14). Thus, Paul could speak of "we Jews" (Jewish believers in Jesus, such as Peter and Paul), who were not gentile "sinners" (2:15). Yet because of Christ they became like gentiles in eating with them – and thus through Christ became "sinners" like them (2:17) – if, in fact, these gentiles were "sinners"![27]

---

26. M. W. Jacobus, "Paul and His Teaching in Galatians 2:11–21," *The Biblical World* (1904), 24(5), 358.

27. C. S. Keener, *Galatians* (New York: Cambridge University Press, 2018), 98.

Keener also notes three absurdities that the logic would present if it were not emphatically denied by Paul. First, it is absurd to put forward the premise that it is sinful to eat with Gentiles. Second, to claim that Gentiles alone are sinners must also be absurd. Third, it is absurd to suppose that those made right by faith in Christ (2:16) will behave more sinfully (see 5:13; cf. Rom 6:1–2).[28]

From these theological absurdities, Paul continues in 2:18 by stating that if he were to rebuild the things that he had already torn down, it would then prove that he was wrong to tear them down in the first place. In other words, if he, or any other person for that matter, wants to reinstate these ritual laws that excluded the Gentiles, he would be proving that he was wrong to tear them down and thus had been living in sin. Ngewa notes, "If Paul rebuilds a system that he once destroyed, he is acknowledging that he made a mistake, in which case he broke the law by destroying the law."[29] Hence if this is the case, he ends up not justified but a sinner in need of redemption. However, this is not the way Peter would see himself. He would not consider his relationship with the Gentiles to be a sinful matter, for this was something that God had already convicted him of in Acts 10. In Christ, Peter, Paul, and the other believers had torn down the laws that separated the Jews and Gentiles (Gal 3:28). They had received the Spirit through the resurrection power of Christ (3:1) who worked in them to do God's will.[30]

Dead to the Law, Alive in God (2:19)

Paul notes that he had died to the law, which means that the restrictions of the law do not apply to him. This is because he has been crucified with Christ. The purpose of this is that he may live to God. Paul makes the first steps in defining the implications of the doctrine of justification. This is Paul's reflection on the grand truths in verses 15–18: "I have died to the law" and "I live for God." It is the reflection of a radically changed Christian, a depiction of new life in Christ. According to Dunn, "the strength of Paul's language strongly suggests that he reflects his own experience in coming to Christ as a Jew."[31] Lightfoot renders this reflection in the following manner: "Through my recognition that I could

---

28. Keener, *Galatians*, 98.
29. Ngewa, *Galatians*, 28.
30. Keener, *Galatians*, 99.
31. J. D. G. Dunn, *The Theology of Paul's Letter to the Galatians* (Cambridge: Cambridge University Press, 1993), 143.

not fulfil the law, I came to understand that I must die to it."[32] This is what Galatians 3:24 is aiming at: "the law was our schoolmaster to bring us unto Christ" (KJV, also see Gal 3:13; Rom 7:14–25). Ngewa notes, "'To live for God' has the idea of life under the control of God and for the honour of God."[33]

The Result of Justification (2:20–21)

This subsection seems to many an unconventional fit into the argument of Paul. Cowan observes that this section cannot be understood without factoring in the unity of the section 2:17–20.[34] Central to Cowan's argument is the understanding of the word "live" which is repeated four times in verse 20, twice being related to Christ and once qualified by σαρχι. He argues that justification in Galatians 2:17 is connected to Paul's description of his relation to Christ in 2:19–20, observing:

> 2.19–20 is a description of the justifying relationship mentioned in 2.17 because the references to "life" in 2.19–20 metonymically represent a positive verdict in the divine courtroom. Furthermore, the phrase "Christ lives ἐν ἐμοί" should be viewed as a reference to Christ's resurrection life as a reality into which Paul has been incorporated rather than as a reference to Christ's presence within Paul by means of the Holy Spirit. Christ's resurrection life represents his own status as righteous before God, and Paul can speak of this life and status as his because of his union with Christ.[35]

We also must observe a key correlation between justification and life. Death to the law produces life toward God. Dying to self produces life. This new life in Paul was an actual death to a former life and a replacement for the actual life of Christ[36] – a life that, though lived this side of eternity, relies on the deep union with the righteous Christ and not on self-emanating righteousness. He thus can claim the righteousness of Christ (attested to by his resurrection), and by it he stands justified before God. This section thus provides us with the

---

32. Lightfoot, *Epistle of St. Paul*, 118.
33. Ngewa, *Galatians*, 85.
34. J. A. Cowan, "The Legal Significance of Christ's Risen Life: Union with Christ and Justification in Galatians 2.17–20," *Journal for the Study of the New Testament* 40, no. 4 (2018): 453–72.
35. Cowan, "Legal Significance," 466.
36. Jacobus, "Paul and His Teaching," 358.

grounds for justification that Paul has been arguing about. It is the reality of the union with Christ and fellowship with other believers (the body of Christ). On these grounds, Peter and the Judaizers are found to be at fault, for by their insistence on circumcision they deny this essential unity with and in Christ that they share with their brothers and sisters who are Gentiles, for neither Jews nor Gentiles have done anything to warrant their union with Christ.

Paul concludes this long discourse by noting that he does not in any way nullify the grace of God, for if justification came by the law, then Christ died for nothing. We find here a statement that a true appreciation of grace is understanding that Christ is sufficient to justify the sinner and that there is no other obligation laid on Christians to earn their righteousness or their position in Christ.

Bridging the Horizons

In our discussion above, we have noted several things. First, there is nothing greater than the work of Christ in justifying his people by faith. Second, the grounds of justification is believers' union with Christ. Believers can claim the attested righteousness of Christ. Thus, there is no barrier between brothers and sisters redeemed by this merciful savior.

It is hence reasonable for Paul to state that the Jews are not to cling to the law, for the law does not bring life; only Christ does. The divisions highlighted in the text seem at first sight to be superficial and social, and yet Paul labors to provide a theological polemic to them. Paul's opponents might accuse him of overreacting to the situation in Antioch, but Paul demonstrates that this "social" issue reflected their theology. It thus comes to us today as a discourse that we cannot ignore. Our understanding of justification as believers is of paramount importance. It is not only a matter of how accurately we can express it to others and affirm it in our confessions, but how its understanding shapes our orthopraxy.

The Galatian church needed to be confronted with the truth of justification. Other teachers were teaching wrongly, and this matter was affecting not simply the confessional faith but, to a large extent, how they were living it out in practice. They needed to see the disunity brought about by the distortion of this doctrine of justification by Peter and the others in Antioch as they succumbed to the fear of the circumcision party. For those of us in the church in Africa, we too are in need of this polemic. Our application of this text will, without doubt, look somewhat different, for the division in question is not brought about by the issue of circumcision. Division in the church is caused by various things, but here we will focus in particular on the division that the Kenyan church experiences during elections.

At election time we see congregants turning against each other and dividing into political factions, and this plays out silently in the church. Believers who are justified as Paul was take up tribal "cohorts" that jeopardize their unity as a body.[37] Fellowship becomes tough because we are of different political minds. The extreme example of this was in 2007/8 when we saw congregations turning on each other and upholding their tribal allegiances as primary. Some clergy could not serve in certain places because they were not of a particular ethnicity. In fact, in a rather sad irony, the rumors of a certain tribe being uncircumcised raised serious suspicion among fellow believers.

The truth is that we need to hear the polemical presentation of Paul and face the challenge whether we truly understand the extent of the confession we make as believers who are justified in Christ. The divisions we face, albeit social, challenge the genuineness of our confession. If we truly understand that we are justified by faith on the grounds of the union we have in the resurrection life of Christ, then our allegiance would be to none other than Christ, who has made it possible for us to be justified and whose righteous life we can claim as ours. This would then mean that no tribe would be greater than the people with whom we share the same spiritual life.

We may even adapt the *Ubuntu* philosophy "I am because we are": *We are because he is.* Our life as a community is drawn from one source through whom we can claim to be alive. This idea is not far from the conceptual idea of community in the African setting. A community, which we refer to as a tribe, identifies itself not only by sharing common beliefs and traditions but through the commonality of the people's origin, their ancestry. This ancestry points to a common life source, and a great deal of their unity is attributable to this. As a case in point, the popular Kikuyu saying "*mundu wa Nyumba*" is literally translated as "a person of the house." The meaning here is that the person who is of the same tribe belongs to the same house of Mumbi, and, in a sense, that the life of everyone in the community started there.

This understanding of community in the African mind mirrors to a great extent what Paul shares in the text. If we were to think of what Paul writes as a Kikuyu, we would basically say that all Christians are "*adu a nyumba*," translated as "people of the house," irrespective of their tribe. The common ground uniting us is not human ancestry but Christ and our union with him.

---

37. By the term "tribe," we do not necessarily imply only ethnic tribalism but also tribes formed by commonalities shared among certain people.

This commonality transcends human tribes and ancestry, forming what we might term a "supra-tribe."

The applications that follow are not the main focus of this chapter; however, given the text at hand they are useful reflections.

The church in Kenya must be wary of the resurgence of African Traditional Religion. While we cannot compare the rituals there to those of the Jews, those who pray to mountains and shrines seem to indicate that, unless something is followed to the core, we are not fully redeemed. For example, take the discourse of family altars that is prevalent today. Proponents will share that there are things that need to be done so that one may be fully "delivered." One of those things may involve the practice of certain rituals for "deliverance." Since we claim the righteousness of Christ and are one with him, there is no other ritual, ordinance, or practice needed to grant freedom. Freedom is guaranteed in the justification we have by faith in Christ and in the union we have in him.

The passage challenges us to always be champions of the truth, for it is greater than any person's reputation. Paul confronted Peter, who was perceived to be a pillar of the church. The nature of the confrontation was such that the source of condemnation was outside them and superior: it was the gospel. With the "man of God" syndrome prevalent in the church in Kenya, we must be wary that no one is perceived as being above correction. It must be noted, however, that any correction that needs to be delivered to people when they are wrong should be based not on feelings but on an objective standard of Scripture that condemns their errors. Since such errors affect the public outlook of the faith, they must be corrected publicly yet with wisdom. Let truth reign over all.

Conclusion

Justification is an issue that has been heavily debated in the recent past, and the debate still continues. However, amid the debate, we must see that it is central to the Christian faith both in soteriological and in ecclesiological matters. With regard to soteriology, we are saved by grace alone and not by works. This must affect our lives now, as we respond to what has already happened to us by living lives consistent with the new nature.

Ecclesiologically, justification affects how we perceive other people in the faith. They are our brothers and sisters in Christ, and nothing should hinder our true fellowship with them. Just as in Paul's day, we should remember that there is no one who is less justified than another, for we all have the same Lord who is the means of justification – the Lord Jesus Christ. Thus in the African church we should look to the Scriptures for a solution to ethnic divisions both inside and outside the church. Our justification has implications for the unity of the church and how we treat each other.

Bibliography

de Boer, M. C. "Paul's Use and Interpretation of a Justification Tradition in Galatians 2:15–22." *Journal for the Study of the New Testament* 28, no. 2 (2005): 189–216.

Cowan, J. A. "The Legal Significance of Christ's Risen Life: Union with Christ and Justification in Galatians 2.17–20." *Journal for the Study of the New Testament* 40, no. 4 (2018): 453–72.

Dunn, J. D. G. *Jesus, Paul, and the Law: Studies in Mark and Galatians.* Louisville: Westminster John Knox, 1990.

———. "The Justice of God: A Renewed Perspective on Justification by Faith." *Journal of Theological Studies* 43, no. 1 (1992): 1–22.

———. "The New Perspective on Paul." *Bulletin of the John Rylands Library of Manchester* 65, no. 2 (1983): 95–122.

———. *The Theology of Paul's Letter to the Galatians.* Cambridge: Cambridge University Press, 1993.

Jacobus, M. W. "Paul and His Teaching in Galatians 2:11–21." *The Biblical World*, Vol. 24, No. 5 (Nov., 1904): 351–58.

Keener, C. S. *Galatians.* New York: Cambridge University Press, 2018.

———. *The IVP Bible Background Commentary: New Testament.* Downers Grove: InterVarsity, 1993.

Lightfoot, J. B. *The Epistle of St. Paul to the Galatians.* Zondervan Commentary. Grand Rapids: Zondervan, 1997.

Moo, D. J. *Galatians.* Baker Exegetical Commentary on the New Testament. Grand Rapids: Baker Academic, 2013.

Ngewa, S. M. *Galatians.* Nairobi: HippoBooks, 2010.

Schreiner, T. R. "Justification: The Saving Righteousness of God in Christ." *Journal of the Evangelical Theological Society* 54, no. 1 (2011): 19–34.

Wright, N. T. *Justification: God's Plan and Paul's Vision.* Downers Grove: IVP Academic, 2009.

7

Past, Present, and Future

Paul's View of Salvation in the Thessalonian Correspondence

Gift Mtukwa
Chair of Department and Lecturer, School of Religion and Christian Ministries of Africa Nazarene University, Nairobi, Africa

Abstract

In his writings, Paul uses various images to speak about the salvation we have in Christ. The Thessalonian letters are no exception; the verb σώζω and its cognates appears only twice in these letters (1 Thess 2:16; 2 Thess 2:10), whereas the noun σωτηρίας appear four times (1 Thess 5:8, 9; 2 Thess 2:13). However, Paul has other ways that express the idea of salvation; for instance, the idea of turning/repentance in 1 Thessalonians 1:9. This chapter seeks to investigate what salvation entails; in other words, what exactly are people saved from and for? Is salvation in the past, present, or future? The chapter will use African biblical hermeneutics, particularly the Shona perspective, as a lens through which to read particular passages from the Thessalonian letters, namely, 1 Thessalonians 1:9-10; 1 Thessalonians 5:8-10; and 2 Thessalonians 2:10-14, where soteriological references are apparent. The study will contribute to our understanding of salvation in Paul's earliest letters as well as our understanding of salvation in Africa.

Key words: salvation, soteriological, sin, Shona, Thessalonians, deliverance, hope

Introduction

The African landscape presents many problems, which include crime, disease, racism, poverty, ignorance, oppression, hatred, war, tribalism, and many others.[1] If salvation is to be presented in such a context, it must make sense to the African person confronted by these issues. Henry J. Mugabe says concerning these problems, "they are not peripheral to the gospel, they are inextricable ingredients kernel [sic] to the gospel."[2] This chapter will present an African perspective on salvation before we embark on a study of Pauline texts in the Thessalonian correspondence that deal specifically with salvation, for the purpose of ensuring that the proclamation of salvation in Africa can take into consideration some of the concerns of the African peoples.

Salvation in Traditional African Society

Scholars have long noted the need to do theology contextually. African Christian theology ought to take seriously the cultural, social, political, religious, and economic landscape of African life and thought forms.[3] The same call has been made in relation to how we read the biblical text. The Bible ought to be read contextually since there is no such thing as a universal reading of the text. Each reader of the Bible reads within a particular cultural milieu. It is our contention that our understanding of salvation in the Thessalonian letters can benefit immensely from an African biblical hermeneutics – more specifically a Shona perspective of reading the biblical text.

As is the case in most African communities (Akan, Zulu, Kikuyu), in African Traditional Religion (Shona perspective) salvation is concerned not only with the afterlife but also with the here and now – in other words, it is "anthropocentric; it is life-affirming."[4] As such, its concerns are "protection, restoration, preservation, survival and the continuance of human, societal and environmental life in the world."[5] Mbiti speaks along the same lines when he says,

---

1. Brian Raftopoulos, "The Zimbabwean Crisis and the Challenges for the Left," *Journal of Southern African Studies* 32, no. 2 (2006): 203–19.
2. Henry J. Mugabe, "Salvation from an African Perspective," *The Indian Journal of Theology* 36, no. 1 (1994): 40.
3. Mugabe, "African Perspective," 31.
4. Mugabe, 32.
5. Mugabe, 32.

> Salvation in African religion has to do with physical and immediate dangers (of the individual and more often of the community) – dangers that threaten individual or community survival, good health and general prosperity or safety.... Salvation is not just an abstraction; it is concrete, told in terms of both what has happened and is likely to be encountered by people as they go through daily experiences.[6]

The Shona word *ruponeso*, which is translated as "salvation," has the meaning "to give birth, to survive, to sustain life, to rescue, or to deliver a baby."[7] This is akin to the Akan perspective, where "the central soteriological concern . . . has to do with protection, preservation of life both physical and spiritual from the threats of evil doers like witches, sorcerers, vengeful spirits and all those who seek to destroy life."[8] From this perspective, anything that threatens or destroys life and general well-being is addressed adequately.[9]

The question that should be posed is: What are we being saved from and saved for? Among the Shona, the notion of *chivi* (sin) is an important category for which salvation is needed. "Sin" is defined as "any and all antisocial activities that are aimed at hurting individuals and communities."[10] It follows then that *ruponeso*, if it is real, must address the relationships among members of the community. Salvation in this sense results in harmonious relationships in which persons seek the good of others. As Byang H. Kato notes concerning the Jaba, "if sin is only societal, the so-called social gospel has to be the right solution."[11] *Ruponeso*, in this understanding, consists of things that an individual can do to mend broken relationships. It is assumed that once one is in a right relationship with others, then God is happy. It follows then that this aspect of salvation has to do with proper relationships with others and not with God. Even though the concept of sacrificing oneself for others is present among the Shonas, the idea of a savior who "died for us" is nonexistent. Thus,

---

6. John Mbiti, "Some Reflections on African Experience of Salvation Today," in *Living Faiths and Ultimate Goals* (Geneva: World Council of Churches, 1974), 1–138, quoted in Mugabe, 32.
7. Mugabe, 32.
8. Mugabe, 33, summarizing Abraham Ako Akrong, "An Akan Christian View of Salvation from the Perspective of John Calvin's Soteriology" (PhD diss., Lutheran School of Theology at Chicago, 1991).
9. Akrong, "Akan Christian View," 1–110.
10. Mugabe, "African Perspective," 33.
11. Byang H. Kato, *Theological Pitfalls in Africa* (Nairobi: Evangel, 1987), 42.

as important as the mending of broken relationships is, it does not encompass all that salvation in a biblical perspectives entails.

In summary, the African context has its own understanding of salvation which can aid our understanding of biblical salvation. The dominant theme of salvation in Africa is that of deliverance from physical harm and the mending of broken relationships. Let us now turn to the Thessalonian correspondence to investigate the soteriological references that Paul makes.[12] We will begin our investigation with 1 Thessalonians 1:9b–10.

1 Thessalonians 1:9b–10

Salvation in Scripture denotes several things including healing from disease, safe travel, and protection in times of trouble. The term is also used "for deliverance from sin and for the ultimate deliverance when the saved enter bliss with Christ at the end of the age."[13] Deliverance from sin and life with Christ feature prominently in Paul's understanding of salvation in the Thessalonian letters. Paul enlightens the Thessalonians about the reputation that they have among the people of Macedonia regarding their "faith" (πιστις) (1 Thess 1:8). It is their faithfulness that has become known in all the surrounding regions. Such faithfulness is a result of the conversion that the Thessalonians have experienced. Some scholars see this passage as part of the early church hymn which Paul adopts for his own use.[14] For instance, Morris writes,

> There is very little that is specifically Pauline in the expression. It is difficult, for example, to imagine that Paul would give an account in his own words of people entering into a genuine Christian experience with no mention of their being justified by faith and without any reference to the cross.[15]

---

12. It is assumed here that Paul wrote both letters to the Thessalonians. I have argued elsewhere that we should see these letters as coming from Paul and addressing the same issues within a short period of time; see Gift Mtukwa, *Work and Community in the Thessalonian Correspondence: An African Communal Reading of Paul's Work Exhortations* (Carlisle: Langham Monographs, 2021).

13. Leon Morris, "Salvation," in *Dictionary of Paul and His Writings: A Compendium of Biblical Scholarship*, eds. Gerald F. Hawthorne, Ralph P. Martin, and Daniel G. Reid (Downers Grove: InterVarsity, 1993), 858.

14. Charles A. Wanamaker, *The Epistles to the Thessalonians: A Commentary on the Greek Text*, New International Greek Testament Commentary (Grand Rapids: Eerdmans, 1990), 84.

15. Leon Morris, *The Epistles of Paul to the Thessalonians: An Introduction and Commentary*, rev. ed., Tyndale New Testament Commentaries (Leicester: Inter-Varsity, 1984), 53.

Yet Paul does not need to use the same words to speak of salvation. The language of justification does not appear in the Thessalonian letters for Paul is not dealing with the issue of creating one community consisting of Jews and Gentiles.[16] Be that as it may, whether or not we are dealing with pre-Pauline material is inconsequential; Paul has integrated this material into his letters, and the ideas fit with Paul's rhetorical focus.

Paul reports that the people have noted how the Thessalonians "turned . . . from idols" to "serve the living . . . God" (v. 9b). It is indeed true that words such as "turn," "serve," and "the living God" constitute Old Testament language.[17] Paul here is speaking about their conversion which entailed a "change of direction of the will" resulting in a "reorientation of the whole life."[18] The fact of their having turned from idols is an explanation of the faith (πιστις) of the Thessalonians.[19] The Thessalonians have made a total break with the past in which they worshipped idols.[20] Such a break with the past would have meant disentangling oneself from one's family, workmates, and the gods of the family.[21] For Africans who are accustomed to religion helping them get along, the fact that commitment to Jesus may disentangle family relationships can be unsettling. However, it needs to be made clear that relationships can only be healthy when people are committed to good African values which are consistent with biblical teaching and the message of the gospel.

Given that the God the Thessalonians now worshipped could not be seen, the charge of atheism would have been made against them.[22] Such a charge had social, economic, and political ramifications since religion was not considered merely a personal matter.[23] It is possible that the friction between the house

---

16. I. Howard Marshall, *1 and 2 Thessalonians: A Commentary* (Vancouver: Regent College Pub., 2002), 176.

17. Gary S. Shogren, *1 and 2 Thessalonians*, 1st ed., Zondervan Exegetical Commentary on the New Testament (Grand Rapids: Zondervan, 2013), 72.

18. Morris, *Epistles of Paul*, 52.

19. R. C. H. Lenski, *The Interpretation of St. Paul's Epistles to the Colossians, to the Thessalonians, to Timothy, to Titus, and to Philemon* (Peabody: Hendrickson, 1998), 233.

20. Jeffrey A. D. Weima, *1-2 Thessalonians* (Grand Rapids: Baker Academic, 2014), 109.

21. John M. G. Barclay, *Obeying the Truth: Paul's Ethics in Galatians* (Vancouver: Regent College Pub., 2005), 58.

22. Weima, *1-2 Thessalonians*, 108.

23. Gene L. Green, *The Letters to the Thessalonians*, Pillar New Testament Commentary (Grand Rapids: Eerdmans, 2002), 107.

church and the townspeople resulted from this (1 Thess 2:14).[24] The conversion that the Thessalonians experienced would have had visible manifestations in the Roman world where many gods were worshipped. These would have entailed their "turning away from their 'normal' civic activities," including their duty to the imperial cult.[25] Given that Thessalonica took its status as a free city seriously, officials would not have wanted to jeopardize that status, hence the persecution from their own compatriots.[26]

These believers used to worship idols, and now they had turned from them. The word "idol" appears in Homer's writings, meaning "shadow" or "form."[27] It is used in a derogatory manner by Jews and Christians to denote gentile religion, even though the Gentiles themselves would not have considered their worship idolatry.[28] Since "idols" are frequently associated with gentile religion, scholars see Paul's words as evidence that the Thessalonians themselves are Gentiles.[29] It is more significant that the Thessalonians could "see Mount Olympus, about fifty miles south of their city, where the Greek gods were supposed to live."[30] Paul's converts did not mix their newfound faith with "indigenous religious practices"; thus they could not be accused of being syncretistic.[31] African Christians have much to learn from the Thessalonians who left their traditional gods for "the living God."[32] It was the cruciform story of Christ that transformed Paul and the Thessalonians' story. They could no longer frequent local temples, paying homage to pagan gods. They adopted new rituals and ceremonies and stopped the old ones.[33]

---

24. Green, *Letters to the Thessalonians*, 107. Weima has noted that "such a total renunciation of all pagan deities also meant a complete rejection of a variety of social events closely associated with the worship of these gods. Such action by Christians evoked resentment and anger in their non-Christian family members and friends." Weima, *1–2 Thessalonians*, 108.

25. Andy Johnson, *1 and 2 Thessalonians*, Two Horizons New Testament Commentary (Grand Rapids: Eerdmans, 2016), 52–53.

26. Weima, *1–2 Thessalonians*, 108.

27. Shogren, *1 and 2 Thessalonians*, 72.

28. Shogren, 72.

29. Ben Witherington III, *1 and 2 Thessalonians: A Socio-Rhetorical Commentary* (Grand Rapids: Eerdmans, 2006), 74; Gordon D. Fee, *The First and Second Letters to the Thessalonians* (Grand Rapids: Eerdmans, 2009), 46.

30. John R. W. Stott, *The Message of 1 and 2 Thessalonians: The Gospel and the End of Time*, Bible Speaks Today (Leicester: Inter-Varsity, 1991).

31. Green, *Letters to the Thessalonians*, 106.

32. Witherington, *1 and 2 Thessalonians*, 76.

33. Witherington, 76.

One could not accept Paul's gospel and, at the same time, have a connection with the idols of the Greco-Roman world. For one to have a connection with this world would have meant connecting "with the dark side and the evil being of that realm."[34] As Johnson has noted, "these images do somehow participate sacramentally in the power of the invisible realities they represent."[35] This is the reason why elsewhere "Paul admonishes" the Corinthians "to 'flee from idolatry' (1 Cor 10:14)."[36]

For the Thessalonians, it was not just a matter of leaving idols; for Paul, the end goal was to serve "the living and true God." Scholars have noted an allusion to Jeremiah 10:10, which speaks of God as "the true God," "the living God," and "the everlasting King" (ESV). Jeremiah also makes reference to God's "wrath" and his "indignation" (ESV), which the nations cannot endure. Even though Paul does not cite Old Testament Scripture verbatim in the Thessalonian letters, scriptural allusions and echoes are common. If God is "living and true," the idols in turn are "dead and worthless inventions" and are also false gods.[37] Jewish, pagan, and Christian literature all speak about "serving" or "worshipping" a god.[38] Such service was often rendered in a manner reminiscent of a slave.[39] Johnson has rightly noted that by using "the present tense verb *douleuein*, Paul portrays others as describing the state of the Thessalonian assembly as one of *ongoing enslavement to God*, that is, as exhibiting unconditional obedience and loyalty toward God."[40] Paul makes use of the noun δοῦλος to speak about his calling by Christ to be a slave.[41] The language of calling in speaking of salvation is common in the Thessalonian letters. As such, salvation is not just about being saved; it is being saved for a purpose – namely to "serve the living God."

The Thessalonians' conversion was visible for all to see; in other words, their devotion to God was both inward and outward.[42] Speaking of the "before" and "after" of their conversion, Fee asserts that these "former pagans, who had been worshipers of idols ('dead gods'), have now given themselves 'to

---

34. Witherington, 74.
35. Johnson, *1 and 2 Thessalonians*, 53.
36. Johnson, 54.
37. John Calvin, *1, 2 Thessalonians*, eds. Alister E. McGrath and J. I. Packer (Wheaton: Crossway, 1999), 22.
38. Shogren, *1 and 2 Thessalonians*, 73.
39. Weima, *1–2 Thessalonians*, 109.
40. Johnson, *1 and 2 Thessalonians*, 53.
41. Shogren, *1 and 2 Thessalonians*, 73.
42. Weima, *1–2 Thessalonians*, 109.

serve the living and true God.' The end result of such conversion was a new orientation, an eschatological one, wherein they were now waiting for their final consummation."[43] While serving God, they were also to "wait for his Son from heaven" (v. 10). This, according to Weima, forms the second motivation for their conversion.[44] The word ἀναμένειν is a *hapax legomenon* in the New Testament, appearing only here. However, as Wanamaker has noted, the idea of waiting for Christ is not unusual in the New Testament (Rom 14:18; 16:18; Col 3:24). The verb ἀναμένειν means "to look forward to with patience and confidence."[45] This word (a present infinitive) signifies that "the believers in Thessalonica are constantly awaiting the return of Christ."[46]

The fact that the believers are to wait for God's Son demonstrates that the "gospel message is inherently eschatological: believers await the future intervention of God through his Son."[47] As Shogren asserts, "The Thessalonians have been converted not merely to monotheism, but to a Christological-eschatological faith: they await God's Son."[48] In this sense, "the new lives of believers are eschatologically oriented."[49] Waiting has to do with "the set of observable actions or behaviour to which the expectation gives rise."[50] The moral conduct of the Thessalonians had changed as a result of their conversion. Serving God meant that there were things they could not do and also things that they could do.

In the first letter to the Thessalonians, Paul frames their conduct in terms of holiness. What God requires of them is nothing short of holy living (1 Thess 3:13; 4:4, 7; 5:23). The goals of holiness and anticipation are to be pursued in equal measure. One is not to be sacrificed at the altar of the other.[51] Waiting has "ethical implications," meaning that they ought to live holy lives.[52] The

---

43. Fee, *First and Second Letters*, 49.

44. Weima, *1–2 Thessalonians*, 109.

45. George Milligan, *St. Paul's Epistles to the Thessalonians: The Greek Text, with Introduction and Notes* (London: Macmillan & Co., 1908), 14.

46. Weima, *1–2 Thessalonians*, 109.

47. Shogren, *1 and 2 Thessalonians*, 74; see also Abraham J. Malherbe, *The Letters to the Thessalonians: A New Translation with Introduction and Commentary* (New York: Doubleday, 2000), 132.

48. Shogren, 74.

49. Terence Peter Paige, *1 and 2 Thessalonians: A Commentary in the Wesleyan Tradition* (Kansas City: Beacon Hill, 2017), 69.

50. Anthony Thiselton, *Life after Death* (Grand Rapids: Eerdmans, 2011), 58 as cited in Johnson, *1 and 2 Thessalonians*, 55.

51. Weima, *1–2 Thessalonians*, 110.

52. F. F. Bruce, *1 and 2 Thessalonians*, Word Biblical Commentary (Waco: Word, 1982), 19.

"Son" is identified as Jesus, and he is coming from "the heavens." It should be remembered that the name Jesus has the connotation of "one who saves," basically "the Savior" (Matt 1:21).[53] Here we see a connection between Christology (Jesus, God's Son), soteriology (he rescues us), and eschatology (he is coming from the heavens). Salvation is effected by God's Son Jesus who is our savior. This Son has a unique, intimate relationship with the Father.[54] The Son for whom they wait "rescues us from the coming wrath." The word "ῥύεσθαι ('to save') is not as common in Paul as its synonym σῴζειν, but when it does occur, it refers to being saved or rescued *from* something (cf. Rom 7:24; 11:26; Col 1:13)."[55] It (ῥύεσθαι) can also mean "to deliver" with reference to "evil or danger or enemy."[56]

The emphasis is on the intensity of the danger vis-à-vis the power of the deliverer. The preposition εκ reveals that they were to be delivered from the wrath itself.[57] Here we see similarities with the understanding of salvation in the African setting, where salvation is usually understood in terms of deliverance from some danger. This negative aspect of "salvation *from*" should be emphasized in the African context, without of course neglecting the other aspect of "salvation *to*."[58] Shogren notes that since the word "rescue" is an "attributive participle, it might be rendered 'Jesus who saves us,' 'who will save us,' or even 'who has saved us.'" This way, "it leaves vague whether it denotes past, present, or future deliverance."[59] Africans can find this appealing since salvation is not a once-and-for-all event; the precarious nature of life requires that one experience salvation constantly. The assurance of a Jesus who rescues us not just in the past but also in the present and the future is comforting.

What is the source of "the coming wrath"? God is the source of the eschatological wrath which he metes out on those who "refuse to love the truth and so be saved" (2 Thess 2:10). Wrath should be thought of as originating from God and understood as his activity, which is meted out against those

---

53. Weima, *1–2 Thessalonians*, 111.
54. Weima, 110.
55. Wanamaker, *Epistle to the Thessalonians*, 88.
56. Marvin Richardson Vincent, *Word Studies in the New Testament* (New York: Charles Scribner's Sons, 1887), 20.
57. Leon Morris, *The Epistle to the Romans*, Pillar New Testament Commentary (Grand Rapids: Eerdmans, 1988), 50.
58. Ernest Best, *The First and Second Epistles to the Thessalonians* (Peabody: Hendrickson, 2003), 84.
59. Shogren, *1 and 2 Thessalonians*, 75.

who go against God.[60] In addition, wrath is God's response "to human actions that harm oneself and others, destroying human relationships or God's good created order."[61] As Weima has stated, "God's wrath must be seen in the light of his justice. God is indeed loving and kind, but his justice demands that sin, which is an affront to his holiness and supreme majesty, be punished."[62] The African ancestors can punish individuals who disrupt the harmony of things. The punishment can be thought of in terms of wrath, and in their (the ancestors') case, they have to be appeased to end it. The fact that God and his intermediaries (spirits and ancestors) can get angry and punish people is very much in the psyche of an African. The punishment is not only in the here and now but also eschatological in both African (not being able to live with the ancestors) and Christian (eternal damnation) perspectives.

In summary, the Thessalonians' salvation has to do with "turning" (past) from idols "to serve" (present) the true and living God and "to wait" for his Son who "rescues us" from the coming wrath (future). This verse is loaded with soteriological references. Christ cannot be served alongside other gods, and waiting for him does not preclude serving him. All these soteriological references have to do with the triad of faith, love, and hope (1 Thess 1:3). For, as Stott noted, "the turning to God is certainly faith, and the serving of God could be seen as the fruit of love, while the waiting for Christ is the essence of hope."[63] Let us now turn to our next passage.

1 Thessalonians 5:8–10

The context of 1 Thessalonians 5:8–10 is the eschatological teachings Paul is giving the Thessalonians. In this passage, he is instructing them "concerning the times and the seasons" (1 Thess 5:1 ESV). Since the "day of the Lord" will come like a thief in the night (v. 2), the believers who are not in the dark must live as "children of the light" (v. 5). In verse 8 Paul continues his ethical instructions in the light of the day of the Lord. This verse makes use of military imagery drawn from Isaiah 59:17,[64] which says, "He put on righteousness as a breastplate and a helmet of salvation on his head" (ESV). The "breastplate of

---

60. Weima, *1–2 Thessalonians*, 112.
61. Johnson, *1 and 2 Thessalonians*, 55.
62. Weima, *1–2 Thessalonians*, 112.
63. Stott, *1 and 2 Thessalonians*, 43.
64. Karl P. Donfried, "The Cults of Thessalonica and the Thessalonian Correspondence," *New Testament Studies* 31, no. 3 (1985): 341.

righteousness" and the "helmet of salvation" are parts of the uniform of the divine warrior, whose task is to rescue those who cannot rescue themselves.[65] The day of the Lord will see widespread disobedience against God, with the lawless one leading the way to "usurp the throne of God and claim divine honours for himself."[66] Unlike in Isaiah where the divine warrior is God himself, the believer has become the warrior who must now wear the armor.[67]

The believers are called to be "sober" in the same way that disciplined soldiers conduct themselves.[68] When they are sober, they can put on the breastplate of "faith and love" and the "hope of salvation as a helmet." These are the virtues that will ensure that the Christian is well "prepared for the 'day of the Lord.'"[69] This again recalls the triad of faith, love, and hope we encountered in 1 Thessalonians 1:3. The fact of putting on ἐνδυσάμενοι (aorist participle) makes it possible for them to "be self-controlled."[70] Given that in the expression "the hope of salvation" we are dealing with an objective genitive, Shogren is right to read the phrase "the salvation for which we hope."[71] Salvation here has to do with the future; in other words, we are dealing with eschatological salvation. In the present time, the people of God can hope for it.[72] This hope is not wishful thinking; rather, it is "the settled assurance of future deliverance (see 1:10; Rom 8:24)."[73]

Verse 9 envisions two groups of people who have two different destinies, namely "wrath" and "salvation." The believers are destined to "obtain salvation" (ESV), while the unbelievers are appointed "to suffer wrath." Weima has noted that "the reference to 'wrath' looks back to this passage's earliest description of the judgment that awaits unbelievers, the 'sudden destruction' from which 'they will certainly not escape' (vv. 2–3)."[74] Just as salvation is eschatological, the wrath is also "eschatological (1:10, 'the coming wrath')."[75] The reference to the "day of the Lord" anticipated the appointment to wrath since that day is a

---

65. Johnson, *1 and 2 Thessalonians*, 42.
66. Bruce, *1 and 2 Thessalonians*, 175.
67. Weima, *1–2 Thessalonians*, 363.
68. Bruce, *1 and 2 Thessalonians*, 250.
69. Bruce, 250.
70. D. Michael Martin, *1, 2 Thessalonians*, New American Commentary 33 (Nashville: Broadman & Holman, 1995), 166.
71. Shogren, *1 and 2 Thessalonians*, 209.
72. Wanamaker, *Epistles to the Thessalonians*, 186.
73. Green, *Letters to the Thessalonians*, 241.
74. Weima, *1–2 Thessalonians*, 366.
75. Weima, 367.

"day of wrath."[76] This hope of salvation is for those who will "have persevered, have put on the armour, have stayed alert, have remained faithful and true."[77]

Paul makes it clear that salvation is a gift from the Lord Jesus Christ – his work at Calvary makes it a reality.[78] The fact that God destines the believers does not mean there is no response needed on their part.[79] As Green affirms,

> Christians will not gain this salvation through any merit on their part; it becomes theirs because of God's gracious election. It is not obtained as if it were a salary. This message of grace is both implied in the verb and underlined by the final clause, *through our Lord Jesus Christ*.[80]

God's enablement is through the death of Christ, which was "for us" (v. 10). The death and the resurrection of Jesus are the basis for salvation since in his death, he received God's wrath which was due to his people.[81] The death of Christ "paradoxically results in the life of the believer."[82]

Paul does not say much about Jesus's death; neither does he tell his readers "exactly what Christ's death as a sacrifice accomplished so that it was salvific for the audience of this letter."[83] Paul's focus seems to be the question why Christ died for us, which is the point of verse 10: "so that . . . we may live together with him."[84] Even though we don't learn much about Christ's death from this passage, it is, however, clear that it was substitutionary. His death was not for himself; it was vicarious, meaning that he lived and died for others.

Some scholars interpret γρηγορῶμεν, "keep alert," (translated *awake* in the NIV and ESV) as the opposite of "fall asleep," καθεύδωμεν (v. 10). The implication of such a reading is that "Christ will take the negligent Christian with him."[85] This interpretation is unlikely. We should look to 1 Thessalonians 4:15 for the interpretive key to this passage. As Shogren has noted, "the rendering 'died' is perfectly correct, given that 'sleep' was a fixed metaphor

---

76. Shogren, *1 and 2 Thessalonians*, 210.
77. Witherington, *1 and 2 Thessalonians*, 151.
78. Witherington, 151–52.
79. Johnson, *1 and 2 Thessalonians*, 144.
80. Green, *Letters to the Thessalonians*, 243.
81. G. K. Beale, *1–2 Thessalonians*, IVP New Testament Commentary (Downers Grove: InterVarsity, 2003), 154.
82. Weima, *1–2 Thessalonians*, 371.
83. Johnson, *1 and 2 Thessalonians*, 147.
84. Johnson, 145.
85. Shogren, *1 and 2 Thessalonians*, 210.

for death."[86] It should be remembered that the comfort Paul brings to the believers is that, regardless of whether they are alive or dead when Christ returns, salvation, not wrath, is what they will receive.[87] The implication is that both the dead and the living in Christ share this new life equally.[88] This then is the goal of salvation for Paul; it is to "live together with him" (v. 10). Martin is right to note that such life together with Christ is "eschatological life."[89] This aspect fits perfectly with the African view of the integration that takes place in the community of the ancestors: when an individual joins this community, he or she is said to be truly saved.[90] The fact that a person qualifies through the life he or she has lived on earth to join the ancestors and eventually become one of them is reminiscent of the fact that those who stand firm and live holy lives are those who will "live together with him." Yet it must be noted that the goal for Christians is not only to be with the saints but to be with Christ, who is the hope of resurrection.

In summary, this passage makes it clear that salvation is not just in the past; it is also future. There are two destinies for two groups of people: one is the hope of salvation, and the other is wrath. The believers are appointed for salvation, whereas the unbelievers are appointed for wrath with the "lawless one." Salvation results in living together with the risen Christ, in the same way that Africans look forward to living in the community of the ancestors. Even though this similarity can be used to present the gospel, it must be stressed that living with Christ is qualitatively different from living with ancestors. Let us now turn to our final passage.

2 Thessalonians 2:10–14

The context of this passage is again Paul's eschatological teaching. He is speaking about "the coming of our Lord Jesus" (2:1). It contains the same themes of the revealing of the lawless one (v. 3) and the things which he does (v. 4). The fate of the lawless one is destruction, which the Lord Jesus Christ will unleash on him. The connection between "the working of Satan" and the lawless one is made apparent, as well as the fact that he "uses all power, signs, lying wonders and every kind of deception" (vv. 8–10a NRSV). This

---

86. Shogren, 211.
87. Weima, *1–2 Thessalonians*, 369.
88. Weima, 367.
89. Martin, *1, 2 Thessalonians*, 168.
90. Mugabe, "African Perspective," 34.

verse should caution Africans today, who are often preoccupied with signs and wonders as evidence of God's work; it is clear here that even such can be done by the enemies of God.

Verse 10 spells out the fate of those who "refuse to love the truth." For Paul, the truth is the message of the gospel and not "some philosophical truth" that comes as a result of speculation.[91] Their refusal "is a deliberate" one; as such, "it expresses the attitude of their heart. And it is fraught with eternal consequences."[92] Though Satan and the lawless one deceive the unbelievers, ultimately it is their choice, as indicated by the causal clause.[93] These people are not victims of the deceiver; they are willing participants. The implication of their refusing to accept the truth of the gospel is that it leaves them "vulnerable to the destructive work of Satan's superman."[94] Consequently, they will miss out on God's salvation: since they refuse, they take full responsibility for their fate.

The Thessalonian believers, in contrast, love the truth and, therefore, have obtained salvation. The fact that Paul speaks of "love [of] the truth" (v. 10) signifies that the believers are "personally and fully devoted to the truth."[95] The word "be saved" ($\sigma\omega\theta\tilde{\eta}\nu\alpha\iota$), an aorist infinitive, "simply describes the fact of the action, without regard to time and without giving information concerning the nature of the action."[96] Verses 11 and 12 spell out what God will do to those people who refuse the gospel. Not only will they believe a lie, but also they are the object of God's judgment. In this case, judgment is meted out not only on those who persecute believers but also on those who "refuse to love the truth" (v. 10) and "do not believe" (v. 12).[97] Since they are already allowing themselves to be deceived, "God sends them a powerful delusion," which in turn leads them to "believe what is false" (v. 11 ESV). The implication is that by failing to believe the truth they take "pleasure in unrighteousness" (v. 12 ESV).

Verses 13–14 follow this by contrasting two groups as well, namely those who "will be condemned" (v. 12) and those who will "be saved" (v. 13).[98] This contrast continues in verse 14, where the believers are to "share in the glory

---

91. Weima, *1–2 Thessalonians*, 541.
92. Morris, *Epistles of Paul to the Thessalonians*, 233.
93. Martin, *1, 2 Thessalonians*, 249.
94. Weima, *1–2 Thessalonians*, 540–41.
95. By using the past tense in "they refused," Paul is making a reference to his gospel proclamation in Thessalonica. Weima, 542.
96. Shogren, *1 and 2 Thessalonians*, 293.
97. Shogren, 294.
98. Fee, *First and Second Letters*, 299.

of our Lord" whereas the non-believers will "perish" (cf. v. 10).[99] The believers are those who are "beloved by the Lord" (ESV) and are also chosen by God, to whom Paul gives thanks (v. 13). God's choice of the Thessalonians is clearly prompted by love.[100] Does this mean that God chooses certain individuals and rejects others? Paul would say "by no means" to this question. The choice is not that of individuals as such but of the church in its entirety. As Johnson has noted, "God's electing is not limited to a precreation selection process but is played out in the actual reception of Paul's gospel in active faith/faithfulness to God and love toward others."[101] F. F. Bruce asserts that "it is a travesty of God's electing grace to suppose that, because he chooses some for salvation, all the others are thereby consigned to perdition. On the contrary, if some are chosen for a special blessing, it is in order that others may be blessed through them and with them."[102] We should observe that the call was made "through our gospel," for the preposition εν should be considered instrumental.[103] Paul has already said that the unbelievers "refused to love the truth"; it is their refusal of the truth of the gospel that determines their destiny. God is not responsible for their choice; those who accept the gospel are the chosen ones in this sense.

The believers were chosen as either "firstfruits for salvation" (ἀπαρχὴν εἰς σωτηρίαν) or "from the beginning for salvation" (ἀπ' ἀρχῆς εἰς σωτηρίαν). The manuscript evidence is divided equally between these two options.[104] The same is true of Bible translations: they are also equally divided. The second option is a temporal reading which states that they have been chosen "from the beginning." For instance, Wanamaker says that this is "a reference to the fact that from the beginning God's purpose was to save the elect."[105] The problem with this is that Paul does not usually use this phrase in this manner. We are hard-pressed to find a similar use elsewhere in the Pauline corpus. The weightiest evidence is that "the term 'first fruits' is a Pauline word that occurs in his other writings six times (Rom 8:23; 11:16; 15:5; 1 Cor 15:20, 23; 16:15), two of which occur without a qualifying genitive, as is the case here in 2:13."[106]

---

99. Fee, 299.
100. Beale, *1–2 Thessalonians*, 225.
101. Johnson, *1 and 2 Thessalonians*, 56–57.
102. Bruce, *1 and 2 Thessalonians*, 191.
103. Bruce, 190.
104. Wanamaker, *Epistles to the Thessalonians*, 266; Shogren, *1 and 2 Thessalonians*, 302.
105. Wanamaker, 266.
106. Weima, *1–2 Thessalonians*, 550.

Some scholars object to the "firstfruits" reading on the basis that the Thessalonians were not the first believers in Macedonia since that designation belongs to the Philippians.[107] However, as Weima notes, "this argument assumes that Paul intended something that he does not say: 'firstfruits *of Macedonia.*'"[108] These believers, in Paul's estimation, were to see themselves "more narrowly as God's 'first fruits' *in Thessalonica.*"[109] In addition, the firstfruits should be seen not only chronologically but "also qualitatively [as] the best produce or best animal that one offers to God."[110]

The Thessalonian believers as firstfruits are a small representation of the many people who will ultimately be saved.[111] This has nothing to do with their being "of greater value to God than other Christians"; as suggested by Wanamaker,[112] the firstfruits should be understood as a foretaste of what is to come. This concept fits perfectly in a communal setting, which the African perspective brings. The African communal worldview affirms that "I am because we are," signifying that those who are saved understand that there is a sense in which their salvation is not complete until all are saved; therefore, they do all they can to ensure that all are saved. This can be an impetus for spreading the good news to those who are not saved. Like the man in Luke's parable who, when he realized the fate of unbelievers in hell, requested that someone go and warn his brothers and sisters (Luke 16:27), Africans feel the need to lead their kith and kin to salvation. However, it should not be just kith and kin; salvation should be spread to all people who are lost.

The purpose for which the believers have been chosen as firstfruits is literally "for salvation" (εἰς σωτηρίαν); this is their raison d'être.[113] The verb σώζω, the noun also encapsulates being secure, safe, delivered, and preserved, usually from situations in which mortal danger is an imminent probability.[114] With this word, Paul was able to comfort his readers at Thessalonica by contrasting them with those who were persecuting them.[115] The assurance Paul's readers

---

107. Bruce, *1 and 2 Thessalonians*, 190.
108. Weima, *1–2 Thessalonians*, 550.
109. Fee, *First and Second Letters*, 302.
110. Weima, *1–2 Thessalonians*, 551; Ceslas Spicq, "Les Thessaloniciens «inquiets» étaient-ils des paresseux?," *Studia Theologica – Nordic Journal of Theology* 10, no. 1 (1956): 1–13.
111. Johnson, *1 and 2 Thessalonians*, 202.
112. Wanamaker, *Epistles to the Thessalonians*, 266.
113. Bruce, *1 and 2 Thessalonians*, 190.
114. Beale, *1–2 Thessalonians*, 226.
115. Weima, *1–2 Thessalonians*, 551; see also 554.

receive is that God has guaranteed "their future salvation and glory."[116] Yet this does not exclude the present since the deliverance is also from deception by the lawless one and his associates.[117]

The Trinitarian shape of salvation is evident in this text. It is God who has "chosen" and "called" the believers; they are "loved by the Lord" and are "saved through the sanctifying work of the Spirit."[118] Part of the reason Paul writes in this way is to emphasize that salvation is purely God's activity. God is the one who saves the Thessalonians, and their response is a result of divine initiative. God brings salvation to his people "through the sanctifying work of the Spirit."[119] We can understand this phrase to mean what the Holy Spirit does to make "the whole person holy."[120] As such, God's work of salvation is not complete until the sanctifying work of the Spirit has been done, the result of which is the holiness of the people of God. As Johnson has asserted, "the audience's salvation occurs in the *ekklesia*, in a network of relationships where the Spirit is active in sanctifying ways."[121]

The purpose for which they have been saved is that they "might share in the glory of our Lord Jesus Christ" (v. 14). Glory should not be thought of in secular ways in the sense of "fame, recognition, renown, honour, prestige."[122] The people of the Mediterranean world in the first century were part of an honor-based culture in which honor was the chief preoccupation for many.[123] Considering that the believers at Thessalonica suffered dishonor (1 Thess 2:14) due to their neglect of the family gods, the fact that they might "share in the glory of our Lord Jesus Christ" was good news for them.[124] We should, however, think of the Old Testament meaning of "'divine glory,' the visible radiance and majesty of God."[125] The phrase "of our Lord Jesus Christ" should be considered

---

116. Weima, 551; see also 554.

117. Beale, *1–2 Thessalonians*, 226; see also Bruce, *1 and 2 Thessalonians*, 190.

118. Fee, *First and Second Letters*, 300; Wanamaker, *Epistles to the Thessalonians*, 266; Shogren, *1 and 2 Thessalonians*, 303.

119. Beale, *1–2 Thessalonians*, 228.

120. Morris, *Epistles of Paul to the Thessalonians*, 239.

121. Johnson, *1 and 2 Thessalonians*, 203.

122. Frederick W. Danker et al., *Greek-English Lexicon of the New Testament and Other Early Christian Literature*, 3rd ed. (Chicago: University of Chicago Press, 2000), 257.3.

123. Bruce J. Malina, *The New Testament World: Insights from Cultural Anthropology* (Louisville: Westminster John Knox, 2002), 28–32; Jerome H. Neyrey and Eric C. Stewart, *The Social World of the New Testament: Insights and Models* (Peabody: Hendrickson, 2008), 25–65.

124. Green, *Letters to the Thessalonians*, 328.

125. Weima, *1–2 Thessalonians*, 554.

both a descriptive genitive and a genitive of source. The glory is the same as that of Jesus Christ qualitatively, but also it derives from him.[126]

The "divine glory" is much better than the honorific titles people clamored for. To share in the glory (δόξα) of God is integral to Paul's conception of salvation in the Thessalonian correspondence.[127] Johnson has rightly stated that to partake in the glory of the Lord is also constitutive of sharing

> in the visible manifestation of his holiness . . . to be "blameless in holiness" (1 Thess 3:13), and finally to experience the culmination of the whole process of sanctification (1 Thess 5:23). Ultimately, it is to be conformed to the image of the Son and thus to reflect the character of the Triune God.[128]

In this sense, it should be observed that the faith to which they have committed themselves is "not human-centered but God-centered."[129]

In summary, Paul has instructed his readers concerning two groups of people, namely those who refuse to love the truth and those who believe the truth. The unbelievers are deceived by the lawless one and Satan, yet they are ultimately responsible for their choice. The believers have experienced εἰς σωτηρίαν in the present and will experience it in the future as well. The ultimate goal of salvation is to participate in the divine glory.

Synthesis

We began our analysis by looking at salvation in the African context, particularly in the Shona community. We noted that the emphasis is on present deliverance from anything that causes one to be less than human. Yet the future aspect of salvation is also present (though it is not as dominant as we see in Paul's teaching) since the Shonas look forward to joining the ancestors and being one with them. The Thessalonian correspondence also understands salvation as multifaceted. Salvation is turning from idols, escaping the coming wrath, living a holy life with the Lord Jesus Christ, and sharing in the divine glory. As such, we should not focus only on what Howard A. Snyder calls "impoverished views of salvation that focus only mainly on inner spiritual

---

126. Contra Shogren, *1 and 2 Thessalonians*, 304, who accepts only a descriptive genitive.
127. Johnson, *1 and 2 Thessalonians*, 203.
128. Johnson, 203.
129. Beale, *1–2 Thessalonians*, 226.

experience, an eternity in heaven."[130] True Christian salvation ought to be holistic: Jesus himself "provided not only spiritual salvation but also physical and emotional healing."[131] Being rescued from the lawless one and the coming wrath is important for a wholesome view of salvation. As we noted above, the African view focuses on deliverance from danger, an aspect of Christian salvation that should not be sacrificed. If we are to "scratch where it is itching," we must address the concerns of the African man and woman.

Yet we must also not forget the fact that we are saved from sin. Thus, "the Christian message of total deliverance from the original and practical sins of the individual is what the African people and the whole world need."[132] African religions are incapable of offering "a way of 'escape,' a message of 'redemption.'"[133] Jesus is the Savior of humanity par excellence, who rescues us not only from danger but also from sin and death, the twin enemies of humanity. Salvation also entails "wholeness, wellness, health, goodness."[134] The aspect of a changed life permeates the entire Thessalonian correspondence; to experience salvation is to be transformed. This transformation affects every area of life, encompassing the spiritual, social, economic, and political. We cannot have experienced salvation and go on in sin (understood as social [neighbour] and theological [God]) as if nothing has happened. Yet it must be affirmed that salvation in the Pauline perspective can be experienced even in the midst of persecution, as the Thessalonians experienced. Africans should not assume, if they experience bad health or poverty, that they have not experienced salvation. Paul speaks about how his converts had changed and were no longer frequenting the pagan temples. Such change was visible for all the people of Macedonia to see and acknowledge their faithfulness. This should be the case for African Christians: faith in Jesus cannot exist alongside certain elements of African Traditional Religions. As Tokunboh Adeyemo has stated, "Christianity cannot cohabit with idolatry."[135] The Thessalonians avoided syncretism, and African Christians should do the same.

---

130. Howard A. Snyder with Joel Scandrett, *Salvation Means Creation Healed: The Ecology of Sin and Grace – Overcoming the Divorce between Earth and Heaven* (Eugene: Cascade, 2011), 1.

131. Samuel Waje Kunhiyop, *African Christian Theology* (Grand Rapids: HippoBooks, 2019), 105–6.

132. Kato, *Theological Pitfalls*, 43.

133. John S. Mbiti, *African Religions and Philosophy*, repr. (Nairobi: East African Educational, 2015), 128–29.

134. Morris, "Salvation," 862.

135. Tokunboh Adeyemo, *Salvation in African Tradition* (Nairobi: Evangel, 1997), 14.

Conclusion

We should not be too quick to emphasize the differences between African understandings of salvation and Christian views of salvation. Our analysis of the Thessalonian correspondence has demonstrated that the aspects that are important in the African milieu are also emphasized in the two letters to the Thessalonians, particularly the aspect of deliverance from harm. Yet this must not be seen as encompassing all of salvation: deliverance should also be understood as deliverance from sin (both social and theological), which in turn should result in holy living. Even though salvation according to Paul has to do with the past (the turning from idols), the present (seen in holy living), and the future (the coming wrath), Paul says more about the future than about the past or the present since the Thessalonians lacked hope for the future. With regard to the understanding of salvation, there is no difference between the two Thessalonian letters.

Bibliography

Adeyemo, Tokunboh. *Salvation in African Tradition*. Nairobi: Evangel, 1997.

Akrong, Abraham Ako. "An Akan Christian View of Salvation from the Perspective of John Calvin's Soteriology." PhD diss., Lutheran School of Theology at Chicago, 1991.

Barclay, John M. G. *Obeying the Truth: Paul's Ethics in Galatians*. Vancouver: Regent College Pub., 2005.

Beale, G. K. *1–2 Thessalonians*. IVP New Testament Commentary. Downers Grove: InterVarsity, 2003.

Best, Ernest. *The First and Second Epistles to the Thessalonians*. Peabody: Hendrickson, 2003.

Bruce, F. F. *1 and 2 Thessalonians*. Word Biblical Commentary. Waco: Word, 1982.

Calvin, John. *1, 2 Thessalonians*. Edited by Alister E. McGrath and J. I. Packer. Wheaton: Crossway, 1999.

Danker, Frederick W., Walter Bauer, William F. Arndt, and F. Wilbur Gingrich. *Greek-English Lexicon of the New Testament and Other Early Christian Literature*. 3rd ed. Chicago: University of Chicago Press, 2000.

Donfried, Karl P. "The Cults of Thessalonica and the Thessalonian Correspondence." *New Testament Studies* 31, no. 3 (1985): 336–56.

Fee, Gordon D. *The First and Second Letters to the Thessalonians*. Grand Rapids: Eerdmans, 2009.

Green, Gene L. *The Letters to the Thessalonians*. Pillar New Testament Commentary. Grand Rapids: Eerdmans, 2002.

Johnson, Andy. *1 and 2 Thessalonians*. Two Horizons New Testament Commentary. Grand Rapids: Eerdmans, 2016.

Kato, Byang H. *Theological Pitfalls in Africa*. Nairobi: Evangel, 1987.

Kunhiyop, Samuel Waje. *African Christian Theology*. Grand Rapids: HippoBooks, 2019.

Lenski, R. C. H. *The Interpretation of St. Paul's Epistles to the Colossians, to the Thessalonians, to Timothy, to Titus, and to Philemon*. Peabody: Hendrickson, 1998.

Malherbe, Abraham J. *The Letters to the Thessalonians: A New Translation with Introduction and Commentary*. New York: Doubleday, 2000.

Malina, Bruce J. *The New Testament World: Insights from Cultural Anthropology*. Louisville: Westminster John Knox, 2002.

Marshall, I. Howard. *1 and 2 Thessalonians: A Commentary*. Vancouver: Regent College Pub., 2002.

Martin, D. Michael. *1, 2 Thessalonians*. New American Commentary 33. Nashville: Broadman & Holman, 1995.

Mbiti, John S. *African Religions and Philosophy*. Reprint, Nairobi: East African Educational, 2015.

Milligan, George. *St. Paul's Epistles to the Thessalonians: The Greek Text, with Introduction and Notes*. London: Macmillan & Co., 1908.

Morris, Leon. *The Epistles of Paul to the Thessalonians: An Introduction and Commentary*. Rev. ed. Tyndale New Testament Commentaries. Leicester: Inter-Varsity, 1984.

———. *The Epistle to the Romans*. Pillar New Testament Commentary. Grand Rapids: Eerdmans, 1988.

———. "Salvation." In *Dictionary of Paul and His Writings: A Compendium of Biblical Scholarship*, edited by Gerald F. Hawthorne, Ralph P. Martin, and Daniel G. Reid, 858–62. Downers Grove: InterVarsity, 1993.

Mtukwa, Gift. *Work and Community in the Thessalonian Correspondence: An African Communal Reading of Paul's Work Exhortations*. Carlisle: Langham Monographs, 2021.

Mugabe, Henry J. "Salvation from an African Perspective." *The Indian Journal of Theology* 36, no. 1 (1994): 31–42.

Neyrey, Jerome H., and Eric C. Stewart. *The Social World of the New Testament: Insights and Models*. Peabody: Hendrickson, 2008.

Paige, Terence Peter. *1 and 2 Thessalonians: A Commentary in the Wesleyan Tradition*. Kansas City: Beacon Hill, 2017.

Raftopoulos, Brian. "The Zimbabwean Crisis and the Challenges for the Left." *Journal of Southern African Studies* 32, no. 2 (2006): 203–19.

Shogren, Gary S. *1 and 2 Thessalonians*. 1st ed. Zondervan Exegetical Commentary on the New Testament. Grand Rapids: Zondervan, 2013.

Snyder, Howard A., with Joel Scandrett. *Salvation Means Creation Healed: The Ecology of Sin and Grace – Overcoming the Divorce between Earth and Heaven*. Eugene: Cascade, 2011.

Spicq, Ceslas. "Les Thessaloniciens «inquiets» étaient-ils des paresseux?" *Studia Theologica – Nordic Journal of Theology* 10, no. 1 (1956): 1–13.

Stott, John R. W. *The Message of 1 and 2 Thessalonians: The Gospel and the End of Time*. Bible Speaks Today. Leicester: Inter-Varsity, 1991.

Thiselton, Anthony. *Life after Death*. Grand Rapids: Eerdmans, 2011.

Vincent, Marvin Richardson. *Word Studies in the New Testament*. New York: Charles Scribner's Sons, 1887.

Wanamaker, Charles A. *The Epistles to the Thessalonians: A Commentary on the Greek Text*. New International Greek Testament Commentary. Grand Rapids: Eerdmans, 1990.

Weima, Jeffrey A. D. *1–2 Thessalonians*. Grand Rapids: Baker Academic, 2014.

Witherington, Ben, III. *1 and 2 Thessalonians: A Socio-Rhetorical Commentary*. Grand Rapids: Eerdmans, 2006.

8

How Can Women Be Saved?

A Reinterpretation of 1 Timothy 2:15 Within a Nigerian Context

Moses Iliya Ogidis
*Serving with Evangelical Church Winning All in Nigeria and
PhD Candidate, St. Paul's University, Limuru, Kenya*

Abstract

Marriage is God's institution to provide companionship between a man and a woman, as affirmed in Genesis. However, when such a relationship is interpreted within the context of the punishment resulting from the fall in Genesis, an understanding of the salvation of a woman often focuses on her womb, based on 1 Timothy 2:15. This begs the question: What is the place of an infertile woman in 1 Timothy 2:15 within the context of salvation in Africa? Women who cannot conceive or whose wombs have been removed for medical reasons often experience discrimination in Africa. In Nigeria, many women are in this complex situation within the church and society due to cultural expectations and biblical interpretations of marriage and procreation. It also appears that the church is silent on this issue. This chapter uses a "hermeneutics of life" within African women's theologies as its framework, but also includes other approaches such as storytelling, in order to address the matter of the womb as a means of salvation and to affirm the place of infertile women in the heart of God, even though they cannot give birth and Paul said they would be saved through childbearing.

Key words: infertile, African woman, salvation, interpretation, childbirth, liberation, oppression, marginalized

Introduction

Infertility is a challenge that confronts many marriages on the African continent, and the church is not excluded from this. Assimeng has noted that even though African women have made immense contributions to the development of the family and the nation, they still face inequities that limit their potential to promote personal and collective well-being within society and beyond.[1] This is especially the case for infertile women in Africa and specifically Nigeria, the focus of this chapter. Infertility is an issue that affects both the husband and the wife, but women are usually singled out, and the religious interpretation of certain texts, such as 1 Timothy 2:15, appears to cement their predicament and oppression.

Christianity plays a vital role in nurturing people physically, emotionally, mentally, and spiritually; in other words, it is holistic in its approach to the followers of Christ. The Christian approach includes the interpretation of the Bible for the daily realities of the members/followers of Christ. Rev. Dr. Marie Fortune and Rabbi Cindy Enger say that

> through texts, traditions, teachings, and doctrine, religious communities and institutions convey values and belief systems to their members. In addition, members often have direct support or counseling relationships with religious leaders who may provide guidance or instruction.[2]

Biblical texts and teachings serve as resources to assist those experiencing subordination, marginalization, and oppression in finding safety and healing. However, the interpretation of the Bible has been and is being misused to excuse or condone abusive behaviour between the genders. In the New Testament, the Pauline letters such as 1 Timothy constitute a group called the Pastoral Epistles; this suggests that the letters have pastoral implications for the church's current challenges – in this case, those within Nigeria. Abiola Mbamalu observed that as part of the pastoral letters,

---

1. M. Assimeng, "Women in Ghana: Their Integration in Socio-Economic Development," *Research Review* 6, no. 1 (1990): 57–68.

2. Rev. Dr. Marie M. Fortune and Rabbi Cindy G. Enger, "Violence against Women and the Role of Religion," Applied Research Forum: National Electronic Network on Violence Against Women (2005), 1.

1 Timothy is a veritable tool in the hands of Pauline scholars who are interested in the development of Pauline thought and ideas. The Pastoral Epistles, in general, provide the occasion for noting the similarities and dissimilarities between Paul's authentic letters and those that bear his name without his usual charismatic flair.[3]

The letter of 1 Timothy deals with gender debates, false teachers, and other challenges that the recipient (young Timothy) faced in the church at Ephesus. This chapter does not focus on the debates over authorship of the letter but instead addresses the gender aspect concerning the salvation of the infertile woman[4] as noted in the letter at 1 Timothy 2:15. Salvation, in this chapter, is considered to be the act of deliverance from a wrong interpretation of the Bible that oppresses women who are unable to conceive, or saving or protecting them from harm or from dire situations brought about by cultural norms. Therefore, this chapter engages the "hermeneutics of life" by African women theologians in reinterpreting the idea of salvation for African married women who cannot conceive.

African women's theologies are an aspect of contextual liberation theology that recognizes the full humanness and equity of women and men made in the image and likeness of God, not considering factors such as race, ethnicity, nationality, and marital status. They seek an understanding of God that is not bound by the limitations of the patriarchal system that shapes and, in most cases, determines women's lives in the church or home. Isabel Phiri avers that

> African women's theologies are a critical academic study of the causes of women's oppression, particularly in their struggle against societal, cultural, and religious patriarchy found within Africa. The approach is committed to purging all forms of oppression and subordination of women through a critique of African culture's social and religious dimensions and the interpretation of the Bible, church traditions, and doctrine.[5]

---

3. A. I. Mbamalu, "'The Woman Was Deceived and Became a Sinner': A Literary-Theological Investigation of 1 Timothy 2:11–15," *HTS Teologiese Studies/Theological Studies* 70, no. 3 (2014), 1, Art. #2062, 7 pages.

4. In this chapter, an infertile woman is a woman who is unable to conceive or whose womb has been removed for medical reasons. Infertility is the inability to reproduce by natural means. S. J. Dyer, N. Abrahams, M. Hoffman, & Z. M. Van der Spuy. "Infertility in South Africa: women's reproductive health knowledge and treatment-seeking behaviour for involuntary childlessness." *Human Reproduction* (7) Issue 6 (2002). 1657–62.

5. Isabel Phiri, "Doing Theology in Community: The Case of African Women Theologians in the 1990s," *Journal of Theology for Southern Africa* 99 (1997): 68–76.

And again,

> The approach takes women's experiences and realities as its starting point, focusing on the oppressive areas of life caused by injustices such as patriarchal interpretation and culture, rereading those texts that appear oppressive to women, and finding liberating ways. It sees a need to include the voices of all women, not just theologians, because it acknowledges that most African women are engaging in oral and experiential theology.[6]

The theoretical framework of African women's theologies has the following characteristics. First, the approach focuses on women's liberation from all forms of oppression and injustice, particularly through a patriarchal interpretation of the Bible motivated by culture and societal expectations. Second, it provides a critical analysis and interpretation of the Bible through the "hermeneutics of life" to address the causes of oppression, particularly in Christianity and African culture. Third, the hermeneutics of life interpretation of 1 Timothy 2:15 follows an inclusive approach focusing on women of all statuses in order to represent all women's voices (married, single, barren, or fertile). Finally, African women theologians must be bilingual, "speaking the language of the academy and that of their communities not just linguistically, but culturally and socially," as noted by Phiri and Nadar.[7]

In such an interpretation of the biblical text, the interpreter needs to consider the diversity of women in Africa, as expressed in the range of different methodologies and religious affiliations represented by African women theologians. This chapter focuses on the reality of women who cannot conceive and the misinterpretation of the biblical text to support their oppression. However, the interpretation has to contend with the fact that Western Christian culture and patriarchal ideology have blended to enhance the power of men and the misinterpretation of the biblical text. Therefore this approach fits this chapter because it deals with the reality for African women that tradition and a patriarchal interpretation of the Bible cement their oppression. The words of 1 Timothy 2:15 regarding the salvation of women through childbirth need to be reinterpreted through the lens of infertile women within the African context.

---

6. Phiri, "Doing Theology," 69.

7. Isabel Apawo Phiri and Sarojini Nadar, "African Women's Theologies," in *African Theology on the Way: Current Conversations*, ed. Diane Stinton, SPCK International Study Guide 46 (London: SPCK, 2012), 90–100.

Infertility within the Nigerian Church

Infertility – also known as barrenness or involuntary childlessness – is a health problem that affects many couples culturally, socially, religiously, and psychologically. Hollos states that the prevalence of infertility varies across Africa, affecting 9 percent of couples in the Gambia, 21.2 percent in northwestern Ethiopia, between 20 and 30 percent in Nigeria, and 11.8 percent of women and 15.8 percent of men in Ghana. However, men are commonly excluded in infertility discourse.[8] It is also difficult to get statistics from within the states in Nigeria. Nevertheless, with the above statistics, the "blame" for infertility falls mostly on the women, and society often looks down on them, even when they are not at fault, with religious interpretations making their situation more complex.

The Bible, for instance, presents several barren women, such as Hannah, Sarah, and Elizabeth. These women through divine intervention eventually conceived and gave birth. The Bible appears to be silent about those who never conceive. The Bible talks of children as a blessing from God, so a married woman who is not able to conceive presents a significant challenge for her, her in-laws, the family, the society, and even the church. In the words of Kathryn Lilla Cox:

> In the ancient world, a childless man solved his problem by having children with a second wife or with a surrogate. A childless woman, on the other hand, suffered reproach, shame, and disgrace. Infertility was perceived as a sign that the woman had somehow displeased God. Conception and a child affirmed that God was pleased, and assured the woman's place in the ancient household. Thus the word emerging from Scripture can be experienced as both a blessing and a curse.[9]

When they go to church, people hear sermons concerning what Christian marriage entails, and they hear how God instituted marriage for companionship and then procreation. God said to Adam and Eve in Genesis 1:28: "Be fruitful and increase in number; fill the earth and subdue it. This declaration by God in Genesis has made some Christians within the Nigerian church deny the reality of infertility. The fact that infertile women have existed since time immemorial is not considered within twenty-first-century Nigeria. With the institution of

---

8. M. Hollos and B. Whitehouse, "Women in Limbo: Life Course Consequences of Infertility in a Nigerian Community," *Human Fertility* 17, no. 3 (2014): 188–91.

9. Kathryn Lilla Cox, "Toward a Theology of Infertility and the Role of *Donum Vitae*," *Horizons* 40 (2013): 3.

marriage comes the expectation of the blessings of the womb. For instance, in weddings in the Evangelical Church Winning All (ECWA), after the joining/solemnization, there is a moment when the newly wedded couples are prayed for by the clergy present. Most of these prayers end with a declaration of the blessing of children, such as "By this time next year, we will come to celebrate with the family for the addition of a child/children."[10]

Marriage in West African countries, specifically Nigeria, is understood as joining groups – two different families – not just individuals; it involves the exchange of wealth, which cements relationships in religious and spiritual terms and enables public witness to the reality of a marriage. Such marriage comes with many expectations. For instance, in most cultures in Nigeria, men, once married, are seen as having "nothing to lose but all to gain (a wife [or wives, as the case may be], children, respect in the society and even a wife-personified-housekeeper. Demand is not placed on the man in any way."[11] Yet women within Nigeria face many challenges, both within the church (interpretation of the Bible) and in the culture that tends to oppress women with regard to giving birth to children.[12]

The challenge of infertility within marriage has become a silent pandemic, killing the joy and happiness of many weddings. Infertility has always been a serious issue throughout history. It is a global health challenge, and this has led to the development of technological ways to help women conceive, such as artificial insemination. Nevertheless, the problem of infertility or childlessness remains significant and can cause marital instability, especially in Nigeria.[13] While it affects both men and women, the cause is often placed on the woman in the marriage since she is the one to become pregnant, and people see the evidence in her – even though it may be the man who is impotent. This is in

---

10. From discussion with a woman in Lafia in Nasarawa State who has been married for ten years but is still childless, just like Mercy Amba Oduyoye who also remains childless after several years of marriage, which motivated her to become a writer; see Mercy Amba Oduyoye, "A Coming Home to Myself: The Childless Woman in the West African Space," in *Liberating Eschatology*, eds. Margaret A. Farley and Serene Jones (Louisville: Westminster John Knox, 1999), 105–20.

11. Morire OreOluwapo Labeodan, "The Family Lifestyle in Nigeria," paper for School of Statistics and Actuarial Science, University of the Witwatersrand, Johannesburg, South Africa [n.d.], 8.

12. S. O. Ademiluka, "Taking a Holistic View of the Biblical Perspectives on Childlessness: Implications for Nigerian Christians and the Church in Nigeria," *HTS Teologiese Studies / Theological Studies* 77, no. 4 (2021), a6083, 1–2.

13. S. N. Covington and L. H. Burns, "Psychology of Infertility," in *Infertility Counseling: A Comprehensive Handbook for Clinicians*, 2nd ed. (Cambridge: Cambridge University Press, 2006), 1–19.

large part because Nigeria traditionally has a patriarchal structure of marriage characterized by inequality between males and females. Larsen observes that "patriarchy refers to social relations with a material base that enables men to dominate women in virtually all aspects of life."[14] Socially, patriarchy is constructed based on sex roles that gives advantages to men over women in society, even in religious space. This can be especially the case within Nigerian context where women face severe constraints often related to childbearing.

In Nigeria, people get married for several reasons; and Dorcas Ofosu-Budu and Vilma Hanninen state that one of the most significant reasons is reproduction (childbearing).[15] Children are considered to be blessings; they bring joy and happiness to the parents and the entire family, and they signify that the lineage will continue. Children play a vital role in the traditional Nigerian family. Chimbatata and Malimba state, "Children are a source of power and pride, and children act as a potential source of support for their parents in old age. The other major aspect of childbearing is that it is an assurance of family continuity."[16] The absence of children due to infertility therefore comes with many challenges.

One response for women who are struggling to deal with the pain of their infertility is to avoid hurtful situations. For instance, they may avoid holidays to the village (rural areas) and gatherings where there are children present, or where topics around parenting are being discussed or parents are complaining about their children. Morire OreOluwapo Labeodan observes that families will go to any lengths to have children. They may visit diviners, shrines, prayer houses, new generation churches, or even practice polygamy. To the outside observer, it seems "that both the educated and the uneducated have been reduced to the same without any societal class just because of the bid to have children or, in some cases, male children."[17]

This high view of children within Nigerian culture supports the church's interpretation of the Bible regarding the place of children in marriage which is normally emphasized during premarital counseling. During such counseling

---

14. U. Larsen, "Primary and Secondary Infertility in Sub-Saharan Africa," *International Journal of Epidemiology* 29 (2000): 285–91.

15. Dorcas Ofosu-Budu and Vilma Hanninen, "Living as an Infertile Woman: The Case of Southern and Northern Ghana," *Reproductive Health* 17, Art. 69 (2020), 1–2.

16. N. B. W. Chimbatata and C. Malimba, "Infertility in Sub-Saharan Africa: A Woman's Issue for How Long? A Qualitative Review of Literature," *Open Journal of Social Sciences* 4, no. 8 (2016), 98.

17. Labeodan, "Family Lifestyle," 8.

sessions, engaged couples are not asked about the possibility of being unable to conceive.

> Couples do not hear the question, "Are you willing to accept the possibility of infertility or the inability to bear biological children?" What happens, then, as the marriage progresses and biological children do not arrive? How is one to understand the inability to become or remain pregnant? Where does the infertile couple fit in the theological picture of love, marriage, and children?[18]

For these reasons, this chapter discusses 1 Timothy 2:15 through the lens of infertile women within the Nigerian context in order to provide an interpretation of how they can be saved even when they cannot conceive. Furthermore, how can they be protected from marginalization, oppression, and suppression through culture and the interpretation of marriage regarding reproduction or bearing of children?

The Context of 1 Timothy

To interpret 1 Timothy 2:15 with regards to infertile women, the interpreter first needs to understand the purpose of the letter as a whole. Although there are debates concerning the authorship of the first letter to Timothy, that is not the focus of this chapter. We take the view that the apostle Paul wrote this letter to Timothy when the Ephesian church was struggling under increased attack from false teachers from within. Köstenberger observes that the city was "a centre of pagan worship; Ephesus presented a considerable challenge for the Christian mission."[19] In the city of Ephesus, the pagan cult of Artemis was very influential. Artemis was considered the main goddess in Asia Minor and had sanctuaries as far away as Gaul and Spain. Eckhard Schnabel says that the Ephesians were not permitted to erect a temple to Tiberius or Caligula because they already had the temple of Artemis.[20] It was believed that Artemis was the daughter of Zeus and Leto, and that instead of looking for relationships with other male gods, she sought human men instead. This made Artemis and all her female adherents superior to men, and was dramatized at the feast of the

---

18. Cox, "Theology of Infertility," 3.

19. Andreas Köstenberger, "1 Timothy," in *Expositor's Bible Commentary*, vol. 12: *Ephesians – Philemon*, eds. Tremper Longman III and David E. Garland (Grand Rapids: Zondervan, 2006), 490.

20. Eckhard J. Schnabel, *Acts*, Zondervan Exegetical Commentary on the New Testament (Grand Rapids: Zondervan, 2012), 804.

Lord of Streets when the priestess of Artemis pursued a man, pretending she was Artemis herself.[21] In the cult (temple) of Artemis, women were therefore exalted and considered superior to men.

Van Dooren states that "Paul wrote when he was an old man, and he writes out of a rich experience as a missionary, evangelist, pastor, and teacher. The Pastoral Epistles deal with some of the problems that the pastors or servants of the Lord faced."[22] For instance, the letter of 1 Timothy is believed to have been written to Timothy, the spiritual son of the apostle Paul, as indicated in 1 Timothy 1:2. According to van Dooren, "it is certain that a close friendship sprang up between them. Paul was a spiritual father to Timothy, and Timothy was a son in the faith."[23] Paul played a vital role in the spiritual upbringing of Timothy, although in 2 Timothy 1:5 it is made clear that Timothy's mother Eunice and grandmother Lois also played a key role in his life; nothing is said here about his father.

The letter of 1 Timothy, one of the "Prison Epistles," gives Paul's counsel regarding dealing with the challenges of false teachers to help restore order in the Ephesian church. The church was dealing with false teachers who were influencing the unlearned women. These women were then spreading the teaching in the church and causing turmoil. In his letter to Timothy, Paul was "doing damage control on a church in crisis."[24] Van Dooren argues that the immediate purpose of the letter was to encourage the young man Timothy. The letter warned him about the false teaching, and also instructed him – and indeed all Christian workers and ministers – to live a holy and godly life and to stand fast in the faith and preach sound doctrine.[25]

The main theme of 1 Timothy is therefore false teaching/doctrine. Paul's first command to Timothy is that he should teach against the false doctrine (1:3–11) being spread in the church. The apostle condemns Hymenaeus and Alexander (1:20), some elders need to be rebuked (5:20), Paul gives Timothy instructions about false teaching (6:3–10), and Paul says how some in the church have already followed after the false teaching (5:15; 6:20–21).[26] Chapter

---

21. Ronald W. Pierce, Rebecca Merrill Groothuis, and Gordon D. Fee, eds., *Discovering Biblical Equality: Complementarity without Hierarchy*, 2nd ed. (Downers Grove: InterVarsity, 2005), 219.

22. L. A .T. van Dooren, *Introducing the New Testament* (Carnforth: Latimer, 1972), 72.

23. van Dooren, *Introducing the New Testament*, 72.

24. Robert Black and Ronald McClung, *1 and 2 Timothy, Titus, and Philemon: A Commentary for Bible Students* (Indianapolis: Wesleyan House, 2004), 61.

25. van Dooren, *Introducing the New Testament*, 73.

26. Pierce, Groothuis, and Fee, *Discovering Biblical Equality*, 206.

2 of 1 Timothy supports this theme of false teaching. As van Dooren asserts, one of the heresies that Paul sought to combat was Gnosticism, such as he dealt with in the epistle to the Colossians. The gnostics believed in angels mediating between a holy God and sinful people. They taught that there were different ranks of angels, and they reduced the Lord Jesus to the position of one of the higher angels.[27]

Dennis Mock avers that the purpose of the letter was "so that people would know how to conduct themselves in the church concerning proper belief and behaviour."[28] The apostle Paul wasted no time in 1 Timothy in addressing the matter of teaching and living correct doctrine. Because of the false doctrines being spread in Ephesus, the teachers had wandered away from "a pure heart and a good conscience and a sincere faith" (1 Tim 1:5). In 1 Timothy 2, Paul encourages all the Ephesians to pray for those in authority and to live lives of peace. He instructs that prayer should be "without anger or disputing," and that women should not dress extravagantly or cause dissension within the church body.

1 Timothy 2:15 and the Salvation of Infertile Nigerian Women

We have seen that the purpose of the letter of 1 Timothy was to address the false teaching that was being spread in the church at Ephesus. Turning now to our key verse of 1 Timothy 2:15, we discover several grammatical and interpretative problems. There are several interpretations of the Greek noun τεκνογονίας (in the feminine singular genitive, meaning "childbirth, childbearing, or rearing of the family"). First is the interpretation which, with the Greek verb σωθήσεται (third person singular future indicative passive, meaning "to save, heal, preserve, or rescue"), suggests the physical preservation of the body during childbirth. A second view is the interpretation of being kept safe from deception, with the idea taken from Genesis 3 of being saved from the devil. Most proponents of this interpretation consider τεκνογονίας as a synecdoche that goes beyond solely the act of childbirth to refer to the scope of women's role in the home.[29] Furthermore, there is a christological or messianic interpretation, interpreting the verse literally to mean that through

---

27. van Dooren, *Introducing the New Testament*, 73.

28. Dennis J. Mock, *New Testament Survey* (Atlanta: Bible Training Centre for Pastors, 2002), 193.

29. Gordon D. Fee. *1 and 2 Timothy, Titus*, New International Biblical Commentary (Peabody: Hendrickson, 1984), 75.

the divine child Jesus women will be saved. Thus, women will be spiritually and eternally saved "by the great childbearing, by that which has produced the Saviour, the childbearing of Mary, which has undone the work of Eve."[30] However, one cannot deny that the apostle Paul appears to be influenced by the social, cultural, and religious values of his day to accept women's subordination and the inclusion of verse 15 of women being saved from childbirth.

Scholars and commentators such as Black and McClung,[31] Guthrie,[32] Hamilton and Cunningham,[33] and Köstenberger[34] approach the pericope through a gender lens with regard to the inclusion of women in the church. Other scholars approach the pericope as regarding women being saved through childbirth from God's punishment. Scholars such as Schreiner,[35] Mounce,[36] and Mouton[37] interpret the Greek noun τεκνογονίας either physically or spiritually. However, the above scholars with whom this chapter engages pay little attention to an "infertile woman" who cannot conceive or give birth or whose womb may have been removed for medical reasons; their interpretations exclude such women. This raises the following questions: If the interpretation is literal, how can we understand 1 Timothy 2:15 so that African infertile married women can also be saved? How can single virgin ladies be saved if they die without having given birth? This chapter addresses these intriguing questions with a focus on married infertile women within the context of Africa.

The problem arises from the Greek verb σωθήσεται – in the imperative future passive third-person singular form of σῴζω: meaning "to save, keep safe and sound, to rescue from danger or destruction," and "to deliver from

---

30. Walter Lock, *A Critical and Exegetical Commentary on the Pastoral Epistles* (Edinburgh: Morrison & Gibb, 1973), 33.

31. Black and McClung, *1 and 2 Timothy*.

32. Donald Guthrie, *The Pastoral Epistles* (Grand Rapids: Eerdmans, 1990).

33. David J. Hamilton and Loren Cunningham, *Why Not Women? A Fresh Look at Scripture on Women in Missions, Ministry, and Leadership* (Seattle: YWAM, 2000).

34. Köstenberger, "1 Timothy."

35. T. Schreiner, "An Interpretation of 1 Timothy 2:9–15: A Dialogue with Scholarship," in *Women in the Church: An Analysis and Application of 1 Timothy 2:9–15*, eds. A. Köstenberger and T. Schreiner (Grand Rapids: Baker Academic, 2005), 85–120.

36. W. D. Mounce, *The Pastoral Epistles*, Word Biblical Commentary (Nashville: Thomas Nelson, 2000).

37. E. Mouton, "Reading a Pastoral 'Text of Terror' in Africa Today? 1 Timothy 2:8–15 as a Context-Specific Appropriation of the Creation Story," in *Men in the Pulpit, Women in the Pew? Addressing Gender Inequality in Africa*, eds. H. Hendricks, E. Mouton, L. Hansen, and E. le Roux (Stellenbosch: SUN Press, 2012), 115–28.

the penalties of the Messianic judgment."[38] The verb is without an expressed nominal or pronominal subject. The question then is: Does the verb refer back to "Eve," or does it refer back to the "woman" in the earlier verses (10–11)? The rest of the verse indicates that the reference goes beyond Eve to all women in general, especially within Ephesus, since the second verb (μείνωσιν: to remain, to stay, abide; live, dwell; last, endure, continue) is in the plural.

To correctly interpret the word σῴζω, there is a need to consider the meaning in classical Greek – that is, to rescue or deliver from some danger, such as the dangers of war, the danger of the sea, and the dangers of sickness. In religious contexts, the gods were usually involved in saving human beings from some life-threatening peril.[39] In New Testament usage, the concept of σῴζω refers to deliverance from physical danger, as Paul used it in Acts 27:20, 31, 34. It is also used in Mark 15:29–31 and Luke 23:29. In other places, the meaning relates to physical healing, as noted by Colin Brown.[40] A Pauline concept of σῴζω relates to the salvation of the body (1 Cor 15) and the spirit (1 Cor 5:5), and not just for now but for all eternity. Therefore, salvation has the idea of well-being in all its forms, from the soundness of the body to the highest ideal of deliverance from all forms of marginalization, stigmatization, oppression, and suppression. This chapter uses the idea of σῴζω as discussed above to include infertile Nigerian women in the context of the challenges they face in society.

However, Bruce Winter suggests that the statement in 1 Timothy 2:15 is a response to women in Ephesus who put their health at risk by seeking abortions. The message to any woman who did such was that she "would be preserved by continuing in her pregnant condition."[41] The reality of what women went through in Ephesus due to abortion practices shows that the interpretation of 1 Timothy 2:15 gives space for the inclusion of infertile women, and that the interpretation of τεκνογονίας should not be taken literally or biologically but ideologically, since not all women can give birth in this life. Infertile women within Africa need to interpret τεκνογονίας from the ideological point of view

---

38. https://kingjamesbibledictionary.com/StrongsNo/G4982/save (Accessed on 04/05/2023).

39. D. McCain, "God's Design of Salvation for Africa: A Biblical Perspective," *Journal of Biblical Studies* 15, no. 1 (2000): 100.

40. Colin Brown, "Redemption, Loose, Ransom, Deliverance, Release, Salvation, Saviour," in *The New International Dictionary of New Testament Theology*, vol. 3 (Grand Rapids: Zondervan, 1978), 212.

41. Bruce W. Winter, *Roman Wives, Roman Widows: The Appearance of New Women and the Pauline Communities* (Grand Rapids: Eerdmans, 2003), 110–11.

because Paul began by discussing how women are to appear modestly in worship and learn in quietness. Therefore, the idea behind the verse is not to say that the salvation of women is attached to giving birth – which may not be possible. But women who seek abortion put their lives in danger; therefore, to be saved from death, they should keep the baby and give birth.

G. Neufeld Redekop notes how the charge in verse 15 to women has elicited various interpretations, specifically regarding the meaning of τεκνογονίας. Redekop states that this verse may be a continuation of Paul's typological use of the Old Testament. In that case, both verbs in verse 15 are addressed to the women Paul discusses in 1 Timothy regarding false teaching and the reality of women going for abortions in Ephesus or looking to Artemis to bless them with children. Therefore, the verse is cautionary; the warning is that false teachers must not deceive these women as the serpent deceived Eve in Genesis 3.[42] The subject of the second verb which is in the plural can be understood as the children who are born, or the husband and wife. The first is difficult, since it would mean that a woman will be saved simply by bearing children without manifesting any Christian qualities herself: her salvation depends on her children's conduct. But what about the infertile woman who cannot give birth to children?

The verb in the beginning of verse 15 σωθήσεται is in the imperative, future passive third singular, from the root word σῴζω referring to "to save, keep safe and sound, to rescue from danger or destruction, to deliver from the penalties of the Messianic judgment."[43] The phrase in verse 15, δὲ διὰ τῆς τεκνογονίας, is the heart of the matter and means "but through childbearing." It is possible to translate "δέ as the copulative conjunction 'and,' indicating that an additional argument following verses 13–14 supports the command in verse 12."[44] The Greek participle δέ could also be translated as the adversative conjunction "but," expressing contrast between the way women perceived salvation and how Paul comprehended it. Some consider there to be a reference to the influence of the temple of Artemis, where women might go in search of fruit from the womb.[45]

---

42. G. Neufeld Redekop, "Let the Women Learn: 1 Timothy 2:8–15 Reconsidered," *Studies in Religion/Sciences Religieuses* 19, no. 2 (1990): 244.

43. F. W. Danker, *The Concise Greek-English Lexicon of the New Testament* (Chicago: University of Chicago Press, 2009), 345 and see also Teresa Chateia David, "Women, Teaching and Leadership in 1 Timothy 2:11-15: A rhetorical critical study, with reference to Angola," Thesis presented in partial fulfilment of the requirements for the degree of Master of Theology (New Testament) in the Faculty of Theology at Stellenbosch University 2019, 4.

44. Danker, *The Concise Greek-English Lexicon of the New Testament*, 84.

45. Teresa Chateia David, "Women, Teaching and Leadership", 25.

This could also mean that the women believed that Artemis could save them by giving them children, which the author now tries to address. However, as discussed above, salvation within Christianity should be understood as saving people from oppression, marginalization, abuse, subordination, and other things which cause pain. An interpreter needs to consider that the salvation of Christ is not attached to any conditions. Therefore, the text should not be interpreted as literal or patriarchal to oppress women, but in line with how salvation is depicted in John 3:16: as being offered to all who believe in Christ Jesus – which means that infertile women are included.

Similarly, it is essential to understand the concept of salvation elsewhere in the Pastoral Epistles. Salvation was Christ's mission, as he "came into the world to save sinners" (1 Tim 1:15), bestowing mercy on Paul as a king might pardon a criminal.[46] Most noteworthy is that the universal view of salvation in this letter to Timothy is related to the social norms and realities of their day. Universal salvation is God the Savior's goal, but it cannot be accomplished unless the Christian community leads a "peaceful and quiet life" (2:2). Salvation is God's wish for humanity (2:4) and the reason why Jesus came into the world. To be saved is the overarching goal for the believer and involves access to the heavenly kingdom of God (2 Tim 4:18) – in other words, eternal life after death (Titus 3:7). Understanding the concept of salvation in general gives a better insight into the interpretation that includes infertile women in the plan for salvation; it is not necessary to give birth to children biologically, as interpreters note.

In the letter of 1 Timothy Paul asserts that Jesus Christ is the agent of salvation; he is the one "who gave himself as a ransom for all people . . . at the proper time" (1 Tim 2:6). Given Paul's developing argument in 1 Timothy 2, the most natural reading of 2:15 should align with the mention of salvation in 2:4. If this is the case, spiritual salvation is in view throughout this section of the epistle. Furthermore, Vine (as cited in David 2019) "understands the meaning of the text concerning bearing children as accomplishing the plan appointed for the woman through her acceptance of maternity."[47] By doing so, she will be saved from becoming a target of the social evils of the time and will take her part in preserving the testimony of the local church.[48] The social evil here is

---

46. G. M. Wieland, *The Significance of Salvation: A Study of Salvation Language in the Pastoral Epistles* (Eugene: Wipf & Stock, 2006), 21.

47. W. E. Vine, *An Expository Dictionary of New Testament Words*. 4 Vols (Westwood: Revell, 1940), 47. See also Teresa Chateia David, "Women, Teaching and Leadership," 24.

48. R. Earle, "1 Timothy," in *The Expositor's Bible Commentary*, vol. 11: *Ephesians – Philemon*, eds. F. E. Gaebelein and J. D. Douglas (Grand Rapids: Zondervan, 1991), 362.

probably a woman's infertility since it is the societal expectation and even the mandate given by God to be fruitful and multiply. Therefore, when she gives birth, she is saved from the oppression and marginalization she otherwise would have faced in the Greco-Roman world in which the letter was written.

As we have discussed, when a woman cannot bear children, it becomes a significant challenge for the family and society. Even the interpretations of the biblical text of 1 Timothy 2:15 tend to silence infertile women. David, following Scholer, avers that, "women treasured their place among the saved through the maternal and domestic roles that were unquestionably assumed to constitute correctness for women in the Greco-Roman culture of Paul's day."[49] Therefore, the goddess Artemis played a significant role in the lives of women in Ephesus, because she was the goddess of wild animals, hunting, vegetation, chastity, and childbirth; the Romans identified her with Diana.[50]

In interpreting τεκνογονίας in 1 Timothy 2:15, one needs to consider the fact that some women in Ephesus were looking to Artemis for help to conceive and also for safe delivery during labor.[51] It is believed that the allusion to Eve was a response to the false teaching in Ephesus. David, following Newsom, observes that "a woman obtained honor through being a mother in ancient cultures . . . cultural values are applied as the means of salvation. Since the verb means to rescue from danger, the author means that women in Ephesus were in danger or were the target of the false teaching which were affecting the women's responsibility as mother and wife."[52] Similarly, verse 15 is an allusion to Genesis 3:16: although women must bear children in pain as part of the punishment God placed on them, nevertheless they will come through it safely if they continue in faith, love, and holiness with propriety.

Interpreting the pericope with the idea of an infertile woman recognizes another interpretation of the verse as suggested by Jebb: "she may be *saved from falling away into this error* of usurping authority and thus being deceived by Satan, by keeping to the proper function for which she was made. Bearing

---

49. See also Teresa Chateia David, "Women, Teaching and Leadership in 1 Timothy 2:11–15: A rhetorical critical study, with reference to Angola," 24–26. See also: D. M. Scholer, "1 Timothy 2:9–15 and the Place of Women in the Church," in *Women, Authority and the Bible*, ed. A. Mickelsen (Downers Grove: IVP Academic, 1986), 197.

50. Encyclopaedia Britannica online, "Artemis: Greek Goddess," accessed 10th January 2022, www.britannica.com/topic/Artemis-Greek-goddess.

51. David, "Women, Teaching and Leadership," 63–64.

52. David, "Women, Teaching and Leadership," 24. See also: C. A. Newsom and S. H. Ringe, eds., *Women's Bible Commentary* (Louisville: Westminster John Knox, 1998), 599.

children will save her from being tempted to 'lord it' over the man."[53] By implication, the Greek verb σωθήσεται, which is from σῴζω, suggests the idea that women had wrong views that were influenced by the false teachers and the belief in Artemis that probably warranted them to think they would be saved through childbirth. Therefore, for an infertile woman, it means to be saved and rescued from the discrimination of being childless and unable to conceive, since bearing children does not determine one's salvation. Furthermore, as David argues, "the discussion above reinforces the idea that the instruction in verse 12 relates to married women, for childbirth as the condition for salvation cannot be applied to all women because not all are married, others might be widows, still others married but childless,"[54] and finally some have had their wombs removed.

In considering other Pauline letters regarding salvation, there is no condition attached, including for women. David affirms that salvation can only be achieved through God's grace, not by our own effort. As a result, it would be incorrect to interpret this verse literally and suggest that salvation for women depends on the process of childbirth, whereby it is implied that childbirth is the means to salvation for women.[55] Despite what some ascetics believed, the apostle Paul wanted the Christian women of Ephesus to know that getting married and having children was not a matter of salvation.[56] Verse 15 attaches moral purity to childbearing due to Ephesus church members' teachings that forbade marriages and praised celibacy (1 Tim 4:3).[57] The apostle corrected other radical and ascetic teachings that emphasized sexual immorality. Having been created in the image and likeness of God, Paul wishes women to know that they do not lose their salvation if they become pregnant, but he also wishes them to exercise self-control in the process.[58]

The Implications for the Church in Africa

Biblical scholars, interpreters, and teachers have a difficult time interpreting this text in the context of the contemporary African church since they must

---

53. S. Jebb, "A Suggested Interpretation of 1 Timothy 2:15," *Expository Times* 81 (1970): 221.
54. David, "Women, Teaching and Leadership," 64.
55. David, 64.
56. David, 64–65.
57. R. C. Kroeger and C. C. Kroeger, *I Suffer Not a Woman: Rethinking 1 Timothy 2:11–15 in Light of Ancient Evidence* (Grand Rapids: Baker Academic, 1998), 171–77.
58. David, 65.

read against the grain of historical interpretations to allow it to speak afresh in its multidimensional context and the women's reality.[59] Equally, Teresa Okure,[60] in agreement with Oduyoye,[61] as quoted in Dube Zorodzai's paper "coined the phrase 'Biblical Hermeneutics of Life' to argue that the interpretation of the Bible should be for the liberation of humanity from all forms of oppression," including the plight of infertile women within Africa, and be life-affirming.[62] Furthermore, Mouton notes that "in continuation with the dynamic processes represented and stimulated by the text, such spaces invite an ongoing, faithful struggle to interpret God's radical presence in the world"[63] that discriminates and oppresses infertile women. Even some churches within Africa need to approach the biblical text through the hermeneutics of life to enhance the lives of all, especially women.

Similarly, Okure as quoted in Dube's paper (2016) states that the interpretation of the Bible (here, 1 Tim 2:15) should seek to better the living conditions of infertile women within the church and society. Thus we need to search for the liberative strands to life in 1 Timothy 2:15; in this case, infertile women should recognize their dignity as women created in the image and likeness of God, and that their salvation is not attached to childbearing.[64] Oduyoye, a childless woman, has written from her experience to challenge the Christian church's silence about this reality. She states that

> the "child factor" in Africa (and perhaps elsewhere) is complex, and its public faces are daunting. Still, nothing is more oppressive than the ordinary meanings imposed on the absence of children in a marriage. The silence that shrouds the issue compounds its potential for the disempowering of women. Shall we continue to be silent, or shall we shape a life-giving theology in a situation that

---

59. Elna Mouton, "Reading a Pastoral 'Text of Terror' in Africa Today," in *Men in the Pulpit, Women in the Pew* (South Africa: Sun Press, 2013), 128.

60. T. Okure, "First Was Life, Not the Book," in *To Cast Fire upon the Earth: Bible and Mission Collaborating in Today's Multicultural Global Context*, ed. T. Okure (Pietermaritzburg: Cluster, 2000), 194.

61. Mercy Amba Oduyoye, "The Christ for African Women," in *With Passion and Compassion: Third World Women Doing Theology; Reflections from the Women's Commission of the Ecumenical Association of Third World Theologians*, eds. V. Fabella and M. A. Oduyoye (Maryknoll: Orbis, 1988), 32.

62. Z. Dube, 2016, "The African Women Theologians' contribution towards the discussion about alternative masculinities," *Verbum et Ecclesia* 37(2), a1577. http://dx.doi.org/10.4102/ve.v37i2.1577 (page 4).

63. Elna Mouton, "Reading a Pastoral 'Text of Terror' in Africa Today," 8.

64. Okure, "First Was Life," 194.

is otherwise a context of death? The one who sits on the throne says, "See, I am making all things new" (Rev 21:5). Shall we not seek a new life for the childless?[65]

The church in Africa needs to change its ecclesial practices, doctrine, interpretation, and traditions and meet the needs of the faithful, which could foster the awareness of a theology of infertility and be life-affirming. By implementing changes, Christian communities should rise to Oduyoye's challenge to address the pain and suffering of infertility by breaking the church's silence. This is important because, as Ryan highlights, infertility is not only a "medical or social crisis" but also a "spiritual crisis, a deep confrontation of meaning and belief." This is a difficult challenge given that the Judeo-Christian tradition emphasizes the importance of children within marriage rather than counseling engaged couples on the possibility of not conceiving or giving birth to children after the wedding. The need to talk about childlessness resulting from infertility also means examining the implicit "norms" that govern the practice of parenthood and marriage.

The church in Africa also needs to adopt new marriage vows. The possibility of not having children should be considered. For instance, in the vows that couples take on the wedding day, along with the words "in sickness and in health, for richer or poorer," there is a need to add words like "with or without biological children." Infertility may be caused by sickness or it may be God's design for the couple not to conceive. In such cases, the woman needs to hold on to her faith, as the concluding part of 1 Timothy 2:15b suggests.

Conclusion

This chapter has examined how 1 Timothy 2:15 can be read through the lens of infertile women within the church in Africa and reinterpreted using African women theologies. It has discussed the reality of infertility within the church in Africa at large and Nigeria specifically; no matter how religious we claim to be, many marriages experience very painful difficulties. The idea of "being saved through childbirth" needs to be interpreted through the hermeneutics of life to enhance the lives of women who cannot conceive. Therefore, infertile women need to understand that the text of 1 Timothy 2:15 should not be understood literally or through a patriarchal interpretation that tends to oppress, suppress, or marginalize. Instead, they need to consider the concept of salvation in Paul's

---

65. Oduyoye, "Coming Home to Myself," 119.

letters generally. Salvation must be considered universally, in line with John 3:16 and other New Testament passages.

Bibliography

Ademiluka, S. O. "Taking a Holistic View of the Biblical Perspectives on Childlessness: Implications for Nigerian Christians and the Church in Nigeria." *HTS Teologiese Studies / Theological Studies* 77, no. 4 (2021), a6083, 1–2. https://doi. org/10.4102/hts.v77i4.6083.

Assimeng, M. "Women in Ghana: Their Integration in Socio-Economic Development." *Research Review* 6, no. 1 (1990): 57–68.

Black, Robert, and Ronald McClung. *1 and 2 Timothy, Titus, and Philemon: A Commentary for Bible Students*. Indianapolis: Wesleyan House, 2004.

Brown, Colin. "Redemption, Loose, Ransom, Deliverance, Release, Salvation, Saviour." In *The New International Dictionary of New Testament Theology*. Vol. 3. Grand Rapids: Zondervan, 1978.

Chimbatata, N. B. W., and C. Malimba. "Infertility in Sub-Saharan Africa: A Woman's Issue for How Long? A Qualitative Review of Literature." *Open Journal of Social Sciences* 4, no. 8 (2016): 96–102. http://dx.doi.org/10.4236/jss.2016.48012.

Covington, S. N., and L. H. Burns. *Infertility Counseling: A Comprehensive Handbook for Clinicians*. 2nd ed. Cambridge: Cambridge University Press, 2006.

Cox, Kathryn Lilla. "Toward a Theology of Infertility and the Role of *Donum Vitae*." *Horizons* 40 (2013): 1–25.

Danker, F. W. *The Concise Greek-English Lexicon of the New Testament*. Chicago: University of Chicago Press, 2009.

David Teresa Chateia, "Women, Teaching and Leadership in 1 Timothy 2:11–15: A rhetoricalcritical study, with reference to Angola," Thesis presented in partial fulfilment of the requirements for the degree of Master of Theology (New Testament) in the Faculty of Theology at Stellenbosch University 2019.

Dube, Z., 2016, "The African Women Theologians' contribution towards the discussion about alternative masculinities," *Verbum et Ecclesia* 37(2), a1577. http://dx.doi. org/10.4102/ ve.v37i2.1577.

Dyer, S. J., N. Abrahams, M. Hoffman, & Z. M. Van der Spuy. 2002. Infertility in South Africa: women's reproductive health knowledge and treatment-seeking behaviour for involuntary childlessness. *Human Reproduction* (7) Issue 6, 1657–62.

Earle, R. "1 Timothy." In *The Expositor's Bible Commentary*. Vol. 11: *Ephesians – Philemon*, edited by F. E. Gaebelein and J. D. Douglas, 339–90. Grand Rapids: Zondervan, 1991.

Encyclopaedia Britannica online. "Artemis: Greek Goddess." Accessed 10th January 2022. https://www.britannica.com/topic/Artemis-Greek-goddess.

Fee, Gordon D. *1 and 2 Timothy, Titus.* New International Biblical Commentary. Peabody: Hendrickson, 1984.

Fortune, Rev. Dr. Marie M., and Rabbi Cindy G. Enger. "Violence against Women and the Role of Religion." Applied Research Forum: National Electronic Network on Violence Against Women, 2005. http://www.ncdsv.org/images/vawnet_vawandtheroleofreligion_3-2005.pdf.

Guthrie, Donald. *The Pastoral Epistles.* Grand Rapids: Eerdmans, 1990.

Hamilton, David J., and Loren Cunningham. *Why Not Women? A Fresh Look at Scripture on Women in Missions, Ministry, and Leadership.* Seattle: YWAM, 2000.

Hollos, M., and B. Whitehouse. "Women in Limbo: Life Course Consequences of Infertility in a Nigerian Community." *Human Fertility* 17, no. 3 (2014): 188–91. http://dx.doi.org/10.3109/14647273.2014.936052.

Jebb, S. "A Suggested Interpretation of 1 Timothy 2:15." *Expository Times* 81 (1970): 221–22.

https://kingjamesbibledictionary.com/StrongsNo/G4982/save (Accessed on 04/05/2023).

Köstenberger, Andreas. "1 Timothy." In *Expositor's Bible Commentary.* Vol. 12: *Ephesians – Philemon,* edited by Tremper Longman III and David E. Garland, 487–562. Grand Rapids: Zondervan, 2006.

Kroeger, R. C., and C. C. Kroeger. *I Suffer Not a Woman: Rethinking 1 Timothy 2:11–15 in Light of Ancient Evidence.* Grand Rapids: Baker Academic, 1998.

Labeodan, Morire OreOluwapo. "The Family Lifestyle in Nigeria." Paper for School of Statistics and Actuarial Science, University of the Witwatersrand, Johannesburg, South Africa [n.d.].

Larsen, U. "Primary and Secondary Infertility in Sub-Saharan Africa." *International Journal of Epidemiology* 29 (2000): 285–91.

Lock, Walter. *A Critical and Exegetical Commentary on the Pastoral Epistles.* Edinburgh: Morrison & Gibb, 1973.

Mbamalu, A. I. "'The Woman Was Deceived and Became a Sinner': A Literary-Theological Investigation of 1 Timothy 2:11–15." *HTS Teologiese Studies/Theological Studies* 70, no. 3 (2014), 1, Art. #2062. 7 pages. https://doi.org/10.4102/hts.v70i3.2062.

McCain, D. "God's Design of Salvation for Africa: A Biblical Perspective." *Journal of Biblical Studies* 15, no. 1 (2000): 97–124.

Mock, Dennis J. *New Testament Survey.* Atlanta: Bible Training Centre for Pastors, 2002.

Mounce, W. D. *The Pastoral Epistles.* Word Biblical Commentary. Nashville: Thomas Nelson, 2000.

Mouton, E. "Reading a Pastoral 'Text of Terror' in Africa Today? 1 Timothy 2:8–15 as a Context-Specific Appropriation of the Creation Story." In *Men in the Pulpit, Women in the Pew? Addressing Gender Inequality in Africa,* edited by H. Hendricks, E. Mouton, L. Hansen, and E. le Roux, 115–28. Stellenbosch: SUN Press, 2012: 115–128.

Musa, Dube, ed. *Other Ways of Reading: African Women and the Bible*. Geneva: WCC, 2001.
Newsom, C. A., and S. H. Ringe, eds. *Women's Bible Commentary*. Louisville: Westminster John Knox, 1998.
Oduyoye, Mercy Amba. "The Christ for African Women." In *With Passion and Compassion: Third World Women Doing Theology; Reflections from the Women's Commission of the Ecumenical Association of Third World Theologians*, edited by V. Fabella and M. A. Oduyoye, 35–46. Maryknoll: Orbis, 1988.
———. "A Coming Home to Myself: The Childless Woman in the West African Space." In *Liberating Eschatology*, edited by Margaret A. Farley and Serene Jones, 105–20. Louisville: Westminster John Knox, 1999.
Ofosu-Budu, Dorcas, and Vilma Hanninen. "Living as an Infertile Woman: The Case of Southern and Northern Ghana." *Reproductive Health* 17, Art. 69 (2020). https://doi.org/10.1186/s12978-020-00920-z.
Okure, T. "First Was Life, Not the Book." In *To Cast Fire upon the Earth: Bible and Mission Collaborating in Today's Multicultural Global Context*, edited by T. Okure, 194–214, Pietermaritzburg: Cluster, 2000.
Phiri, Isabel. "Doing Theology in Community: The Case of African Women Theologians in the 1990s." *Journal of Theology for Southern Africa* 99 (1997): 68–76.
Phiri, Isabel Apawo, and Sarojini Nadar. "African Women's Theologies." In *African Theology on the Way: Current Conversations*, edited by Diane B. Stinton, 90–100. SPCK International Study Guide 46. London: SPCK, 2012.
Pierce, Ronald W., Rebecca Merrill Groothuis, and Gordon D. Fee, eds. *Discovering Biblical Equality: Complementarity without Hierarchy*. 2nd ed. Downers Grove: InterVarsity, 2005.
Redekop, G. Neufeld. "Let the Women Learn: 1 Timothy 2:8–15 Reconsidered." *Studies in Religion/Sciences Religieuses* 19, no. 2 (1990): 235–45.
Ryan, Maura. *The Ethics and Economics of Assisted Reproduction: The Cost of Longing*. Washington, DC: Georgetown University Press, 2001.
Schnabel, Eckhard J. *Acts*. Zondervan Exegetical Commentary on the New Testament. Grand Rapids: Zondervan, 2012.
Scholer, D. M. "1 Timothy 2:9–15 and the Place of Women in the Church." In *Women, Authority and the Bible*, edited by A. Mickelsen, 98–121. Downers Grove: IVP Academic, 1986.
Schreiner, T. "An Interpretation of 1 Timothy 2:9–15: A Dialogue with Scholarship." in *Women in the Church: An Analysis and Application of 1 Timothy 2:9–15*, edited by A. Köstenberger and T. Schreiner, 85–120. Grand Rapids: Baker Academic, 2005.
van Dooren, L. A. T. *Introducing the New Testament*. Carnforth: Latimer, 1972.
Wieland, G. M. *The Significance of Salvation: A Study of Salvation Language in the Pastoral Epistles*. Eugene: Wipf & Stock, 2006.
Winter, Bruce W. *Roman Wives, Roman Widows: The Appearance of New Women and the Pauline Communities*. Grand Rapids: Eerdmans, 2003.

9

Understanding the Soteriological Conceptualization of the Early Church Fathers

An Exploration of the Legacy of Athanasius and Its Relevance to African Christianity

Henry Marcus Garba

Evangelical Church Winning All (ECWA), Nigeria, Africa International University, Nairobi, Kenya, Center for the Study of World Christianity

Abstract

The doctrine of salvation remains fundamental in the theological development of the early church fathers. Among the patristic fathers, Athanasius is ranked high in soteriological conceptualization. He was an outstanding character whose theological contribution helped confront the soteriological heresies of the fourth century and understand and preserve the soteriological implications of Christ's incarnation. This study adopts the historical qualitative methodology that explores the legacy of Athanasius with its integration into contemporary African Christianity. The growth of Christianity in Africa is plagued by concerns regarding its soteriological implications. This concern is due to doctrinal diversities in the perceptions and emphases of the various Christian traditions about the subject matter. Thus, there is a need to examine the soteriological conception of Christianity during the classical era from the lenses of the early church fathers in which Athanasius played such a critical role in its development in order to fathom and integrate its relevance for contemporary African Christianity.

Key words: African Christianity, Athanasius, conceptualization, early church fathers, exploration, soteriological

Introduction

The fourth century AD witnessed the proliferation of different doctrines that questioned the very fabric of Christian identity and its soteriological implications. Indeed, the fourth century was characterized as the era of soteriological debates due to the rise of doctrines that denied the divinity of Christ, which in turn threatened the work of salvation and its implications for humanity.[1] By implication, the fourth-century Christological engagements emphasized the person of Christ; his divinity, and his humanity in relationship to the Father, with a focus on the application of redemption. Thus, Christ's entire work included his incarnation, death, and resurrection and his relationship with each person of the Trinity, with other Christians, with the rest of creation, and with those outside the church. Therefore, Christology in a broader sense discourses a theology of the incarnation, while soteriology in a narrow sense explores the salvific work of the incarnate son, particularly his atoning death on the cross.

Besides, the fourth century recorded the numerous responses of the church fathers to offer a better interpretation of the doctrine of salvation. Soteriology overwhelmed the theological discourse of the fourth century because of the proliferation of different kinds of heresies regarding salvation. Thus, great emphasis was placed on the divinity of Christ and the salvific implications for all who believe in him. Accordingly, at the center of the church fathers' soteriological debates was, as Prahlow writes, their quest to understand the redemptive "implications of orthodox Christian Christology":

> Soteriology is quite literally "the doctrine of salvation." But by the fourth century, there were many doctrines of salvation. Some Christians, such as Paul of Samosata, denied that Jesus was fully divine; the Gnostics denied that Jesus was human; Arius proclaimed that while Jesus was God, he was created and not eternal. In this

---

1. Jacob J. Prahlow, "Early Christian Soteriology," Pursuing Veritas, 24 June 2014, accessed 19 July 2021, https://pursuingveritas.com/2014/06/24/early-christian-soteriology/.

debate about the divinity of Christ, salvation became a significant concern, as the various sides of the debate used soteriology to support their respective positions. Christianity's kerygma (proclamation) had always centered on Jesus Christ as the source of the good news of the true God and salvation for all who believed in him. Therefore, it is not surprising that amid the most technical and philosophical debates, the early church was greatly concerned with understanding the soteriological implications of orthodox Christian Christology. Since each competing Christological claim appealed to the words of Scripture for support, the church looked to its history to answer the question of what salvation meant for earlier followers of Jesus.[2]

Consequently, the patristic doctrines of salvation were not unified systematic proposals by the fathers of the church; instead, the church fathers wrote with consistency, thus articulating pastoral and practical doctrine that certainly included the teachings on salvation so it would be helpful to their audience to articulate what salvation implied. First and foremost, the focus of patristic soteriology was on the giver of salvation, namely Christ, rather than the receiver of salvation, the individual.[3] Therefore, a renewal of interest in patristics as a field of theological rather than purely historical inquiry can serve as retrieval and the inseparability of theology, exegesis, and spirituality.

The Choice of Athanasius

Athanasius of Alexandria (c. 295–373) is one of the most important church fathers. He is often described as the most influential theologian of the fourth century. Athanasius was one of the four doctors of the Eastern Church who defended with clarity the full divinity of the Son of God and its soteriological implications.[4] He is often called "Athanasius the Great" or "Athanasius the Confessor" because he was the shaper of Christian tradition.[5] He is also described as the theological and ecclesiastical center because his greatness was

---

2. Prahlow, "Early Christian Soteriology."

3. Justin S. Holcomb, ed., *Christian Theologies of Salvation: A Comparative Introduction* (New York: New York University Press, 2017), 3.

4. Thomas G. Weinandy, *Athanasius: A Theological Introduction* (Washington: Catholic University of America Press, 2018), vii.

5. John R. Tyson, *The Great Athanasius: An Introduction to His Life and Work* (Eugene: Wipf & Stock, 2017).

intellectual and moral; he proved himself through suffering and years of warfare against errors, the powerful, and the imperial court. Indeed, Athanasius was a theologian and church father of the highest rank, a bishop, and an Alexandrian church leader. He played a role in theology and politics, and in his ecclesiastical career was a spiritual father and pastor. He is also described as the "Father of Orthodoxy," being a prominent spokesperson on behalf of orthodoxy in the first half of the fourth century. He adopted the traditional hermeneutic meaning and defended the Nicene orthodoxy and Creed. Athanasius proved influential in discussions around the one substance of the Father and Son among the council fathers because of his clarity, orthodoxy, and spirit.[6] He supported and defended the orthodox faith as the Council of Nicaea had defined it. Indeed, it was his articulation and defense of the theology behind the Nicene Creed which made him stand out among his peers. Thomas G. Weinandy and Daniel Keating have noted that while most bishops, theologians, and emperors stood against Athanasius on theological, ecclesiastical, and political grounds, he resolutely endorsed and championed the Nicene Creed as a true expression of the Catholic faith.[7]

The choice of Athanasius is because of his soteriological articulation. His theological contributions provided the church with a roadmap to conceptualize soteriology. Athanasius demonstrated that from creation to the second coming of Christ was about salvation.[8] Holcomb writes,

> Athanasius constructs a vision of reality determined by the fact of the incarnation, cross, and resurrection of the Word of God, aiming to offer a holistic interpretation of the Scripture, which Athanasius says is "sufficient for the exposition of the truth." On the one hand, the work functions almost like a catechism, offering a primer in Nicene theology in a form that could inspire people to faith to live and proclaim the gospel. At the same time, it constitutes an *apologia cricis*, a response to those who object to the scandal of the cross, showing, based on whole gospel rationality, that "the cross was not the ruin but the salvation of creation" and that "he who ascended the cross is the Word of God and the

---

6. Brian T. Kelly, "The Father of Orthodoxy: Why We Read Athanasius," Thomas Aquinas College, accessed 19 January 2022, https://www.thomasaquinas.edu/news/father-orthodoxy-why-we-read-athanasius.

7. Thomas G. Weinandy and Daniel A. Keating, *Athanasius and His Legacy: Trinitarian-Incarnational Soteriology and Its Reception* (Minneapolis: Fortress, 2017), 7.

8. Weinandy, *Athanasius*, vii.

Savior of the universe." This distinctive Athanasian vision remains consistent from one end of Athanasius's career to the other.[9]

Hence, the contributions of Athanasius to the Christian faith and theology remain an essential dialogue partner in the contemporary Christian struggle to understand the soteriological question of the relationship between God the Father and the Son and the bearing of the incarnation of the Word of God upon the understanding of salvation.

Furthermore, Athanasius was immersed in a theological agenda. He reaffirmed the use of *homoousion*.[10] In the refutation of Arius, he argues that salvation is not external but takes place within Christ's incarnate constitution.[11] Accordingly, the relationship between the Father and the Son is presented through the notion of "participation." Khaled Anatolios has noted two aspects of this participation: *terminus a quo* (the "whence" of that which partakes) and a *terminus ad quem* (that which is partaken).[12] In analyzing these two notions, Athanasius demonstrated that what is participated in is the very essence of the Father and not something external to it. As Anatolios continues:

> Athanasius pointed out that what participated in the Father is none other than the very essence of the Son; therefore, there is something between what is from the Father and the essence of the Son. Thus, in Athanasius' viewpoint, there is no gap between that which participates and that which is participated. Therefore,

---

9. Holcomb, *Christian Theologies*, 77.

10. The word *homoousion* means "consubstantial" or "one in substance." The word implies that God the Son is "of one essence" with the Father. There was contention about the use of *homoousios*; many argued that the word was not found in the Scriptures and therefore there was no need to use it. Arius argued that the Father and the Son are not of one essence; however, Athanasius defended the Nicene doctrine of *homoousios*, affirming that the Father and the Son share the same essence. When Athanasius became bishop, *homoousios* became the standard for understanding the relationship between the Father and the Son. Athanasius was concerned about the unity of the Son and the Father, which preserves our salvation in God. In Athanasius's view, if the Son were a creature, humanity would remain mortal and would never be joined to God. Doru Costache, Philip Kariatlis, and Mario Baghos, eds., *Alexandrian Legacy: A Critical Appraisal* (Newcastle upon Tyne: Cambridge Scholars, 2015), 144, 149; Clint Tibbs, *Religious Experience of the Pneuma: Communication with the Spirit World in 1 Corinthians 12 and 14* (Eugene: Wipf & Stock, 2012), vii.

11. Alexandra Sophie Radcliff, *The Claim of Humanity in Christ: Salvation and Sanctification in the Theology of T. F. and J. B. Torrance* (Eugene: Wipf & Stock, 2016), 50.

12. Khaled Anatolios, *Athanasius: The Coherence of His Thought* (London: Routledge, 2004), 107.

the relationship between the Father and the Son connects with immediacy in the relationship between God and the world.[13]

Appropriately, Athanasius's theology regarding the relationship of the Father to the Son in the matter of salvation was straightforward, elaborate, and articulative. For this reason Athanasius has been described as the "Pillar of the Church" and "Champion of Christ's Divinity."[14] His soteriological conception offered a perfect explanation of mediation between humanity and God; thus, his legacy helped the people of Alexandria to resist the Arian pretender and the doctrine of subordinationism.[15] As he was known to be the chief defender of Trinitarian doctrine, Athanasius played a vital role in shaping the theological identity of the fourth century, which were formative years of the church, which made him the bearer par excellence of the church's consciousness on "one essence" and "three hypostases."[16] Thus, as one of the pivotal figures in developing Christian doctrine, Athanasius's soteriology offers contemporary African Christianity a constructive way forward in the quest for a genuine African Christian theology.

The Early Life of Athanasius of Alexandria

There are no substantial records about the early life of Athanasius. However, the evidence available on his upbringing suggests that he was born at the close of the third century around AD 293 not long before the dangerous days of the Great Persecution. Different accounts suggest he was either from a humble background in Alexandria with parents who were not Christian or he was the son of an eminent rich woman who was an idol worshipper.[17] Athanasius became an exceptionally learned teacher with an ascetic spirituality. He spoke Coptic and Greek and was revered by the ordinary people of Alexandria and the monks of the Egyptian desert. However, he was reviled by his theological

---

13. Anatolios, *Athanasius*, 109.

14. Athanasius faced an onslaught from theological enemies in both church and state in the fourth century. However, he withstood these onslaughts by promoting and shaping the theological ground of the Christian faith, championing the full divinity of Christ and his true humanity, which were open questions for the Christian church at that time. Rosemary Guiley, *The Encyclopedia of Saints* (New York: Infobase, 2001), 33.

15. Edward J. Watts, *Riot in Alexandria: Tradition and Group Dynamics in Late Antique Pagan and Christian Communities* (Berkeley: University of California Press, 2017), 185.

16. Pavel Florensky, *The Pillar and Ground of the Truth: An Essay in Orthodox Theodicy in Twelve Letters* (Princeton: Princeton University Press, 2004), 43.

17. Gerald J. Donker, *The Text of the Apostolos in Athanasius of Alexandria* (Atlanta: Society of Biblical Literature, 2011), 7.

opponents as "a black dwarf," a hint that he was from the native Egyptian Coptic population as opposed to the Greek upper classes who made up the city's aristocracy. Perhaps Athanasius was born outside the city near the Nile Delta.[18]

The life of Athanasius is connected to Alexander, the bishop of Alexandria, who discovered the young Athanasius and took him under his wing. Alexander helped shape the life of Athanasius. Forbes asserts that Alexander noted the broad, intelligent brow, the keen eyes, and the clear-cut face of Athanasius, and suggests that Alexander was caught up by the frankness and fearlessness of Athanasius, his strength of will, and his keenness of intellect. Such charisma assured the bishop that the lad was born for significance, and he resolved to take Athanasius, bring him up in his way, and let him serve as his secretary.[19] Forbes further asserts,

> Athanasius was still very young when he began to act as secretary to the patriarch, accompanying him on all his journeys throughout his vast diocese, and he tells us how he stayed for a time among the monks in the desert of Egypt and how his young soul was on fire by the holiness of their lives. Neither science nor logic nor philosophy offered any difficulty to the brilliant young scholar, whose knowledge of Scripture and theology astonished the men of his time. As he grew older, Alexander learned more and more on Athanasius, consulting him, young as he was, on the most critical matters. So, the years rolled on, and the boy grew into manhood, "gentle and strong," as we are told by one who knew him, "high in prowess, humble in spirit, full of sympathy, angelic in mind and face." Few who knew him doubted that he would make his mark on the world of his time, but of the dauntless soldier-spirit that slumbered behind that gentle mien, of the steadfast will that no human power could shake, they knew but little. God's moment had not yet come.[20]

Meanwhile, Athanasius was taught religious habits and practices and educated in ancient literature and philosophy. Penelope Lawson describes

---

18. Mark Ellingsen, *African Christian Mothers and Fathers: Why They Matter for the Church Today* (Eugene: Wipf & Stock, 2015), 130.
19. Francis Alice Forbes, *Saint Athanasius: The Father of Orthodoxy* (Hamburg: BoD – Books on Demand, 2020), 4–5.
20. Forbes, *Saint Athanasius*, 4–5.

Athanasius as Egyptian by birth and Greek by education.[21] Shortly after the death of Alexander, Athanasius was elected bishop, a position in which he faced severe opposition. Peter Crawford opines that Athanasius was opposed as bishop because he forced himself into that position after his mentor died.[22] Forcing himself into the position of a bishop and using force against the Meletians made the Meletians ally with Eusebius of Nicomedia. This alliance raised various allegations against Athanasius that forced him into exile.[23] Though he served as bishop for almost half a century (forty-five years), Athanasius was exiled five times within a span of seventeen years, mainly because of the stern position he took against Arius's agitation.[24] However, even in exile and under the emperor's ban, Athanasius was still the bearer of truth. During these periods of exile, he built support for pro-Nicene theology and was named the "father of orthodoxy."[25]

Understanding the Background to Athanasius's Soteriology

Athanasius lived during a period of fundamental change in the Roman Empire and Christianity. He was alive at the time of the conversion of Constantine, who became the first Christian Roman emperor.[26] The reign of Emperor Constantine was the formative years of Christian theology; it opened the door to serious theological debates, which became a matter of public concern. This period is also when the patristic fathers flourished and made significant impacts theologically and politically because serious theological issues were debated and resolved at this time. This period of Christian liberation brought the rise of great theologians like Athanasius, among others, to offer their voices on theological matters. Also, for the first time in many years, theologians had the freedom to work without fear of persecution, and the church as a whole was also free

---

21. Penelope Lawson, *On the Incarnation: The Treatise De Incarnatione Verbi Dei* (Crestwood: St Vladimir's Seminary Press, 1996), 17.

22. Peter Crawford, *Constantius II: Usurpers, Eunuchs and the Antichrist* (Barnsley: Pen & Sword, 2016), n.p.

23. Crawford, *Constantius II*.

24. Charles Kannengiesser, ed., *Early Christian Spirituality* (Minneapolis: Fortress, 1986), 10–11.

25. Muhammad Wolfgang G. A. Schmidt, *"And on This Rock I Will Build My Church." A New Edition of Philip Schaff's "History of the Christian Church": From Nicene and Post-Nicene Christianity to Medieval Christianity A.D. 311–1073* (Hamburg: disserta Verlag, 2017), 371.

26. David M. Gwynn, *Athanasius of Alexandria: Bishop, Theologian, Ascetic, Father* (Oxford: Oxford University Press, 2012), ix.

from this threat.²⁷ Alister E. McGrath submits that following the conversion of Constantine, the persecution of the church ceased, thus reconciling the church and the empire.²⁸ Forman similarly avers that the fourth century was a time for the rise and works of great scholars and religious movements. However, the period was undoubtedly stressful and theologians soon became enmeshed in exhausting doctrinal debates that divided the church.²⁹ The fourth century was thus marked by disputes, polemics, and violence over doctrinal issues and rivalry between regional power bases. Different controversies arose, such as the Meletian, Arian, Origenist, and Nestorian controversies.³⁰

Consequently, throughout the fourth and fifth centuries, the church struggled to address the different controversies that brought endless rivalry and pain. For instance, Arianism, a view spread by Arius, erupted in the first quarter of the fourth century. Its primary concern was the Christian understanding of the nature of the Logos in relation to God. This controversy occasioned the convening of the Council of Nicaea, whose theological decisions became the standard of orthodox faith for most churches. It was the reigning orthodoxy of Arianism that brought Athanasius onto the scene of Christian theology. At the Council of Nicaea, Athanasius was the chief defender of the Logos in relation to God.³¹

The discussion was a hermeneutical battle that forced the interpretation of several key biblical passages. According to Thomas C. Ferguson, "Arius questioned the fundamental tenet of the Christian faith, the divinity of Jesus, and because of influences ranging from Judaism, pagan philosophy, or even demonic control, contumaciously deviated from what had always been the church's teaching regarding the Trinity."³² For example, Arius preached that the Father begot the Son, meaning that the Son had a beginning in existence; therefore, Arius taught that there was a time when the Son did not exist.

---

27. Alister E. McGrath, *Christian Theology: An Introduction* (Hoboken: John Wiley & Sons, 2016), 9.

28. McGrath, *Christian Theology*, 9.

29. Mary Forman, ed., *One Heart, One Soul, Many Communities: Proceedings of the 21st Annual Monastic Institute, School of Theology-Seminary, Saint John's University, Collegeville, Minnesota 56321, July 1–7, 2006* (Collegeville: Liturgical, 2009), 7.

30. Donald B. Redford and Edward Bleiberg, *The Oxford Encyclopedia of Ancient Egypt: A–F* (Oxford: Oxford University Press, 2001), 304.

31. Dale T. Irvin and Scott Sunquist, *History of the World Christian Movement*, vol. 1: *Earliest Christianity to 1453* (Edinburgh: T&T Clark, 2002), 156.

32. Thomas C. Ferguson, *The Past Is Prologue: The Revolution of Nicene Historiography* (Leiden: Brill, 2005), 3.

Arianism thus promoted the view that the Son was among the things created by God. The Arian controversy spread throughout the Roman Empire to the extent that Christian supporters "could be heard singing a catchy tune that championed the Arian view."[33] Consequently, the Arian controversy brought fierce contention between bishops. News of the dispute eventually reached Emperor Constantine, who being newly converted to Christianity perhaps wanted church unity more than theological truth, thus promoting unity in his realm.[34] Amid this fierce controversy, Athanasius rose to fame as a mobilizer and the chief architect of the Nicene Creed, which became the theological confession of the divinity of the Word of God personally incarnated in Christ.[35]

In addition, Alexandrian theology, which was Christocentric, played a leading role in the life of Athanasius. Alexandrian Christian theology focused on the role of Jesus as the Logos of God. According to Tyson, the Alexandrian Christian theology "drew upon aesthetic and philosophical impulses," and Scripture "was often interpreted symbolically through the means of allegory."[36] Alexandria became the citadel of Eastern Christian theology, and its bishops were highly revered. While persecution of the church ended, the church faced the danger of heresy. It was such a contributory factor that helped shape the theological scene of Athanasius.

The Soteriological Conceptualization of Athanasius

There are three categories of patristic and medieval soteriology: the soteriology of redemption, sanctification, and deification. Steven C. van den Heuvel has noted that these three soteriological approaches have influenced how Christians engage with society.[37] The soteriology of Athanasius was founded upon the theological meaning of deification and its implications. The soteriology of deification is about participation, which speaks of salvation as sharing in

---

33. "Athanasius: Five-Time Exile for Fighting Orthodoxy," *Christianity Today* online, accessed 18 January 2022, https://www.christianitytoday.com/history/people/theologians/athanasius.html.

34. K. G. Powderly Jr., *One Faith – Many Transitions: Worldviews in Church History* (Lincoln: iUniverse, 2002), 68.

35. John Anthony McGuckin, *The Westminster Handbook to Patristic Theology* (Louisville: Westminster John Knox, 2004), 35.

36. Tyson, *Great Athanasius*, 24.

37. Steven C. van den Heuvel, *Bonhoeffer's Christocentric Theology and Fundamental Debates in Environmental Ethics* (Eugene: Wipf & Stock, 2017), n.p.

God's incorruption and the personal communion between the persons of the Trinity. Deification thus does not mean absorption but adoption: it is not being absorbed into God but being adopted.[38]

Although Athanasius did not invent the doctrine of deification, he speaks of the transforming effect of the incarnation using the language of deification more explicitly than any of his predecessors.[39] For Athanasius, the incarnation of the Logos was originally created to participate in the divine Logos, which was fulfilled in Jesus.[40] Athanasius used synonyms that functioned as equivalents to "deification"; words such as adoption, renewal, salvation, sanctification, grace, transcendence, illumination, and vivification were used to help clarify the meaning of deification and its implications.[41] It was the linguistic approach of Athanasius that distinguished pagan deification from its Christian counterpart.[42] This chapter does not aim to provide an elaborate explanation of Athanasius's soteriology but offers a brief overview of his incarnational soteriology, which can better be summarized under the categories that follow:

The Fallenness of Humanity as Necessary for Salvation

Unlike others who focused on sin and treated Christ as the atoning victim who reverses the fall of Adam, Athanasius argued that the nature of human beings must be changed for salvation to be realized. In his work *Against the Heathen*, Athanasius argued that salvation is found in no one but Christ

---

38. Cyril Orji, *A Semiotic Christology* (Eugene: Wipf & Stock, 2021), 209.
39. Ernst M. Conradie et al., eds., *Christian Faith and the Earth: Current Paths and Emerging Horizons in Ecotheology* (Bloomsbury: A&C Black, 2014), 22.
40. Orji, *Semiotic Christology*, 207.
41. Norman Russell, *The Doctrine of Deification in the Greek Patristic Tradition* (Oxford: Oxford University Press, 2004), 178; Denis Edwards, *Partaking of God: Trinity, Evolution, and Ecology* (Collegeville: Liturgical, 2014), 41.
42. Ruth Coates notes that "The idea of deification predates Christianity" however, deification gained significance during the ruler cult of the Hellenistic and Roman pagan civilizations. Meanwhile, when Christianity was adopted as the state religion under Constantine the Great 272–337, the ruler cult began to be accommodated into the Christian faith. See Ruth Coates, *Deification in Russian Religious Thought: Between the Revolutions, 1905–1917* (Oxford: Oxford University Press, 2019), 27. Also, Christensen and Wittung aver that the essential fallacy of Hellenistic religion, according to Athanasius, is the ontological gap between the created and uncreated, which places the object of pagan worship in the created universe. Athanasius argued that the fundamental falsehood of Hellenistic religion lies in the ontological disparity between what is created and the uncreated, in which the object of pagan worship lies with the created realm. Michael J. Christensen and Jeffery A. Wittung, *Partakers of the Divine Nature: The History and Development of Deification in the Christian Traditions* (Grand Rapids: Baker Academic, 2008), 125; Norman Russell, *The Doctrine of Deification in the Greek Patristic Tradition* (Oxford: Oxford University Press, 2004), 27.

and that accepting the teaching of Scripture is the only way the lost can find salvation. Scripture is the source of true faith in Christ.[43]

For Athanasius, salvation is necessary because of the character of human nature, which is universally and equally in need and capable of salvation through Christ. Langworthy writes:

> The soteriology of Athanasius begins with the incarnation. Having taken on a body, the immutable and transcendent Word is sacrificed in death – the consequence of man's sin. Sin is atoned for through this sufficient sacrifice, which confers the qualities of the Word to the body; through this redemption of the body, the source of sin is nullified. Salvation not only becomes possible through the incarnation, but the assumption of the body becomes of definitive importance – Christology and soteriology run together.[44]

By this, Athanasius emphasized a salvation that is based on the loss of the salvific knowledge of God in man. His view of salvation was that of restoration and recreation; therefore, promoted a physical theory (Christ's conception, birth, baptism, crucifixion, resurrection, ascension, and his return) of Christ becoming man as the remedy from the curse of sin and the restoration of the divine image in man. Therefore, salvation lies in the existential reorientation of rational human souls, i.e., the life of Jesus, in its incarnational form of the Christian faith, is the self-expression of the eternal in time. Thus, the incarnation is a decisive revelatory and demonstrative event, which must be seen as soteriological.[45]

Furthermore, Athanasius affirms that the historical man is responsible for the fall, i.e., Adam and his posterity sinned willingly, which implies that neither Adam nor our responsibilities can be isolated any more than Adam's and our existence. Consequently, "if the responsibility for the fall is to be shared between Adam and his posterity . . . likewise, the undoing of the fall should require action from all men collectively and individually."[46] Hence, Athanasius argued that repentance does not provide adequate ground for salvation because

---

43. John Allen Dearing III, *Will Not Return Void: The Use of Scripture in the Evangelistic Writings in the Greek Patristic Tradition* (Eugene: Wipf & Stock, 2021), n.p.

44. Oliver B. Langworthy, *Gregory of Nazianzus' Soteriological Pneumatology* (Tübingen: Mohr Siebeck, 2019), 39.

45. Timothy John Carter, *The Apollinarian Christologies: A Study of the Writings of Apollinarius of Laodicea* (London: Hamley King, 2011), 25.

46. George Dion Dragas, *Saint Athanasius of Alexandria: Original Research and New Perspectives* (Rollinsford: Orthodox Research Institute, 2005), 83.

of the existential consequences, which deprive human beings of the possibility of being saved by mere repentance. "The impossibility lies with the 'existential' consequences and not with the method of repentance, because repentance is a fundamental aspect of the saving act offered in Christ."[47] Man in his present condition is in a state of nothingness; however, in the Triune God with the Son-Logos in the center, there is the provision of a contrary force against the fallen state of man, which the Son-Logos draws men into the orbit of the divine life and activities, that is capable of restraining them from reaching the logical end of their fallenness.[48]

Additionally, Athanasius viewed salvation as restoring and recreating God's original intention for human existence. Kathryn S. Eisenbise observed that Athanasius argued that though humanity was created in God's image and given a portion of God's power so they might forever abide in his blessedness, they rejected God, resulting in death, the corruptibility of human nature.[49] Therefore, the necessity of the incarnation was God's intention to restore humanity to its original state of communion with him. Furthermore, Athanasius emphasized Christ's death as a sacrifice with the idea of substitution or representation; thus, the death of all mankind was accomplished in the Lord's body so that what we have lost in Adam, the image and likeness of God, is regained through Christ.[50] Therefore, salvation as recreation implies that Christ has banished death from humanity, creating a new man by bringing the knowledge of God everywhere, i.e., redemption is not conceived solely in terms of salvation from death but in terms of salvation from sin.

The Incarnation as Necessary for Human Salvation

Athanasius offered a detailed understanding of the necessity of the Logos taking human form as necessary for the salvation of humanity. In the incarnation, by the divine presence of his entire life, death, and resurrection, Christ reopens the path to salvation.[51] What remains the soteriology of Athanasius is his perspective of the incarnation. Deification is inconceivable without the

---

47. Dragas, *Saint Athanasius*, 83.
48. Dragas, 85.
49. Kathryn S. Eisenbise, *Cooperative Salvation: A Brethren View of Atonement* (Eugene: Wipf & Stock, 2014), n.p.
50. Thomas P. Rausch, *Who Is Jesus? An Introduction to Christology* (Collegeville: Liturgical, 2016), n.p.
51. Philip Kariatlis, "Soteriological Insight in St. Athanasius' *On the Incarnation*," *Phronema* 28, no. 2 (2013): 27.

incarnation. For Athanasius, the Father and the Son are distinct, yet their unity is implied within their designation as Father and Son, i.e., the Father acts through the Son, and the Son makes present the Father.[52] Athanasius reaffirms the genuineness of Jesus's body and his human experience as authentic and divine immediacy. Jesus's body is a human instrument that offers the Son the ability to do human salvific deeds. By implication, the body allows the Son to do things that he could not have done if he had not become a man, which implies that the divine and human natures of Christ are distinctly different yet complete, and the result of the union is a single person. Nevertheless, Athanasius explicitly considered Christ as a single agent by referring to the agency of his saving work in the divine Word and the man assumed.[53]

Furthermore, Athanasius emphasized that God the Son is not simply incarnated *in* human beings but *as* a human being.[54] By implication, the Son, on the one hand, appropriates the fullness of fallen humanity; on the other hand, by his saving deeds, the Son has exalted humanity to the extent of being deified and adopted by the Father in the Holy Spirit. Christ, in his incarnation, accomplishes the salvific work regarding mankind.[55] The Athanasian soteriological conceptualization encapsulates that the economy of the incarnation and the cross are necessary for salvation because it was not a mere human that died for the salvation of humanity but an infinite God. Hence, if Jesus is not divine, there is no salvation, making Christianity utterly useless. Therefore, the power to turn corruptible into incorruptible is achieved by Christ alone. Thus, to restore humanity from sin requires the work of a person who identifies with mankind in his humanity and with God in his divinity; indeed, Christ must be both God and man. Hence, Athanasius argued that the life Jesus lived in the flesh – his life and death remains the center of Christological interpretation and its soteriological consequence.

Deification: Soteriology in the Sense of a Holistic Restoration

Athanasius promoted deification as necessary for human salvation. The Eastern Fathers related deification as the blessings of salvation – immortality or

---

52. Weinandy, *Athansius*, 46.
53. Alan Spence, *Incarnation and Inspiration: John Owen and the Coherence of Christology* (New York: A&C Black, 2007), 69.
54. Matthew Baker and Todd H. Speidell, eds., *T. F. Torrance and Eastern Orthodoxy: Theology in Reconciliation* (Eugene: Wipf & Stock, 2015), 75.
55. Thomas F. Torrance, *Theology in Reconstruction* (Eugene: Wipf & Stock, 1996), 230.

incorruption – gradually experienced by the believer in this life.[56] Deification describes the personal encounter of the believer with God and his work of grace, whereby believers experience communion with God and are regarded as his children. In his description of salvation as deification, Athanasius affirms that Christ's work is to restore the divine image in humanity.[57] In his soteriological perspective, Athanasius reacted against any notion of an intermediate being. "His soteriology was a powerful motive in the working out of his Trinitarian theology. The savior must be none other but God. He could not be an intermediary."[58]

Furthermore, Athanasius argued that the Logos was revered in his theology of deification, noting that God's Word later became a human being that humanity may be divinized.[59] Weinandy asserts that Athanasius' conception of the full divinity of the Son is essential to his soteriology. Only if the Word is truly God can he reveal the Father through his actions in creation and redemption.[60] Also, Christ's divinity is necessary for human salvation. If Christ were a mere creature, he could have been powerless as a savior. Foremost, Athanasius argues that the incarnation is essential for man's union with God, and from the beginning of creation, God's soteriological motive is to deify humanity.[61] Daniel E. Wilson observes that Athanasius describes man's fall as necessary for salvation, noting that God planned the incarnation within salvation history before he created the world because he knew the need for the incarnate Christ would arise to bring about humanity's deification.[62] Summarily, McKim has this to say,

> Athanasius provided a vivid description of salvation as deification, noting that the goal of Christ's work was to restore the divine image in humanity, for Christ took on the human body to make man divine. Christ made us sons of the Father, deified us by himself, and became man by becoming a man. Also, for the Father

---

56. Donald K. McKim, *Theological Turning Points: Major Issues in Christian Thought* (Louisville: Westminster John Knox, 1988), 84.

57. McKim, *Theological Turning Points*, 84.

58. Hubert Cunliffe-Jones, ed., *A History of Christian Doctrine* (London: A&C Black, 2006), 106.

59. Edwards, *Partaking of God*, 41.

60. Weinandy, *Athansius*, 46.

61. George Thomas Kurian and James D. Smith III, eds., *The Encyclopedia of Christian Literature*, vol. 2 (Lanham: Scarecrow, 2010), 189.

62. Daniel E. Wilson, *Deification and the Rule of Faith: The Communication of the Gospel in Hellenistic Culture* (Bloomington: WestBow, 2015), n.p.

to restore the original condition of man's original model, God had to sit on the damaged portrait once again, making it crucial for Christ to be indeed God. God must be the model, and Christ as the agent of salvation, must be truly God. The ultimate result of the incarnation and salvation is divinization by the grace of God. Thus, humanity is deified as they are restored to God's image.[63]

The Soteriological Contribution of Athanasius

The contribution of Athanasius is against Arian's subordinationism, which denied the Trinity and its soteriological implication to humanity. In Athanasius' viewpoint, Christ is not like a substance to God, but the same substance. The argument between Athanasius and Arius continued that over 300 bishops convened, and the Nicene Creed was reviewed. Consequently, Arius was declared a heretic, and his works were prohibited.

However, Arianism played a decisive role in shaping Christian thought. As a pivotal figure against Arianism, Athanasius was able to use his ability to command the support of the Western bishops. His readiness to dialogue with a broader range of theologians led to the growing consensus in the East about the coequal deity of the Logos.[64] Athanasius' treatise on the incarnation laid the foundation for orthodox theology. His writings were apologetical, dogmatic, historico-polemical, and ascetic, or letters were written to defend his actions and beliefs. He attacked the actions of his enemies and false doctrines and used Scripture to expound on correct doctrine.[65] Such writings provided clear evidence of his theological stand. Moreover, Athanasius built a complete system of religious thought, and Christ is always the central place in that system. Finally, he offered with clarity the purpose of the incarnation, which is to prove that the Word is genuinely divine and eternal.

Athanasius remains the theological giant of the fourth century, whose theological conception of deification was used to prove other doctrines.[66] His theological position has become the standard of Christian theology. For instance, Célestin Musekura noted that before Athanasius, there was no explicit

---

63. McKim, *Theological Turning Points*, 84.
64. McGuckin, *Westminster Handbook*, 29.
65. Donald K. McKim, ed., *Historical Handbook of Major Biblical Interpreters* (Downers Grove: InterVarsity, 1998), 18.
66. Timothy E. G. Bartel, *Glimpses of Her Father's Glory: Deification and Divine Light in Longfellow's Evangeline* (Eugene: Wipf & Stock, 2019), 84.

doctrine of salvation or redemption of man in the early stage of the church. However, his treatise *On the Incarnation* offered the church the fundamental perspective on the doctrine of salvation through the concept of divinization.[67] Foremost, contemporary theologians have continued to emphasize the divinity of Christ for salvation. As the champion of the doctrine of the incarnation, Athanasius' soteriology ushered in a new understanding of the implication of the incarnation, which affirms the incarnation as not only a temporary state but represents the beginning of a new and a permanent state of affairs in the life of the Son of God.[68]

Trends in the Soteriology of African Christianity

In a narrow sense, soteriology is a consideration of Christology. Soteriology deals not merely with the person of Christ but also with the concept of redemption because the view of Christian salvation influenced how the person of Christ was conceived.[69] Consequently, the incarnation remains the center of Christian confession, and the area grappled with Christians, including theologians. In the contemporary era, soteriology has been the focus of many scholars, especially in Africa. Over the years, Africans have struggled to understand and integrate Christ's events into their everyday lives. Chinua Achebe reiterated this concern in his classic African literature when he wrote,

> After the singing, the interpreter spoke about the Son of God, whose name was Jesu Kristi. Okonkwo, who only stayed in the hope that it might come to chasing the men out of the village or whipping them, now said:
>
> "You told us that there was only one God with your mouth. Now you talk about his son. He must have a wife then."
> The crowd agreed.[70]

This classic (fictional) literature demonstrates the concerns in Africa's theological development. The question of the identity and meaning of Christ

---

67. Célestin Musekura, "Soteriology in Athanasius of Alexandria," paper, Dallas Theological Seminary (n.d.), 9, accessed 4 February 2022, https://www.academia.edu/5553683/Soteriology_in_Athanasius_of_Alexandria.

68. Richard A. Holland Jr., *God, Time, and the Incarnation* (Eugene: Wipf & Stock, 2012), 68.

69. Pieter J. Lalleman, *The Acts of John: A Two-Stage Initiation into Johannine Gnosticism* (Leuven: Peeters, 1998), 153, 155.

70. Chinua Achebe, *Things Fall Apart* (New York: Anchor, 1994), 147–48.

has remained the concern of African Christianity. Notably, Africa believed in God before the advent of missionaries and did not need a serious explanation about him. However, the message of the Son was the new message brought by western missionaries, which African Christians embraced.[71] With the tremendous shift of Christianity from the northern hemisphere to the south, Christology and its soteriological implication have remained the driving force of new quests among African Christian theologians. Therefore, African Christian soteriology seeks to contextualize the alien and expatriate image of the incarnate Christ in Africa.

It is worth noting that the rise of African Indigenous Churches (AICs), Pentecostal, and Charismatic movements have shaped how Africans interpret and contextualize Christology. Likewise, salvation in Africa is about redeeming the soul and its application to the everyday life of Africans. Consequently, African theologians have proposed several Christological titles from African cultures to interpret Christology and its soteriological implication.[72] Furthermore, the comprehensive nature of African Christian soteriology has made African Christian theologians resort to innovative forms of conceptualizing the person of Christ that designate him as "the agent of historic salvation."[73] Also, three adopted models have helped shape African soteriological conceptions: inculturation, indigenization, and contextualization. These models are moved toward contextual Christianity that seeks to communicate with the African heritage. Accordingly, Michael Matthew asserts that in an attempt for continuity between Christianity and traditional African religion, the effort is made to reevaluate classical Christian theology for self-identification and adequate integration among Africans.[74]

Furthermore, African Christianity seeks to engage traditional African images to integrate its soteriological implication. In the studies of modern African theology, scholars argue for two theoretical mediations, which can be described as social-analytical arbitration and hermeneutical mediation. Henry Garba observes that these two theoretical mediations see Jesus as Savior and the

---

71. Nicholas Ibeawuchi Mbogu, *Jesus in Post-Missionary Africa: Issues and Questions in African Contextual Christology* (Munich: GRIN Verlag, 2012), 2.

72. Frances M. Young, *From Nicaea to Chalcedon: A Guide to the Literature and Its Background* (London: SCM, 2013), 68.

73. Komi Ahiatroga Hiagbe, *Reconciled to Reconcile: An African View of John Calvin's Doctrine of Salvation* (Frankfurt: Peter Lang, 2008), 168.

74. Matthew Michael, *Christian Theology and African Traditions* (Eugene: Wipf & Stock, 2013), n.p.

Word of revelation, which seeks to express the divinity of Christ in the human and temporal experiences of all aspects of Christology to African reality.[75]

Other trends in understanding African soteriology are fourfold – comparative, systematic, liberationist, and community-based approaches.

> A comparative approach examines Christology with a strong interest in African culture. Systematically, they connect the various mysteries of Christ and the church, which seeks to present the deposit of faith in an African manner. On the liberationist, interest is focused on the worship of Christ and spirituality, which enables change and transformation in the social situations of Africans. The Community-based approach informs the people's Christian living and integrates the Bible intimately. Aversely, these Christological elaborations do not focus on the death of Jesus as a sacrifice that brought salvation but is also linked with the resurrection in a dynamic process of initiation or perfecting the risen Lord.[76]

Meanwhile, from the late 20th to early 21st centuries, many Africans have adopted multidimensional approaches to apply soteriology. Portraits of Jesus as savior, liberator, and redeemer have been adopted to address various forms of oppression that Africans suffer, including socioeconomic and political issues. Thus, soteriology in Africa is not only about salvation from sin but committed to critical reflection and praxis. It is not an abstract academic pursuit but a grappling with concrete issues. According to Rudolf K. Gaisie, the universal significance of Jesus as the savior of the world gives a universal value to a local image applied to him. The enlarged scope opens and broadens the local context that produced the image. Although no single image can claim to say or reveal everything about Jesus, these images are complimentary and neither monopolistic nor exclusive.[77] Hence, Africans connect Christology to the conversion of souls and everyday life.

---

75. Henry Marcus Garba, "African Spirituality: A Paradigmatic Study of Selected Christological Perspectives with Relevance to African Christianity," *Impact: Journal of Transformation* 3, no. 1 (6 May 2020): 9.

76. Karl Muller et al., eds., *Dictionary of Mission: Theology, History, Perspectives* (Eugene: Wipf & Stock, 2006), 12–14.

77. Rudolf K. Gaisie, *Jesus Christ as Logos Incarnate and Resurrected Nana (Ancestor): An African Perspective on Conversion and Christology* (Eugene: Wipf & Stock, 2020), 7.

The Applicability of Athanasius' Soteriology to African Christianity

Soteriology is essential for the understanding of Christian theology. It is focused on the doctrine of salvation and its implication. Emphasis on Christology focuses more on the Christological synthesis of the Trinitarian framework, in which soteriology is fundamental. It is considerably accurate that the three conceptions of Athanasius' soteriology offer the African theologian the models of engaging with the concerns of the present church and society. Meanwhile, the willpower to set the Christian traditions right on track is deficient in many African theologians due to a lack of interest in understanding the mystery of Christ. Therefore, there is a need for a collaborative dialogical reflection on soteriology in the language of Athanasius' soteriology, which is vital for response to the contemporary needs of African Christianity.

Accordingly, the soteriology of Athanasius helps reopen the path to salvation. In Athanasius' soteriological view, the incarnation has two distinguishing effects – the manifestation of God's knowledge and the reversal of human corruption.[78] Hence the incarnated Word is our warrant and foundation. Furthermore, Athanasius sees Christ as eternal in his person and position as Son. Therefore, his soteriology and meaning of humanity's salvation are that the redeemed are participants in the Son's divine nature.[79] Thus, the hermeneutical principles of Athanasius offer contemporary African Christianity the basic standard of exegesis because he promoted the principle and character of the Bible from the angle of contextualization as the standard of interpretation.

For Athanasius, the central message of the Bible reveals Christ as both human and divine. Accordingly, the Bible is the product of a single divine mind that speaks about the incarnate Christ as the eternally preexistent Son of the Father. Therefore, the Athanasian principle of the unity of Scripture offers contemporary Christianity a recreative and transforming effect of the incarnation, which is neither obtained by its educational forces nor dependent on the political and cultural downwind. The truth of incarnation does not need to be confirmed by a historical process but by biblical truth.[80]

Furthermore, some basic tenets of African theology include the divinity of Christ, the efficacy of the atonement, the Trinity, and the acceptance of the

---

78. Terrence Merrigan and Jacques Haers, eds., *The Myriad Christ: Plurality and the Quest for Unity in Contemporary Christology* (Leuven: Peeters, 2000), 212.

79. Marvin Jones, ed., *Recovering Historical Christology for Today's Church* (Eugene: Wipf & Stock, 2019), 74.

80. Johannes Roldanus, *The Church in the Age of Constantine: The Theological Challenges* (London: Routledge, 2006), 95.

word of God. The standard of Athanasius' soteriology that emphasizes the Lordship of Christ, his victory over the powers, and the efficacy of his death in delivering humankind from these powers is an important part that African theology ought to promote.[81] Consequently, African Christian theologians should examine the economy (Christ's incarnation) and the nature of God who became incarnate (theology). While contemplation is necessary for understanding the whole concept of soteriology, exegesis must proceed with it.[82]

Conclusion

The soteriological conceptualization of Athanasius offers a continuing historical development of Christology, and African Christian theologians need to appropriate this historical fact. The starting point of biblical soteriological conceptualization begins with the deity of Christ about atonement. As African theologians seek a balanced theology, the focus must be on the incarnation central to Christianity, which must be monumental in promoting the doctrine of salvation. Africans must appreciate the foundational vitality of Athanasius's soteriology in this present age, which affirms three incarnational truths – Christ being God who came to exist in the flesh, the Son must be fully human and truly human (deified) for salvation to be authentic. A critical evaluation of these truths will provide the African theologian with an opportunity to investigate the soteriological implications of the incarnation. Consequently, African Christianity must seek to explore and articulate the soteriological conceptualization of Athanasius from a historical perspective. Appropriately, one can assert that this historical reality provides contemporary scholars with the need for historical revitalization.

Bibliography

Achebe, Chinua. *Things Fall Apart*. New York: Anchor, 1994.
Anatolios, Khaled. *Athanasius: The Coherence of His Thought*. London: Routledge, 2004.
"Athanasius: Five-Time Exile for Fighting 'Orthodoxy.'" Christianity Today online. Accessed 18 January 2022. https://www.christianitytoday.com/history/people/theologians/athanasius.html.

---

81. William A. Dyrness and Veli-Matti Kärkkäinen, eds., *Global Dictionary of Theology: A Resource for the Worldwide Church* (Downers Grove: InterVarsity, 2009), 9.

82. Craig A. Carter, *Contemplating God with the Great Tradition: Recovering Trinitarian Classical Theism* (Grand Rapids: Baker, 2021), n.p.

Baker, Matthew, and Todd H. Speidell, eds. *T. F. Torrance and Eastern Orthodoxy: Theology in Reconciliation*. Eugene: Wipf & Stock, 2015.

Bartel, Timothy E. G. *Glimpses of Her Father's Glory: Deification and Divine Light in Longfellow's Evangeline*. Eugene: Wipf & Stock, 2019.

Carter, Craig A. *Contemplating God with the Great Tradition: Recovering Trinitarian Classical Theism*. Grand Rapids: Baker, 2021.

Carter, Timothy John. *The Apollinarian Christologies: A Study of the Writings of Apollinarius of Laodicea*. London: Hamley King, 2011.

Christensen, Michael J., and Jeffery A. Wittung. *Partakers of the Divine Nature: The History and Development of Deification in the Christian Traditions*. Grand Rapids: Baker Academic, 2008.

Coates, Ruth. *Deification in Russian Religious Thought: Between the Revolutions, 1905–1917*. Oxford: Oxford University Press, 2019.

Conradie, Ernst M., Sigurd Bergmann, Celia Deane-Drummond, and Denis Edwards, eds. *Christian Faith and the Earth: Current Paths and Emerging Horizons in Ecotheology*. Bloomsbury: A&C Black, 2014.

Costache, Doru, Philip Kariatlis, and Mario Baghos, eds. *Alexandrian Legacy: A Critical Appraisal*. Newcastle upon Tyne: Cambridge Scholars, 2015.

Crawford, Peter. *Constantius II: Usurpers, Eunuchs and the Antichrist*. Barnsley: Pen & Sword, 2016.

Cunliffe-Jones, Hubert, ed. *A History of Christian Doctrine*. London: A&C Black, 2006.

Dearing, John Allen, III. *Will Not Return Void: The Use of Scripture in the Evangelistic Writings in the Greek Patristic Tradition*. Eugene: Wipf & Stock, 2021.

Donker, Gerald J. *The Text of the Apostolos in Athanasius of Alexandria*. Atlanta: Society of Biblical Literature, 2011.

Dragas, George Dion. *Saint Athanasius of Alexandria: Original Research and New Perspectives*. Rollinsford: Orthodox Research Institute, 2005.

Dyrness, William A., and Veli-Matti Kärkkäinen, eds. *Global Dictionary of Theology: A Resource for the Worldwide Church*. Downers Grove: InterVarsity, 2009.

Edwards, Denis. *Partaking of God: Trinity, Evolution, and Ecology*. Collegeville: Liturgical, 2014.

Eisenbise, Kathryn S. *Cooperative Salvation: A Brethren View of Atonement*. Eugene: Wipf & Stock, 2014.

Ellingsen, Mark. *African Christian Mothers and Fathers: Why They Matter for the Church Today*. Eugene: Wipf & Stock, 2015.

Ferguson, Thomas C. *The Past Is Prologue: The Revolution of Nicene Historiography*. Leiden: Brill, 2005.

Florensky, Pavel. *The Pillar and Ground of the Truth: An Essay in Orthodox Theodicy in Twelve Letters*. Princeton: Princeton University Press, 2004.

Forbes, Francis Alice. *Saint Athanasius: The Father of Orthodoxy*. Hamburg: BoD – Books on Demand, 2020.

Forman, Mary, ed. *One Heart, One Soul, Many Communities: Proceedings of the 21st Annual Monastic Institute, School of Theology-Seminary, Saint John's University, Collegeville, Minnesota 56321, July 1–7, 2006*. Collegeville: Liturgical, 2009.

Gaisie, Rudolf K. *Jesus Christ as Logos Incarnate and Resurrected Nana (Ancestor): An African Perspective on Conversion and Christology*. Eugene: Wipf & Stock, 2020.

Garba, Henry Marcus. "African Spirituality: A Paradigmatic Study of Selected Christological Perspectives with Relevance to African Christianity." *Impact: Journal of Transformation* 3, no. 1 (6 May 2020): 1–23.

Guiley, Rosemary. *The Encyclopedia of Saints*. New York: Infobase, 2001.

Gwynn, David M. *Athanasius of Alexandria: Bishop, Theologian, Ascetic, Father*. Oxford: Oxford University Press, 2012.

Hiagbe, Komi Ahiatroga. *Reconciled to Reconcile: An African View of John Calvin's Doctrine of Salvation*. Frankfurt: Peter Lang, 2008.

Holcomb, Justin S., ed. *Christian Theologies of Salvation: A Comparative Introduction*. New York: New York University Press, 2017.

Holland, Richard A., Jr. *God, Time, and the Incarnation*. Eugene: Wipf & Stock, 2012.

Irvin, Dale T., and Scott Sunquist. *History of the World Christian Movement*. Vol. 1: *Earliest Christianity to 1453*. Edinburgh: T&T Clark, 2002.

Jones, Marvin, ed. *Recovering Historical Christology for Today's Church*. Eugene: Wipf & Stock, 2019.

Kannengiesser, Charles, ed. *Early Christian Spirituality*. Minneapolis: Fortress, 1986.

Kariatlis, Philip. "Soteriological Insight in St. Athanasius' *On the Incarnation*." *Phronema* 28, no. 2 (2013): 21–34.

Kelly, Brian T. "The Father of Orthodoxy: Why We Read Athanasius." Thomas Aquinas College. Accessed 19 January 2022. https://www.thomasaquinas.edu/news/father-orthodoxy-why-we-read-athanasius.

Kurian, George Thomas, and James D. Smith III, eds. *The Encyclopedia of Christian Literature*. Vol. 2. Lanham: Scarecrow, 2010.

Lalleman, Pieter J. *The Acts of John: A Two-Stage Initiation into Johannine Gnosticism*. Leuven: Peeters, 1998.

Langworthy, Oliver B. *Gregory of Nazianzus' Soteriological Pneumatology*. Tübingen: Mohr Siebeck, 2019.

Lawson, Penelope. *On the Incarnation: The Treatise De Incarnatione Verbi Dei*. Crestwood: St Vladimir's Seminary Press, 1996.

Mbogu, Nicholas Ibeawuchi. *Jesus in Post-Missionary Africa: Issues and Questions in African Contextual Christology*. Munich: GRIN Verlag, 2012.

McGrath, Alister E. *Christian Theology: An Introduction*. Hoboken: John Wiley & Sons, 2016.

McGuckin, John Anthony. *The Westminster Handbook to Patristic Theology*. Louisville: Westminster John Knox, 2004.

McKim, Donald K., ed. *Historical Handbook of Major Biblical Interpreters*. Downers Grove: InterVarsity, 1998.

———. *Theological Turning Points: Major Issues in Christian Thought*. Louisville: Westminster John Knox, 1988.

Merrigan, Terrence, and Jacques Haers, eds. *The Myriad Christ: Plurality and the Quest for Unity in Contemporary Christology*. Leuven: Peeters, 2000.

Michael, Matthew. *Christian Theology and African Traditions*. Eugene: Wipf & Stock, 2013.

Muller, Karl, Theo Sundermeier, Stephen B. Bevans, and Richard H. Bliese, eds. *Dictionary of Mission: Theology, History, Perspectives*. Eugene: Wipf & Stock, 2006.

Musekura, Célestin. "Soteriology in Athanasius of Alexandria." Paper, Dallas Theological Seminary (n.d.). Accessed 4 February 2022. https://www.academia.edu/5553683/Soteriology_in_Athanasius_of_Alexandria.

Orji, Cyril. *A Semiotic Christology*. Eugene: Wipf & Stock, 2021.

Powderly, K. G., Jr. *One Faith – Many Transitions: Worldviews in Church History*. Lincoln: iUniverse, 2002.

Prahlow, Jacob J. "Early Christian Soteriology." Pursuing Veritas. 24 June 2014. Accessed 19 July 2021. https://pursuingveritas.com/2014/06/24/early-christian-soteriology/.

Radcliff, Alexandra Sophie. *The Claim of Humanity in Christ: Salvation and Sanctification in the Theology of T. F. and J. B. Torrance*. Eugene: Wipf & Stock, 2016.

Rausch, Thomas P. *Who Is Jesus? An Introduction to Christology*. Collegeville: Liturgical, 2016.

Redford, Donald B., and Edward Bleiberg. *The Oxford Encyclopedia of Ancient Egypt: A–F*. Oxford: Oxford University Press, 2001.

Roldanus, Johannes. *The Church in the Age of Constantine: The Theological Challenges*. London: Routledge, 2006.

Russell, Norman. *The Doctrine of Deification in the Greek Patristic Tradition*. Oxford: Oxford University Press, 2004.

Schmidt, Muhammad Wolfgang G. A. *"And on This Rock I Will Build My Church." A New Edition of Philip Schaff's "History of the Christian Church": From Nicene and Post-Nicene Christianity to Medieval Christianity A.D. 311–1073*. Hamburg: disserta Verlag, 2017.

Spence, Alan. *Incarnation and Inspiration: John Owen and the Coherence of Christology*. New York: A&C Black, 2007.

Tibbs, Clint. *Religious Experience of the Pneuma: Communication with the Spirit World in 1 Corinthians 12 and 14*. Eugene: Wipf & Stock, 2012.

Torrance, Thomas F. *Theology in Reconstruction*. Eugene: Wipf & Stock, 1996.

Tyson, John R. *The Great Athanasius: An Introduction to His Life and Work*. Eugene: Wipf & Stock, 2017.

van den Heuvel, Steven C. *Bonhoeffer's Christocentric Theology and Fundamental Debates in Environmental Ethics*. Eugene: Wipf & Stock, 2017.

Watts, Edward J. *Riot in Alexandria: Tradition and Group Dynamics in Late Antique Pagan and Christian Communities*. Berkeley: University of California Press, 2017.

Weinandy, Thomas G. *Athanasius: A Theological Introduction*. Washington: Catholic University of America Press, 2018.

Weinandy, Thomas G., and Daniel A. Keating. *Athanasius and His Legacy: Trinitarian-Incarnational Soteriology and Its Reception*. Minneapolis: Fortress, 2017.

Wilson, Daniel E. *Deification and the Rule of Faith: The Communication of the Gospel in Hellenistic Culture*. Bloomington: WestBow, 2015.

Young, Frances M. *From Nicaea to Chalcedon: A Guide to the Literature and Its Background*. London: SCM, 2013.

10

The Sacrifice of Christ in African Perspective

A Contribution to the Atonement Debate

Samuel K. Bussey

Doctoral Student in Intercultural Theology, Protestant Theological University, Groningen

Abstract

The notion of "sacrifice" is highly controversial in the contemporary Western evangelical discussion. In recent debates about the doctrine of atonement, two American theologians and leading critics of penal substitution – Mark Baker and Joel Green – have argued that the concept of sacrifice is of limited value for explaining the meaning of atonement in Western contexts. Although they recognize that the concept of sacrifice powerfully communicates the saving work of Christ in African contexts, they believe that there are limitations as to what African reflection on sacrifice can contribute to substantive theological issues. In Africa, however, the notion is prevalent across a wide range of theological traditions. The work of three African theologians – John Ekem, Edison Kalengyo, and Mercy Oduyoye – challenges Baker and Green's understanding of sacrifice in five important ways. First, they challenge their metaphorical approach to sacrifice with their dialogical typological approaches. Second, they challenge their focus on ritual sacrifice with their attention to both ritual sacrifice and self-sacrifice. Third, they challenge their reduction of sacrifice to moral self-giving with their emphasis on multiple themes. Fourth, they challenge their association of sacrifice and death with their strong association of sacrifice and life. Finally, they challenge their focus on understanding and articulation with their deep concern for worship and everyday life.

Key words: African theology, atonement, Lord's Supper, ritual sacrifice, salvation, sacrifice, sacrifice of Christ, self-sacrifice

Introduction[1]

The notion of "sacrifice" is highly controversial in the contemporary Western evangelical discussion. In recent years there have been heated debates about the doctrine of atonement, especially the theory of penal substitution, which is seen by many evangelicals as central to their theology, but which has come under increasing criticism from within the evangelical constituency. In the course of these debates, some of the leading critics of penal substitution have argued that the concept of sacrifice is of limited value in explaining the meaning of the atonement in Western contexts. Mark Baker, an American theologian, and Joel Green, an American biblical scholar, argue that because ritual sacrifice is foreign to most Westerners, the metaphor of sacrifice has little impact on their lives, except in the sense of moral self-giving. Although they recognize that the concept of sacrifice powerfully communicates the saving work of Christ in African contexts, they believe that there are limitations as to what African reflection on sacrifice can contribute to substantive theological issues.[2] In Africa, however, the notion is highly popular across a wide range

---

1. Some of the material in this chapter was originally published in Samuel K. Bussey, "Stories of Sacrifice from Below: From Girard to Ekem, Kalengyo and Oduyoye," *Stellenbosch Theological Journal* 6, no. 4 (2020): 183–212, https://doi.org/10.17570/stj.2020.v6n4.a8. It has been revised for publication in this volume. The novelty of this chapter lies in its comparison of treatments of sacrifice in the atonement debate and African theology. Special thanks to the organizers of the ASET Conference for the opportunity to present this paper; to the Protestant Theological University for making it financially possible for me to participate in the conference; and to Maartje Bussey for looking after the girls while I was away. I am grateful to Martin Bussey and Kwabena Asamoah-Gyadu for sending me some of the books that I consulted in writing this chapter. Thanks also to audiences at the Protestant Theological University, the ASET Conference, and Saint Paul's University for their positive responses and helpful questions. I am very grateful for detailed feedback on earlier versions of this chapter from Joseph Mutei, Benno van den Toren, Renée van Riessen, Lieke Werkman, and two anonymous reviewers for ASET Publications.

2. Baker and Green have been major voices in the evangelical atonement debate from the very beginning. See Mark D. Baker and Joel B. Green, *Recovering the Scandal of the Cross: Atonement in New Testament and Contemporary Contexts* (Downers Grove: IVP, 2000); Mark D. Baker, "Contextualizing the Scandal of the Cross," in *Proclaiming the Scandal of the Cross: Contemporary Images of Atonement*, ed. Mark D. Baker (Grand Rapids: Baker Academic, 2006), 13–36; Joel B. Green, "Kaleidoscopic View," in *The Nature of the Atonement: Four Views*, eds. James K. Beilby and Paul R. Eddy (Downers Grove: InterVarsity, 2006), 157–85; Joel B. Green, "Must

of theological traditions. Since the third wave of evangelization first reached African shores in the middle of the eighteenth century, sacrifice has been a key theme in missionary and African theological discourse. Biblical scholars have wrestled with the relation between biblical and African concepts of sacrifice, liturgical theologians have focused on the appropriation of Christ's sacrifice in the celebration of the Eucharist, and systematic theologians have reflected on the meaning of Christian sacrifice in African social contexts.[3]

In this chapter, I explore how African stories of sacrifice challenge Western stories of sacrifice by examining how the work of three African theologians challenges Baker and Green's understanding of sacrifice, as well as their rather disparaging assessment of what African theological reflection can contribute on substantive theological issues. I take an intercultural approach, setting up an

---

We Imagine the Atonement in Penal Substitutionary Terms? Questions, Caveats and a Plea," in *The Atonement Debate: Papers from the London Symposium on the Theology of Atonement*, eds. Derek Tidball, David Hilborn, and Justin Thacker (Grand Rapids: Zondervan, 2008), 153–71. In this chapter I refer to their most recent joint publication, Mark D. Baker and Joel B. Green, *Recovering the Scandal of the Cross: Atonement in New Testament and Contemporary Contexts*, 2nd ed. (Downers Grove: IVP Academic, 2011). The work of Baker and Green has generated a considerable response, some of it quite critical, from other evangelical theologians. See Hans Boersma, "The Disappearance of Punishment: Metaphors, Models and the Meaning of the Atonement," *Books and Culture: A Christian Review* (March/April 2003): 32–34, https://www.booksandculture.com/articles/2003/marapr/16.32.html; Kevin J. Vanhoozer, "The Atonement in Postmodernity: Guilt, Goats and Gifts," in *The Glory of the Atonement: Biblical, Historical and Practical Perspectives*, eds. Charles E. Hill and Frank A. James III (Downers Grove: IVP Academic, 2004), 367–404; Thomas R. Schreiner, "Penal Substitution View," in Beilby and Paul Eddy, *Nature of the Atonement*, 67–98; Steve Jeffrey, Mike Ovey, and Andrew Sach, *Pierced for Our Transgressions: Rediscovering the Glory of Penal Substitution* (Nottingham: Inter-Varsity, 2007); Garry Williams, "Penal Substitution: A Response to Recent Criticisms," in Tidball, Hilborn, and Thacker, *Atonement Debate*, 172–91.

3. On the relation between biblical and African concepts of sacrifice, see Harry Sawyerr, "Sacrifice," in *Biblical Revelation and African Beliefs*, eds. Kwesi A. Dickson and Paul Ellingworth (London: Lutterworth, 1969), 57–82; Justin S. Ukpong, *Sacrifice, African and Biblical: A Comparative Study of Ibibio and Levitical Sacrifices* (Rome: Urbaniana University Press, 1990); and Samuel Ngewa, "The Biblical Idea of Substitution versus the Idea of Substitution in African Traditional Sacrifices: A Case Study of Hermeneutics for African Christian Theology" (PhD diss., Westminster Theological Seminary, 1987). On eucharistic sacrifice, see Francis A. Arinze, "Ibo Sacrifice as an Introduction to the Catechesis of Holy Mass" (PhD diss., Urbaniana University, Rome, 1960), the first part of which was later published as *Sacrifice in Ibo Religion* (Ibadan: Ibadan University Press, 1970); Ted Nelson-Adjakpey, "Penance and Expiatory Sacrifice among the Ghanaian-Ewe and Their Relevance to the Christian Religion" (PhD diss, Urbaniana University, Rome, 1982); and Sithembele Sipuka, "The Sacrifice of the Mass and the Concept of Sacrifice among the Xhosa: Towards an Inculturated Understanding of the Eucharist" (ThD diss., University of South Africa, 2000). On Christian sacrifice, see Emmanuel Katongole, *The Sacrifice of Africa: A Political Theology for Africa* (Grand Rapids: Eerdmans, 2011); and Olumuyiwa O. Familusi, "Voluntary or Subtle Compulsion? An Ethical Context of Giving as Sacrifice in Contemporary Christianity," in *Sacrifice in Religious Traditions: Essays in Honour of Ven. Prof. J. Omosade Awolalu*, eds. Deji Ayegboyin and Adekunle O. Dada (Ibadan: University of Ibadan, 2018), 173–88.

"encounter" between thinkers from different times and places for comparison.[4] First, I discuss the notion of sacrifice, explaining why it is so controversial and developing an interpretive framework for a theological approach. Next, I examine the story of sacrifice in the work of Mark Baker and Joel Green, arguing that their approach does not do justice to the notion of sacrifice in either Western or African cultures. Finally, I examine the stories of sacrifice in the work of John Ekem, a Ghanaian mother-tongue biblical scholar, Edison Kalengyo, a Ugandan inculturation theologian, and Mercy Oduyoye, a Ghanaian women's theologian. I argue that they challenge Baker and Green's understanding of sacrifice in five important ways. First, they challenge their metaphorical approach to sacrifice with their dialogical typological approaches. Second, they challenge their focus on ritual sacrifice with their attention to both ritual sacrifice and self-sacrifice. Third, they challenge their reduction of sacrifice to moral self-giving with their emphasis on multiple themes. Fourth, they challenge their association of sacrifice and death with their strong association of sacrifice and life. Finally, they challenge their focus on understanding and articulation with their deep concern for worship and everyday life.

The Notion of Sacrifice

One reason that the notion of sacrifice is so controversial in Western discussions is related to the question of metanarrative. In modern thought, there are several overarching accounts of sacrifice that make competing claims about the acceptability of the concept.[5] The first metanarrative of sacrifice is a Christian one. African church fathers, such as Origen, Athanasius, and Augustine, played a key role in developing the idea that the sacrifice of Christ ends and fulfils all sacrifice. As John Rogerson writes,

> Christian interpretation of Old Testament sacrifice was necessarily allegorical from an early period. On the one hand, the sacrifice of Christ had summed up and rendered unnecessary all the sacrifices of the Old Testament; on the other hand, the details of

---

4. Mark J. Cartledge and David A. Cheetham, eds., *Intercultural Theology: Approaches and Themes* (London: SCM, 2011), 2–3. This encounter is necessarily a metaphorical one. The "debate" or "conversation" is a classic method in theology for conceiving the relationship between two or more thinkers that goes back to Aquinas. While it is frequently used to compare thinkers from different times, it is equally useful in an intercultural approach for comparing contemporary thinkers from different places.

5. John Milbank, "Stories of Sacrifice: From Wellhausen to Girard," *Theory, Culture & Society* 12, no. 4 (Nov. 1995): 15–46.

all sacrifices . . . could be interpreted in terms of the Incarnation and Passion.[6]

Augustine, for example, interprets both Isaac and the ram in the story of the *Akedah* as types of Christ.[7] During the European Reformations, both Protestant and Catholic Reformers generally followed this account: "Reformation interpretation of sacrifice, while being less allegorical and more concerned to describe the rituals themselves, nonetheless regarded Old Testament sacrifice as a synchronic scheme looking forward to the sacrifice of Christ."[8] Both Protestant and Catholic Reformers, however, treated the concept of sacrifice as an immanent and fully grasped principle. For Luther, Christian sacrifice was primarily the penitential offering of the self with and in Christ; for the Council of Trent, it was the offering of Christ in the Mass. Both superimposed their respective concepts of sacrifice on Hebrew beliefs and practices, which limited the extent to which the latter could enrich the former.[9] During the modern era, theologians have continued to use the Christian metanarrative as an interpretive framework for understanding sacrifice, both in the Bible and in other cultural traditions. Furthermore, allegorical interpretation has been given fresh impetus with the development of typology and figural interpretation.[10]

In the modern era, a new evolutionist metanarrative of sacrifice emerged. Early anthropologists, such as Edward B. Tylor, drew on the work of Charles Darwin and earlier thinkers to construct general theories of religion. Over time, "lower" forms of sacrifice, such as ordinary gift giving, were understood as necessarily giving way to "higher" forms, such as abnegation. Furthermore, "higher critics" of the Old Testament, such as Julius Wellhausen, took a similar approach to the history of Hebrew sacrifice. Originally sacrifice was a natural, spontaneous, private affair which involved giving to God and sharing

---

6. John W. Rogerson, "Sacrifice in the Old Testament: Problems of Method and Approach," in *Sacrifice*, eds. Michael F. C. Bourdillon and Meyer Fortes (London: Academic, 1980), 50.

7. Augustine, *De civitate Dei* 16.32.

8. Rogerson, "Sacrifice in the Old Testament," 51.

9. Martin Luther, "First Sunday after Epiphany," in *The Precious and Sacred Writings of Martin Luther*, ed. John N. Lenker, vol. 8, *Luther's Epistle Sermons*, vol. 2: *Epiphany, Easter and Pentecost*, trans. John N. Lenker (Minneapolis: Luther Press, 1909), 10; Council of Trent, Session 22, "Doctrine Concerning the Sacrifice of the Mass" (17 Sep. 1562), in *Canons and Decrees of the Council of Trent: Original Text with English Translation*, trans. Henry J. Schroeder (London: B. Herder Book Co., 1941), 149.

10. See Jean Daniélou, *From Shadows to Reality: Studies in Biblical Typology of the Fathers* (London: Burns & Oates, 1960); and Erich Auerbach, *Scenes from the Drama of European Literature: Six Essays* (New York: Meridian, 1959), 11–76.

a meal.[11] Through a process of centralization and spiritualization, sacrifice was transformed into moral self-giving.[12] For Wellhausen, the true sacrifice is "resultless self-sacrifice and resigned obedience" for others, the church, and ultimately the nation state.[13] The idea of spiritualization, which assumes an essence of sacrifice, a spiritual and ethical kernel that can be freed from the shell of ritual practice, has continued to be influential. The evolutionist account of sacrifice, however, has been criticized for merely historicizing and reconceptualizing the Christian metanarrative. Consequently, some theorists argue that the concept of sacrifice should be renounced entirely. As the historian of Greek religion Marcel Detienne writes,

> the notion of sacrifice is indeed a category of the thought of yesterday, conceived of as arbitrarily as totemism – decried earlier by Lévi-Strauss – both because it gathers into one artificial type elements taken from here and there in the symbolic fabric of societies and because it reveals the surprising power of annexation that Christianity still subtly exercises on the thought of these historians and sociologists who were convinced they were inventing a new science.[14]

Nevertheless, the ethnographer of African religion Luc de Heusch argues that this conclusion may be too hasty and suggests that a minimum definition of sacrifice, such as "the immolation of a human or animal victim," enables a researcher to study a phenomenon that occurs in many different contexts.[15] As he writes, "one must listen patiently to the ideological speeches of a multitude of sacrificers, in the most diverse societies, before reaching a conclusion."[16]

A second reason that the notion of sacrifice is so controversial in Western discussions is the question of class. Many researchers have approached sacrifice as a conventional monothetic class. In such a class, members must have a certain characteristic or series of characteristics in common in order to belong to that class. In recent years, however, there has been a growing consensus that sacrifice

---

11. Julius Wellhausen, *Prolegomena to the History of Israel*, trans. J. Sutherland Black and Allan Menzies (Edinburgh: A&C Black, 1885), 71.

12. Wellhausen, *Prolegomena*, 81.

13. Wellhausen, 513.

14. Marcel Detienne, "Culinary Practices and the Spirit of Sacrifice," in *The Cuisine of Sacrifice among the Ancient Greeks*, eds. Marcel Detienne and Jean-Pierre Vernant, trans. Paula Wissing (Chicago: University of Chicago Press, 1989), 20.

15. Luc de Heusch, *Sacrifice in Africa: A Structuralist Approach*, trans. Linda O'Brien and Alice Morton (Manchester: Manchester University Press, 1985), 15.

16. de Heusch, *Sacrifice in Africa*, 23.

is actually a polythetic class.¹⁷ In a polythetic class, members may share a number of characteristics that occur commonly in other members, but no single characteristic is essential for belonging to that class. Ludwig Wittgenstein's notion of family resemblance is helpful here. I am the eldest of five brothers. Although people often claim that it is easy to tell that we are all Busseys, they find it difficult to say precisely why. No one feature is common to us all; rather, there are a series of overlapping similarities. As the Anglican theologian John Milbank argues, "sacrifice is not a pure, intact genus."¹⁸ A minimum definition of sacrifice, like that of de Heusch, can identify "a cultural feature nearly always present, and sufficiently distinctive to be recognizable," but "it does not at all follow that a universal feature must possess a universal identity, and then a universal meaning and explanation."¹⁹ If sacrifice is a polythetic class, a theological approach to sacrificial phenomena must resolutely avoid modern essentializing and generalizing tendencies. As Stephen Sykes writes, "the first thing a Christian theologian must learn is to resist the temptation to try to create a basic structure to which they all conform."²⁰

A third reason that the notion of sacrifice is so controversial in Western discussions is related to the question of scale.²¹ As the historian of religion Jeffrey Carter observes, "the process of understanding is always comprised of a series of choices over how to construct generalities out of diversity."²² For the researcher approaching the subject of sacrifice, the singularity and variability of the empirical data are simply bewildering. The sociologist Michael Bourdillon indicates that there is a multitude of ideas and practices associated with it – for example, a gift to a deity, a means of controlling death, substitution, a communal meal, and a means of releasing or getting rid of power.²³ Different theorists make different decisions about what themes to include and what to ignore. Large-scale approaches involve significant generalization to account

---

17. See Rodney Needham, "Polythetic Classification: Convergence and Consequences," *Man* 10, no. 3 (Sep. 1975): 349–69; John W. Burton, "Sacrifice: A Polythetic Class of Atuot Religious Thought," *Journal of Religion in Africa* 11, no. 2 (1980): 93–105; and Kathryn McClymond, *Beyond Sacred Violence: A Comparative Study of Sacrifice* (Baltimore: Johns Hopkins University Press, 2008).

18. Milbank, "Stories of Sacrifice," 16.

19. Milbank, 16.

20. Stephen W. Sykes, "Sacrifice in the New Testament and Christian Theology," in Bourdillon and Fortes, *Sacrifice*, 61.

21. Jeffrey Carter, ed., *Understanding Religious Sacrifice: A Reader* (London: Continuum, 2003), 451.

22. Carter, *Understanding Religious Sacrifice*, 41.

23. Michael C. F. Bourdillon, "Introduction," in Bourdillion and Fortes, *Sacrifice*, 10–23.

for as much diversity as possible. Small-scale approaches pay attention to the complexity of a particular case. As Carter writes, "there are different, and equally legitimate, ways to answer the question of scale. How a researcher answers this question, the choices he or she makes regarding which details (differences) can be legitimately generalized (seen as similar), lies at the root of diverging understandings."[24] Small wonder, then, that those different understandings of sacrifice abound, from the grand theories of sacrifice of the modern era to more modest recent attempts. If sacrifice can be approached using a variety of scales, a theological approach must be sufficiently dialogical if it is to do justice to the wide variety of stories, practices, and concepts of sacrifice in different cultures and come to a fuller understanding of the sacrifice of Christ. As Milbank writes, "in the face of many different cultures Christian sacrifice discovers many different modes of fulfilment, and so itself again, as possibly arrived at by an *infinity* of different narrative routes."[25]

The Atonement Debate: Mark Baker and Joel Green

Next, we turn to the work of Mark Baker and Joel Green.[26] In their book *Recovering the Scandal of the Cross*, Baker and Green bring together their New Testament expertise and contextual experience to address the question of how to understand and communicate the saving significance of Jesus's death in the twenty-first century. As they observe,

> As is often the case in our use of the New Testament, our use of tradition frequently falters because, rather than learn how the theological task has been undertaken and exemplified, we attempt instead to carry into our own lives and pronouncements models and metaphors that belong to another age and that are dead to us. Metaphors work within cultures where a shared encyclopedia, or cultural narrative, can be assumed. Crossing cultures sometimes requires new idioms, working with fresh ways of conceptualizing and communicating.[27]

---

24. Carter, *Understanding Religious Sacrifice*, 451–52.
25. Carter, 32; emphasis original.
26. Mark Baker is an American Mennonite minister and academic who was born in 1957. He is currently a professor of Mission and Theology at Fresno Pacific Biblical Seminary in Fresno, California. Joel Green is an American Methodist minister and academic who was born in 1956. He is currently a professor of New Testament Interpretation at Fuller Theological Seminary in Pasadena, California, and a member of the prestigious Studiorum Novi Testamenti Societas.
27. Baker and Green, *Scandal of the Cross*, 38.

On the one hand, they call attention to the multiplicity of metaphors in the New Testament; on the other hand, they argue that not all the metaphors and models found in the Scriptures and Christian tradition are equally suitable in contemporary contexts. In particular, they argue that the penal substitution model and the metaphor of sacrifice often associated with it are of limited value for explaining the meaning of the atonement in Western contexts.

Baker and Green take a metaphorical approach to sacrifice. They introduce their main section on metaphor as a response to concerns raised by feminist theologians about atonement imagery, especially its implications for our understanding of who God is and how we approach human relationships. They argue that these concerns are legitimate but observe that their criticism of atonement theology "reflects our common problem of dependence on metaphorical language to communicate what is beyond language."[28] Drawing on the work of George Lakoff and Mark Johnson, Baker and Green state that metaphors "highlight and hide" certain aspects of a concept.[29] Two interpretive principles follow from this. First, "no one metaphor will capture the reality of the atonement." Interestingly, they use sacrifice as an example: "Metaphors from Israel's sacrificial system communicate something important about the death of Jesus, but they cannot contain the profundity of the cross of Christ."[30] Second, "not all properties are necessarily embraced or legitimated in a given use of a metaphor."[31] The ransom saying in Mark 10:45, for example, does not explicitly address who pays the ransom, or to whom it is paid. Furthermore, following Lakoff and Johnson, they emphasize the contextual nature of metaphor: "metaphors for the atonement in the New Testament are implicit comparisons that rely on larger systems of thought and are grounded in life in the world."[32] Consequently, a metaphor must be read "according to the right frame."[33] Baker and Green's metaphorical approach is helpful in that it calls for careful attention to atonement metaphors in contemporary culture and causes them to engage with perspectives from around the world, but it seems to contribute to a spiritualizing tendency in their treatment of sacrifice.

---

28. Baker and Green, 117.
29. Baker and Green, 118. See George Lakoff and Mark Johnson, *Metaphors We Live By* (Chicago: University of Chicago Press, 1980), 10–13.
30. Baker and Green, 118.
31. Baker and Green, 118.
32. Baker and Green, 120.
33. Baker and Green, 120.

Baker and Green's story of sacrifice is set within a narrative of contextual atonement: Since the fall, the relationship between God and humans has been broken by sin. To resolve this estrangement, atonement is necessary. God provides a sacrificial system for Israel through which atonement can be made. But ritual sacrifice is not the only way of restoring or maintaining the relationship with God. In the history of Israel, the notion of the "sacrifice of obedience" emphasizes acts of obedience rather than acts of ritual sacrifice. Outside Israel, there are also notions of heroic self-giving and human sacrifice. Jesus's faithfulness and obedience to death, even death on a cross, becomes the exemplar of moral self-giving.[34]

In Baker and Green's view, the New Testament interpretations of Christ's saving work as a sacrifice are primarily related to concepts of ritual sacrifice, which poses problems for using the notion of sacrifice to explain the meaning of the atonement today.[35] As they write,

> Sharply put, to speak of "sacrifice" today may be to use the same terms as those used in the first-century world, but spoken in the context of modern-day America, those words can hardly mean the same thing. Unlike those who were trafficked in the temples of Israel and the Roman world, we are people for whom the butchery of animals lies outside the realm of common experience.[36]

On the other hand, Baker and Green recognize that the concept of sacrifice powerfully communicates the saving work of Christ in African contexts. Drawing on the autobiography of Kisare, a Mennonite bishop from Tanzania, Baker and Green write, "The concept of the cleansing and reconciling power of Jesus' death on the cross was easily understood by the people because of the role blood sacrifice had played in the traditional religion and culture of the predominant tribe – the Luo."[37] In contrast to Western contexts, where sacrifice is often understood in terms of satisfaction or penal substitution as a payment to God, in the Luo context sacrifice is understood as "a way of removing a barrier or curse – a cleansing of the consequences of an evil action."[38] Nevertheless, Baker and Green stress that although articulating the sacrifice of Jesus in terms of sacrificial ritual might be helpful in a Luo

---

34. Baker and Green, 64–68, 72–77, 128–31.
35. Baker and Green, 130–31.
36. Baker and Green, 136.
37. Baker and Green, 226.
38. Baker and Green, 227.

context, it would not have the same impact in a North American context. Rather, "Kisare's story challenges us to find images and models as effective in our setting of mission as this sacrificial imagery was in his."[39] The only notion of sacrifice they find helpful is the idea of ethical self-sacrifice in C. S. Lewis's *The Lion, the Witch, and the Wardrobe*. In this story, Aslan, the great lion and a Christ figure, willingly dies in a human traitor's place to save his life. For Baker and Green this shows that "Jesus was willing to sacrifice himself, suffer death in our place according to the rules of the world, to release us from the grasp of evil."[40]

Baker and Green have been major voices in the evangelical atonement debate from the beginning, and their work has generated considerable response.[41] They argue that the concept of sacrifice is of limited value for explaining the meaning of the atonement in Western contexts. Still, their approach does not do justice to sacrifice in either Western or African cultures. Their use of metaphor theory seems to contribute to a spiritualizing tendency in their treatment of sacrifice, which drives a wedge between ritual sacrifice and self-sacrifice. They focus on the former in their understanding of the atonement and are quick to label sacrifice a "dead metaphor" in Western contexts because ritual sacrifice is unfamiliar to most people.[42] Nevertheless, even a cursory glance at the news suggests that it continues to be an important concept in many different spheres of life, from politics to sport, to the coronavirus pandemic.[43] Moreover, the notion of "sacrifice" is discussed across a wide range of academic fields, from biblical studies to philosophy, to anthropology, psychology, and even evolutionary biology. Furthermore, while they allow for an understanding of sacrifice as moral self-giving, they mainly associate sacrifice with death

---

39. Baker and Green, 228.

40. Baker and Green, 234. Interestingly, Green appears to be more open to the notion of sacrifice than Baker. See Green, "Kaleidoscopic View," 177–78. Nevertheless, their most recent joint publication maintains their earlier understanding of sacrifice.

41. See note 2 above.

42. As Lakoff and Johnson observe, systematic metaphorical expressions "are 'alive' in the most fundamental sense: they are metaphors we live by. The fact that they are conventionally fixed within the lexicon of English makes them no less alive." Lakoff and Johnson, *Metaphors We Live By*, 55.

43. BBC News online, "General Election 2019: Labour and Tories Make Armistice Day Vows to Forces," last modified 11 November 2019, https://www.bbc.com/news/election-2019-50369104; Stanley Kwenda, "Sadio Mane: Liverpool Players Have to 'Sacrifice' Themselves to Win Title," BBC Sport, last modified 27 December 2019, https://www.bbc.com/sport/football/50920736; Nikki Fox and Julian Sturdy, "Coronavirus: Essex GP with 'Textbook Symptoms' Dies," BBC News online, last modified 27 March 2020, https://www.bbc.com/news/uk-england-essex-52040991.

and do not explore the kind of life that results from sacrifice. Their focus is strongly on understanding and articulation, with little attention to worship and everyday life. For this, we must turn to some African stories of sacrifice.

Mother-Tongue Biblical Theology: John Ekem

First, we turn to the work of John Ekem.[44] In his book *New Testament Concepts of Atonement in an African Pluralistic Setting*, Ekem reflects on "the vital subject of atonement" from an explicitly African Christian perspective.[45] He begins with a working definition of atonement. Rather than confining himself to one particular theory, he casts his net as wide as possible, describing atonement as "an all-inclusive soteriological concept involving the entire scope of God's redemptive work in Christ from the Incarnation to Christ's present heavenly ministry, and even beyond that."[46] He views it as "a holistic, multifaceted event that transcends time and space."[47] Furthermore, he observes that "a death-centred approach to atonement is . . . woefully inadequate for the African situation where life leads into death and death into life."[48] In his work, he seeks not only to contribute to New Testament scholarship on biblical concepts of atonement but also to reevaluate the translation of several biblical texts into Ghanaian languages. In the process, he develops a programmatic hermeneutical approach for African biblical interpreters and highlights the need for contextual insights to be made available to nonacademic African readers through commentaries and study notes.[49]

Ekem develops his hermeneutical approach through discussions of the cosmic Christology in Colossians and the priestly Christology in Hebrews. He explores the relationship between "Christ" and "culture," opting for what Emmanuel Martey has described as a dualist view, in which they exist in a paradoxical relationship.[50] Ekem argues that although Christ can be

---

44. Ekem is a Ghanaian Methodist minister and academic who was born in 1959. He is a professor of New Testament and director of the Institute for Mother-Tongue Biblical Hermeneutics at Trinity Theological Seminary in Legon, Accra, and a member of the prestigious Studiorum Novi Testamenti Societas.

45. John D. K. Ekem, *New Testament Concepts of Atonement in an African Pluralistic Setting* (Accra: SonLife Press, 2005), iv.

46. Ekem, *Concepts of Atonement*, 3.

47. Ekem, 4.

48. Ekem, 123.

49. Ekem, 63–64, 93, 121–22.

50. Ekem, 89.

encountered in any human culture, "he does not necessarily superimpose himself on those cultures, but is perceived with the eye of faith and borne witness to within a people's existential circumstances."[51] Ultimately, he finds a model for African biblical hermeneutics in the creative typological approach of the author of Hebrews. He argues that the author was "an innovative thinker, aware of, and in dialogue with alternative world-views within his community."[52] In particular, the author treats Old Testament characters and events as "types of Christ and temporary anticipations of the Gospel" in a context characterized by religious pluralism.[53] In addition to his hermeneutical approach, Ekem has developed a novel exegetical method, which he terms "dialogical exegesis."[54] In short, his method involves the following:

1. An examination of texts from a cross-cultural hermeneutical perspective whereby the biblical and other worldviews (e.g. African) are brought face to face with the principle of reciprocal challenge (*intercultural/cross-cultural hermeneutics*).

2. Dialogue between the translated texts and their "originals" with a view to ascertaining their points of convergence and divergence as well as their impact on the community of faith (*intertextual dialogue*).

3. Bringing the insights of (1) and (2) to bear on the development of context-sensitive study Bible notes and commentaries (*applied hermeneutics*).[55]

Ekem's hermeneutical approach and method are important for understanding his "dialogical typological" approach to sacrifice. In contrast to Baker and Green's approach, which superimposes the notion of ethical self-giving on other sacrificial systems, Ekem stresses the need for constructive dialogue with other stories, practices, and concepts of sacrifice in a dynamic and open-ended encounter that enables a richer understanding of Christ's sacrifice.

Ekem's story of sacrifice is set within a narrative of cosmic salvation: since the fall, humans and the entire created universe have been corrupted by sin. For humanity and the cosmos to be saved, reconciliation must occur. Sacrifice is one of several ways in which reconciliation can be achieved. Before the birth

---

51. Ekem, 94.
52. Ekem, 94.
53. Ekem, 107.
54. John D. K. Ekem, "A Dialogical Exegesis of Romans 3:25a," *Journal for the Study of the New Testament* 30, no. 1 (2007): 75.
55. Ekem, "Dialogical Exegesis," 77.

of Jesus, God revealed something of his saving activity in the history of Israel and the histories of other nations. This saving activity reached its fulfillment in the life, ministry, death, resurrection, and glorification of Jesus. Now humans can do the will of their Creator through the empowerment of the Holy Spirit and the continuing intercessory ministry of Jesus.[56]

Ekem's most detailed discussion of sacrifice is in his article on Romans 3:25a, in which Paul describes Jesus as a *hilastērion*. Western debates on this verse often remain at an impasse as to whether the term *hilastērion* should be interpreted in a propitiatory or an expiatory sense.[57] Ekem suggests that these options hardly exhaust the meaning of the term.[58] He presents translations of the verse into European and Ghanaian languages, examining how they render *hilastērion*. Some Ghanaian translations bring out interesting aspects of the term but none are quite satisfactory. Ekem then analyses the sacrificial concepts among the Abura-Mfantse of Ghana.[59] There is a general word for sacrifice which can be understood as "an expression of gratitude for what the benevolent spirit world has done," but also as "that act of giving which expects nothing in return."[60] The sacrificial system also includes a number of concepts related to propitiation, expiation, and reconciliation. Furthermore, there are popular legends about people who willingly gave themselves to be offered as sacrificial victims to save their people from a calamity.[61] Consequently, Ekem argues that a better translation of *hilastērion* would be *ahyɛnanmuadze*. This term refers to the object of replacement or substitution on behalf of the group or individual. As he writes,

> considering the idea that God takes the initiative to "put Jesus forward" as a means of *hilastērion* through his blood, which event should be *appropriated by faith for justification to be operational in a person's life*, it seems to me that *ahyɛnanmuadze* offers the most

---

56. Ekem, *Concepts of Atonement*, 1–4.

57. Against propitiation, see Charles H. Dodd, "*Hilaskesthai*, Its Cognates, Derivatives, and Synonyms, in the Septuagint," *The Journal of Theological Studies* 32, no. 128 (1931): 352–60. For propitiation, see Leon Morris, "The Use of *Hilaskesthai* etc. in Biblical Greek," *The Expository Times* 62, no. 8 (1951): 227–33; and Roger Nicole, "C. H. Dodd and the Doctrine of Propitiation," *Westminster Theological Journal* 17, no. 2 (1955): 117–57. For a more recent assessment of the evidence, see Daniel P. Bailey, "Jesus as the Mercy Seat: The Semantics and Theology of Paul's Use of *Hilasterion* in Romans 3:25" (PhD diss., University of Cambridge, 1999). The last resource is freely accessible.

58. Ekem, "Dialogical Exegesis," 79.

59. Ekem, 88.

60. Ekem, 88.

61. Ekem, 89.

appropriate register for the process described in Rom. 3.25a. In this sense, Jesus becomes God's means of *ahyɛnanmuadze* through his sacrificial death. Precisely, he functions as God's potent revelatory means of atonement through his vicarious, substitutionary and representative death on the cross.[62]

Thus, *hilastērion* becomes "a representative revelatory sacrifice."

Ekem's main contribution is his dialogical typological approach. This allows him to envisage more clearly the significance of Christ's sacrifice within the Christian tradition than in the Abura-Mfantse tradition. He pays careful attention to both concepts of ritual sacrifice and stories of self-sacrifice in his interpretation of Jesus's sacrifice. Translating *hilastērion* as "a representative revelatory sacrifice" leads to a richer understanding of Christ's sacrifice, both for Abura-Mfantse Christians and Christians around the world. Jesus's sacrifice is not merely a pacifying sacrifice, but "God's potent revelatory means of atonement."[63] Ekem's dialogical typological approach also means that he pays attention to multiple themes related to Abura-Mfantse sacrifice, including the notion of the gift, propitiation, expiation, and reconciliation. Furthermore, he shows that a central concern in Abura-Mfantse sacrifice is safeguarding community life. Finally, a key factor in Ekem's choice to translate *hilastērion* as *ahyɛnanmuadze* is his concern for appropriating Christ's sacrifice among Abura-Mfantse Christians. The stories of self-giving in Abura-Mfantse tradition suggest ways in which Abura-Mfantse Christians might live out notions of sacrifice.

Inculturation Theology: Edison Kalengyo

Second, we turn to the work of Edison Kalengyo.[64] Kalengyo has made the theme of sacrifice his life's work, exploring it from biblical, cultural, and liturgical angles.[65] As he observes, "for all Christianity has meant to Africa, the

---

62. Ekem, 90; emphasis added.
63. Ekem, 90.
64. Kalengyo is a Ugandan Anglican priest who was born in 1959. He is an Associate Professor of the New Testament at Uganda Christian University in Mukono. He has also served as the director of theology and interfaith relations at the All Africa Conference of Churches (AACC).
65. Edison Kalengyo, "The Sacrifice of Christ and Ganda Sacrifice: A Contextual Interpretation in Relation to the Eucharist," in *The Epistle to the Hebrews and Christian Theology*, ed. Richard Bauckham (Grand Rapids: Eerdmans, 2009), 302–18; Edison Kalengyo, *Sacrifice in Hebrews and the Pauline Epistles* (Nairobi: Acton, 2015); Edison Kalengyo, *Celebrating the Lord's Supper: Ending the Eucharistic Famine* (Carlisle: HippoBooks, 2018); Edison Kalengyo, "The

Christian understanding of sacrifice has not been clarified in societies for which sacrifice lay at the heart of their traditional religion."[66] In his Ugandan context, this is an urgent need because of its implications for Christian identity and practice, especially as traditional ritual sacrifices remain common. He writes,

> The elaborate sacrificial system of the Ganda has, by and large, remained intact to date (albeit some of the sacrificial rituals being performed in great secrecy). There is even a reported increase in the once abandoned ritual of human sacrifice. This is despite clearly defined and stated Church dogma backed by extensive preaching of the gospel of Christ and relentless condemnation of the traditional practice of sacrifice from the pulpits every Sunday.[67]

Kalengyo seeks to address this pressing need by demonstrating how Jesus's sacrifice can be appropriated in the Ugandan context through the contextual celebration of the Lord's Supper.[68]

Kalengyo combines an inculturation approach, drawing on the work of Brian Hearne, with a tripolar interpretive process, drawing on the work of Christina Grenholm, Daniel Patte, and Jonathan Draper.[69] Following Hearne, Jesus is a "completely 'inculturated' human being, a Jew, a Galilean, brought up in the religious and cultural traditions of his people."[70] At the same time, "Jesus the Jew is now the universal man, the 'transcultural person,' the one who is the everlasting home for all peoples of all cultures."[71] For Kalengyo, this means that Christ "is able to effectively communicate with people of all nations and effect the eternal salvation for which he came in the first place."[72] Kalengyo is very aware of the dangers of syncretism and emphasizes the need for biblical contextual interpretations. As he writes, "All contextual inculturation studies and practices of the sacrificial death of Christ must have as their foundation a

---

Understanding and Practice of Sacrifice among the Ganda," in Ayegboyin and Dada, *Sacrifice in Religious Traditions*, 315–51.

66. Kalengyo, "Sacrifice of Christ," 302.
67. Kalengyo, 303.
68. Kalengyo, 303.
69. Kalengyo, 303 n. 3, 312–13.
70. Brian Hearne, "Christology and Inculturation," *African Ecclesial Review* 22 (1980): 338, quoted in Kalengyo, 312.
71. Hearne, "Christology and Inculturation," 339, quoted in Kalengyo, 313.
72. Kalengyo, 313.

clear understanding of the sacrifice of Christ in the New Testament."[73] First, he examines the biblical text, arguing that sacrifice is a key concept in the Pauline Epistles and the Epistle to the Hebrews for explaining the death of Jesus and its benefits for believers.[74] Then he analyses the context, examining Ganda culture, especially the sacrificial system. He deliberately avoids espousing one theory of sacrifice as he observes that Ganda sacrifices are often "multifunctional": "What was a gift was at the same time a thanksgiving sacrifice that ended in a communal meal that enhanced communication, friendship and communion with the deity."[75] Finally, he addresses the question of appropriation. Jesus's words at the Last Supper draw heavily on the language of sacrifice, suggesting that the Lord's Supper is the key to appropriating the sacrifice of Christ.[76]

Kalengyo's story of sacrifice is set within a narrative of incarnation, and the concept of culture plays a larger role: Since the fall, human nature and culture have been tainted by sin. For humans to be saved and culture transformed, sin must be dealt with through sacrifice. Before the incarnation, God was at work in Jewish culture and other cultures to create an understanding of who he is and what salvation is. This process reached its fulfillment in Jesus, especially at the cross. Now the process of incarnation continues, primarily through the inculturation of the Lord's Supper.[77]

For Kalengyo, the Lord's Supper is the interface between Jesus's sacrifice and Ganda sacrifice. Historically, Anglican missionaries in Uganda avoided using sacrificial language in the liturgy, but this needs to be reassessed in light of the Scriptures.[78] The sacrificial language used at the Last Supper suggests that Christ's sacrifice should be understood in terms of gift, atonement, substitution, covenant, and communion.[79] Kalengyo therefore argues that language from the Ganda sacrificial system should be used to convey the meaning of Jesus's sacrifice as clearly as possible in the eucharistic celebration. He observes that *ekitambiro*, the general word for sacrifice, is multivocal and is associated with well-being, protection, and healing. Given this, he suggests that the Lord's

---

73. Kalengyo, *Sacrifice in Hebrews*, 232.
74. Kalengyo, 1. See also Kalengyo, "Sacrifice of Christ," 304–9.
75. Kalengyo, "Understanding and Practice," 348. See also Kalengyo, "Sacrifice of Christ," 309–11.
76. Kalengyo, *Celebrating the Lord's Supper*, 47–99. See also Kalengyo, "Sacrifice of Christ," 311–18.
77. Kalengyo, "Sacrifice of Christ," 312–13; Kalengyo, *Celebrating the Lord's Supper*, 31–33, 38–39, 44.
78. Kalengyo, *Celebrating the Lord's Supper*, 47–52.
79. Kalengyo, 52–56.

Supper should be called *Ekitambiro eky'Okwebaza*, "a sacrifice of thanksgiving."[80] He also suggests that *ekyonziira*, the word for a traditional scapegoat sacrifice, should be used to convey the atoning aspect of Jesus's sacrifice.[81] Furthermore, Kalengyo notes that there is also a word for nonritual sacrifices that can be used to translate the concept of living sacrifice in Romans 12:1, but he does not explore this further.[82]

Envisaging the significance of Jesus's sacrifice in relation to Ganda sacrifice has important implications for celebrating the Lord's Supper. First, Kalengyo argues that locally available food and drink, such as banana bread and banana beer or wine,[83] should be presented by members of the congregation to show that "they are not merely called to participate in Christ's sacrifice, but also to continue it by offering the fruits of their labour to God."[84] Second, believing ancestors should be acknowledged during the prayers offered at the eucharistic celebration.[85] Third, Kalengyo suggests that the daily concerns of the people, such as well-being, protection, and healing, should be sought in the blood of Jesus, and one of the ways of doing this is by invoking the blood of Jesus in prayer.[86] Finally, just as sacrificial meals in Ganda culture included every clan member, so the Lord's Supper should include the members of God's extended family from other denominations.[87]

Like Ekem, Kalengyo gives a dialogical typological account of sacrifice. In line with inculturation theology, he understands the sacrifice of Christ as ending and fulfilling Ganda sacrifice. He also notes that there is a word for nonritual sacrifice, although he does not pursue this further because his focus is on the Lord's Supper. Furthermore, he emphasizes multiple aspects of sacrifice, including the notion of the gift, the communal meal, and the strong association in Ganda culture between sacrifice and life, especially well-being, protection, and healing. Finally, Kalengyo's main contribution is in the area of appropriation. Understanding Christ's sacrifice in terms of Ganda sacrifice suggests important ways in which Ganda Christians can celebrate the Lord's Supper in a more biblical and contextual way.

---

80. Kalengyo, 60.
81. Kalengyo, 60–61.
82. Kalengyo, 54.
83. Kalengyo, 66–73.
84. Kalengyo, 65.
85. Kalengyo, 75–81.
86. Kalengyo, 83–89.
87. Kalengyo, 91–99.

Women's Theology: Mercy Oduyoye

Third, we turn to the work of Mercy Oduyoye.[88] In one of her earliest papers, presented at the first Ecumenical Association of Third World Theologians (EATWOT) conference in Accra, Oduyoye highlights the theme of communal sacrifice. As she pointedly observes,

> African women have a traditional belief in the benefit of sacrifice for the community. Sacrifice, taken seriously, can lead to social reforms and to lifestyles that are less wasteful and more mindful of humanity's stewardship of life and ultimate dependence on the Source-Being. But I have difficulty understanding why it is the prerogative of only one sex to sacrifice for the community's well-being.[89]

In the same paper, she connects this notion of sacrifice with the doctrine of atonement. As she writes,

> In both African religion and Christianity, when life is sacrificed, when it is given back to God, it is made sacred and harmony is restored. This belief is embodied in the Christian doctrine of atonement. A fresh statement of this belief, which uses African ideas of sacrifice and covenants, will enable African religion to contribute to humankind's religious development.[90]

Sacrifice has been a recurring theme in her work ever since. Given that Baker and Green see their work as a response to feminist criticism of atonement theology, it is noteworthy that Oduyoye offers a carefully nuanced defense of the notion of sacrifice.

Oduyoye's work responds to both inculturation theology and liberation theology and draws on aspects of both in her attempt to give African women

---

88. Mercy Oduyoye is a Ghanaian Methodist theologian born in 1934 and is affectionately known as the grandmother of African Women's Theologies. She has been active in the World Council of Churches since 1966, serving as deputy general secretary from 1987 to 1994, and the Ecumenical Association of Third World Theologians (EATWOT) since 1977, serving as the president from 1996 to 2001. In 1989 she cofounded the Circle of Concerned African Women Theologians to give African women a voice in theological discussion. She is currently the director of the Institute of African Women in Religion and Culture at Trinity Theological Seminary in Legon, Accra, Ghana.

89. Mercy A. Oduyoye, "The Value of African Religious Beliefs and Practices for Christian Theology," in *African Theology en Route: Papers from the Pan-African Conference of Third World Theologians, December 17–23, 1977, Accra, Ghana*, eds. Kofi Appiah-Kubi and Sergio Torres (Maryknoll: Orbis, 1979), 112.

90. Oduyoye, "African Religious Beliefs," 113.

a voice in theological discussion. Her main starting point is her experience of the sacrifice of women in the African church, but she is also appreciative of the sacrifices that the missionaries made in their work.[91] As she writes, "The spirit of sacrifice and dedication found among workers in the missionary institutions was unique . . . it was this spirit that the African appreciated. The missionaries did not just preach sacrifice; they acted it out."[92] For Oduyoye, mission and sacrifice are closely connected. In her understanding of the church in mission, Christians are sent by Christ, which always means "forgoing one thing in order to undertake another."[93] Therefore, "Christians individually and corporately as the church are called to a life of sacrifice."[94] Nevertheless, she acknowledges that this takes on different forms in different times and places. For Oduyoye, African sacrificial beliefs and practices are fulfilled in the sacrifice of Christ. First, she examines ritual sacrifice in African Traditional Religion and self-sacrifice in African society to situate her discussion in its particular context.[95] Second, she examines the sacrifice of women in the African church. Third, she turns to the example of Christ in the Scriptures and its implications for the African church.

Oduyoye's story of sacrifice is set within a narrative of liberation: Since the fall, humans have found themselves in oppressive and dehumanizing situations. In order to be saved, they need to be liberated and formed into a new community. In Jewish and African cultures, God atoned for and reconciled people to each other by making covenants with them. Jesus proclaimed a new covenant in his blood at the Last Supper, forming a new community. The process of community building continues through participation in the sacraments, especially the Lord's Supper, and the sacrifice of the whole community of women and men.[96]

Like Kalengyo, Oduyoye sees the Lord's Supper as central to appropriating the sacrifice of Christ. As she observes, "From the perspective of Africa, an interpretation of the Eucharist that highlights the aspect of sacrifice is one that

---

91. Mercy A. Oduyoye, "Churchwomen and the Church's Mission," in *New Eyes for Reading: Biblical and Theological Reflections by Women from the Third World*, eds. John Pobee and Barbel von Wartenberg-Potter (Geneva: World Council of Churches, 1986), 68; Mercy A. Oduyoye, *Hearing and Knowing: Theological Reflections on Christianity in Africa* (Maryknoll: Orbis, 1986), 42.

92. Oduyoye, *Hearing and Knowing*, 42.

93. Oduyoye, "Churchwomen," 70.

94. Oduyoye, 70.

95. Oduyoye, 71.

96. Oduyoye, *Hearing and Knowing*, 70–119.

will touch people's spirituality in such a way as to affect their lives."[97] Oduyoye, however, goes further than Kalengyo in her discussion of Christian sacrifice. She observes that in African Traditional Religions, sacrifices are made in response to crises that could harm the community's life, which includes both stories of human sacrifice and practices of nonhuman sacrifice. In the former, "in dire circumstances human beings have been sacrificed to restore health, wholeness and safety to whole communities."[98] In the latter, "what is given up has no will of its own; yet the sacrifice is, or is expected to be, efficacious, because it represents the willingness of the human-offerers to 'give up' what they see as their possession in order to bring about more good."[99] There are also sacrifices of thanksgiving that cultivate the gift economy, unity, and identity within a group, all of which are essential for communal life. In traditional African society, the sacrifices of women are closely related to this notion of sacrifice for the community.[100] Nevertheless, Oduyoye distinguishes between making a sacrifice and being sacrificed. Many women are sacrificed against their will – in the home, in society, and even in the church – but there are also women who deliberately choose to give up their lives for others, making a "reasonable sacrifice" that can be characterized as "a process of 'self-emptying.'"[101] Oduyoye suggests that men and women are called to make this kind of sacrifice. As she argues,

> If the church can begin to function more effectively as an instrument of Christ, it must follow the sacrificial life of the woman. Not as the sacrificed, but as the one consciously and deliberately becoming a living sacrifice, taking up the cross voluntarily. In this way, it will be following its Lord, who dedicated his whole life to the announcement of the kingdom by word and deed.[102]

For Oduyoye, such a vision has important implications for the question of women's ministry and how the church practices hospitality.[103]

---

97. Oduyoye, 119.
98. Oduyoye, "Churchwomen," 71.
99. Oduyoye, 71.
100. Oduyoye, 72.
101. Oduyoye, 73.
102. Oduyoye, 79.
103. Oduyoye, 78–79. Mercy A. Oduyoye, *Introducing African Women's Theology* (Cleveland : Pilgrim, 2001), 90–109.

Like Ekem and Kalengyo, Oduyoye gives a dialogical typological account of sacrifice, but she explicitly makes women's experiences the starting point for her approach. She pays close attention to concepts of both ritual sacrifice and self-sacrifice in African cultures in order to discover how they have shaped the sacrificial lives of African women. Like Ekem and Kalengyo she emphasizes multiple aspects of sacrifice, including reconciliation, expiation, and the notion of the gift, and stresses that the goal of sacrifice is always the fullness of life. Oduyoye offers a carefully nuanced articulation of Christian sacrifice that involves both women and men and has direct consequences for the life of the church, especially women's ministry and Christian hospitality.

Conclusion

Baker and Green are yet to engage more deeply with African theologians. If they were to do so, it could lead to an important reassessment of their understanding of sacrifice, as well as their rather disparaging assessment of what African reflection on sacrifice can contribute to substantive theological issues. First, Baker and Green's metaphorical spiritualizing approach needs to become more typological if it is to do justice to the sheer diversity of sacrificial concepts in cultures worldwide. Ekem, Kalengyo, and Oduyoye's dialogical typological approaches avoid superimposing an essentialized and generalized notion of sacrifice on other systems of sacrifice, allowing the universal and the particular to be brought together in a way that enriches the sense of the Christian tradition. Second, Baker and Green focus primarily on ritual sacrifice in their understanding of the atonement and overlook the rich notions of self-sacrifice in Western and African cultures. Ekem, Kalengyo, and Oduyoye pay careful attention to both. Third, Baker and Green's reduction of sacrifice to moral self-giving ignores other themes that need to be explored in order to develop a fuller polythetic concept of sacrifice. Ekem, Kalengyo, and Oduyoye explore multiple themes, such as the gift, the communal meal, and reconciliation, which help to bring out further aspects of Christ's sacrifice. Fourth, Baker and Green strongly associate sacrifice with death, whereas Ekem, Kalengyo, and Oduyoye see it as the key to the fullness of life. Finally, Baker and Green's focus on understanding and articulation needs to be given a more ecclesial form. Intellectual comprehension is no substitute for liturgical and spiritual formation. For Ekem, "appropriability" is an important criterion when choosing how to translate biblical concepts of sacrifice into African languages. For Kalengyo, the contextual celebration of the Lord's Supper is where "the incarnate and risen Lord Jesus Christ meets with the Ganda and bestows the benefits of his sacrificial death to the faithful through faith."[104] For Oduyoye, "the Christ-event calls *both men and women* to the twin experience of cross and resurrection.... We risk sacrifice and cross, we struggle against evil and endure many scars, because armed with hope we already see life defeating death."[105] I hope that this "encounter" will encourage more engagement between Western and African theologians on the concept of sacrifice.

Bibliography

Arinze, Francis A. "Ibo Sacrifice as an Introduction to the Catechesis of Holy Mass." PhD diss., Urbaniana University, Rome, 1960.

———. *Sacrifice in Ibo Religion*. Ibadan: Ibadan University Press, 1970. https://archive.org/details/sacrificeinibore0000arin.

Auerbach, Erich. *Scenes from the Drama of European Literature: Six Essays*. New York: Meridian, 1959. http://archive.org/details/scenesfromdramao00auer.

Bailey, Daniel P. "Jesus as the Mercy Seat: The Semantics and Theology of Paul's Use of *Hilasterion* in Romans 3:25." PhD diss., University of Cambridge, 1999. https://doi.org/10.17863/CAM.17213.

Baker, Mark D. "Contextualizing the Scandal of the Cross." In *Proclaiming the Scandal of the Cross: Contemporary Images of Atonement*, edited by Mark D. Baker, 13–36. Grand Rapids: Baker Academic, 2006.

Baker, Mark D., and Joel B. Green. *Recovering the Scandal of the Cross: Atonement in New Testament and Contemporary Contexts*. Downers Grove: IVP, 2000.

———. *Recovering the Scandal of the Cross: Atonement in New Testament and Contemporary Contexts*. 2nd ed. Downers Grove: IVP Academic, 2011.

BBC News online. "General Election 2019: Labour and Tories Make Armistice Day Vows to Forces." Last modified 11 November 2019. https://www.bbc.com/news/election-2019-50369104.

Boersma, Hans. "The Disappearance of Punishment: Metaphors, Models and the Meaning of the Atonement." *Books and Culture: A Christian Review* (March/April 2003): 32–34, https://www.booksandculture.com/articles/2003/marapr/16.32.html.

Bourdillon, Michael C. F. "Introduction." In *Sacrifice*, edited by Michael C. F. Bourdillon and Meyer Fortes, 1–27. London: Academic, 1980.

Burton, John W. "Sacrifice: A Polythetic Class of Atuot Religious Thought." *Journal of Religion in Africa* 11, no. 2 (1980): 93–105. https://doi.org/10.2307/1581259.

Carter, Jeffrey, ed. *Understanding Religious Sacrifice: A Reader*. London: Continuum, 2003.

---

104. Kalengyo, "Sacrifice of Christ," 318.
105. Oduyoye, *African Women's Theology*, 118; emphasis added.

Cartledge, Mark J., and David A. Cheetham, eds. *Intercultural Theology: Approaches and Themes*. London: SCM, 2011.
Council of Trent. Session 22, "Doctrine Concerning the Sacrifice of the Mass." 17 September 1562. In *Canons and Decrees of the Council of Trent: Original Text with English Translation*, 144–49. Translated by Henry J. Schroeder. London: B. Herder Book Co., 1941.
Daniélou, Jean. *From Shadows to Reality: Studies in Biblical Typology of the Fathers*. London: Burns & Oates, 1960. http://archive.org/details/fromshadowstorea0000dani_b2k8.
Detienne, Marcel. "Culinary Practices and the Spirit of Sacrifice." In *The Cuisine of Sacrifice among the Ancient Greeks*, edited by Marcel Detienne and Jean-Pierre Vernant, 1–20. Translated by Paula Wissing. Chicago: University of Chicago Press, 1989.
Dodd, Charles H. "*Hilaskesthai*, Its Cognates, Derivatives, and Synonyms, in the Septuagint." *The Journal of Theological Studies* 32, no. 128 (1931): 352–60. https://doi.org/10.1093/jts/os-XXXII.128.352.
Ekem, John D. K. "A Dialogical Exegesis of Romans 3:25a." *Journal for the Study of the New Testament* 30, no. 1 (2007): 75–93. https://doi.org/10.1177/0142064X07081547.
———. *New Testament Concepts of Atonement in an African Pluralistic Setting*. Accra: SonLife Press, 2005.
Familusi, Olumuyiwa O. "Voluntary or Subtle Compulsion? An Ethical Context of Giving as Sacrifice in Contemporary Christianity." In *Sacrifice in Religious Traditions: Essays in Honour of Ven. Prof. J. Omosade Awolalu*, edited by Deji Ayegboyin and Adekunle O. Dada, 173–88. Ibadan: University of Ibadan, 2018.
Fox, Nikki, and Julian Sturdy. "Coronavirus: Essex GP with 'Textbook Symptoms' Dies." BBC News online. Last modified 27 March 2020. https://www.bbc.com/news/uk-england-essex-52040991.
Frei, Hans. *The Eclipse of Biblical Narrative: A Study in Eighteenth and Nineteenth Century Hermeneutics*. New Haven: Yale University Press, 1974.
Green, Joel B. "Kaleidoscopic View." In *The Nature of the Atonement: Four Views*, edited by James K. Beilby and Paul R. Eddy, 157–85. Downers Grove: InterVarsity, 2006.
———. "Must We Imagine the Atonement in Penal Substitutionary Terms? Questions, Caveats and a Plea." In *The Atonement Debate: Papers from the London Symposium on the Theology of Atonement*, edited by Derek Tidball, David Hilborn, and Justin Thacker, 153–71. Grand Rapids: Zondervan, 2008.
Hays, Richard B. *Reading Backwards: Figural Christology and the Fourfold Gospel Witness*. Waco: Baylor University Press, 2014.
de Heusch, Luc. *Sacrifice in Africa: A Structuralist Approach*. Translated by Linda O'Brien and Alice Morton. Manchester: Manchester University Press, 1985.
Jeffrey, Steve, Mike Ovey, and Andrew Sach. *Pierced for Our Transgressions: Rediscovering the Glory of Penal Substitution*. Nottingham: Inter-Varsity, 2007.

Kalengyo, Edison M. *Celebrating the Lord's Supper: Ending the Eucharistic Famine.* Carlisle: HippoBooks, 2018.

———. *Sacrifice in Hebrews and the Pauline Epistles.* Nairobi: Acton, 2015.

———. "The Sacrifice of Christ and Ganda Sacrifice: A Contextual Interpretation in Relation to the Eucharist." In *The Epistle to the Hebrews and Christian Theology*, edited by Richard Bauckham, 302–18. Grand Rapids: Eerdmans, 2009.

———. "The Understanding and Practice of Sacrifice among the Ganda." In *Sacrifice in Religious Traditions: Essays in Honour of Ven. Prof. J. Omosade Awolalu*, edited by Deji Ayegboyin and Adekunle O. Dada, 315–51. Ibadan: University of Ibadan, 2018.

Katongole, Emmanuel. *The Sacrifice of Africa: A Political Theology for Africa.* Grand Rapids: Eerdmans, 2011.

Kwenda, Stanley. "Sadio Mane: Liverpool Players Have to 'Sacrifice' Themselves to Win Title." BBC Sport. Last modified 27 December 2019. https://www.bbc.com/sport/football/50920736.

Lakoff, George, and Mark Johnson. *Metaphors We Live By.* Chicago: University of Chicago Press, 1980.

Luther, Martin. "First Sunday after Epiphany." In *Luther's Epistle Sermons.* Vol. 2, *Epiphany, Easter and Pentecost*, translated by John N. Lenker, 7–19. Vol. 8 of *The Precious and Sacred Writings of Martin Luther*, edited by John N. Lenker. Minneapolis: Luther Press, 1909. https://archive.org/details/precioussacredwr08luth.

McClymond, Kathryn. *Beyond Sacred Violence: A Comparative Study of Sacrifice.* Baltimore: Johns Hopkins University Press, 2008.

Milbank, John. "Stories of Sacrifice: From Wellhausen to Girard." *Theory, Culture & Society* 12, no. 4 (Nov. 1995): 15–46.

Morris, Leon. "The Use of *Hilaskesthai* etc. in Biblical Greek." *The Expository Times* 62, no. 8 (1951): 227–33.

Needham, Rodney. "Polythetic Classification: Convergence and Consequences." *Man* 10, no. 3 (Sep. 1975): 349–69. https://doi.org/10.2307/2799807.

Nelson-Adjakpey, Ted. "Penance and Expiatory Sacrifice among the Ghanaian-Ewe and Their Relevance to the Christian Religion." PhD diss., Urbaniana University, Rome, 1982.

Ngewa, Samuel. "The Biblical Idea of Substitution versus the Idea of Substitution in African Traditional Sacrifices: A Case Study of Hermeneutics for African Christian Theology." PhD diss., Westminster Theological Seminary, 1987.

Nicole, Roger. "C. H. Dodd and the Doctrine of Propitiation." *Westminster Theological Journal* 17, no. 2 (1955): 117–57.

Oduyoye, Mercy A. "Churchwomen and the Church's Mission." In *New Eyes for Reading: Biblical and Theological Reflections by Women from the Third World*, edited by John Pobee and Barbel von Wartenberg-Potter, 68–80. Geneva: World Council of Churches, 1986. https://archive.org/details/neweyesforreadin00john.

———. *Hearing and Knowing: Theological Reflections on Christianity in Africa.* Maryknoll: Orbis, 1986. https://archive.org/details/hearingknowingth0000oduy.

———. *Introducing African Women's Theology.* Cleveland: Pilgrim, 2001. https://archive.org/details/introducingafric0000oduy.

———. "The Value of African Religious Beliefs and Practices for Christian Theology." In *African Theology en Route: Papers from the Pan-African Conference of Third World Theologians, December 17–23, 1977, Accra, Ghana,* edited by Kofi Appiah-Kubi and Sergio Torres, 109–16. Maryknoll: Orbis, 1979. https://archive.org/details/africantheologye0000pana.

Rogerson, John W. "Sacrifice in the Old Testament: Problems of Method and Approach." In *Sacrifice,* ed. Michael F. C. Bourdillon and Meyer Fortes, 45–59. London: Academic, 1980.

Sawyerr, Harry. "Sacrifice." In *Biblical Revelation and African Beliefs,* edited by Kwesi A. Dickson and Paul Ellingworth, 57–82. London: Lutterworth, 1969. https://archive.org/details/biblicalrevelati0000unse_l4g2.

Schreiner, Thomas R. "Penal Substitution View." In *The Nature of the Atonement: Four Views,* edited by James K. Beilby and Paul R. Eddy, 67–98. Downers Grove: InterVarsity, 2006.

Sipuka, Sithembele. "The Sacrifice of the Mass and the Concept of Sacrifice among the Xhosa: Towards an Inculturated Understanding of the Eucharist." ThD diss., University of South Africa, 2000. http://hdl.handle.net/10500/16045.

Sykes, Stephen W. "Sacrifice in the New Testament and Christian Theology." In *Sacrifice,* edited by Michael F. C. Bourdillon and Meyer Fortes, 60–83. London: Academic, 1980.

Ukpong, Justin S. *Sacrifice, African and Biblical: A Comparative Study of Ibibio and Levitical Sacrifices.* Rome: Urbaniana University Press, 1987.

Vanhoozer, Kevin J. "The Atonement in Postmodernity: Guilt, Goats and Gifts." In *The Glory of the Atonement: Biblical, Historical and Practical Perspectives,* edited by Charles E. Hill and Frank A. James III, 367–404. Downers Grove: IVP Academic, 2004.

Wellhausen, Julius. *Prolegomena to the History of Israel.* Translated by J. Sutherland Black and Allan Menzies. Edinburgh: A&C Black, 1885.

Williams, Garry. "Penal Substitution: A Response to Recent Criticisms." In *The Atonement Debate: Papers from the London Symposium on the Theology of Atonement,* edited by Derek Tidball, David Hilborn, and Justin Thacker, 172–91. Grand Rapids: Zondervan, 2008.

11

Critical Analysis of the Doctrine of Adoption through the Honor and Shame Paradigm

An African Perspective

Kenosi Molato

Researcher at SHINE Africa Project, Gaborone, Botswana

Abstract

The doctrine of adoption is central to Calvinistic soteriology in the so-called "order of salvation." However, in Calvinistic churches in Africa the doctrine is mostly presented using legal metaphors which represent Western legal aspects of salvation. This neglects the way in which the concept of adoption is usually perceived in African ways of life. Though African culture is understood as involving honor and shame, those who have tackled the doctrine of adoption from an African perspective have neglected this important aspect, which is found at the heart of the doctrine of adoption in both the Pauline letters and African cosmology. This chapter reconstructs the doctrine of adoption, taking it from the Western perspective to look at it through the lens of African honor and shame. It engages with the biblical text that formulates the doctrine of adoption, and demonstrates how Western perspectives have shaped the understanding of this doctrine. Furthermore, it shows how this doctrine should be applied in the African context borrowing from the communal aspects of the African honor and shame cultural paradigm.

Key words: doctrine of adoption, honor-shame, guilt-innocence, cultural paradigm, communal cultures, kinship fostering, Western cultures

Introduction

The notable Kenyan theologian Andrew Mbuvi once said that African theology has been struggling to find the appropriate means to speak conspicuously in African accents to address the pertinent needs of African churches.[1] This suggests that the African church has been, and is still, speaking with foreign accents to address African maladies. By using foreign accents the African theology practitioner is teasing African issues rather than addressing them. It might be perceived that African problems are being addressed, but in reality the problems remain like gangrene, eating away from the inside. The question is, how should African theology speak with an accent which addresses African churches? Most answers given to this question tend to lean toward identifying African religious practices and then proposing that the church should adhere to African Traditional Religions. It is therefore incumbent upon African theologians to seek ways to articulate African theology in a way that African people can grasp. The purpose of this chapter is to propose a theoretical framework by which to explain the doctrine of adoption from an African cultural paradigm perspective, thereby deconstructing the Western cultural perspective. This chapter chooses to use an honor-shame cultural paradigm to both speak with accents of soteriology which resonate with sub-Saharan people, and engage with the doctrine of adoption.

This chapter has the following structure: first, definitions of the doctrine of adoption which have been raised over the years are presented. Second, the sub-Saharan cultural paradigm of honor-shame is presented as a framework for studying theology in an African environment. Third, the African community is outlined in relation to how the concept of adoption is perceived in African societies. Fourth, an evaluation of the Greco-Roman culture's view of adoption is presented. Fifth, the apostle Paul's usage of the expression *huiothesia* in Galatians 4:5 and Romans 8:15, 23 is discussed. The chapter then provides a concluding analysis with the major findings of this research.

---

1. Andrew Mbuvi, "African Theology from the Perspective of Honor and Shame," in *The Urban Face of Mission: Ministering the Gospel in a Diverse and Changing World*, eds. Harvie M. Conn, Manuel Ortiz, and Susan S. Baker (Phillipsburg: P&R, 2002), 279–95.

Toward a Definition of the Doctrine of Adoption

Canadian New Testament scholar and Catholic priest Peter Hugh Davids, in an article published in the *Evangelical Dictionary of Theology*, states that the term "adoption" is "relatively infrequent in the Scriptures." The doctrine often occurs in Old Testament literature in conceptual form, but it is not fully developed. As such, the term "adoption" and the doctrine of adoption as it is known in the twenty-first century – with an emphasis on the legal metaphor – does not appear in the Old Testament.[2] Furthermore, Davids argues that the concept of adoption does not appear in the nation of Israel, and the provision of adoption is not presented in the Levitical laws and codes. Trevor Burke supports Davids in that he points out that the concept of adoption as presently understood does not appear in the Jewish literature, nor in the LXX.[3] However, there are some examples which resemble the doctrine of adoption as understood today. Scriptures such as Genesis 15:1–4 undergird the consciousness of adoption for Israel as a whole, bringing the idea that God had chosen them, therefore implying that they are God's children.[4] This sense of adoption appears in Psalm 2:7; 89:27; and 2 Samuel 7:14, and thus seems also to form the base of the New Testament concept on which Paul builds his theology. Though Davids and other scholars argue that the doctrine of adoption is infrequent in the Old Testament, they also affirm that the significance of this doctrine cannot be ignored in Christian theology.

Systematic theologian Millard Erickson argues that the doctrine of adoption signifies the means whereby a believer is transferred from a status of alienation from God to a position of acceptance and favor with God.[5] The undergirding principle, which is pivotal in Erickson's use of the concept of status, moves away from a legal metaphor to emphasize position. Church historians Mark Jones and Joel Beeke point out that the doctrine of adoption is more developed now in the twenty-first century than it was in the sixteenth century, when several Puritan theologians, such as William Perkins, William Ames, Thomas Watson, and Herman Witsius, contributed to its understanding.[6] This implies that the later development of the doctrine and the framework in which it is used have

---

2. P. H. Davids, "Adoption," in *Evangelical Dictionary of Theology*, ed. Walter A. Elwell (Grand Rapids: Baker Academic, 2004), 25–26.

3. Trevor Burke, "Pauline Adoption: A Sociological Approach," *The Evangelical Quarterly* 73, no. 2 (2001): 119–34.

4. Davids, "Adoption," 25–26.

5. Millard J. Erickson, *Christian Theology* (Grand Rapids: Baker Academic, 2012), 961.

6. Joel R. Beeke and Mark Jones, *A Puritan Theology: Doctrine for Life* (Grand Rapids: Reformation Heritage, 2012), 537.

been influenced by modern developments in secular societies. William Perkins, for example, stated:

> the childe or heir of any earthly Prince [since] the son of the greatest Potentate may be the child of wrath: but the child of God by grace, hath Christ Jesus to bee his eldest brother, with whom he is fellow heir in heaven; he hath the holy Ghost also for his comforter, and the kingdom of heaven for his everlasting inheritance.[7]

Perkins's definition is grounded upon the privileges that come with adoption into God's family. Furthermore, John Murray adds to the above definition, stating that "by adoption the redeemed become sons and daughters of the Lord God almighty; they are introduced into and given the privileges of God's family."[8] The key phrase in Murray's definition is "the redeemed become sons and daughters." This phrase combines the idea of justification with that of the transformation of sinners to be accepted and placed in the position of children of God. As such, at the center of adoption are multiple actions of God taking place at once, such that to separate these actions would do injustice to the whole activity of God in salvation. This separation of the actions has led some within Reformed theology to conflate the doctrine of justification with that of adoption in the sense that justification is perceived as a public declaration or announcement.[9] In this way, justification and adoption are both understood as the event of the announcement of the honorable status in entering the family of believers.[10]

Current African Scholarship on the Honor-Shame Cultural Paradigm in Sub-Saharan Africa

Former Cambridge University Professor of African History John Iliffe published one of the most important works on honor and shame with regard to sub-Saharan Africa.[11] He covers various honor concepts in different African

---

7. Quoted in John Murray, *Redemption Accomplished and Applied* (Carlisle: Banner of Truth, 1979), 6.

8. Murray, *Redemption*, 6.

9. Murray, 6.

10. Abraham Kuyper, *The Work of the Holy Spirit* (Spain: Hard Press Publishing, 2012), 367–68.

11. John Iliffe, *Honour in African History* (Cambridge: Cambridge University Press, 2005), 1.

genres, including poems and songs. He came across the idea of honor and shame when trying to understand Christianity in the kingdom of Buganda on the northern shore of Lake Victoria,[12] noting that even though the people were fiercely persecuted, they endured without resistance, yet quarreled among themselves and took pleasure in the sufferings of their enemies.[13] His colleague Michael Twaddle then suggested that he should study the heroic behavior of the ancient Greeks in order to understand the behavior of the people of Buganda.[14] Iliffe states that through his study he found similarities between the Greeks and the people of Buganda.[15]

Iliffe's book builds on the work done on honor and shame in sub-Saharan Africa by Boubakar Ly in his doctoral thesis. This work approaches honor and shame from a sociological point of view.[16] Though his thesis is fundamental for the study of honor and shame in sub-Saharan Africa, it has not been published in book form. In this dissertation, Ly laments the lack of publications about honor and shame in sub-Saharan Africa and urges his fellow Africans to carry out research into honor and shame in their societies. Catherine Ver Eecke built on Ly's work, focusing on the Fulani ethnic group.[17] She argues that the social interactions of the Fulani are driven by a strong sense of shame, respect for aloofness, and a desire for domination.[18] She writes, "They are sensitive to shame to the extent of avoiding any individual assertiveness even while going to great lengths of asserting their collective ability to rule."[19] Lund responded to Ly's plea by studying the question of honor in property disputes and brokerage in Burkina Faso.[20] In this study, Lund investigates the conflict over land in Burkina Faso. He notes that when people are fighting over land, they will go to the extent of paying bribes of greater worth than the value of the land itself in order to get the land.[21] He mentions a parallel situation in Tanzania whereby

---

12. Iliffe, *Honour in African History*, 1.
13. Iliffe, 1.
14. Iliffe, 1.
15. Iliffe, 1.
16. Boubakar Ly, *L'honneur et les valeurs morales dans les sociétés Ouolof et Toucouleur du Sénégal* (Paris: Université de Paris, 1967), 39.
17. Catherine Ver Eecke, "Pulaaku: Adamawa Fulbe Identity and Its Transformation" (diss., University of Pennsylvania, 1988).
18. Ver Eecke, "Pulaaku," 8.
19. Ver Eecke, 1.
20. Christian Lund, "A Question of Honour: Property Disputes and Brokerage in Burkina Faso," *Africa* 69, no. 4 (1999): 576.
21. Lund, "Question of Honour," 575.

"people's litigation costs bore no relation to the value of the disputed land."[22] Lund argues that these seemingly irrational scenarios can be perceived as rational only through the lens of the local meaning of honor.[23]

Mahlangu is one of the first scholars to engage the concepts of honor and shame from a biblical studies perspective.[24] Mahlangu uses the Mediterranean cultural concepts of honor and shame as a hermeneutical lens for comparing the honor and shame cultural values of the African community. She concludes, "The African view of honor and shame could be an interpretative tool which . . . the ordinary African reader of the biblical text could employ. The need of such a paradigm is strongly felt in modern times."[25] Building on the biblical studies perspective on honor and shame, Mbuvi, an African Bible scholar, uses honor and shame hermeneutics in reading the book of Job.[26] He argues that the book of Job goes beyond the so-called wisdom of daily life to the reality of putting God's honor at the center of Job's struggle.[27] In the same way, Congolese Bible scholar Rukundwa uses honor and shame hermeneutics in interpreting the book of Matthew and analyses the commitment of the Banyamulenge Christian in light of the honor and shame cultural paradigm.[28]

From a theological perspective, one of the first works to engage with the concept of honor and shame was the work of Joseph Ochola-Omolo, titled *Reconciliation in an African Concept: Paul's Theology of Reconciliation – Engaging Honour and Shame Cultural Elements among the Gusii, Luhya, and Luo people of Kenya*.[29] The objective of Ochola-Omolo's work was to engage with theological discourse in a cultural setting which is dominated by the concept of honor and shame.[30] Mbuvi also developed African theology from an honor and shame perspective. He argues for what he calls "contact

---

22. Lund, 575.

23. Lund, 575.

24. Ellen Mahlangu, "The Ancient Mediterranean Values of Honour and Shame as a Hermeneutical Procedure: A Social-Scientific Criticism in an African Perspective," *Verbum et Ecclesia* 22, no. 1 (2001): 85–101.

25. Mahlangu, "Ancient Mediterranean Values," 99–100.

26. Andrew Mbuvi, "The Ancient Mediterranean Values of 'Honour and Shame' as a Hermeneutical Lens of Reading the Book of Job," *Old Testament Essays* 23, no. 3 (2010): 752.

27. Mbuvi, "Ancient Mediterranean Values," 752.

28. S. L. Rukundwa, "The Banyamulenge people: Their angst, honour and shame in the light of the Matthean Community," *HTS* 60, no 2 (2004): 285–409.

29. Joseph Ochola-Omolo, *Reconciliation in an African Context: Paul's Theology of Reconciliation – Engaging Honour and Shame Cultural Elements among the Gusii, Luhya and Luo People of Western Kenya* (Nairobi: Uzima Publishing, 2008).

30. Ochola-Omolo, *Reconciliation*, 8.

theology."³¹ In this theology, the African theology practitioner avoids using Western theology, instead using biblical theology and the African culture in comparative analyses.³² By doing so, the theology practitioner demonstrates that the African culture is close to the Hebrew culture in which the Bible was written.³³ Mbuvi then demonstrates that the Hebrew culture is a shame and honor-oriented culture, similar to African societies.³⁴ Martin Munyao builds from contact theology in that he recognizes that the language of honor and shame pervades both Bible and African societies.³⁵ Moreover, he advances contact theology by developing a contextual theology of honor and shame in which he explores Kenyan Baptist theology for missional praxis.

Kenosi Molato and Sandra Freeman realized the importance of honor and shame in discipleship, publishing a devotional discipleship book addressing the concept of honor-shame.³⁶ They devote the first half of the book to addressing the question of who God is. They argue that the concept of "who God is" is crucial in discipleship, especially in honor-shame cultures.

The Background of Adoption in African Societies

The key identity marker of honor-shame communities is that they are societies that value a community lifestyle rather than individualism. Thus, everything in the African community is executed in a way that will foster the community members' bond. For example, when a marriage occurs in the community, it is not only for the couple but is perceived as joining two families together. In this way, a representative family's honor is considered and upheld. The young woman getting married is warned by her uncle never to bring the reputation and honor of their name to the ground (soil), defiling it in the community. The young man is informed that from now on, he has a family on his spouse's side; therefore, he is encouraged to maintain the honor of being a man. From a young age, it is instilled in him that he should provide for his family, and failure to do so will bring shame to the family name. Writing about the Basotho traditions

---

31. Mbuvi, "African Theology," 279.
32. Mbuvi, 281.
33. Mbuvi, 283.
34. Mbuvi, 287.
35. Martin Munyao, "Linking Ancient Mediterranean with Contemporary Kenyan Pivotal Values of Honor-Shame: A Missional Appraisal of Baptist Theology in Kenya through Honor-Shame Lenses" (PhD diss., Concordia Seminary, 2017).
36. Kenosi Molato and S. E. Freeman, *Highest Honor: 60 Days toward Honoring God with Your Whole Life* (Nairobi: CLC Kenya, 2018).

in southern Africa, Keketso Sepere notes that if a man fails to provide for his family and the people under his care, he will fall under public condemnation.[37] In this case, Sepere uses honor-shame rhetoric by emphasizing the term "public condemnation," in the sense that public condemnation brings shame to the man who fails to provide for his family. This drives him to be an honorable man who protects the honor of his masculinity by taking care of his family.

In the Setswana cultural tradition in southern Africa, a man who lacks resources to provide for his family will often be given some cows (mafisa) to feed his family.[38] This is so that the family's honor will be maintained, as it is shameful for a man and his family if he cannot provide for them. Thus, there is a strong kinship bond which ties the community together. It is also tied to the blood of the culture, which must be maintained and kept pure. At the center of these ties is the web of honor-shame, which controls and guides the community.

In relation to the concept of adoption, Judith Gibbons argues that the practice of adoption differs in Western societies from what takes place in traditional African communities, as seen in child-sharing, child circulation, and kinship fostering.[39] This kind of child-rearing or fostering revolves around the family relationship. Therefore, a phrase like "kinship care," according to Tumani Malinga and Poloko Ntshwarang, refers to "the full-time nurturing and protection of children who must be separated from their parents by relatives, members of their tribes, clans, godparents, step-parents or other adults who have a kinship bond with a child."[40] This kind of childcare represents the idea of adoption which is often used in Western culture. However, given the family ties and the responsibilities of the family members toward other members of the group, the concept of a child being taken by nonfamily members is unusual in African societies. The honor of the family must be preserved; thus for someone to leave his or her family to be taken by outsiders brings shame to the family lineage. African culture emphasizes a strong connection with the ancestors,

---

37. Keketso Christina Sepere, "The Impact of Western Culture on the Basotho Family Structure and the Erosion of African Values in Lesotho," in *Law, Religion and the Family in Africa*, eds. M. Christian Green and Faith Kabata (Stellenbosch: African Sun Media, 2021), 43.

38. Sepere, "Impact of Western Culture," 39.

39. Judith Gibbons, "Adoption and Fostering: Traditional and Contemporary Child Welfare Strategies in Sub-Saharan Africa" (2013), 2–6, https://www.researchgate.net/publication/256835417_Adoption_and_fostering_Traditional_and_contemporary_child_welfare_strategies_in_Sub-Saharan_Africa.

40. Tumani Malinga and Poloko N. Ntshwarang, "Alternative Care for Children in Botswana: A Reality or Idealism?" (2011), https://ejournals.bib.uni-wuppertal.de/index.php/sws/article/view/277/593.

and the ancestors will torment such a family for generations until the child is brought back into the family. The shame of being tormented by the ancestors promotes the idea of child fostering in African societies.

Moreover, in African society, when a child is "adopted" by his or her uncle to be taken care of, the child does not assume a new status of honor since he or she already possesses the family's status. In this way, the family's honor is maintained and magnified by other family groups so that they can see that the family can take care of their family members. Consequently, because of the honor-shame worldview in the background, African societies have a strong desire to eradicate Western-style adoption, for it brings shame on the family name. If we imagine a hypothetical case of another family adopting a child, that child will be forced to speak highly about his or her former family's honor, to avoid shaming the family of origin. In this way, there will be an honor conflict that brings pain to the child, because the child knows he or she cannot turn his or her back on the ancestral honor connected to the biological family.

Ethical issues concerning religious allegiance are also crucial in analyzing the concept of adoption in African societies. Unlike the Western form of adoption, in African cultures a child who is moved from one family to another does not need to learn a new religious orientation because the way of life and religious orientation are the same in every community. In African societies, an adopted child is not given to faraway family members; instead, an uncle will adopt and raise the child. In this way, the honor of the family is preserved and enhanced by the continuity from one generation to another. Priscilla Gerrand argues that the imposition of the Western concept on African societies has not been well received. The adopters tend to be secretive about the adoption because they do not want to expose the adopted child to public ridicule.[41] This highlights the honor-shame framework in relation to adoption in sub-Saharan communities. A foreign adopter coming into an African society with a Western understanding of adoption might see it as a way of transforming the society by a humanitarian act. But, in reality, it exposes children to a form of shame. Moreover, it can be hard for such children to recover from the shame, because they are exposed to public condemnation and are forever reminded of their biological family's failure to take care of them.

---

41. Priscilla Gerrand, "An African Community's Attitude towards Modern, Western Adoption" (Master's diss., Rand Afrikaans University, 1997), 1.

A Critical Evaluation of the Western Analysis of Adoption in Theological Studies

The Western model of adoption is usually used as the main metaphor in explaining the doctrine of adoption in African churches, to the extent that, whenever this metaphor is challenged, it is perceived as a challenge to the concept of adoption as outlined by the apostle Paul.[42] Trevor Burke argues that the metaphor used in Western society to envisage or explain the doctrine of adoption in fact differs from the metaphor Paul used to articulate the doctrine of adoption in the first century. As such, this chapter argues that a metaphor of a concept is not the ultimate truth but rather a framework used to depict aspects of that truth. However, some take the metaphor as the ultimate truth, such that if someone points out a loophole in the metaphor, that person is considered a heretic who has abandoned orthodoxy or the evangelical tradition. Theologian Colin Gunton argues that "biblical metaphors are an imaginative expression of the human experience of the world rather than . . . a means by which we speak about the reality of God."[43] As such, the Western metaphor of adoption, outlined below, has been formulated through human experience in Western society to express the doctrine of adoption in the Western context. Therefore, this Western expression should not be perceived as the only accent in which the soteriological aspect of adoption can be expressed, for by doing so the theology practitioner will be robbing non-Westerners of the opportunity to fully grasp and apply this doctrine in their own context, such as in African societies.

Western theology emerges from the guilt-innocence cultural paradigm, which has less emphasis on family orientation but focuses attention on individualism. As such, the concepts of individualism in salvation are common. As already demonstrated, such emphases make the concept of adoption different from that in African societies and from Greco-Roman culture, as the next section will show. Moreover, the legal aspect is one of the central emphases of the doctrine of adoption in the Western theological enterprise. A critique of this legal aspect was made by Nathan Vigil, who argues that legal aspects of the doctrine of adoption in Western theology are derived from the secular notion of adoption; therefore, they do not represent the biblical concept of adoption.[44]

---

42. Christopher Flanders, *About Face: Rethinking Face for 21st Century Mission* (Eugene: Pickwick, 2011), 218.

43. Colin E. Gunton, *The Actuality of Atonement: A Study of Metaphor, Rationality and the Christian Tradition* (Grand Rapids: Eerdmans, 1988), 42.

44. Nathan Vigil, "The Conflicted Theological Construct of Adoption," *Affirmation & Critique* 7, no. 2 (2002), 124.

The Background to Paul's Doctrine of Adoption

Burke argues that adoption in the first century was practiced around the concept of the family. As such, adoption could occur only within the framework of kinship.[45] Family within the Roman structure was considered the bedrock of society. Any individual honor was derived from and enjoyed within the family. Subsequently, there was a fear of having no family. To be cut out of the family structure was equivalent to death. Judge argues that the context of family in the first century was greater than how a family is understood in the twenty-first century.[46] Judge points out the family in Roman times encompassed (1) the nuclear family, (2) wife and husband, (3) unmarried children, (4) slaves, (5) freedmen, and (6) foster children.[47]

The family structure revolved around the *paterfamilias* (head of the family). It was mainly within this context that adoption from the outside might occur. This was based on the fear that when the head of the family had no son, there would be no one to lead the family. Thus, adoption was a means for the family to look for someone to be the head of the family. Therefore, the family might look outside the boundaries of the family for someone with leadership abilities. Burke argues that this was the main reason why adoption occurred in Greco-Roman society.[48] This also suggests that adoption in that context was not usually like that of the twenty-first century, whereby children are relieved from poverty because their biological family cannot provide for them. Adoption in the first century was not a humanitarian act.

Furthermore, Crook argues that in Greco-Roman societies, adoption was practiced in relation to religious orientation in the sense that it was called upon when a family lacked an heir who could lead the family cult.[49] Adoption of this nature implies that the person who was to be adopted had to be an older person who knew the nitty-gritty of leading a religious cult.

Burke argues that in Greco-Roman culture, certain procedures needed to be adhered to for the adoption to occur. These procedures depended upon the honor and status that the adopter held in the community. As such, based on the honor-shame web that controlled Greco-Roman societies, the people made sure that it was not just anyone who could adopt but someone who had

---

45. Burke, "Pauline Adoption," 119–34.
46. E. A. Judge, *The Social Pattern of Christian Groups in the First Century* (London: Tyndale, 1960), 30–32.
47. Judge, *Social Pattern*, 30–32.
48. Burke, "Pauline Adoption," 122.
49. J. A. Crook, *Law and Life of Rome* (London: Thames & Hudson, 1967), 7.

the means and the ability to do so. The first procedure was known as *abrogatio*. Burke writes, "In such cases, a preliminary investigation was carried out to ensure the suitability of the family interested in adopting as well as the security of the family about to lose a member."[50] The second procedure was known as *adoptio*. In this procedure, a son who was still under the guidance of the head of the family was placed on sale in the role of the adoptee.[51] Then the son would be released back into the hands of his biological family or the head of the family. Upon his third release the son would be fully accepted into the new family under the headship of the *paterfamilias*.[52]

Three main ideas resurface around the issue of adoption in Greco-Roman culture: (1) Adoption was a religious concept linked with the running of the family cult. (2) The adopter was supposed to be a person with honor and status in the community. Thus, cultural notions of honor and shame set the background to adoption. (3) Those who were adopted were often older people who had the capability to lead the cult. As such, this again differs from the modern-day kind of adoption which is done as a humanitarian act.

Moreover, adoption brought a radical change to the person who was adopted. It brought a new way of life, and the person acquired a new state of honor in the community. As such, the person who was adopted was of equal status with a biological son. Lyall notes:

> The profound truth of Roman Adoption was that the adoptee was taken out of his previous state and was placed in a new relationship of a son to his father, his new *paterfamilias*. All his old debts were cancelled, and in effect, the adoptee started a new life as part of his new family. From that time on, the *paterfamilias* had the same control over his new "child" as he had over his natural offspring.[53]

Paul's Usage of *Huiothesia*

In Paul's writings in Galatians 4:5 and Romans 8:15, 23 he uses the expression *huiothesia*, which is interpreted as "adoption." Burke argues that this expression is unique to Pauline usage and does not appear in the biblical data except in

---

50. Burke, "Pauline Adoption," 123.
51. Burke, 123.
52. Burke, 123.
53. Francis Lyall, "Roman Law in the Writings of Paul: Adoption," *Journal of Biblical Literature* 88, no. 4 (1969): 458–66.

Paul's letter.⁵⁴ Vine, in his famous dictionary, states that the word *huiothesia* is a compound word made of two words, namely *huis*, translated as son, and *thesis*, translated as "a placing."⁵⁵ Nigel Tomes presents a survey of the New Testament translations of the occurrences of *huiothesia* which shows that the vast majority – 90 percent – of translators translate it as "adoption" or "adopted as sons." The question then is, why do the vast majority of translators translate *huiothesia* as "adoption" if the term does not refer to adoption? Is it because the Western concept of adoption has influenced the interpreters to use a familiar metaphor in interpreting this concept? Vine argues, "Adoption (*huiothesia*) is a term involving the dignity of the relationship as a son; it is not putting into the family by spiritual birth, but a putting into the position of sons."⁵⁶ Vine's definition does not follow the route of the Western adoption motif but instead emphasizes the honor or status of adoption. In this way, Vine also does not follow the regeneration formula which is common in the Western metaphor. He perceives the honor-shame worldview which influenced the apostle Paul's usage of the term *huiothesia*. Moreover, other scholars, such as Nathan Vigil, have heavily criticized the idea that God adopts sinners into his family, stating that "the concept that God brings sinners into His family by means of a legal transaction parallel to the human practice of adoption is not found in the Scriptures and is contrary to the Bible's revelation concerning our divine sonship. . . . [It is] imposing this erroneous theological construct upon the Scriptures."⁵⁷ In this line of thought, Vigil separates the Pauline thought of *huiothesia* from what is commonly referred to as the doctrine of adoption today. He points out that the latter is influenced by the legal metaphor of adoption practiced in Western culture. In this way, Vigil comes close to what the apostle Paul presents when he uses the term *huiothesia*.

However, Nathan Vigil and William Lee take the Pauline concept of *huiothesia* to an extreme by arguing that this term refers to a "coming of age" or "maturing to sonship."⁵⁸ In their view, the doctrine of adoption included the concept of coming of age in the sense that a son would not enjoy the full rights of adoption until he reached maturity; only when he was mature would

---

54. Burke, "Pauline Adoption," 119.
55. W. E. Vine, *Vine's Complete Expository Dictionary of Old and New Testament Words* (London: Thomas Nelson, 1970), 13.
56. Vine, *Complete Expository Dictionary*, 13.
57. Vigil, "Conflicted Theological Construct," 124.
58. William Lee, *Life Study of Romans* (Anaheim: Living Stream Publisher, 1984), 224.

he be able to enjoy the full rights of a son.[59] Nigil Tomes, who has written a major critique of both Nathan Vigil and William Lee, argues that their view has significant implications, such as that Christians cannot enjoy the full benefits of their salvation until they reach a certain form of maturity.[60] However, what this form of maturity is neither Nathan Vigil nor William Lee clearly outline. Consequently, it is left to Christians to figure out if they have reached the level of maturity.

Therefore, this chapter argues that the Western understanding of the doctrine of adoption, which emphasizes the legal aspects borrowed from a secular concept of adoption, needs to be reconstructed, as the metaphor used is not cross-cultural, and neither does it tally with the Pauline usage of the term *huiothesia*. As such, the metaphor employed by the Western doctrine of adoption fails to be contextualized in cultures such as in Africa, which are built upon the framework of honor and shame.

The Pauline term *huiothesia* is an honor term, thereby emphasizing the state of honor which believers have in Christ. It is a place or sphere of dignity, a position in which believers are dignified to appropriate their privileges in Christ. Rather than it being a place of maturing to sonship, believers are placed in this position because of their allegiance to Christ. In this way, the shame orientation that believers in African societies experience is dealt with. The doctrine of adoption within an honor-shame framework means being placed in the sonship of Christ, which is a place of the highest honor; thus the shame of sin and the experience of shame no longer have a hold on believers because they are accepted into this place of honor. They are identified with Christ and are one with him in his honorable state. Consequently, presenting this line of thought on the doctrine of adoption unhitches it from the secular notions of legal frameworks and makes it tally with the honor-shame communities of sub-Saharan Africa. Furthermore, this accent of the soteriology of adoption is grounded upon the Pauline understanding, and it is also contextual in the sense that it links the Pauline term *huiothesia* with the African culture of honor. In this way, the Western notion of adoption does not play a mediatory role in linking Paul with African culture.

---

59. Though this view has a certain Jewish cultural background, it has to be investigated regarding how it fits a Christian worldview of soteriology.

60. Nigel Tomes, "Paul's *Huiothesia*: LSM's 'Coming-of-Age' Sonship or Adoption as Sons?" (2010), 7, http://concernedbrothers.com/Truth/HUIOTHESIA.pdf.

Conclusion

This chapter has presented a critical analysis of the doctrine of adoption as presented in Western theological discourse. The major findings that have surfaced are as follows.

First, the influence of the Western secular concept of adoption is conspicuous in the presentation of the doctrine in that the legal framework which grounds the doctrine is evident. In this way, the doctrine of adoption as it is articulated cannot be perceived as cross-cultural, as it has been contextualized to fit into Western cultures that practice adoption from a legal sense. This chapter has demonstrated that African cultures are community-based and focused on family structure. Consequently, to infer the doctrine of adoption as it is presented in Western theological studies as the benchmark for how this doctrine should be taught is to do injustice to alternatives that can be presented in non-Western cultures.

Second, this chapter has presented the background to the apostle Paul's concept of adoption in the first century. As such, the concept of "adoption" entails the adoption of an adult, especially a male, with a view to leading the family cult. The Western secular concept of adoption does have some similarities with the first-century secular concept of adoption. However, the passages written by the apostle Paul which are used to formulate the Western doctrine of adoption use the term *huiothesia*, which this chapter has demonstrated is a term of honor that emphasizes the placing of believers in an honorable state in Christ.

Third, while changing the emphasis in the doctrine of adoption from the individualistic to the corporate – especially family-oriented – might seem small, the ramifications are significant at both an exegetical and a practical level. As such, there are levels of similarity between African notions of the concept of adoption and Paul's understanding, especially concerning honor-shame emphases. Through noticing these similarities, the contextualization of the doctrine of adoption becomes easier to implement in African society since the legal metaphor of Western theology can be eliminated from the picture. A Western theology of adoption has no role to play in reconciling the Pauline concept of adoption with the African understanding of adoption.

Finally, this chapter has argued that the emphasis on sonship in the doctrine of adoption speaks with a soteriological accent which resonates with the African worldview of honor and shame, thereby engendering a heartfelt transformation to Christlikeness in African believers. It has demonstrated that this soteriology of honor gives Africans tools to deal with the issues of shame that are rampant in African societies. Moreover, this heartfelt transformation is grounded upon a biblical understanding rather than what is perceived to be cultural. This entails that for Christianity to take root in African societies, it must get rid of the secondary metaphors that define Western theology and examine the Scriptures and original sources without entering the gates of Western theology. In this sense, the African theologian is faced with the task of sifting that which is biblical from that which is Western in order to contextualize biblical doctrine in African society.

Bibliography

Beeke, Joel R., and Mark Jones. *A Puritan Theology: Doctrine for Life*. Grand Rapids: Reformation Heritage, 2012.
Burke, Trevor. "Pauline Adoption: A Sociological Approach." *The Evangelical Quarterly* 73, no. 2 (2001): 119–34.
Crook, J. A. *Law and Life of Rome*. London: Thames & Hudson, 1967.
Davids, P. H. "Adoption." In *Evangelical Dictionary of Theology*, edited by Walter A. Elwell, 25–26. Grand Rapids: Baker Academic, 2004.
Erickson, Millard J. *Christian Theology*. Grand Rapids: Baker Academic, 2012.
Flanders, Christopher. *About Face: Rethinking Face for 21st Century Mission*. Eugene: Pickwick, 2011.
Gerrand, Priscilla. "An African Community's Attitude towards Modern, Western Adoption." Master's diss., Rand Afrikaans University, 1997.
Gibbons, Judith. "Adoption and Fostering: Traditional and Contemporary Child Welfare Strategies in Sub-Saharan Africa." 2013. https://www.researchgate.net/publication/256835417_Adoption_and_fostering_Traditional_and_contemporary_child_welfare_strategies_in_Sub-Saharan_Africa.
Gunton, Colin E. *The Actuality of Atonement: A Study of Metaphor, Rationality and the Christian Tradition*. Grand Rapids: Eerdmans, 1988.
Iliffe, John. *Honour in African History*. Cambridge: Cambridge University Press, 2005.
Judge, E. A. *The Social Pattern of Christian Groups in the First Century*. London: Tyndale, 1960.
Kuyper, Abraham. *The Work of the Holy Spirit*. Spain: Hard Press Publishing, 2012.
Lee, William. *Life Study of Romans*. Anaheim: Living Stream Publisher, 1984.
Lund, Christian. "A Question of Honour: Property Disputes and Brokerage in Burkina Faso." *Africa* 69, no. 4 (1999): 575–94.
Ly, Boubakar. *L'honneur et les valeurs morales dans les sociétés Ouolof et Toucouleur du Sénégal*. Paris: Université de Paris, 1967.
Lyall, Francis. "Roman Law in the Writings of Paul: Adoption." *Journal of Biblical Literature* 88, no. 4 (1969): 458–66.

Mahlangu, Ellen. "The Ancient Mediterranean Values of Honour and Shame as a Hermeneutical Procedure: A Social-Scientific Criticism in an African Perspective." *Verbum et Ecclesia* 22, no. 1 (2001): 85–101.

Malinga, Tumani, and Poloko N. Ntshwarang. "Alternative Care for Children in Botswana: A Reality or Idealism?" 2011. https://ejournals.bib.uni-wuppertal.de/index.php/sws/article/view/277/593.

Mbuvi, Andrew. "African Theology from the Perspective of Honor and Shame." In *The Urban Face of Mission: Ministering the Gospel in a Diverse and Changing World*, edited by Harvie M. Conn, Manuel Ortiz, and Susan S. Baker, 276–95. Phillipsburg: P&R, 2002.

———. "The Ancient Mediterranean Values of 'Honour and Shame' as a Hermeneutical Lens of Reading the Book of Job." *Old Testament Essays* 23, no. 3 (2010): 752–68.

Molato, Kenosi, and S. E. Freeman. *Highest Honor: 60 Days toward Honoring God with Your Whole Life*. Nairobi: CLC Kenya, 2018.

Munyao, Martin. "Linking Ancient Mediterranean with Contemporary Kenyan Pivotal Values of Honor-Shame: A Missional Appraisal of Baptist Theology in Kenya through Honor-Shame Lenses." PhD diss., Concordia Theological Seminary, 2017.

Murray, John. *Redemption Accomplished and Applied*. Carlisle, PA: Banner of Truth, 1979.

Ochola-Omolo, Joseph. *Reconciliation in an African Context: Paul's Theology of Reconciliation – Engaging Honour and Shame Cultural Elements among the Gusii, Luhya, and Luo People of Western Kenya*. Nairobi: Uzima Publishing, 2008.

Rukundwa, S. L. "The Banyamulenge people: Their angst, honour and shame in the light of the Matthean Community." *HTS* 60, no. 2 (2004): 285–409.

Sepere, Keketso Christina. "The Impact of Western Culture on the Basotho Family Structure and the Erosion of African Values in Lesotho." In *Law, Religion and the Family in Africa*, edited by M. Christian Green and Faith Kabata, 35–45. Stellenbosch: African Sun Media, 2021.

Tomes, Nigel. "Paul's *Huiothesia*: LSM's 'Coming-of-Age' Sonship or Adoption as Sons?" 2010. http://concernedbrothers.com/Truth/HUIOTHESIA.pdf.

Ver Eecke, Catherine. "Pulaaku: Adamawa Fulbe Identity and Its Transformation." Diss., University of Pennsylvania, 1988.

Vigil, Nathan. "The Conflicted Theological Construct of Adoption," *Affirmation & Critique* 7, no. 2 (Oct. 2002): 124–28.

Vine, W. E. *Vine's Complete Expository Dictionary of Old and New Testament Words*. London: Thomas Nelson, 1970.

12

A Balanced Approach to Understanding the Concept of Salvation in Contemporary African Christianity

Joseph Mavulu

Adjunct Faculty, International Leadership University

Abstract

The concept of salvation is found in virtually all religions and cultures of the world. It is broadly understood as a religious attempt to respond to a wide range of perplexing issues we find in human societies all over the world. In fact, the concept can be regarded as the bedrock of all world religions and cultures. There is something inside all of us, whether we live in the most advanced cultures of the world or the most primal cultures, that seeks to be delivered from the vagaries of life. In fact, the big question is not the "what" of salvation but the "how." We seem to be in unanimous agreement that something is seriously wrong with human society and that we need to be delivered from it. What we don't seem to be in agreement about is how to be delivered from, or how to fix, the brokenness in our world and our personal lives. The concept of salvation introduced to African Christianity by Western missionaries was largely that of deliverance from personal sin and of restoration to relationship with God. It did not adequately address the existential predicaments of the African people. Before the advent of European Christianity in Africa, salvation was viewed primarily in temporal and this-worldly terms in accordance with

African cosmology. Although the concept of salvation as deliverance from personal sin and restoration of relationship with God as introduced by Western missionaries has not been entirely lost in African Christianity, the emphasis of salvation is still largely informed by African traditional cosmology. Salvation has retained primarily the idea of deliverance from all that which does not contribute to wholeness of life in the here and now.

This conceptualization of salvation in African Christianity has won the hearts of many African Christians today, as demonstrated by the overwhelming following in Pentecostal, charismatic, and African Independent Churches whose emphasis with regard to salvation is largely temporal and this-worldly. The big question is whether the Bible, especially the New Testament, emphasizes a holistic, a temporal, or only a spiritual salvation. What informs the concept of salvation in most communities in Christian Africa today? How can we have a balanced biblical approach to the concept of salvation that works well for African Christianity? These questions will be answered by exegeting a relevant text from the New Testament using the intercultural hermeneutical methodology.

Key words: salvation, African Traditional Religion, wholeness, African Christianity

Introduction

The idea of salvation is key to every major world religion. In fact, ostensibly the main reason religions exist is to give hope to people and make their idea of temporal and eschatological existence meaningful. Salvation is "the deliverance of humankind by religious means from sin or evil . . . [and] all religions strive towards restoring humans to their truest state which leads to eternal blessedness."[1] Adelakun similarly opines that "the quest for salvation is at the heart of every religion."[2] This is as true of Christianity as it is of African Traditional Religion. However, the concept of salvation in African Traditional Religion is more anthropocentric than theocentric as it is in Christianity. Since salvation in contemporary African Christian thought is informed by African Traditional Religion, there needs to be a balance between the concept of

---

1. Omaka K. Ngele et al., "*Sōtēria* [Salvation] in Christianity and *Ubandu* [Wholeness] in Igbo Traditional Religion: Towards a Renewed Understanding," *HTS Theological Studies* 73, no. 3 (2017): a4639 quoted from Goring (2017).

2. Adewale Adelakun, "A Theological Reflection on Mbiti's Conception of Salvation in African Christianity," *Nebula* 8, no. 1 (Dec. 2011): 25.

salvation in contemporary African Christianity and that of biblical Christianity. This has far-reaching implications for the practices, beliefs, and witness of African Christians. The purpose of this chapter is therefore to argue for a balanced approach to the concept of salvation for the African church so that the church may earn its rightful place in global orthodox Christianity and become a powerful witness to biblical Christianity on the continent and beyond.

Understanding Salvation

The complexity of the concept of salvation is evident even from its definition. A complete definition of the term not only brings out various meanings and nuances but also depends to a great extent on the linguistic and cultural contexts in which the word is used and who is using it and for what purpose. The problem of defining the term is compounded by the lack of unanimity in the way it is used in the Bible. As Ogunkule states, "there is a fundamental difference between the concept of salvation in the Old and New Testaments."[3]

General Understanding of the Concept of Salvation

It is important to note that salvation is not necessarily a religious concept, but when it is used religiously it assumes religious connotations. In virtually all religions and cultures of the world salvation answers to a wide range of concepts. Since words are culturally conditioned the word "salvation" "may denote one thing in one culture and connote something entirely different in another culture context."[4]

In general terms, salvation may mean "deliverance from physical calamities, such as oppression, sickness, fear, death."[5] It may also mean "freedom from distress and the ability to pursue one's own objectives."[6] In New Testament Greek the word for salvation is *sōtēria*, and it was originally used "in the sense of an acutely dynamic act in which gods or even men snatch others by force from serious peril."[7] It signifies preservation from danger or peril when

---

3. C. O. Ogunkule, "An African Perspective of the Concept of Salvation in the Psalter," *Africa Journal of Evangelical Theology* 28, no. 1 (2009): 57.
4. Teresia M. Hinga, "An African Understanding of Salvation" (diss., University of Nairobi, 1980), 19.
5. Ogunkule, "African Perspective," 57.
6. Ogunkule, 57.
7. Gerhard Kittel and Gerhard Friedrich, eds., *Theological Dictionary of the New Testament*, Vol. 7, trans. Geoffrey W. Bromiley (Grand Rapids: Eerdmans, 1971), 967.

it is used to mean "to keep men from want and perishing; to remain in good condition."[8] It is also used to mean conferring benefits by keeping someone "from threat . . . not only to be cured but to be or stay in good health, well-being."[9]

Salvation in Christian Theology

Christian theologians define the term "salvation" in various ways. When discussing the subject of salvation, Grudem does not define the term as such but is careful to classify salvation into common grace and saving grace.[10] He defines common grace as "the innumerable blessings that are not part of salvation."[11] By this he means that God, out of his magnanimity and great love for all his creation, even though it is without merit, gives good health, rain, children, prosperity, protection from danger, and general well-being (Matt 5:44–45). This poses a challenge for understanding the concept of salvation since it appears as though physical well-being is not part of salvation. In fact, in his categorization of salvation Grudem seems to argue for two different sets of salvation – temporal and eternal. According to this categorization, healing and deliverance from danger fall under common grace, or temporal salvation. When Jesus healed sinners, for example, he did not require "all of them to believe in him or to agree that he was the Messiah before he granted them physical healing (Luke 4:40)."[12] The other category of salvation according to Grudem is saving grace, which "brings people to salvation."[13] By this he means the salvation of the soul or spiritual salvation, as is the case in, for example, Romans 1:16; 10:9–10; and Luke 19:9. The big question is whether the Bible requires such a categorization of the concept of salvation, or whether this is only the work of theologians.

Erickson says without further qualification of the term that "salvation is the application of the work of Christ to the life of the individual."[14] However, he is not clear about the extent of this work. Does it cover physical well-being? Erickson further says, "It pertains to the most crucial need of the human

---

8. Kittel and Friedrich, *Theological Dictionary*, Vol. 8, 967.
9. Kittel and Friedrich, Vol. 7, 967.
10. Wayne Grudem, *Systematic Theology* (Grand Rapids: Zondervan, 1994), 657.
11. Grudem, *Systematic Theology*, 657.
12. Grudem, 662.
13. Grudem, 662.
14. Millard J. Erickson, *Christian Theology* (Grand Rapids: Baker, 1985), 887.

person."[15] Most likely, by "the most crucial need of the human person" he means sin. Unlike Grudem, Erickson does not appear to be concerned with the categorization of salvation into general and saving grace.

In the *Evangelical Dictionary of Theology*, Hughes, like Grudem, proffers two types of grace – common grace and special grace. By common grace he means grace that is common to all humankind: "whose benefits are experienced by the whole human race without discrimination between one person and another."[16] This is similar to Grudem's understanding of common grace. By special grace is meant "the grace by which God redeems, sanctifies, and glorifies his people."[17] Again, this is similar to Grudem's saving grace.

The *New Dictionary of Theology* appears closer to the contemporary African understanding of the concept of salvation. It defines salvation as "any kind of situation in which a person is delivered from some danger, real or potential; as in healing a person from illness (Matthew 5:28), from enemies (Psalm 44:7) or from the possibility of death (Matthew 8:25)"[18] This general definition of salvation is partly informed by the Old Testament and is the concept widely held in contemporary traditional African religious thought. It "is quite concrete and covers more than spiritual blessings."[19]

Salvation in the Old Testament

In the Old Testament, the concept of salvation is slightly different from that of the New Testament. The principal term used for salvation in the Old Testament is the Hebrew word *yēšaʻ* and its cognates, whose basic meaning is to "bring into a spacious environment where one is at one's ease, free to develop without hindrance."[20] Metaphorically, "it conveys the sense of freedom from limitations and the means to that; i.e. deliverance from factors which constrain or confine" (cf. Pss 18:36; 66:12).[21] In most cases where salvation is mentioned in the Old Testament, God is depicted as the agent, such that persons are not in a position to save themselves: "Yahweh alone is the author of all deliverance. Even when he

---

15. Erickson, *Christian Theology*, 887.
16. P. E. Hughes, "Grace," in *Evangelical Dictionary of Theology*, ed. Walter A. Elwell (Grand Rapids: Baker, 1984), 482.
17. Hughes, "Grace," 482.
18. I. Marshall, "Salvation" in *The New Dictionary of Theology*, eds. Sinclair B. Ferguson, J. I. Packer, and D. F. Wright (Leicester: Inter-Varsity, 1991), 610.
19. Marshall, "Salvation," 610.
20. Hinga, "African Understanding," 2.
21. J. D. Douglas, ed., *The New Bible Dictionary* (Leicester: Inter-Varsity, 1982), 1057.

sends . . . intermediaries to save on his behalf, Hebrews generally acknowledged that, ultimately, it was Yahweh who saved (Isaiah 37:14–20; Hosea 1:7)."[22]

Salvation in the New Testament

In the New Testament, the word used for salvation is the Greek term *sōtēria* and in most usages it adopts almost a wholly religious sense. Its reference to "moral/spiritual deliverance becomes almost dominant."[23] Jesus Christ is depicted as the agent of moral/spiritual salvation in the New Testament (Matt 1:21; Acts 2:21; 4:12; 1 Tim 1:15; Titus 2:11–14; 1 Thess 5:9–10). Nonspiritual usages are however employed to mean deliverance "from acute danger to life" (Acts 27:20, 31; Mark 15:30).[24]

Factors That Inform the Concept of Salvation in Contemporary African Christianity

The concept of salvation in contemporary African Christianity is, to a large extent, informed by the idea of wholeness. Much of this understanding is in turn informed by a number of factors.

Salvation in African Traditional Religions

The concept of salvation for the majority of contemporary African Christians has been largely influenced by African Traditional Religions. In the African Traditional Religious cosmology, salvation is largely viewed as physical wholeness. Henry J. Mugabe opines, "The discussions about African perception of salvation [should] be taken seriously from African traditional viewpoints of wholeness and well-being which helped Africans to appreciate, appropriate and interpret the theme of salvation preached by missionaries."[25] Mugabe concurs with Mbiti who says: "In these religious considerations of the concept of salvation, we take note that salvation in African religion has to do with physical immediate dangers (of the individual and more often the

---

22. Hinga, "African Understanding," 21.
23. Hinga, 21.
24. Hinga, 21.
25. Henry J. Mugabe, "Salvation from African Perspective," *Indian Journal of Theology* (1994): 32.

community) – dangers that threaten individual or community survival, good health and general prosperity or safety."[26]

Salvation in contemporary African Christianity is also viewed as deliverance or protection from mystical powers and their effects. It involves "deliverance or protection from witchcraft and evil spirits and the possession of life force."[27] It encompasses deliverance and relief from conditions brought about by situations such as sickness, hunger, disasters, misfortunes, oppression, distress, witchcraft, sorcery, magic, barrenness, failure, malevolent spirits, danger, death, drought, foreign domination, slavery, locust invasions, epidemics, floods, and earthquakes, the cause of which is believed to be malignant mystical powers. Generally speaking, salvation is rescue from material, physical, and spiritual problems. According to African religious cosmology (the African religious worldview), "God does not save because he is Savior; rather, he becomes Savior when he does save."[28] The question is, if in African Traditional Religion there is no clear concept of a savior who saves, then who does save? Adeyemo comes close to answering the question when he states that "in African Traditional Religion, a worshipper believes that through divination and prescribed sacrifices he can be delivered from his enemies (real or potential), secure the help of his *ancestors* and the *gods*, and be prosperous in life."[29] According to this view, "ancestors" and "the gods" are the agents of salvation.

Salvation in traditional African cosmology is not individualistic but collective and corporate. No one is truly saved until all are saved. The African ontological worldview considers God, spirits, humans, animals, plants, and inanimate creation to be interconnected. To interfere with any one of them

---

26. John Mbiti, "Some Reflections of African Experience of Salvation Today," in *Living Faiths and Ultimate Goals*, ed. S. J. Samartha (Geneva: World Council of Churches, 1974), 112.

27. Wilbur O'Donovan, *Biblical Christianity in African Perspective* (Carlisle: Paternoster, 1996), 126. The *Collins Dictionary* online defines "life force" as "the energy that some people believe exists in all living things and keeps them alive" (*Collins COBUILD Advanced Learner's Dictionary*, accessed 7 March 2023, https://www.collinsdictionary.com/dictionary/english/life-force). It is also referred to as "vital force" which is "the energy or spirit which animates living creatures." Oladele Abiodun Balagun equates "life force" with "meaningful life" in his article "The Traditional Yoruba Conception of a Meaningful Life," *South African Journal of Philosophy* 39, no. 2 (2020): 166–78, when he opines that "the dominant Yoruba conception of a meaningful life among the Yoruba is the manifestation of some rational valuable ends: material comfort symbolized with monetary possession; long healthy life; children; a peaceful spouse; and victory over life's vicissitudes." Life in Yoruba cosmology, and by extension many parts of Africa, is not truly life unless it is a vital or meaningful life devoid of its unpleasant side.

28. Ogunkule, "African Perspective," 60.

29. Tokunboh Adeyemo, "The Idea of Salvation in Contemporary World Religions," in *Issues in African Christian Theology*, eds. S. Ngewa and M. Shaw (Nairobi: E. A. Edu, 1998), 199–209.

is to interfere with this unity and to destroy one or more of these modes of existence; to destroy one is in effect to destroy them all. To restore and preserve that interconnectivity is tantamount to salvation.

The Influence of the Prosperity "Gospel"

The prosperity gospel – the "health-and-wealth" or "claim-it-possess-it" brand of Christianity – is a recent phenomenon on the African Christian landscape. It is a brand of Christianity propagated mainly by Pentecostalism and the charismatic movement that has captured the imagination of many people in Africa. This brand of Christianity has contributed significantly toward informing a concept of salvation in contemporary African Christianity which is contrary to the traditional biblical concept. O'Donovan describes it as a "Prosperity Theology" based on "the teaching that God does not want any of His children to be poor or lack anything they may desire."[30] David Ngong calls this brand of Christianity "New Christianity" "because of its emphasis on material well-being in its soteriology . . . whose emergence has been attributed to 'unresolved questions' facing the African Church, questions about the place of success and prosperity, healing and material provision, and the 'holistic dimension of salvation.'"[31] The emphasis in this brand of Christianity is on general well-being, good health, and material prosperity as evidence of a right relationship with God. Kwabena Asamoah-Gyadu cites soteriology as one of the emphases of Pentecostalism in African Christianity with its call to turn to God for "salvation that is interpreted in very practical terms."[32] Prayers are often conducted to deliver people from conditions that prevent them from enjoying temporal blessings that are believed to be indispensable to the salvation "package." People are therefore not truly saved unless they are free from that which prevents them from enjoying physical and spiritual wholeness.

This concept of salvation which predominates in contemporary African Christianity resonates well with African Traditional Religious thought. It is anthropocentric in its approach in terms of being utilitarian and pragmatic, unlike the theocentric nature of the biblical concept of salvation. Religion

---

30. Wilbur O'Donovan, *Biblical Christianity in Modern Africa* (Carlisle: Paternoster, 2006), 230.

31. David T. Ngong, "The Material in Salvific Discourse: A Study of Two Christian Perspectives" (PhD diss., Baylor University, 2007), 2.

32. J. Kwabena Asamoah-Gyadu, "Growth and Trends in African Christianity in the 21st Century," in *Anthology of African Christianity*, eds. Isabel Apawo and Dietrich Werner (Oxford: Regnum, 2016), 70.

according to this school of thought exists to serve human beings, and not the other way round. Religion exists primarily to promote human well-being. Whatever people do with religion must be beneficial to them. No wonder salvation is viewed in terms of the temporal physical benefits it confers, which encompass personal well-being in all its manifestations, rather than primarily spiritual well-being with or without such temporal benefits.

The Concept of Sin

The concept of salvation in contemporary African Christianity is incomplete without factoring in the concept of sin. The concept of sin is in turn informed by the way sin is understood in African Traditional Religion. The African traditional understanding of sin is quite unlike the biblical one.

Sin in traditional African religious thought is conceptualized as a violation of prescribed cultural guidelines and norms related to personal and social conduct, taboos, and rituals.[33] Sin is rarely perceived as individual violation of God's laws, but rather is understood as acts done against others in particular and the society in general. Witchcraft is viewed as the epitome of sin in many communities, and witches and wizards are feared and hated at the same time since they harm people and destabilize communities. The consequences of sin from which people are saved are therefore viewed as being temporal and rarely spiritual. They are seen in terms of fractured interpersonal human relationships among the living and between the living and the dead; rarely is sin seen as being against God. Ancestors are viewed as custodians of societal morality and as the ones who reward or punish people according to how they appropriate societal moral norms.

Any imbalance occasioned by an infringement of societal norms is restored through observance of proper rituals. Restoration of people to their pre-sin situation "is ritualistic and utilitarian."[34] Once the offenders are restored, shame is removed and they are again able to enjoy the benefits of being useful members of the community. This paints a picture of salvation in African Traditional Religious thought as focused on dealing with the temporal rather than spiritual consequences of sin.

---

33. Abraham Olutoye Odeloye, "Comparative Ethical Analysis of Sin in African Traditional Religion and Christianity," *International Journal of Innovative Social Research and Humanities Research* 8, no. 2 (April–June 2020): 7–12.

34. Tokunboh Adeyemo, *Salvation in African Tradition* (Nairobi: Evangel, 1997), 85.

A wrong concept of sin inevitably leads to a wrong or unbalanced concept of salvation. Yet as Byang Kato states, "the nature of man's fundamental dilemma does not lie in mere physical suffering. It does not lie primarily in horizontal relationships with his fellow man. All human tragedies, be they sickness, poverty or exploitation, are mere symptoms of the real cause, which the Bible call sin."[35] This concept of sin is lacking in traditional African religious thought, and therefore so is salvation from sin.

Illustration from an Exegetical Study on Mark 5:34

Mark 5:34 can be used to illustrate a biblically balanced concept of salvation. Related texts include Matthew 9:22; 12:22; Mark 9:22; 10:52; Luke 7:50; 8:48; 17:19.

Background Information

The Gospel of Mark is believed by most scholars to have been "the first gospel written."[36] It was probably written in AD 57–59. Another suggestion is AD 64, coinciding with the great persecution of Christians in Rome under Emperor Nero.[37]

The author of the gospel is not clearly stated anywhere. According to Grassmick, the title "'According to Mark' (*Kata Markon*) was added some time before AD 125."[38] However, both internal and external evidence point to Markan authorship (see Acts 15; Col 4:10; 1 Pet 5:13). Moreover, church tradition over the centuries has strongly held to Markan authorship and no credible dissenting voice has been registered. Mark was not a close associate of Jesus so was not a firsthand witness to his life and ministry, but he relied on material from the apostle Peter with whom he was a close ministry associate (Acts 12:12, 25; 1 Pet 5:13).

The Gospel of Mark was written in the context of suffering by believers in the gentile region of Rome. It was written partly to help Christians grasp the power of Jesus to deal with such eventualities. It was to help them understand

---

35. Byang Kato, "The Theology of Eternal Salvation," in *Issues in African Christian Theology*, ed. Samuel Ngewa (Nairobi: East African Educational, 1998), 192–98.
36. John Grassmick, "Mark," in *The Bible Knowledge Commentary*, eds. J. F. Walvoord and R. B. Zuck (Colorado Springs: David C. Cook, 1983), 95.
37. Craig Keener, *The IVP Bible Background Commentary: New Testament* (Downers Grove: InterVarsity, 1993), 132.
38. Grassmick, "Mark," 95.

that "God heard prayers and would work through their witness and faith."³⁹ In the gospel, Jesus is depicted as the servant par excellence who came to serve humankind by alleviating their physical and spiritual needs (Mark 10:45). There is a deliberate attempt by the author to keep the true identity of Jesus as the promised Old Testament Jewish Messiah a guarded secret so as not to unnecessarily raise people's expectations.

Faith is a key theological theme in the gospel. The Christians in Rome needed to be reminded about the "implications of the good news of God's saving power . . . for their lives in a dissolute and often hostile environment," and the necessity of living by faith.⁴⁰

Literary Context

The text of Mark 5:34 is situated in the wider context of Jesus's ministry in Galilee of the Gentiles (Mark 5:21 – 6:6). The events recorded in Mark 5:21–43, namely the healing of the woman and of Jairus's daughter, happened concurrently. The woman who was healed by Jesus was among the crowd who followed him on that day. She had been sick from an unspecified hemorrhage for twelve years (5:25), the same length of time Jairus's daughter had been alive (Luke 8:42). Her situation was so dire that Jesus had to temporarily suspend his planned mission of attending to Jairus's daughter to first attend to the immediate and more urgent need of the woman (5:22–23). The woman was so desperate for healing that "she came up behind him in the crowd and touched his cloak," believing that by so doing she would be delivered from her suffering (5:27–28). True to her expectations, she was dramatically healed (5:29).

The literary genre of Mark's gospel is that it is the good news of salvation through Jesus Christ.

Rendering of Mark 5:34 in Greek

In Greek, Mark 5:34 is transliterated as follows: *o de eipen autē thugatēr ē pistis sou sesōken se upage eis eirēnēn kai isthi ugiēs apo tēs mastigos sou.*

---

39. Keener, *Bible Background Commentary*, 133.
40. Grassmick, "Mark," 101.

Literally translated, this gives the following: "And he said to her: Daughter, the faith of thee has healed thee; go in peace and be whole from the plague of thee."[41]

Exegesis

Jesus addressed the woman as "daughter" (Greek, *thugatēr*), an endearing feminine noun which communicated warmth, care, and concern for her. She must have been elated to hear Jesus address her in this way. Jesus earnestly sought out the woman who had touched him and had hidden in the crowd probably out of fear that she would be found out. The Greek verb *perieblepeto*, which literally means "he looked round about,"[42] is in the imperfect tense, meaning that he "kept on looking around for the woman" (v. 32).[43] Jesus proceeded to pronounce healing to the woman on the basis of her faith by saying to her, *ē pistis sou sesōken* ("your faith has healed you"). The word *sesōken* means "has healed." It is the perfect tense of the word *sōdzō* (to save). The perfect tense denotes "an action already completed whose results continue to the present."[44] By using the perfect tense, he was emphatic that the woman "had indeed been 'made well.'"[45] The primary rendering here is "healed," but according to the Greek text what the woman heard Jesus say was "your faith has saved you." Jesus appears to have meant physical healing when he used the phrase *isthi ugiēs apo tēs mastigos sou*, variously translated as "be healed of your affliction" (NKJV); "your suffering is over" (NLT); "be freed from your suffering" (NIV); "be whole of thy plague" (KJV). Jesus further said to the woman, *upage eis eirēnēn* ("go in peace"). "Going in peace is more than a dismissal formula.... It means to go as one restored to a proper relationship with God."[46] It can also mean wholeness. The woman's healing, though certainly from physical illness, "involved more than simply the physical dimension of her existence.... It involved her spiritual dimension as well."[47] The aspect of faith (Greek *pistis*) is key to this episode as it is throughout the Gospel of Mark.

---

41. Alfred Marshall, *The NIV Interlinear Greek-English New Testament* (Grand Rapids: Zondervan, 1976), 158.
42. Marvin R. Vincent, *Word Studies in the New Testament*, vol. 1 (Peabody: Hendrickson, 1985), 190.
43. Vincent, *Word Studies*, 190.
44. Robert Guelich, *Mark 1 – 8:26*, Word Biblical Commentary (Dallas: Word, 1989), 299.
45. Guelich, *Mark 1 – 8:26*, 299.
46. Guelich, 299.
47. Guelich, 300.

It was not her grasping Jesus's garment but her faith in Jesus which effected the healing.[48]

A similar text is Mark 10:52, where Jesus heals Bartimaeus and uses the same word, *sesōken* ("has saved"), as used in 5:34. In his commentary Cooper states, "Mark probably intended a double meaning. The man was healed physically and saved spiritually. The latter is implied by the fact that he began to follow Jesus."[49] Grassmick agrees, stating, "Bartemaeus' physical 'salvation' (i.e. deliverance from darkness [blindness] to light [sight]) was an outward picture of his spiritual 'salvation.'"[50] Similarly, Cole says, "All miracles of Jesus may have been in the [light of the healing of the soul] and so they could be regarded as 'signs.'"[51]

A number of questions are raised by our text. Why would Jesus have used the word "saved" when he meant "healed"? Did he want to be understood to mean both "saved" and "healed" at the same time? Which one of the two words did the woman (and Bartimaeus) actually understand Jesus to mean? Did the woman get "saved" after being "healed," or did she just get healed and not "saved," contrary to the assertion of Mark? It may be safe to conclude from the study of Mark 5:34 and other related texts that Jesus was deeply concerned about people's spiritual as well as physical well-being. However, he placed greater emphasis on their spiritual well-being since it had eternal implications. He was well aware that people's unwholesome physical conditions were brought about by a bigger problem of sin. Many of his interventions in human predicaments were therefore not just about making people's lives more bearable but about pointing to the bigger problem of sin in their lives – the problem he had come to deal with once and for all.

Conclusion

First and foremost, it is important to emphasize that Jesus was, and still is, concerned about all forms of human suffering, whether physical or spiritual. As Peter Kanyandogo puts it, "a [careful] reading of the Gospels does not leave any shred of doubt that right from the beginning of his public ministry Jesus

---

48. W. D. Davies and D. C. Allison, *A Critical and Exegetical Commentary on the Gospel According to Matthew*, vol. 2 (Edinburgh: T&T Clark, 1991), 130.
49. Rodney Cooper, *Mark*, Holman New Testament Commentary, General Ed. Max Anders (Nashville: Broadman & Holman, 2000), 173.
50. Grassmick, "Mark," 154.
51. R. A. Cole, *The Gospel According to Mark* (Leicester: Inter-Varsity, 1989), 162.

fights against all forms of [human] suffering."[52] As the true representative of Jesus in Africa, the African church should be at the forefront in alleviating human suffering in all its manifestations. This is vital when we bear in mind how much suffering there is on the continent, some of which is moral and some natural. It is the will of God that people live in wholeness of life: in body and spirit, and in harmony with themselves, others, and God.

However, we should be wary of overemphasizing the physical well-being of life at the expense of the spiritual well-being of the soul, and vice versa. Jesus was concerned about the whole person – body, mind, spirit, and social and economic – and so should we be. The task of the church in Africa is to strive to maintain such a balance. This should not be interpreted to mean that all human suffering can ever be eradicated before the end of this age. Some human suffering is a necessary part of life without which our sanctification as Christians would be incomplete. God's desire is that, more than anything else, Christians would be increasingly conformed to the image of Christ in this life (Rom 5:1–5; Jas 1:2–8). Jesus, the pioneer of our salvation, learned obedience through suffering, and the Christian should not expect anything less (Heb 5:8). The great extent of human suffering in Africa should not be an excuse for us not to preach the whole counsel of God (Acts 20:27 NKJV) and instead to present to our people a lopsided gospel message. We don't want to give our people false hope that their unfavorable conditions will go away at the snap of a finger! Right human conditions are not necessarily part of the "salvation package." Some unpleasant conditions will require hard work, diligence, and observance of right rules and procedures, and not just responding to an altar call after evangelistic preaching; others will persist a while longer, and may even defy all human attempts to remedy them, even after we have heeded the gospel message of salvation.

Bibliography

Adelakun, Adewale. "A Theological Reflection on Mbiti's Conception of Salvation in African Christianity." *Nebula* 8, no. 1 (Dec. 2011): 25–33.
Adeyemo, Tokunboh. "The Idea of Salvation in Contemporary World Religions." In *Issues in African Christian Theology*, edited by S. Ngewa and M. Shaw, 199–209. Nairobi: E. A. Edu, 1998.
———. *Salvation in African Tradition*. Nairobi: Evangel, 1997.

---

52. Peter Kanyandogo, "The Cross and Suffering in the Bible," in *The Bible in African Christianity: Essays in Biblical Theology*, eds. Hannah W. Kinoti and John Mary Waligoo (Nairobi: Acton, 1997), 127.

Anderson, Allan. "The Newer Pentecostal and Charismatic Churches: The Shape of Future Christianity in Africa?" *Pneuma: Journal of the Society for Pentecostal Studies* 24, no. 2 (Fall 2002): 167–84.

Asamoah-Gyadu, J. Kwabena. "Growth and Trends in African Christianity in the 21st Century." In *Anthology of African Christianity*, edited by Isabel Apawo and Dietrich Werner, 65–75. Oxford: Regnum, 2016.

Balagun, Oladele Abiodun. "The Traditional Yoruba Conception of a Meaningful Life." *South African Journal of Philosophy* 39, no. 2 (2020): 166–78.

Cole, R. A. *The Gospel According to Mark*. Leicester: Inter-Varsity, 1989.

Cooper, Rodney. *Mark*. Holman New Testament Commentary. General editor Max Anders. Nashville: Broadman & Holman, 2000.

Davies, W. D., and D. C. Allison. *A Critical and Exegetical Commentary on the Gospel According to Matthew*. Vol. 2. Edinburgh: T&T Clark, 1991.

Douglas, J. D., ed. *The New Bible Dictionary*. Leicester: Inter-Varsity, 1982.

Erickson, Millard J. *Christian Theology*. Grand Rapids: Baker, 1985.

Ferguson, Sinclair B., J. I. Packer, and David F. Wright, eds. *New Dictionary of Theology*. Leicester: Inter-Varsity, 1991.

Grassmick, John. "Mark." In *The Bible Knowledge Commentary*, edited by J. F. Walvoord and R. B. Zuck, 95–197. Colorado Springs: David C. Cook, 1983.

Grudem, Wayne. *Systematic Theology*. Grand Rapids: Zondervan, 1994.

Guelich, Robert. *Mark 1 – 8:26*. Word Biblical Commentary. Dallas: Word, 1989.

Hinga, Teresia M. "An African Understanding of Salvation." Diss., University of Nairobi, 1980.

Hughes, P. E. "Grace." In *Evangelical Dictionary of Theology*, edited by Walter A. Elwell, 479–82. Grand Rapids: Baker, 1984.

Kanyandogo, Peter. "The Cross and Suffering in the Bible." In *The Bible in African Christianity: Essays in Biblical Theology*, edited by Hannah W. Kinoti and John Mary Waligoo, 123–44. Nairobi: Acton, 1997.

Kato, Byang. "The Theology of Eternal Salvation." *Issues in African Christian Theology*, edited by Samuel Ngewa, 192–98, Nairobi: East African Educational, 1998.

Keener, Craig. *The IVP Bible Background Commentary: New Testament*. Downers Grove: InterVarsity, 1993.

Kittel, Gerhard, and Gerhard Friedrich, eds. *Theological Dictionary of the New Testament*. Vol. 7. Translated by Geoffrey W. Bromiley. Grand Rapids: Eerdmans, 1971.

Marshall, Alfred. *The NIV Interlinear Greek-English New Testament*. Grand Rapids: Zondervan, 1976.

Mbiti, John. "Some Reflections of African Experience of Salvation Today." In *Living Faiths and Ultimate Goals*, edited by S. J. Samartha, 108–19. Geneva: World Council of Churches, 1974.

Mugabe, Henry J. "Salvation from African Perspective." *India Journal of Theology* 36.1 (1994): 31–42.

Ngele, O. K., et al. "*Sōtēria* [Salvation] in Christianity and *Ubandu* [Wholeness] in Igbo Traditional Religion: Towards a Renewed Understanding." *HTS Theological Studies* 73, no. 3 (2017): 1–7. https://doi.org/10.4102/hts.v73i3.4639.

Ngong, David T. "The Material in Salvific Discourse: A Study of Two Christian Perspectives." PhD diss., Baylor University, 2007.

Odeloye, Abraham Olutoye. "Comparative Ethical Analysis of Sin in African Traditional Religion and Christianity." *International Journal of Innovative Social Research and Humanities Research* 8, no. 2 (April–June 2020): 7–12.

O'Donovan, Wilbur. *Biblical Christianity in African Perspective.* Carlisle: Paternoster, 1996.

———. *Biblical Christianity in Modern Africa.* Carlisle: Paternoster, 2006.

Ogunkule, C. O. "An African Perspective of the Concept of Salvation in the Psalter." *Africa Journal of Evangelical Theology* 28, no. 1 (2009): 57–70.

Vincent, Marvin R. *Word Studies in the New Testament.* Vol. 1. Peabody: Hendrickson, 1985.

13

An Exploration of Understanding Seven Dimensions of Salvation in African Christianity

David K. Ngaruiya
Associate Professor, International Leadership University

Abstract

The African Christian understanding of the holistic concept of salvation impacts the way the doctrine is taught, upheld, and lived out in Christian communities. A misunderstanding of the doctrine gives rise to heresy, as is explicit in the prosperity gospel or in criticism of churches being lukewarm. As a cardinal doctrine for evangelical Christianity, salvation can be understood in various ways. From the New Testament, the concept of salvation can be understood in seven dimensions, namely: salvation from God's wrath; salvation that is eschatological; salvation from sin; salvation from being lost; salvation from physical ailments; salvation from life's pollution; and salvation from danger.

The purpose of this chapter is to explore the extent to which holistic salvation is understood in these seven dimensions in African Christianity by means of a case study of selected African churches. In this study, data from participants at two African churches was collected and analyzed as a way to elicit the varied ways in which the concept of salvation is understood by Christians in those churches. The results of this study are preceded by an exegesis of relevant biblical passages on the concept of salvation. The results of the study provide specific correctives for the African church in its proclamation and expression of the gospel.

Key words: holistic salvation, African Traditional Religion, African Christianity, multidimensional

Introduction

This chapter examines the concept of salvation in African Traditional Religions (ATR) as well as in selected passages of Scripture. I argue that although the idea of salvation in both ATR and the gospel is holistic, African Christian understandings of salvation are sometimes distorted, possibly influenced by a presentation of a "spiritual" gospel in mission Christianity. In this study, we will explore the understandings of salvation in ATR and Lukan expressions of the gospel, as well as the convergence of these two perspectives. Data obtained from selected churches will then be analyzed before drawing conclusions.

Salvation in ATR

That humans are created beings who became proud before their creator, fell to death, and were eventually rescued from death is not an alien idea to African people. There are numerous varied myths about this. One such myth is from the Fulanis of West Africa:

> At the beginning there was a huge drop of milk. Then Doondari came and he created the stone. Then the stone created iron; And iron created fire; And fire created water; And water created air. Then Doondari descended the second time. And he took the five elements. And he shaped them into man. But man was proud. Then Doondari created blindness and blindness defeated man. But when blindness became too proud, Doondari created sleep, and sleep defeated blindness; But when sleep became too proud, Doondari created worry and worry defeated sleep; But when worry became too proud, Doondari created death and death defeated worry. But when death became too proud, Doondari descended for the third time, And he came as Gueno, the eternal one, and Gueno defeated death.[1]

---

1. Ulli Beir, ed., *The Origin of Life and Death: African Creation Myths* (Nairobi: Heinemann Educational, 1966), 1–2.

As a created being, according to African myths, "man also comes into the picture as husband and wife, male and female."² The issue to consider in this myth, which is a part of ATR, is how humankind is rescued or how death is defeated in order that human beings might be saved by their creator. In the myth quoted above, Doondari created man, man fell spiritually through pride, man experienced both physical and spiritual consequences, but the Creator intervened to overcome death, and man was holistically restored. Thus, this myth largely illustrates holistic salvation.

In this chapter, we acknowledge that the term "salvation" is complex and not easily defined. Nevertheless, it is an important term, and different languages use different ways in their cultural contexts to express the idea. In 1975, the World Council of Churches Fifth Assembly that met in Nairobi declared that even though Christians have cultural differences and even though church and society have structures where confession of Christ is obscured, both agree that "Christ is not alien to any society."³

In ATR, salvation is expressed in many aspects of day-to-day life. These expressions are primarily "salvific," be they sacrifices, prayers, or offerings arising out of the human necessity for divine intervention.⁴ In a world plagued by challenges, divine help is often called for, whether from danger, drought, war, disaster, barrenness, conflict, flooding, or pandemics. Thus, salvation can be understood in many categories.

The first category of salvation in ATR is largely physical. In calling for this divine help, ritual is critical. Specifically, ATR is not only ritualistic but also utilitarian.⁵ Therefore, the offering of animal and other sacrifices is a core part of realizing salvation. There are, of course, also cases where human sacrifice has played a part.

A second category for understanding salvation in ATR pertains to geography. Sanctuaries such as sacred mountains, caves, shrines, or rocks serve as arenas where people or animals in the proximity will not be harmed or destroyed.⁶ Mbiti notes the paradox here that, though such places provide

---

2. John Mbiti, *African Religions and Philosophy* (Nairobi: East African Educational, 2002), 93.

3. John Mbiti, "Christianity and Culture in Africa," in *Facing the New Challenges: The Message of PACLA, December 9-19, 1976, Nairobi*, edited by Michael Cassidy and Luc Verlinden, 308-13. Kisumu: Evangel, 1978, 273.

4. John Mbiti, "Some Reflections of African Experience of Salvation Today," in *Living Faiths and Ultimate Goals*, ed. S. J. Samartha (Geneva: World Council of Churches, 1974), 3.

5. Tokunboh Adeyemo, *Salvation in African Tradition* (Nairobi: Evangel, 1997), 69.

6. Adeyemo, *Salvation in African Tradition*, 3.

safety for lives, they are also places of sacrifice. Thus salvation in ATR has a geographical dimension and concretization.

A third aspect is that of time which ties in with history. From Mbiti's perspective, salvation for any generation is a "now" reality. Salvation of course has a past aspect, since it is God who has sustained the present generation, having upheld the ancestors in the past.

A fourth aspect is spiritual. This spiritual aspect is multifaceted. On the one hand is the world of mediators in ATR. Rainmakers, priests, diviners, medicine men, and healers play mediatory roles offering spiritual interventions on behalf of their clients, be they individuals, families, communities, or even a nation. These mediators are believed to intervene on behalf of others to obtain favor from a god or gods or to appease malevolent spirits. On the other hand, some may claim the role that is played by witches, even though within clans in certain communities witchcraft is not condoned, to the extent that suspected witches are burned. The role of witches and sorcerers as part of ATR is contested. Some assert that witchcraft and sorcery are not a part of ATR and that they are regarded as antisocial and reprehensible.[7] This is not to deny the existence of these two practices which are found not only in Africa but around the globe.

Salvation is holistic in ATR. There is no single area of life, whether physical, cultural, or spiritual – and in fact all areas are intertwined – where Africans do not perceive the need for salvation. Are Africans well fed? They will praise their god(s). Are Africans hungry? They will call on their god(s) for rain. Are Africans encountering misfortune? They will call on their diviners. Are Africans ill? They will call on their herbalists or traditional healers. Do Africans see themselves cursed in a certain area? They will seek mediation and peace with their ancestors. In other words, salvation in ATR seeks to restore the human being's relationship with others and his or her environment. Rather than see such practices as creating a battlefield with the gospel, these practices can be seen and used as areas of contextualization in which Christ, the redeemer and refiner of African and all cultures, is presented as all-sufficient for human needs.

A study of the Annang people of Nigeria illustrates the holistic nature of salvation. Annang refer to salvation as *"edinyanga,"* a word that encompasses at least six basic connotations.[8] First it has the connotation of movement to

---

7. Eric O. Ayisi, *An Introduction to the Study of African Culture* (Nairobi: East African Educational, 1992), 75.

8. Kenneth Enang, *Salvation in a Nigerian Background: Its Concepts and Articulation in the Annang Independent Churches* (Berlin: Verlag von Reimer, 1979), 107.

a state of safety from a state of danger. Second, it connotes being free from physical attack. Third, salvation is safety from that which would inflict harm. Fourth, in salvation one flourishes numerically in an environment that is safe, glorious, and prosperous. Fifth, salvation encompasses a harmonious relationship and coexistence with people and objects in one environment. Sixth, one should act in ways that bring about salvation. "Thus the Annang can only say that he has been saved when the different eventualities which, on his behalf and because of him, took place have produced a successful outcome in the end."[9] This again illustrates that in ATR, salvation is holistic. An adherent of ATR cannot be saved and at the same time be in a bad state of health.

To ignore contextualization is to invite unnecessary consequent misunderstandings of salvation. In the so-called independent churches, lack of proper contextualization is both affirmative of the work of Christ and also distortive of it. In positive affirmation, salvation in these churches is understood as deliverance from the power of evil; wholeness; having children, good health, and economic prosperity; and it encompasses the totality of the human being, including judgment of soul and body; it is pragmatic, with the church encouraging followers to have full confidence in God; and that extensiveness of salvation is "world affirming."[10]

In distortion, salvation is seen as consisting in good health and having children. This cannot always be the case, and moreover, Jesus neither was married nor had physical children. In addition, Paul of Tarsus, a saved man, had a "thorn" in the flesh that God did not heal. It is helpful to note that though Jesus had no physical children, he nevertheless had, and continues to have, many spiritual children.

The focus on making many African cultural practices in ATR a battleground between Christianity and culture has led to an unhealthy perception of African culture among Africans, well meant as it may be. Consider, for example, the African generations who embraced Christianity at the time of the East African Revival. Many who became Christians uncritically created areas of conflict between Western cultural practices and African cultural practices, thinking that African culture was evil. For example, it was believed that men should have their beards shaved and women should wear long dresses, among other practices.

---

9. Enang, *Salvation in a Nigerian Background*, 107.
10. John S. Mbiti, *Bible and Theology in African Christianity* (Nairobi: Oxford University Press, 1986), 152–53.

Western missionary Christianity tended to emphasize the value of the soul to the neglect of the body. This was to some extent reflective of the Hellenistic thinking of a disembodied soul, where matter is seen as evil. In this way of thinking, social, economic, and political concerns are "sins" in which the Christian should not be involved. This is of course a way by which Christians can blind themselves and ignore the real challenges of the day, such as poverty, negative ethnicity, injustice, and corruption, by spiritualizing them rather than providing lasting solutions. In other words, church and politics are seen to be like oil and water; they cannot be mixed.[11] Such a view is not reflective of the true gospel.

Nevertheless, salvation among the revival Brethren is expressed and regarded more highly than one is likely to find in mainline churches. This salvation is characterized by loving one's brothers and sisters; confessing sin; an acceptance of challenging others and being challenged; a heart for unbelievers and the bereaved; witnessing through a team; prayer and preaching freedom; transparency; embracing interracial relationships; joy, laughter, and singing; and safety in homes where Jesus dwells.[12] Even though the person and work of Christ is acknowledged in many African arenas, it is more intensely expressed among the Brethren.

Rites are rife within ATR. Africans undergo elaborate rituals as they pass from one phase of life to another. Whether at birth, circumcision, marriage, death, or reconciliation, among other things, rituals are an important part of ATR. While many of the rituals are celebrated, mourning rituals for the dead are also important and tied to the well-being of the mourner. They are the means by which one transitions from one stage of life to another.

Lukan Expressions of Salvation and Distinctive Features

A comparison of Luke with the other gospels reveals that Luke's gospel carries a number of distinctive features.[13] These include Jesus's compassion for humanity and particularly those who were regarded as social outcasts, such as "sinners," women, and the poor; the dependence of Jesus on the Holy Spirit as well as prayer; use of the term *nomikos* (lawyer), an alteration of Mark's terminology so that Luke could bring contextual understanding to his readers; Luke's

---

11. Henry Okullu, *Church and Politics in East Africa* (Nairobi: Uzima, 1974), 2–3.
12. J. E. Church, *Quest for the Highest* (Exeter: Paternoster, 1981), 258.
13. Walter L. Liefeld, "Luke," in *The Expositor's Bible Commentary*, vol. 8, by Walter L. Liefeld and David W. Pao (Grand Rapids: Zondervan, 1984), 798.

sense of praise and joy for the healing and saving work of God; the practical teaching of Jesus that features dealing with finances; and Luke's clear sense of fulfillment, purpose, and accomplishment. These distinctives have a great appeal as a verisimilitude bringing hope and assurance to African believers.

Authorship and Purpose

Early church tradition attributes the authorship of the third gospel to Paul's companion named Luke.[14] Prior to this, Marcion, a heretic, also held the view that Luke penned this gospel. In addition, Irenaeus not only termed Luke Paul's "inseparable" companion, but also attested that this "inseparable" companion authored the Gospel of Luke.[15] Although it is not explicitly stated that Luke was a Gentile, Colossians 4:10–11, 14 suggests that he may not have been a Jew. It is recognized that there are other claims such as that Luke was Jewish, but such claims have not gained traction as the church tradition that Luke wrote this gospel.

Luke's purpose in writing this gospel is mentioned in the prologue of Luke 1:1–4. Luke had carried out a meticulous investigation regarding the accounts of Christ from eyewitnesses as well as gospel writers. Luke wrote an orderly account to Theophilus, so that he would be certain of having assurance of the things he had been taught regarding the gospel.

The Ministry of Jesus in Luke 4:14–44

In this section Luke narrates the preaching ministry of Jesus. This preaching cannot be stopped, not even by the murderous threat of Jesus's audience in a Jewish synagogue (vv. 29–30) nor by the endeavor of the multitudes in Capernaum to retain him (vv. 43–44). The ministry of Jesus in Nazareth and Capernaum which commenced in Galilee is an exemplification of his entire ministry in Palestine.[16] Recognizing the importance of this passage, some have highlighted it as key regarding the "Message of Mission."[17] Edwards asserts that "the bold repositioning of Jesus' sermon in Nazareth, and its dramatic expansion in comparison with its parallels in Mark 6:1–6 and Matt 13:54–58,

---

14. Liefeld, "Luke," 799.
15. Liefeld, 799.
16. John Nolland, *Luke 1:1–9:20*, Word Biblical Commentary (Dallas: Word, 1989), 184.
17. Howard Peskett and Vinoth Ramachandra, *The Message of Mission* (Leicester: Inter-Varsity, 2003), 157–71.

distinguishes it as the programmatic cornerstone of Jesus' ministry."[18] Luke 4:14–30 specifically is a programmatic expression of Christ's mission in the Gospel of Luke.

It is notable that this ministry has without ambiguity the Holy Spirit working in concert with Jesus (Luke 3:22; 4:1, 14, 18; 5:17; 10:21). Granted the meanings expressing "Spirit" are varied, but that Jesus is acting in concert with the Holy Spirit with whom he is anointed is not in doubt. Although Luke's expression of this anointing is ambiguous as to whether it is messianic or prophetic (v. 18), Jesus's mission is clear. Nevertheless, Luke's thinking has the two senses in view, but in this particular case the prophetic sense predominates.[19] This position is also supported explicitly by the Targum of Isaiah in the words "The spirit of prophecy from before the Lord Elohim is before me."[20]

Luke does not present Jesus as a social or political reformer but as one who is greatly concerned not only with our physical needs but also with our direct spiritual needs.[21] His understanding of the year of Jubilee includes spiritual restoration, deliverance from demonic forces, moral transformation, and release from disability and illness.[22] Thus from the Gospel of Luke, salvation is presented in a holistic sense. This holism of the gospel is also underscored by scholars. Talbert, for example, asserts that Jesus provided salvation not only for the "whole person" but also in the "whole world."[23]

It is notable that while Jesus was quoting from Isaiah 61:2, he omitted the words "the day of vengeance of our God." Since the Jews were under the Roman Empire, his audience might possibly have assumed that this day of salvation would result as the day of judgment on the Roman and other Gentile pagan enemies of the Jews. It was, however, through the delayed judgment that the Gentiles would in fact become beneficiaries of Jesus's salvation. Some scholars have suggested that it was because he omitted this vengeance phrase from Isaiah that Jesus attracted the hostility mentioned in verse 28.[24]

---

18. James R. Edwards, *The Gospel According to Luke* (Grand Rapids: Eerdmans, 2015), 133.
19. Nolland, *Luke 1:1–9:20*, 196.
20. J. F. Stenning, ed., *The Targum of Isaiah* (Oxford: Clarendon, 1949), 202.
21. Nolland, *Luke 1:1–9:20*, 197.
22. Nolland, 202.
23. Charles H. Talbert, *Reading Luke: A Literary and Theological Commentary*, rev. ed. (Macon: Smyth & Helwys, 2002), 60.
24. Liefeld, "Luke," 867.

It is critical to ask the question: What is the nature of salvation in Luke? Based on Luke, David Bosch asserts,

> Whatever salvation is . . . in every context, it includes the transformation of human life, forgiveness of sin, healing from infirmities and release from any kind of bondage (Luke uses *aphesis* for both "forgiveness" and "release" or "liberation": compare 24:47 with 4:18). This comprehensive understanding of salvation is evident in both the gospel and Acts.[25]

In Luke 4:18, the word "poor" is a seminal one. It is the term under which other terms used in the text – "prisoners," "blind," and "the oppressed" – are understood. Many scholars see the term "poor" as encompassing a larger meaning than just the literal sense. For example, Green argues that the seminal term "poor" can be perceived as a "holistic sense of those who are for any of a number of socio-religious reasons relegated to positions outside the boundaries of God's people."[26] Used in a collective way then, "poor" refers to anyone who is disadvantaged.[27] Jesus comes to the poor to give them "release."

Luke's concern is not only with spiritual issues but also with the social issues of the poor. Holistically, Luke does not ignore the evil and demonic forces in first-century society which stripped men, women, and children of selfhood and dignity, of food and voice, of sight. Such forces also worked to control the poor "for private gain; with the people's own selfishness and servility and with promises and possibilities of the poor and the outcasts."[28]

While quoting Isaiah 61:1–2, Luke inserts the phrase "to set the oppressed free." These words are from Isaiah 58:6, the context of which is fasting which pleases the Lord and where the oppressed are set free. Why did Luke insert this phrase? David Bosch suggests that since Jesus's audience were familiar with the phrase, they would have understood his message.[29]

Salvation as a multidimensional concept is reflected in the work of many theologians. As an example, William Barclay in his commentary on Romans notes the following seven aspects to Christian salvation:

---

25. David J. Bosch, *Transforming Mission: Paradigm Shifts in Theology of Mission* (Maryknoll: Orbis, 1991), 107.

26. Joel B. Green, *The Gospel of Luke* (Grand Rapids: Eerdmans, 1997), 211.

27. John S. Pobee, *Who Are the Poor? The Beatitudes as a Call to Community* (Geneva: World Council of Churches, 1987), 20.

28. Llewellyn Welile Mazamisa, *Beatific Comradeship: An Exegetical Study on Luke 10:25–37* (Kampen: J. H. Kok, 1987), 99.

29. Bosch, *Transforming Mission*, 101.

1. "It was salvation from physical illness" (Matt 9:21; Luke 8:36 – the healing of a demon-possessed man).
2. "It was salvation from danger" (Matt 8:25; 14:30 – Peter cries out to be saved from drowning).
3. "It was salvation from life's infection" (Acts 2:40 – Peter addresses the crowd and urges them, "Save yourselves from this corrupt generation").
4. "It was salvation from lostness" (Matt 18:11; Luke 19:10 – Jesus tells Zacchaeus that salvation has come to his house).
5. "It was salvation from sin" (Matt 1:21 – Jesus's name means that he will save people from sin).
6. "It was salvation from the wrath of God" (Rom 5:9 – believers are reconciled to God).
7. "It was a salvation which is eschatological" (Rom 13:11; 1 Cor 5:5; 2 Tim 4:18; 1 Pet 1:5 – it will be complete beyond time in the final triumph of Jesus Christ).[30]

The Commission on World Mission and Evangelism (CWME) conference in Bangkok in 1973 focused on "Salvation Today" as its theme. In this conference attended by zealous conservative evangelicals, Orthodox Christians, Pentecostals, and the Kimbanguist Church as well as Roman Catholics, salvation was articulated in four dimensions.[31] In this articulation, salvation is a manifestation of a struggle to attain economic justice as opposed to exploitation; human dignity as opposed to oppression; solidarity as opposed to alienation; and hope as opposed to hopelessness in individual life. While these advocacy and liberating dimensions are solely this-worldly, it is noteworthy that salvation was understood as multidimensional. According to David Bosch, violence in all its various forms – war, hatred, oppression, and injustice – is a manifestation of evil, and a heart for humaneness in the conquest of illness, famine, and purposelessness is an aspect of salvation for which believers not only hope but also labor. Although these four dimensions are deficient in making the person of Christ the liberator central to salvation and from which

---

30. William Barclay, "Good News of Which to Be Proud: Romans 1:16–17," William Barclay's Daily Study Bible, Bible Portal, https://bibleportal.com/commentary/section/william-barclay/good-news-of-which-to-be-proud-romans-116-17-8049.

31. Bosch, *Transforming Mission*, 396–97.

the four dimensions can be derived, the idea of salvation as multidimensional is apparent in this thinking.

Convergence of Salvation in ATR with the Gospel

The gospel and ATR have many points of convergence. Some areas of convergence are the desire and need for worship, the fact that human beings and society experience evil, the belief that humans are spiritual beings, and the reality of good and bad spirits.

Both Scripture and ATR feature worship. That humans long for and seek a deep connection with God is important in both. The question often arises whether Africans in ATR worship the God of the Bible or not. Although that is an important question requiring a comprehensive response, suffice it to say here that humans are made in God's image and, although that image has been marred since the fall, it should not be a surprise when it is asserted that "God the Father of our Lord Jesus Christ is the same God who for thousands of years has been known and worshipped in various ways within the religious life of African peoples."[32] Worshipping is "an imperative urge in man" traceable to the basic "instinct" in humans evoked by their encounter "with the numinous," a "Power" that is greater than humans. Such a "Power" not only dominates but also controls the unseen realm in which humans are encased.[33] This is not to deny that those practicing ATR can worship other gods, but the point is that the human desire and need to worship emanates from God himself.

The idea and practice of sacrifice is also common to Scripture and ATR. The epitome of sacrifice in Scripture is that of Jesus Christ by God the Father and yet in concert with Christ himself. In ATR, sacrifice is made to gods or ancestors. When the Kikuyus sacrifice, it is required that an animal of one color comes from an individual who has not engaged in "murder, theft or rape" or witchcraft. In the company of those making sacrifice for rains to fall must be two children aged below eight years, as such children are understood to be "pure in heart, mind, and body, and . . . free from worldly sins." Moreover, the elders making such sacrifices must refrain from sexual intercourse for eight

---

32. John W. Kinney, "The Theology of John Mbiti: His Sources, Norms and Method," *International Bulletin of Mission Research* 3, no. 2 (1979): 65–67.
33. Bolaji E. Idowu, *Olodumare: God in Yoruba Belief* (London: Crowe & Sons, 1962), 61.

days: six of those days being before the sacrifice and two of those days after the sacrifice.[34] Thus, holiness is a prerequisite for offering this kind of sacrifice.

Scripture and ATR both recognize that there is evil in humans and society. Such evil includes murder, stealing, lying, greed, corruption, sexual immorality, and injustice, among many other vices. That evil is undesirable is also common to ATR and Christianity.

Both ATR and Scripture perceive humans as more than merely physical beings. They are spiritual beings. As such, humans have a spiritual hunger and thirst that needs to be met.

The reality of spirits in Scripture is also reflected in ATR. Such spirits can manifest themselves as abnormalities in people's lives. For example, madness may be understood as caused by a spirit. According to Hood, the biblical perspective of spirits is similar to the African worldview of spirits in many ways. First, just as God's Spirit does not speak without God's authority, so Africans believe that spirits act as directed by God. Second, just as the Spirit inspired God's prophets, so spirits are power-giving according to Africans. Third, just as the seven spirits stand before God's throne, so spirits in African religion are God's messengers. Fourth, though not in every situation, God is considered sovereign over all spirits by Africans, just as the Bible recognizes that God is sovereign over all spirits.[35]

The death of humans in ATR is also readily recognized in Scripture. In both, humans are vulnerable, and at one time or another they will die physically. However, though the death of human beings is inevitable according to both ATR and Scripture, this death is not inconsequential. The aftermath of death carries the serious consequences of the preceding life, spelling either doom or flourishing for the dead person.

Deviation and Deficiencies of Salvation in ATR in Light of Scripture

There are theologians who argue that salvation is not "total" and is a matter more of the soul than of anything else. Foerster and Fohrer, for example, assert that in the New Testament, *sōtēria* is not used in reference to deliverance

---

34. Jomo Kenyatta, *Facing Mount Kenya* (London: Secker & Warburg, 1938), 244, 234. See also John Mbiti, *Concepts of God in Africa* (Nairobi: Acton 2012), 73.

35. Stephen B. Bevans, *Models of Contextual Theology* (Maryknoll: Orbis, 2002), 63. See also Robert E. Hood, *Must God Remain Greek? Afro Cultures and God-Talk* (Minneapolis: Fortress, 1990), 186–88.

from powers of demons, "physical health, political liberation."³⁶ Not achievable by either contrition or reason, salvation, according to Foerster and Fohrer, is strictly about the human being's relationship with God. This salvation is both present and future. Positively, this salvation can be described as attaining "glory," while negatively it can be described as deliverance from God's wrath.

While some Westerners and the legacy of mission Christianity embrace this view, the New Testament portrays a more comprehensive or holistic view of salvation, and we have seen how this is brought out by the Gospel of Luke. We note that Luke also brings the Old Testament notion of salvation into the New Testament. This is by no means surprising since in the Old Testament we see God as the deliverer of Israel from Egypt in the exodus and God healing Naaman; and in the New Testament, Jesus delivers a demon-possessed boy (Matt 17), heals a bleeding woman (Matt 9), and liberates Matthew from the corrupt life of the tax collectors of his day.

To assert that the gospel is holistic is in no way to agree with the tenets of the prosperity gospel or ATR. To some, it may seem so, but that is not the intention of this chapter. Salvation in ATR has deviations and deficiencies in light of Scripture.

ATR is anthropocentric, thus deviating from the critical place occupied by the cross of Christ at the heart of biblical salvation. Thus, the deviation of ATR is idolatry in light of Scripture and draws God's wrath rather than his blessing. Furthermore, ATR minimizes the perspective of God's kingdom, which is larger than the adherents of ATR in light of those who receive the gospel of our Lord Jesus Christ. By this I mean that whether numerically or in terms of ethnic diversity, God's kingdom is larger than ATR's domain. ATR is also deficient as a means of salvation since God has provided only one way of salvation. While ATR may at first seem to value human life, it fails to capture human beings as God's image regardless of their ethnic origin or history.

Contemporary African Christian Understandings of Salvation

Having examined deviations and deficiencies of ATR, we will examine contemporary African Christian understandings of salvation. It has been said that "the church in Africa is a mile wide and an inch deep." This kind of critique may be born out of many factors. One is the "ethnocide" of culture,

---

36. Werner Foerster and Georg Fohrer, "*Sōzo, Sōtēria, Sōtēr, Sōtērios*," in *Theological Dictionary of the New Testament*, eds. Gerhard Kittel and Gerhard Friedrich, trans. Geoffrey Bromiley, vol. 7 (Grand Rapids: Eerdmans, 1985), 1137.

an accompaniment of the colonial legacy. Another is a wrong view of ATR, and yet another emanates from a flawed theory of religion.

Asserting that "the church in Africa is a mile wide and an inch deep" is an insult to God. The statement discredits the sanctifying work of the Holy Spirit and is a way of putting African Christians in the shadows with regard to having a spiritual and prophetic voice. The good news is that the sanctifying work of the Holy Spirit cannot be silenced, discredited, manipulated, or denied.

Biblical salvation is not indifferent to the plight of Africa and the world in addressing negative ethnicity, injustice, poverty, oppression, endemic corruption, suffering, disease, terrorism, and bad governance, among other ills. These realities are dehumanizing and alienating, and they escalate conflict that only the peace of the gospel can resolve.

T. Watson Street asserts that

> liberation can point to conditions and structures from which men today are seeking deliverance such as poverty, injustice, cruelty, and suffering on the one hand, and materialistic affluence, inordinate power, insensitivity, prejudice and complacency on the other hand. All of these alienate men from one another, destroy their humanity, and prevent them from living together in peace.[37]

Watson points to a reality from which humans seek liberation, but only the gospel of Christ can bring the freedom that humankind longs for.

Background of Study Participants

In this study, ninety questionnaires were sent out to two churches. Eighty-eight of the questionnaires were analyzed. The participants were Christians who ranged in age from teenage years to senior citizens. Their education level varied, from primary school certificate holders to one PhD holder, with diverse professions such as nurses, teachers, engineers, accountants, and lawyers. They were drawn from two countries, Kenya and Zimbabwe, and were members or attenders of an evangelical church. The results are presented using William Barclay's 7 aspects of salvation.

Asked when they became Christians, eighteen did not respond. The others responded as follows: five in the period 1985–95; six in 1996–2000; seventeen in 2001–10; thirty-six in 2011–22; and six "since birth." It is not clear why

---

37. T. Watson Street, "Salvation Today: Reflections on the Bangkok Conference," Austin Seminary Bulletin (Faculty ed.) 89, 7 (Apr 1974): 16.

some participants did not wish to respond to the question regarding when they became Christians, and it is notable that some became "Christians" at birth. For the latter, it is possible that they think being born in a Christian family or attending church makes one a Christian, which is a departure from Scripture.

Deliverance from Physical Illness

Asked whether Christian salvation includes deliverance from physical illness, seventeen responded "not at all," while four indicated "a little bit"; twelve indicated "a good bit," and fifty-four indicated "very much." Only one person among the participants did not answer this question. The majority therefore indicated that salvation includes deliverance from physical illness. Again, Jesus was able to heal everyone brought to him physically, even remotely, as in the case of the centurion's son. However, Scripture does not promise that salvation will always be accompanied by deliverance from physical illness, although some may claim so.

Deliverance from Physical Danger

To the question whether Christian salvation includes deliverance from physical danger, one participant did not answer; twenty-one responded "not at all"; six answered "a little bit"; eleven responded "a good bit"; and forty-nine answered "very much." This may mean that the majority of participants believe that salvation is accompanied by deliverance from physical danger. While indeed God is able to deliver from physical danger, he does not necessarily do so, as evidenced by the case of the thief who was crucified with Jesus, narrated in Luke 23:40–43.

Deliverance from Life's Infection

As to whether Christian salvation is accompanied by deliverance from life's infection, one did not respond; twenty participants answered "not at all"; eleven answered "a little bit"; another eleven answered "a good bit"; and forty-five answered "very much." Considering that corruption is endemic in Africa as well as in many other parts of the world, one notes that the majority of the participants in this study seem oblivious to this fact.

Deliverance from Lostness

Asked whether Christian salvation includes deliverance from lostness, one participant did not answer; twelve answered "not at all"; seven answered "a little"; four answered "a good bit"; sixty-four answered "very much." It is notable that the majority of responses here are consistent with Scripture, while at the same time many participants do not have the view that deliverance from lostness is a major work of God in salvation.

Deliverance from Sin

As to the question whether Christian salvation includes deliverance from sin, one respondent did not answer; three answered "not at all"; three answered "a little"; three answered "a good bit"; and seventy-eight answered "very much." The majority of the respondents affirmed the truth that deliverance from sin is a key aspect of salvation, an important aspect of the Christian confession of faith in Africa. This does not in any way deny that sin is present in this world, but it signifies that Christ delivers from the power and penalty of sin.

Deliverance from the Wrath of God

Asked to what extent Christian salvation delivers from the wrath of God, two participants did not respond; seven responded "not at all"; two responded "a little"; nine responded "a good bit"; sixty-eight responded "very much." These responses indicate that the majority of the participants believed that salvation is accompanied by peace from God, though a small proportion of the participants did not believe that God's wrath is fully turned away from those who receive the gift of salvation.

Deliverance from Future Judgment

As to whether Christian salvation includes salvation from future judgment, two respondents did not answer; five responded "not at all"; seven responded "a little"; six responded "a good bit"; sixty-eight responded "very much." The majority of these responses recognize that there is no punitive judgment for Christians in the future.

Implications

The responses above regarding the seven dimensions of salvation (set out in the appendix at the end of this chapter) incline toward a holistic salvation. Although the results raise questions as to the doctrinal nurturing of these Christian study participants, a holistic salvation is part and parcel of their understanding of salvation.

There are several implications of a holistic salvation:

- The African church, while not neglecting the spiritual aspect of salvation, needs to be deliberate in teaching a holistic salvation.
- Evangelists in African churches need training in how to proclaim a holistic gospel while safeguarding themselves from the prosperity gospel.
- Discipleship in the African church needs to reflect that the gospel is holistic and addresses not just the spirit but also the Christian's other needs. This means that African Christians need to use their spiritual gifts to reflect the diversity of these gifts.
- Understanding the concept of salvation in ATR helps with contextualization of the gospel.

Conclusion

Both ATR and Scripture portray a holistic salvation. This holistic salvation is multidimensional, encompassing aspects that are spiritual, physical, and material. Though some may distort the idea of a holistic salvation through teaching the prosperity gospel, this does not negate a biblical holistic gospel. In African Christianity, believers are more inclined toward a holistic salvation than a mere spiritual salvation.

Appendix: African Understanding of Salvation

Age of respondents

		Frequency	Percent	Valid Percent	Cumulative Percent
Valid	Did not answer	1	1.1	1.1	1.1
	15–25 years	53	60.2	60.2	61.4
	26–35 years	13	14.8	14.8	76.1
	36–45 years	11	12.5	12.5	88.6
	46–55 years	7	8.0	8.0	96.6
	56–65 years	3	3.4	3.4	100.0
	Total	88	100.0	100.0	

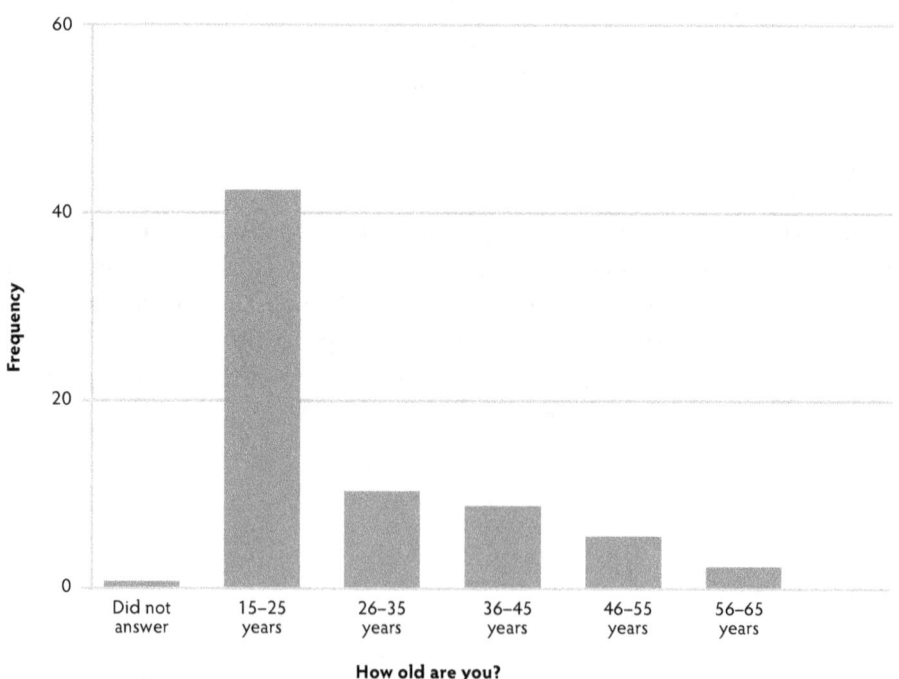

Church belonging

		Frequency	Percent	Valid Percent	Cumulative Percent
Valid	Did not answer	4	4.5	4.5	4.5
	CCK	48	54.5	54.5	59.1
	RG	36	40.9	40.9	100.0
	Total	88	100.0	100.0	

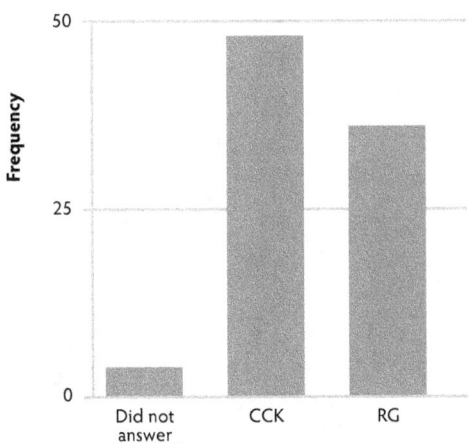

What Church do you belong to?

Level of education

		Frequency	Percent	Valid Percent	Cumulative Percent
Valid	Did not answer	6	6.8	6.8	6.8
	Primary	2	2.3	2.3	9.1
	High School	20	22.7	22.7	31.8
	Diploma	18	20.5	20.5	52.3
	Degree	33	37.5	37.5	89.8
	Master's Degree	8	9.1	9.1	98.9
	PhD	1	1.1	1.1	100.0
	Total	88	100.0	100.0	

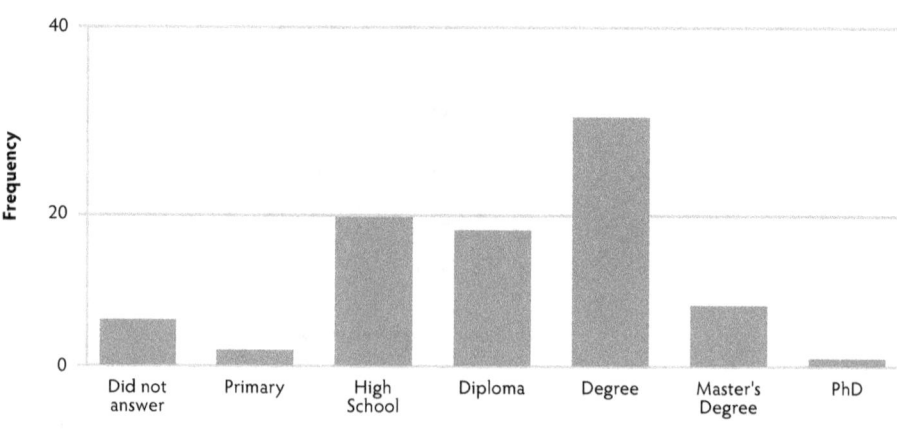

What is your level of education?

Occupation

		Frequency	Percent	Valid Percent	Cumulative Percent
Valid	Didn't answer	29	33.0	33.0	33.0
	Student	18	20.5	20.5	53.4
	Unemployed	3	3.4	3.4	56.8
	Nurse	3	3.4	3.4	60.2
	Engineer	2	2.3	2.3	62.5
	Teacher/Counselor	3	3.4	3.4	65.9
	Accountant	1	1.1	1.1	67.0
	Lawyer	1	1.1	1.1	68.2
	Pastor	6	6.8	6.8	75.0
	Consultant	2	2.3	2.3	77.3
	Others	20	22.7	22.7	100.0
	Total	88	100.0	100.0	

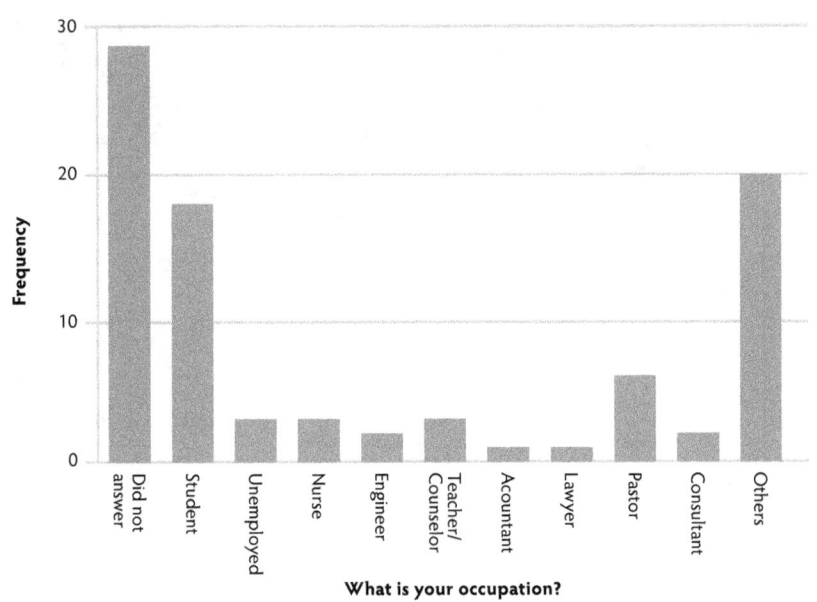

Nationality

		Frequency	Percent	Valid Percent	Cumulative Percent
Valid	Did not answer	8	9.1	9.1	9.1
	Zimbabwe	14	15.9	15.9	25.0
	Kenya	66	75.0	75.0	100.0
	Total	88	100.0	100.0	

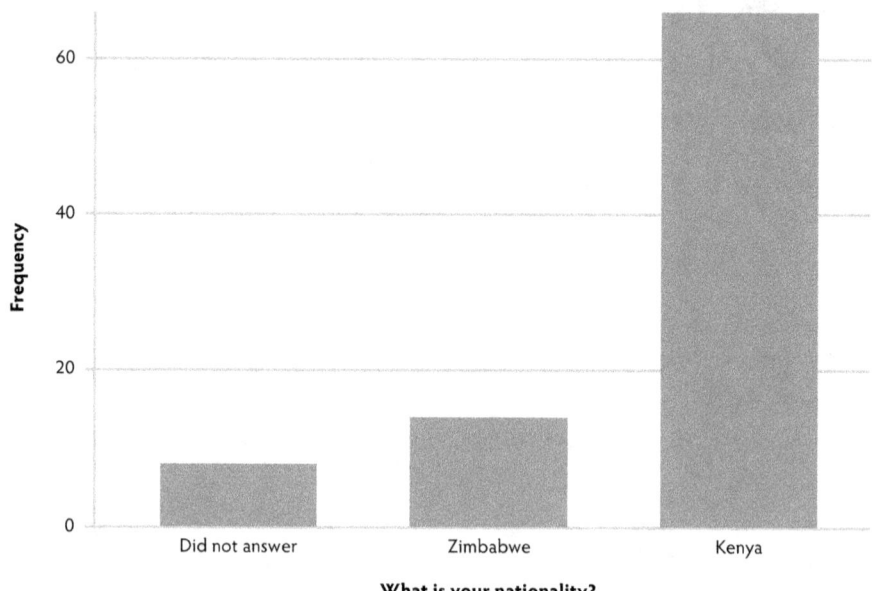

What is your nationality?

When did you become a Christian?

		Frequency	Percent	Valid Percent	Cumulative Percent
Valid	Did not answer	18	20.5	20.5	20.5
	1985–1995	5	5.7	5.7	26.1
	1996–2000	6	6.8	6.8	33.0
	2001–2010	17	19.3	19.3	52.3
	2011–2022	36	40.9	40.9	93.2
	Since birth	6	6.8	6.8	100.0
	Total	88	100.0	100.0	

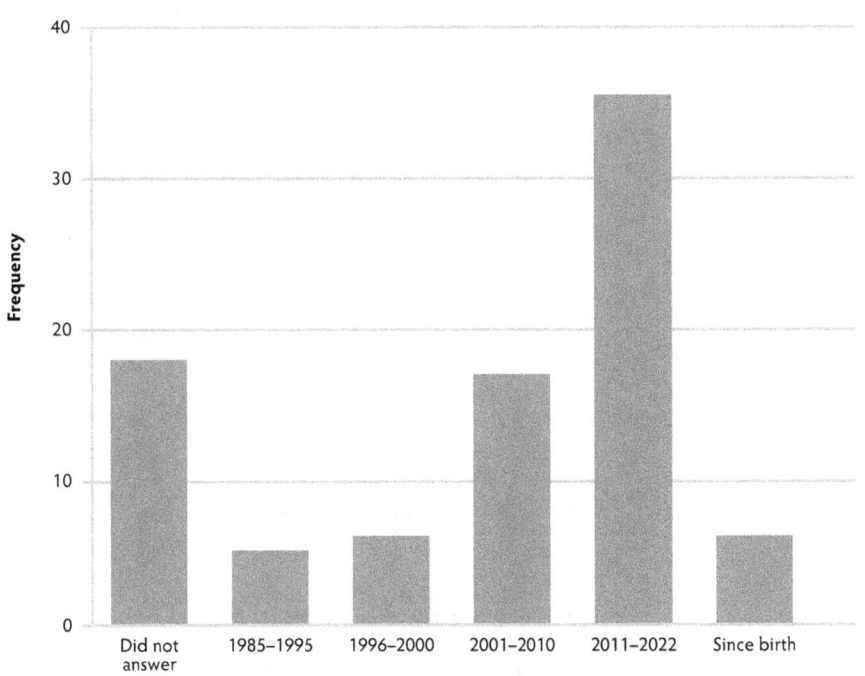

Which year did you become a Christian?

Christian salvation includes deliverance from physical illness

		Frequency	Percent	Valid Percent	Cumulative Percent
Valid	No answer	1	1.1	1.1	1.1
	Not at all	17	19.3	19.3	20.5
	A little	4	4.5	4.5	25.0
	A good bit	12	13.6	13.6	38.6
	Very much	54	61.4	61.4	100.0
	Total	88	100.0	100.0	

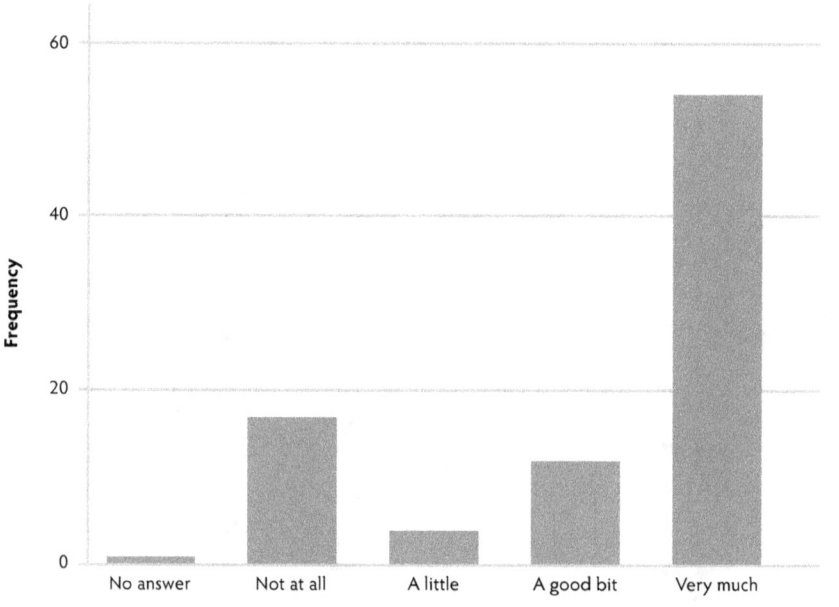

Christian salvation includes deliverance from physical illness

Christian salvation includes deliverance from danger

		Frequency	Percent	Valid Percent	Cumulative Percent
Valid	No answer	1	1.1	1.1	1.1
	Not at all	21	23.9	23.9	25.0
	A little	6	6.8	6.8	31.8
	A good bit	11	12.5	12.5	44.3
	Very much	49	55.7	55.7	100.0
	Total	88	100.0	100.0	

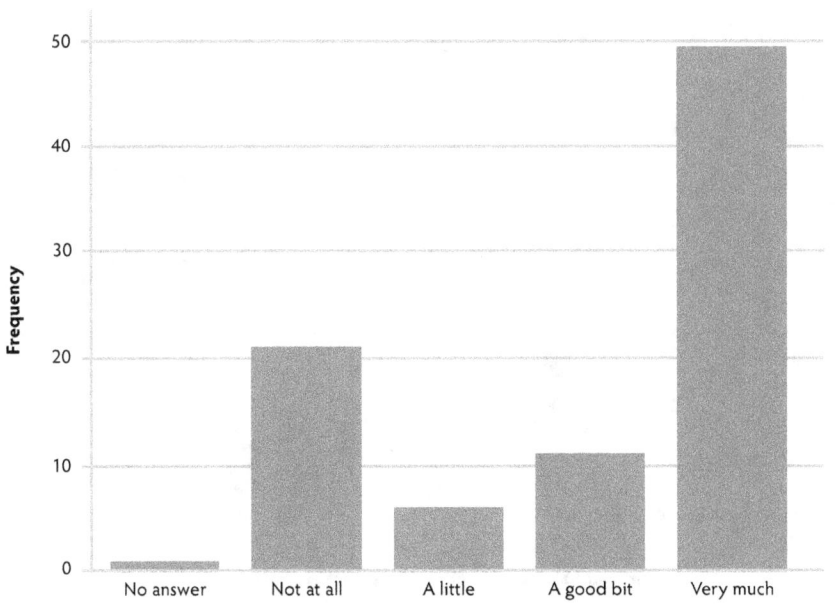

Christian salvation includes deliverance from danger

Christian salvation includes deliverance from life's infection

		Frequency	Percent	Valid Percent	Cumulative Percent
Valid	No answer	1	1.1	1.1	1.1
	Not at all	20	22.7	22.7	23.9
	A little	11	12.5	12.5	36.4
	A good bit	11	12.5	12.5	48.9
	Very much	45	51.1	51.1	100.0
	Total	88	100.0	100.0	

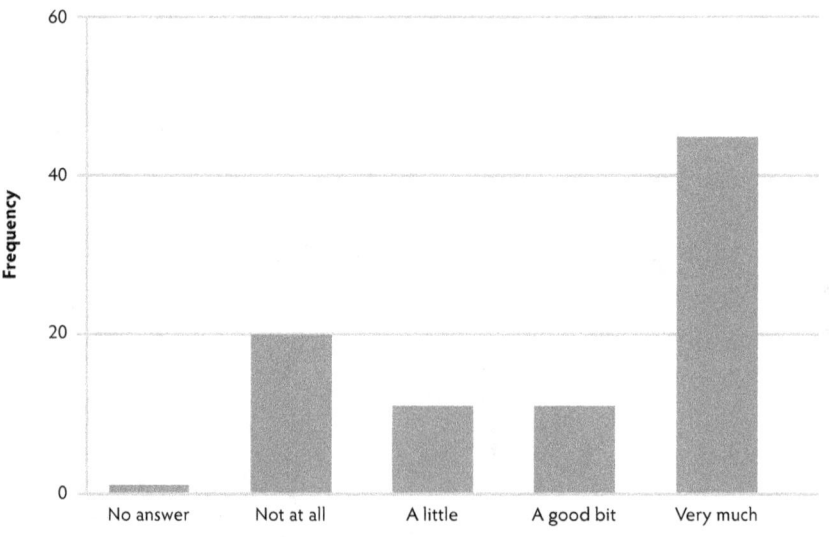

Christian salvation includes deliverance from life's infection

Christian salvation includes deliverance from lostness

		Frequency	Percent	Valid Percent	Cumulative Percent
Valid	No answer	1	1.1	1.1	1.1
	Not at all	12	13.6	13.6	14.8
	A little	7	8.0	8.0	22.7
	A good bit	4	4.5	4.5	27.3
	Very much	64	72.7	72.7	100.0
	Total	88	100.0	100.0	

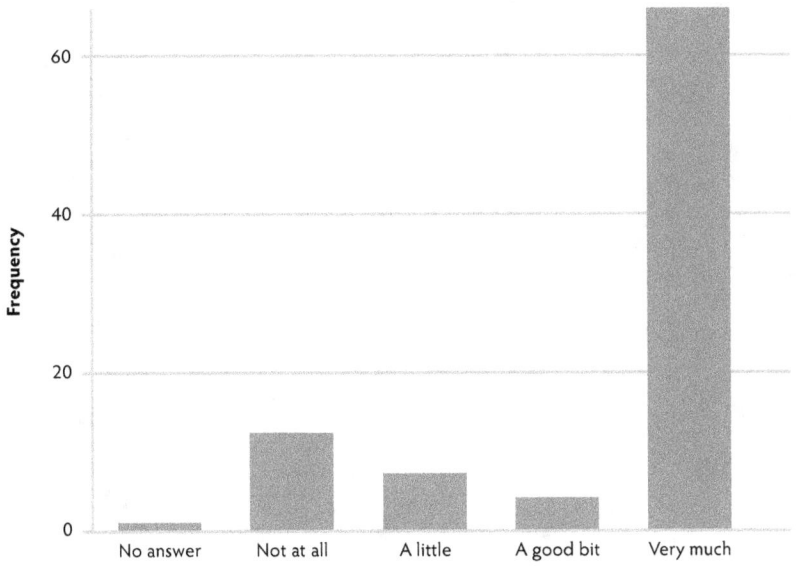

Christian salvation includes deliverance from lostness

Christian salvation includes deliverance from sin

		Frequency	Percent	Valid Percent	Cumulative Percent
Valid	No answer	1	1.1	1.1	1.1
	Not at all	3	3.4	3.4	4.5
	A little	3	3.4	3.4	8.0
	A good bit	3	3.4	3.4	11.4
	Very much	78	88.6	88.6	100.0
	Total	88	100.0	100.0	

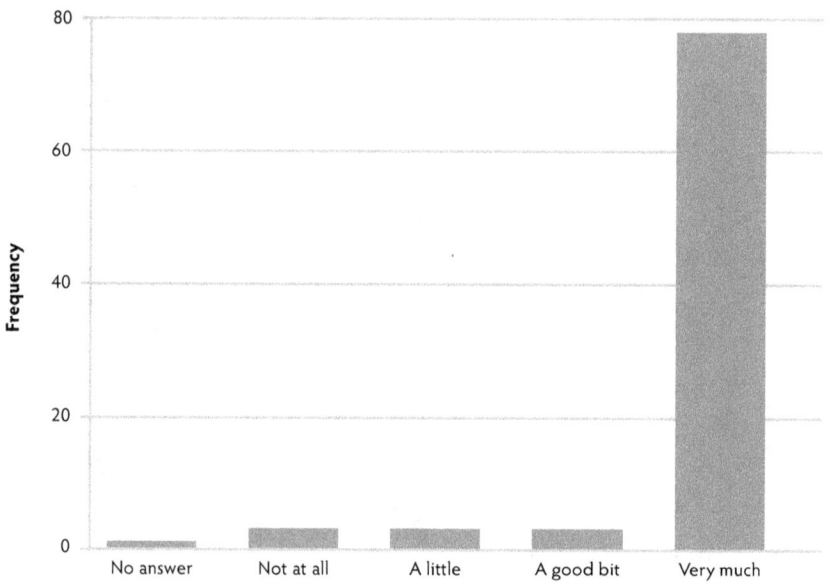

Christian salvation includes deliverance from sin

Christian salvation includes deliverance from wrath of God

		Frequency	Percent	Valid Percent	Cumulative Percent
Valid	No answer	2	2.3	2.3	2.3
	Not at all	7	8.0	8.0	10.2
	A little	2	2.3	2.3	12.5
	A good bit	9	10.2	10.2	22.7
	Very much	68	77.3	77.3	100.0
	Total	88	100.0	100.0	

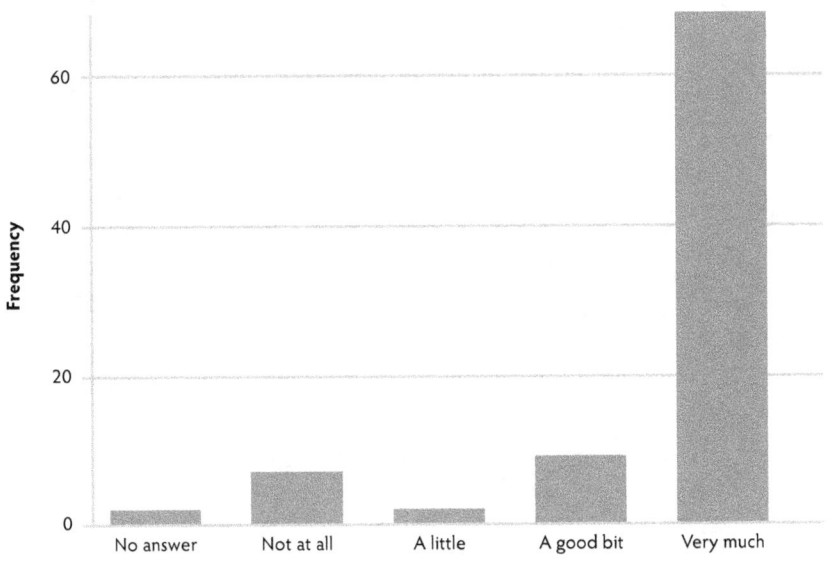

Christian salvation includes deliverance from wrath of God

Christian salvation includes deliverance from future judgment

		Frequency	Percent	Valid Percent	Cumulative Percent
Valid	No answer	2	2.3	2.3	2.3
	Not at all	5	5.7	5.7	8.0
	A little	7	8.0	8.0	15.9
	A good bit	6	6.8	6.8	22.7
	Very much	68	77.3	77.3	100.0
	Total	88	100.0	100.0	

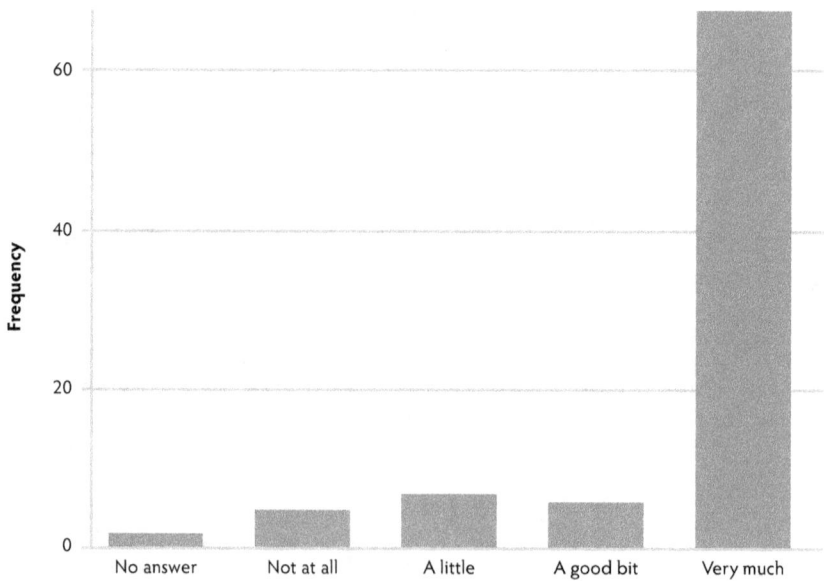

Christian salvation includes deliverance from future judgment

Bibliography

Adamo, David Tuesday. "Africa and Africans in the Old Testament Scheme of Salvation." *Theologia Viatorum* 35, no. 1 (2011): 137–66.

Adeyemo, Tokunboh. "The Idea of Salvation in Contemporary World Religions." *East African Journal of Evangelical Theology* 2, no. 1 (Jan. 1983): 4–12.

Barclay, William. "Good News of Which to Be Proud: Romans 1:16–17." William Barclay's Daily Study Bible. Bible Portal. https://bibleportal.com/commentary/section/william-barclay/good-news-of-which-to-be-proud-romans-116-17-8049.

Beir, Ulli, ed. *The Origin of Life and Death: African Creation Myths*. Nairobi: Heinemann Educational, 1966.
Bevans, Stephen B. *Models of Contextual Theology*. Maryknoll: Orbis, 2002.
Bosch, David J. *Transforming Mission: Paradigm Shifts in Theology of Mission*. Maryknoll: Orbis, 1991.
Chike, Chigor. "The Doctrine of Salvation among African Christians." Fulcrum, 31 October 2007. https://www.fulcrum-anglican.org.uk/articles/the-doctrine-of-salvation-among-african-christians/.
Church, J. E. *Quest for the Highest*. Exeter: Paternoster, 1981.
Edwards, James R. *The Gospel According to Luke*. Grand Rapids: Eerdmans, 2015.
Enang, Kenneth. *Salvation in a Nigerian Background: Its Concepts and Articulation in the Annang Independent Churches* (Berlin: Verlag von Reimer, 1979).
Foerster, Werner, and Georg Fohrer. "Sōzo, Sōtēria, Sōtēr, Sōtērios." In *Theological Dictionary of the New Testament*, eds. Gerhard Kittel and Gerhard Friedrich. Translated by Geoffrey Bromiley. Vol. 7. Grand Rapids: Eerdmans, 1985.
Gehman, Richard J. "Will the African Ancestors Be Saved?" *Africa Journal of Evangelical Theology* 14, no. 2 (1995): 85–97.
Gifford, Paul. "'Africa Shall Be Saved.' An Appraisal of Reinhardt Bonnke's Pan-African Crusade." *Journal of Religion in Africa* 17, no. 1 (1987): 63–92.
Green, Joel B. *The Gospel of Luke*. Grand Rapids: Eerdmans, 1997.
Hood, Robert E. *Must God Remain Greek? Afro Cultures and God-Talk*. Minneapolis: Fortress, 1990.
Idowu, Bolaji E. *Olodumare: God in Yoruba Belief*. London: Crowe & Sons, 1962.
Kenyatta, Jomo. *Facing Mount Kenya*. London: Secker & Warburg, 1938.
Kinney, John W. "The Theology of John Mbiti: His Sources, Norms and Method." *International Bulletin of Mission Research* 3, no. 2 (1979): 65–67.
Liefeld, Walter L. "Luke." In *The Expositor's Bible Commentary*. Vol. 8, by Walter L. Liefeld and David W. Pao. Grand Rapids: Zondervan, 1984.
Mazamisa, Llewellyn Welile. *Beatific Comradeship: An Exegetical Study on Luke 10:25–37*. Kampen: J. H. Kok, 1987.
Mbiti, John S. *African Religions and Philosophy*. Nairobi: East African Educational, 2002.
———. *Bible and Theology in African Christianity*. Nairobi: Oxford University Press, 1986.
———. "Christianity and African Religion." In *Facing the New Challenges: The Message of PACLA, December 9–19, 1976, Nairobi*, edited by Michael Cassidy and Luc Verlinden, 308–13. Kisumu: Evangel, 1978.
———. *Concepts of God in Africa*. Nairobi: Acton, 2012.
———. "Some Reflections of African Experience of Salvation Today." In *Living Faiths and Ultimate Goals*, edited by S. J. Samartha, 108–19. Geneva: World Council of Churches, 1974.
Nolland, John. *Luke 1:1–9:20*. Word Biblical Commentary. Dallas: Word, 1989.

Okullu, Henry. *Church and Politics in East Africa.* Nairobi: Uzima, 1974.

Peskett, Howard, and Vinoth Ramachandra. *The Message of Mission.* Leicester: Inter-Varsity, 2003.

Pobee, John S. *Who Are the Poor? The Beatitudes as a Call to Community.* Geneva: World Council of Churches, 1987.

Sarpongtawiah, Yaw. "Salvation in African Christian Theology: A Critical Comparison of the Views of John Mbiti and Mercy Amba Oduyoye." PhD Dissertation, 2016.

Stenning, J. F., ed. *The Targum of Isaiah.* Oxford: Clarendon, 1949.

Street, T. Watson. "Salvation Today: Reflections on the Bangkok Conference," Austin Seminary Bulletin (Faculty ed.) 89, 7 (Apr 1974): 5–25.

Strohbehn, Ulf. "Theology: Salvation and the Church." In *The Zionist Churches in Malawi*, 274–373. Malawi: Mzuni, 2016.

Talbert, Charles H. *Reading Luke: A Literary and Theological Commentary.* Rev. ed. Macon: Smyth & Helwys, 2002.

Wachege, Patrick N. "The Church: Its Role in God's Plan of Salvation." *AFER* 42, no. 1–2 (2000): 27–51.

14

Holism in Salvation

Philemon Ongole
Overseer of Deliverance Churches in Eastern Uganda

Abstract

The history of salvation in Africa has seen changes in perspectives and practices among African believers at different times and in different cultural contexts. These changes include conflicts with traditional African religions, syncretism, nominalism, dichotomy, and holism. Each of these phenomena has had implications for African Christianity. The current situation seems to be that there are things that are considered to belong to God and things that are considered to belong to the world. This has been called the dichotomy between the sacred and the secular. The factors influencing this dichotomy are identified and addressed in this chapter and include worldviews and value systems.

However, evangelical Christian theology teaches that all things come from God and all things serve God's purposes; therefore, God is involved in everything. The development of this concept in the doctrine and practice of salvation is the core of this chapter. It includes a discussion of the practical challenges that come with it. We also include the advantages and goodness of holism and, conversely, the implications of holding to a contrary position, giving practical illustrations at appropriate points. The aspect of God's kingdom in the African context is also relevantly treated.

The chapter mainly takes a theological approach to the issues discussed, as well as an initial historical approach. Included are a brief historical overview, cultural discussion, theological exposition (including a proper understanding of salvation), practical suggestions, and a conclusive position. The goal of the chapter is to help evangelical African Christian believers be holistic in their understanding and practice of Christianity. This should have a transformational effect on their lives.

Key words: Holism, salvation, sacred, secular, God's kingdom, church, religion, Christianity, syncretism, values

Introduction

The word "holism" in the context of salvation means the involvement of salvation in the whole of one's life. It is a perspective based on the fact that God created all things and is involved in and concerned about all things. Therefore, in salvation, every aspect of one's whole life is committed to God and influenced by him. Pearcey argues in her book *Total Truth* that God is in all things and all things serve his purposes when seen from a divine perspective.[1] This point forms the central argument of this chapter. The division of reality between the sacred and the secular has a historical background which will be explained below. This dichotomy is the chief concern of the chapter, and related factors are discussed.

Holism has some echoes in African Traditional Religions. Scholars of traditional African society, such as Mbiti, bring out the important point that Africans involve their religion in every aspect of their lives.[2] This background serves as an advantage for Christianity: a transformed African believer can allow Christianity to permeate every aspect of his or her life. How this can be done is suggested in the chapter. The challenges involved will also be addressed. Among these challenges is fighting syncretism within African Christianity.

The chapter examines historical factors involved in the subject of its concern, the nature of salvation, the theological significance of holism, challenges to holism in the context of African society (including factors influencing the dichotomy between the sacred and the secular), God's kingdom in Africa, and implications in the context of African Christianity. The chapter concludes with practical suggestions for holism in African Christianity.

---

1. Nancy Pearcey, *Total Truth: Liberating Christianity from Its Cultural Captivity* (Wheaton: Crossway, 2004), 65–66.

2. John S. Mbiti, *African Religions and Philosophy* (Nairobi: East African Educational, 2015), 1.

Historical Background

From the time Emperor Constantine stopped the persecution of Christians in the fourth century and Christianity was made the state religion of the Roman Empire, to sometime during the Middle Ages, Christianity dominated the world. The church was the most powerful institution in society, influencing daily life, activities, and thought systems. The church's leaders were respected, even feared. The church controlled many systems in society. Cairns comments that in the medieval period, especially from 1054 to 1305, the Roman Catholic Church reached the peak of its power when its popes successfully enforced the church's claims to supremacy over the State through the humiliation of the most powerful sovereigns of Europe.[3] It is said of Pope Gregory VII that as a pope, a "vicar of Christ," he claimed that "he could give or take away empires, kingdoms, duchies, marquisates, and the possessions of all men. Everyone on earth, from the emperor down to the humblest peasant, must acknowledge him."[4] State leaders submitted to the church fully because of its divine claims.

However, from the time of the Renaissance and the Enlightenment – that is, from about the fifteenth to the eighteenth centuries – people's way of thinking changed. Science and new learning began to influence society. The authority of the church in society was questioned, and its leaders began to be suspected. The truth was no longer the domain of the church alone; new scientific and intellectual discoveries began to make strong appeals to people's minds. Cairns brings this out clearly in chapter 33 of his book.[5] Moreover, following the Renaissance, nation states began to arise as a form of political organization.[6] Gradually there was a separation between the church and the State. Eventually, the State was considered supreme in all areas of life, and it was subject not to the church but to "the sovereign people."[7] It was only in matters of religion that people turned to the church.

The separation between the church and the State caused a separation between what was considered to be of God and what was considered to be of the world. Eventually, with increased "secular" learning and influence, the church was pushed to a corner of society in its significance. Its authority no longer counted for much. Some of its doctrines, such as creationism and

---

3. Earle E. Cairns, *Christianity through the Centuries: A History of the Christian Church* (Grand Rapids: Zondervan, 1981), 23.
4. A. M. Renwick and A. M. Harman, *The Story of the Church*, 3rd ed. (Nottingham: Inter-Varsity, 2007), 89.
5. Cairns, *Christianity through the Centuries*, 373–87.
6. Cairns, 265.
7. Cairns, 378.

divine sovereignty, were no longer believed in. Instead, humanism emerged, in which people began to take charge of their own lives, determine their own value systems, and take confidence in their own efforts to achieve success in life and decide on their own destinies. This was especially the case during the Enlightenment, which challenged the authority of religious tradition and "celebrated the value of human reason and modern science for human progress."[8] It was felt that through the new learning, humans had been loosed, set free to adventure with their minds into new realms of fulfillment in their lives.

Thus, from the time of the Enlightenment (seventeenth and eighteenth centuries), reality was divided between the "sacred" and the "secular." Religion was "sacred," with all that concerned it. Society was "secular," with all that concerned it. But the so-called "secular" society, with its secular values and lifestyles, had many "good" things in it, such as modern education, science, creativity, freedom of mind, and freedom of choice with regard to values. This perspective on life has influenced humans ever since.

When Christianity, brought by the European missionaries, reached Africa south of the Sahara, especially from about the nineteenth century, it found societies whose traditional cultures were strong and long established. The conflict that ensued was significant. The African cultures were condemned as evil from the Christian perspective. Yet the Africans, in general, held on to those cultures even as they welcomed Christianity and gave it a place among them. This resulted in three things. First, those Africans who fully embraced Christianity were made to abandon their traditional cultures completely. They practically became strangers among their own people. Second, some Africans who became Christians practiced Christianity alongside their traditional cultures. This is called syncretism, a mixture of beliefs and practices from different sources. Third, some similarities were drawn between biblical truths and some African beliefs and practices that were considered appropriate to hold together with Christianity. This was the position of many evangelical African Christians. These three factors continue to exert influence, in some way, on African Christians today.

---

8. C. Taliaferro, "The Enlightenment," in *New Dictionary of Christian Apologetics*, eds. Gavin McGrath and W. C. Campbell-Jack (Leicester: Inter-Varsity, 2006), 233.

The Nature of Salvation

We shall consider the concept of salvation from two perspectives, African and biblical. To Africans who are Christians, salvation usually means going through church ordinances such as water baptism, the celebration of the Lord's Supper, catechesis, participation in church life and programs, and having good behavior. O'Donovan has devoted a chapter in his book to analyzing the kind of Christianity we find in contemporary Africa.[9] He reveals and addresses many phenomena, commenting, "There is much that is accepted as Christianity in Africa today that is not biblical Christianity."[10] This includes a tendency to take works as a means for salvation. In missionary Christianity, Christians are given the impression and even taught that if they avoid wrong acts and adopt good acts and good behavior, they will be accepted in the kingdom of God. This communicates the belief that Christians are saved by what they do, contrary to what Scripture teaches. A church leader in Uganda was once asked to define salvation. His answer was that salvation is when a person leaves bad ways, such as murder, theft, and sexual immorality, and comes to church and becomes an active member.

The biblical perspective of salvation involves what God has done and continues to do, and how humans appropriate it. As Erickson points out, "our salvation is not our achievement. Fellowship with God is not attained by our making our way up to God. That is impossible."[11] Scripture teaches that humans are a fallen race, unable to save themselves or to please God by their own efforts: "for all have sinned and fall short of the glory of God, and are justified by his grace as a gift, through the redemption that is in Christ Jesus, whom God put forward as a propitiation by his blood, to be received by faith" (Rom 3:23–25).[12] This is a cardinal statement of Scripture on the doctrine of salvation. Commenting on this scripture, Kasali rightly says, "Our salvation in its totality is an act of God's grace, freely given, and received by believing in Christ. . . . There is nothing we can do to be justified but believe in Jesus Christ."[13] God's grace is the beginning point of salvation from the biblical standpoint. It is God coming down by his grace to fallen humanity to restore them. The term

---

9. Wilbur O'Donovan Jr., *Biblical Christianity in Modern Africa* (Carlisle: Paternoster, 2000), 217–50.

10. O'Donovan, *Biblical Christianity*, 217.

11. Millard J. Erickson, *Christian Theology* (Grand Rapids: Baker, 1985), 317.

12. Scripture quotations in this chapter are from the ESV.

13. David M. Kasali, "Romans," in *Africa Bible Commentary*, ed. Tokunboh Adeyemo (Nairobi: WordAlive, 2006), 1357.

"grace" means God's "unmerited favor."[14] It defines the basis on which God saves us: it is his sovereign act, completely independent of human merit. In his grace, God carries out his act of redemption upon humankind. In the days of the apostle Paul, the word "redemption" was used, as Kasali explains, "to describe the transaction that allowed one to buy a slave and then set him or her free."[15] In the case of Christian salvation, the believer has been "bought" and set free from condemnation and divine wrath and judgment by Christ's vicarious and atoning death on the cross. He died our death, and so we have been freed from the power and penalty of sin. Following this redemption is God's justification of the believer.

Justification is a central point in the story of salvation. It means God declaring sinners free from their sin and clothing them with the righteousness of Christ. It includes forgiveness of sin, conversion, transformation, and restoration of humanity. Once justified, a believer spiritually experiences all these aspects of salvation. In short, as Erickson puts it, justification "is a restoration of the individual to a state of righteousness."[16] Once in that state, we can relate well to God and serve his purposes. All this is based on the sufficiency of Christ's atoning death; by the same atonement, Christ's righteousness is imputed to the believer; and the believer becomes an heir of eternal life.

Another aspect of the experience of salvation is appropriation by faith of the gift of salvation which results in conversion. It is God who causes a quickening (or awakening) in the human spirit to respond to God's act of salvation; the result is a new birth, a recreation. This is called regeneration. The Bible says the Holy Spirit is the agent of this regeneration (Titus 3:5). And the means by which we receive this new life is faith. Faith is not a "work"; it is a means by which we are saved. But what is faith? What does it mean to believe in Jesus Christ and be saved (Mark 16:16; John 3:16; Acts 16:31; Rom 10:9; 1 John 5:13)? The book of James sheds some light on this for us. According to what we read in James 2:18–26, there is nominal faith and effective faith. Nominal faith consists of mental assent to a fact, such as believing that God exists or that Jesus died. This kind of faith does not save. Effective faith is saving faith. Grudem explains that "saving faith is not just a belief in facts but personal trust in Jesus to save me. . . . The unbeliever comes to Christ seeking to have sin

---

14. Wayne Grudem, *Systematic Theology: An Introduction to Biblical Doctrine* (Grand Rapids: Zondervan, 1994), 729.

15. Kasali, "Romans," 1357.

16. Erickson, *Christian Theology*, 955.

and guilt removed and to enter into a genuine relationship with God that will last forever."[17] Saving faith is a trust which involves a personal commitment to Christ. Grudem rightly comments that one can "believe" something to be true with no personal commitment to it.[18]

However, it may be argued that a person may want to be sure of the truth he or she is being drawn to make a commitment to, that is, the truth of salvation. From an intellectual perspective, this may be expected. In church history, the discipline of Christian apologetics was developed for this very reason, as Christianity interacted with the intellectual world. For example, one of the greatest Christian apologists of the early church, Justin Martyr (second century), wrote to significant people in Roman society to present the rationality and validity of the Christian faith. His lengthiest apology, *Dialogue with Trypho*, was addressed to Jews and explained the Christian faith to them. He wanted to pass the truth of the Christian faith to Jews by rational means rather than by direct preaching. This is an intellectual approach to conversion. It is noted that Martyr himself earnestly sought truth, visiting various places in his search.[19] The apology he wrote to the Jews may be compared to the approach the writer of the biblical Book of Hebrews used; this is also an apologetic piece of work. Similarly, in the prologue to his gospel, Luke states that his work is a researched piece to give Theophilus the truth concerning Jesus and his mission (Luke 1:1–4; cf. Acts 1:1–5). We can imagine that after reading the two volumes of Luke's scholarly work, Theophilus, and all the other readers of that work, could make an informed decision about the Christian faith.

Clement, the head of the Catechetical School of Alexandria in the second century, held that all true learning was given by God and could be used with Scripture for divine purposes. He aimed at "gathering in the treasures of wisdom and knowledge from all sources and using them for Christ."[20] The use of different approaches in the story of salvation – whether emotional or intellectual, homiletical or didactic, prophetic or scholarly – accords with the fact that all things are divine; they are of God and for God. This shows the truth of holism in Christianity.

Saving faith is also transformational. This transformation begins with genuine repentance. Jesus instructed his disciples before he ascended to heaven: "Thus it is written, that the Christ should suffer and on the third day rise from

---

17. Grudem, *Systematic Theology*, 710.
18. Grudem, 710.
19. Renwick and Harman, *Story of the Church*, 29.
20. Renwick and Harman, 45.

the dead, and that repentance for the forgiveness of sins should be proclaimed in his name to all nations" (Luke 24:46–47). Peter told his listeners on the day of Pentecost to "repent and be baptized . . . in the name of Jesus Christ for the forgiveness of your sins" (Acts 2:38). And Paul, in his letters, emphasizes that believers are transformed not only spiritually but also morally and in their character. They should put off their old self and put on their new self (Eph 4:22–24; Col 3:5–11). Transformation also means a change in one's perspective, value system, and life priorities. One should see oneself as a servant of Christ, serving his will and purposes (2 Cor 5:15; Phil 1:21).

When people come to Christ and enter into a personal relationship with him, they start on a lifetime process of growth in Christ. The goal of such growth is for them to be conformed to the image of Christ (Rom 8:29). This means that the character of Christ should be formed in the believer. The Holy Spirit works in the believer toward this goal. Believers need to cooperate with the Holy Spirit if they are to be perfected in Christ. This process is called sanctification. It is the second major stage of salvation after conversion. The final stage is glorification, when believers will experience divine glory in the presence of God and absolute perfection both in themselves and in their experience. There will be total fulfillment for believers in eternity.

Holism

We have noted the tendency to divide reality into compartments which are generally understood not to interfere with each other. This division is between what is considered secular and what is considered sacred; between what is physical and what is spiritual; what is cultural or political and what is ecclesiastical; what is private and what is public; what is holy and what is unholy; what is for God and what is for the world; what is religious and what is nonreligious. The division is influenced by certain factors – historical, cultural, scientific, and philosophical. Historically, in the Middle Ages, as we have seen, the church dominated virtually all spheres of society. However, when corruption and materialism began to characterize the church, people were dismayed. When new learning came in with the Renaissance and the Enlightenment, society broke away from the dominance of the church. The church's authority was questioned and its truths doubted. People's search for truth shifted from the theological to the scientific. Eventually, there was a clear division between church and State, the sacred and the secular.

Culturally, each society and community has its own value system and lifestyle. These are respected by people and adhered to. Matters of culture are divorced from religion in the sense of the Christian religion. Scientifically, contemporary education, with its discoveries and developments, has tended to devalue what is considered to be religious teachings. Educational institutions are geared toward practical matters of society. Religion is considered unpractical, not meeting the practical needs of society, and not scientifically realistic. Philosophically, new ways of thinking have developed through the generations of human history. Humans have had different worldviews and continue to develop new ones. We have seen the development of such worldviews as German Romanticism, French Existentialism, Marxist Communism, secular humanism, the present materialism and postmodernism, and religious worldviews. The limitations of this chapter do not allow a detailed presentation of each of these. Human rights advocacy has also promoted the active influence of the rights of the individual, making life individual and personal and shared only in common concerns. Public institutions may not freely get involved with people's private lives.

From a theological perspective, is this dichotomy of reality valuable? In Africa, before the coming of Christianity and Western education, all life was seen as religious. Mbiti brings this point out clearly in his writings. For example:

> Africans are notoriously religious, and each people has their own religious system with a set of beliefs and practices. Religion permeates all the departments of life so fully that it is not easy or possible always to isolate it. A study of these religious systems is, therefore, ultimately a study of the people themselves in all the complexities of both traditional and modern life.[21]

We note from this extract that for Africans, traditionally, religion and life have been inseparable. All life is religious because life is not just material; it is metaphysical. And it is in the metaphysical that there is a deeper appreciation of the meaning and reality of life. It is also to the metaphysical that ultimate reference is made regarding matters of concern.

Biblical Perspective

When God revealed himself to the Israelites and entered into a covenant relationship with them, he gave them instructions that covered virtually every aspect of their lives. The Pentateuch presents these to us. He gave them an understanding that he was their God in the wholeness of their lives.

---

21. Mbiti, *African Religions*, 1.

Their salvation was not only spiritual; it was also physical, social, political, educational, economic, and everything else. Everything was to be holy to God. Even their battles with other nations involved God. For example, David often had to inquire of the Lord and ask his will before engaging in any battle. Relationships, marriages, worship, personal conduct, health, hygiene, and all other aspects and experiences of life were brought before God. All life was religious.

In the New Testament, we read that in his ministry Jesus touched every aspect of human life. His great invitation recorded in Matthew 11:28–30 saw humanity bearing all kinds of burdens. People needed deliverance, peace, and fulfillment. He preached a whole gospel to the whole person and each person's whole life. His view of salvation in him was holistic. He taught the word, healed the sick, fed the hungry crowds, cleansed lepers, cast out demons from those in bondage, comforted those who had lost loved ones, raised their dead, blessed the children, ministered to tax collectors who were considered sinners by the Jews, challenged the Pharisees and Sadducees, and gave hope to all. He told his disciples to be the salt and the light of the world (Matt 5:13–16). This is a holistic statement of significance. Where salt is present, there is no part of the food that is not influenced by its taste, and where a light has been lit, there is no part that remains dark. In Paul's day, Christians were accused by their enemies of having turned the world "upside down" (Acts 17:6). Although this statement was an exaggeration,[22] apparently no part of society was left untouched by the gospel of Jesus Christ. The Christians themselves walked in the light of God, for God is light (Eph 5:8–9; 1 John 1:5–7).

In church history, among the Christians who have demonstrated well the holistic nature of salvation were the Puritans of the sixteenth and seventeenth centuries in Britain and America. Their zeal for God and passion for his honor came from their hearts through their minds and lives. In his book, in which he highly rates their spirituality and influence, Packer says that their "mature holiness and seasoned fortitude . . . shine before us as a kind of beacon light, overtopping the stature of the majority of Christians in most eras."[23] Their Christianity was all-embracing; all life was "integrated into the single purpose of honouring God. . . . There was for them no disjunction between sacred and secular; all creation, so far as they were concerned, was sacred, and all activities,

---

22. Stanley D. Toussaint, "Acts," in *The Bible Knowledge Commentary: New Testament*, eds. John F. Walvoord and Roy B. Zuck (Wheaton: Victor, 1983), 401.

23. J. I. Packer, *A Quest for Godliness: The Puritan Vision of the Christian Life* (Wheaton: Crossway, 1990), 11.

of whatever kind, must be sanctified, that is, done to the glory of God."[24] For them, the word "holiness" was used in a broad sense to include "every aspect and dimension of the godly life."[25] In a broad sense, their entire life was itself worship – for it was lived for the honor of God. It integrated holiness, devotion, honor, and influence, all to the glory of God. They denounced sin and worldliness and promoted godliness in all areas of life. As Packer states, "in meditation, the Puritan would seek to search and challenge his heart, stir his affections to hate sin and love righteousness."[26] "They applied their understanding of the mind of God to every branch of life," considering that in every sphere of life God must be served and honored. "They saw life whole, for they saw its Creator as Lord of each department of it, and their purpose was that 'holiness to the Lord' might be written over it in its entirety."[27]

The Significance of Holism

If we understand God as the Creator of all things and all things as serving his purposes, then Christianity is necessarily holistic. One of the most important functions of theology is to bring together our various truths of life and existence around God and see him in each of them. Life, with its complexity and mystery, has variety. This variety is not accidental, circumstantial, or arbitrary. It is divinely ordained. From a theological perspective, we can say that human beings vary in many ways, as determined by God. But all their variations have one factor: they are linked to God and serve his purposes. To borrow a phrase from Bray, they all have "a shared mystery" in God.[28] This is true not only of human beings but also of all other things in God's creation. As Erickson puts it, "although we tend at times to think of sacred and secular areas of life, no such division exists from God's standpoint. There are no areas that fall outside the purview of his concern and decision."[29]

Salvation reaches all areas of human life, brings out the divine meaning in them, and seeks to apply that meaning relevantly in the respective contexts of human life. God's restorative program in the salvation of humanity does not leave out some aspects of human life. Human transformation through

---

24. Packer, *Quest for Godliness*, 23–24.
25. Packer, 39.
26. Packer, 24.
27. Packer, 29.
28. Gerald Bray, *The Doctrine of God* (Leicester: Inter-Varsity, 1993), 52.
29. Erickson, *Christian Theology*, 353.

salvation is holistic. Furthermore, God is sovereign. His sovereignty is holistic and universal. It does not leave out some areas of life from his authority. Moreover, whatever is not in his will in his economy does not count. To be outside his will in anything is to waste one's time, resources, and life, and to attract God's judgment. Thus, the division of reality into separate spheres of sacred and secular becomes irrelevant. God is the owner of the whole universe and the whole of life, with their every detail, and in his sovereign design has established all things to serve his purposes. Therefore, some things cannot be said to belong to him (the sacred) while others belong to the world (the secular) or somewhere else; likewise our genuine physical concerns cannot be said to be carnal and our soul concerns spiritual.

Buxton, in his book *Celebrating Life*, explains that the paradigm of splitting reality into two compartments that are distinct and in opposition to each other – the holy and the profane, the sacred and the secular – has important regrettable implications. It makes us fail to appreciate the inherent goodness in all that God has created apart from the sad effects of sin. It discourages Christian involvement in matters of society through fear of "contamination," and thus we fail to influence society with Christian values and truths. From the time of the Renaissance and the Enlightenment to the modern era, the dualism that has pervaded the life of the church has opened the door to the triumph of secularism in Western culture. The growth in humanism and the scientific worldview has pushed the church out to the margins of society as not practically relevant.[30]

This is not to say that Christians should uncritically mix with the world and adopt its values and lifestyles. On the contrary, Christians should permeate society with their influence as the salt and the light of the world (Matt 5:13–16). As Buxton points out, there should be a more holistic theology of the church's engagement with and participation in society. "This perspective," he says, "affirms that God has created a good world, in which he is intimately and necessarily involved, and that his presence is to be celebrated in every area where men and women are active in social, political, cultural and educational discourse and behaviour."[31]

It is true that Scripture warns us not to love the world or the things in the world (1 John 2:15–17) and to "go out from their midst, and be separate from them" (2 Cor 6:14–18). But texts like these should be understood in the sense of not allowing ungodly influence from society into our faith and lives,

---

30. Graham Buxton, *Celebrating Life* (Milton Keynes: Paternoster, 2007), 1–23.
31. Buxton, *Celebrating Life*, 8.

compromising the values and truths God has given us. Furthermore, we should know that even ungodly people living in rebellion against God were created by God for God, and the same is true of the world in which they live, evil as it may be. They are not outside God's sovereign authority. Throughout Scripture, God is seen exercising his sovereign rule over his creatures in various ways. He judges the wicked and destroys their pride. Ultimately his glory is seen as he humbles humanity and glorifies himself.

Pearcey, in her book *Total Truth*, argues that all reality is God's reality. She observes that many believers have adopted the fact/value, public/private, sacred/secular dichotomy, "restricting their faith to the religious sphere while adopting whatever views are current in their professional or social circles."[32] She strongly argues against this tendency and advocates for a holistic Christian view of reality. She contends that evangelicals should not only save souls but also help people to interpret the world around them from a Christian perspective, "providing a set of interrelated concepts that function as a lens to give a biblical view of areas like science, politics, economics, or bioethics."[33] As we mentioned earlier, Pearcey argues that God is in all things and all things serve his purposes if they are seen from a divine perspective.[34] This divine perspective is fundamental to a proper understanding of all realities and how we deal with them.

God's Kingdom in Africa

The doctrine of holism in salvation, if well understood and applied, has a higher view. For African Christians, it is a view of the experience of God's kingdom values in Africa. The kingdom of God is "primarily the dynamic reign or kingly rule of God, and, derivatively, the sphere in which the rule is experienced."[35] In a sense, the kingdom of God has always been present, for God is the sovereign creator, owner, and ruler of the universe; he has ultimate authority over it. But his invisible reign becomes visible as his creatures acknowledge him, submit to him, experience his blessings, and display his glory. God is more concerned about his kingdom and glory than about any other matter on earth and in the universe. Although the full experience of God's kingdom is yet a future phenomenon, the kingdom was inaugurated at Jesus's first coming, when he

---

32. Pearcey, *Total Truth*, 33.
33. Pearcey, 35.
34. Pearcey, 65–66.
35. Grudem, *Systematic Theology*, 863.

said, "The kingdom of God has come upon you" (Matt 12:28). According to the teaching of the New Testament, God's people are in the kingdom and are kingdom agents wherever they are. God's kingdom business is their priority on earth.

In applying the truth of God's kingdom on earth, two factors that are essential are a change of worldview and the application of the concept of dominion. Jerry Rankin, in his book *Empowering Kingdom Growth*, appeals for a change in our worldview if we are truly to be God's kingdom people on earth. Instead of having a worldview that revolves around our own backgrounds, environments, life experiences, and interests, we should change and have what he calls a "kingdom worldview." A kingdom worldview is a perspective on life that is wholly influenced by God's purpose to have all people subject to his sovereign rule and worship him and focus on his glory. Such a perspective drives "kingdom people" to active and passionate involvement in God's kingdom business in life and the world, influencing all things and all people for God. Their greatest desire is to see God acknowledged, served, and glorified, and God's values operate in people's lives.[36] Rankin explains that the vision that guides God's people, whether as individuals or groups, must be shaped by a commitment to fulfill God's will and purpose. And God's purpose for humankind is for them to know him and worship him.[37]

An application of God's kingdom on earth also essentially involves a proper understanding and application of the concept of dominion. Regarding this point, Corrie explains that "God's mission (*missio Dei*) is to reign over the whole of reality so that all creation will be ultimately reconciled to his sovereignty (Eph 1:9–10; Col 1:20; Rom 8:21)."[38] In this mission of God, Corrie adds, we are invited to participate.[39] This means that rulership, or dominion, is part of our divine calling and responsibility on earth as vice-regents of God, the King of all creation. We are to extend the government, authority, and influence of his invisible supernatural realm into the visible realm of the natural world. Created in the image of God and assigned the responsibility of dominion over the earth (Gen 1:26–28), the first human beings were to relate to God, reflect him, and serve him as the leader of the earth. Humankind's disobedience against God

---

36. Jerry Rankin, *Empowering Kingdom Growth: To the Ends of the Earth* (Richmond : International Mission Board, 2005), 195–204.

37. Rankin, *Empowering Kingdom Growth*, 15.

38. John Corrie, "Kingdom of God," in *Dictionary of Mission Theology: Evangelical Foundations*, edited by John Corrie (Nottingham: Inter-Varsity, 2007), 196.

39. Corrie, "Kingdom of God," 196.

made them sadly lose this rule to the devil. But in their redemption in Christ, humans are being restored to their original position and status with God. This includes their dominion over the earth, which means an extension of God's heavenly kingdom on earth through humankind. Given our fallen human nature and the present corruption of things in this world, human dominion over the earth can only be truly realized in and through Christ, our Savior and Redeemer. Scripture says, "For if, because of one man's trespass, death reigned through that one man [Adam], much more will those who receive the abundance of grace and the free gift of righteousness reign in life through the one man Jesus Christ" (Rom 5:17). In Christ we are not only saved, we also "reign in life" through him, for God.

African Christian believers should know that all that God desires to see happen on earth for his glory should be our priority concern and involvement. African believers should be actively involved in God's kingdom business, first in Africa and then in the rest of the world. Holistic ministry and holistic influence by holistically transformed African Christians will go a long way in helping humanity experience God's goodness in every area of life and in glorifying him in every aspect of life. Nothing less than holism in salvation can help realize this phenomenon. Honoring God with our whole lives and our holistic restoration and fulfillment in Christ bring out the whole picture of salvation – total transformation in Christ, with the lordship of Christ over every aspect of life and the glory and blessing of God experienced in everything. It is an encounter with God that involves the whole being and the whole of life.

Implications and Challenges

Holism in salvation is a theological ideal that all genuine believers should embrace. God himself desires that he be acknowledged and submitted to in every aspect of human life. The result will be his abundant blessing on humankind in the totality of their lives. A dividing up of our lives into different areas implies that God is not involved in some areas of human life. This means that we are running our own lives in certain respects. Biblical and general history shows the folly of such a view. For example, the story of the Tower of Babel (Gen 11) shows the confusion and scattering that followed human pride.

However, although holism is a Christian ideal to be desired and worked toward by every genuine believer, there are challenges that stand in its way in the African context. Among them are four key obstacles. First, Africans have a strong attachment to their cultures, with their perspectives, values, and lifestyles. This results in syncretism, whereby believers have Christian faith but also involve traditional beliefs and practices in their lives, many of which are not compatible with the truths and values of the Christian faith, such as immorality, idolatry, and ancestor worship. Byang Kato comments strongly on this in his writings.[40] Akin to this fact is the nominalism that characterizes much of African Christianity. Some people are active in church but do not have a meaningful relationship with Christ. They want the blessings of God in their lives but not the total commitment to Christ the Christian faith requires of its adherents.

Second, a great deal of influence comes into Africa from the West. Much of this influence is unchristian and yet is considered economically and technically helpful to Africans. Some of this influence is related to postmodernism, a worldview that disregards the truths of God. Third, African Christian believers still need much discipleship to help them mature spiritually in the totality of their understanding and lives. This is a long-term process, and a great challenge and responsibility for African Christian leaders and ministers.

Fourth, and perhaps the most significant challenge, are the effects of sin. Like all humanity, Africans are greatly hindered in virtually every aspect of their lives by the impact of sin, which has eaten deep into people's minds, value systems, lifestyles, and perspectives. As Christian theologians generally hold, sin is anathema to the values of God in humanity. Its effects are greater than we often think. Sin has corrupted virtually every system in humans. Erickson says, "Sin is a very serious matter with very serious consequences. . . . Its effects are often both far-reaching and long-lasting."[41] Although saved, Christians still struggle with the effects of sin in their way of thinking and in other areas of their humanity. With minds and lives that have been corrupted by sin, to realize holism in salvation will need real deliverance and a change of worldview on the part of those Africans who become, or are, Christians. This is possible, but it requires serious commitment to God on the part of believers, as well as influence and help from mature Christian leaders and ministers. A practical suggestion to counteract this challenge is for African Christian leaders to disciple their followers until, as Paul says, "we . . . present everyone mature in Christ" (Col 1:28). It is mature believers who do not easily compromise their faith and who can demonstrate holistic commitment to God.

We cited earlier Mbiti's words that Africans are very religious and involve their religions in every aspect of their lives. This background could help with

---

40. Byang Kato, *Theological Pitfalls in Africa* (Nairobi: Evangel, 1975); and *African Cultural Revolution and the Christian Faith* (Jos: Challenge, 1976).

41. Erickson, *Christian Theology*, 601–2.

the inculcation of holism in African believers. However, it is a matter of changing worldview and value system, and of deep Christian influence. As Kato writes, "it is a fundamental Christian principle that Jesus Christ comes first and foremost in the life of the Christian."[42] Kato proclaims, in the form of an aphorism, "Let African Christians be Christian Africans."[43] Those concerned should help bring this change in African Christians.

Conclusion

Holism in salvation is a profound Christian truth that should not be taken lightly. As we have seen, salvation is holistic biblically, theologically, and practically. Holism is in the very nature of God. Among the attributes of God are his omnipotence, omniscience, omnipresence, and infinity. All these point to God's unlimited nature. Accordingly, they also point to his unlimited concern for and involvement in everything in his creation. Inevitably, then, a Christian, as God's servant, must have a divine perspective on all things and relate to them from that perspective. This means holism in the believer's Christianity. People may rebel against God and deny him certain aspects of reality that they assign to themselves in the name of secularism. This is an attempt to run away from God. But as Goldingay states in the conclusion to his exposition of God's omniscience, they cannot hide from him: "You can run, but you cannot hide."[44] If no one can hide from God, then nothing on earth should escape the influence of the Christian faith. It is part of our responsibility toward God on earth, for, as Scripture says, we live for him, not for ourselves (Rom 14:7–8). In any case, as Goldingay notes, "the object of redemption is the restoration of creation. Human beings are redeemed so as to live their created life again before God."[45] It is all about God restoring creation in line with his perfect will, reflecting and serving his glory. Holism in salvation accords perfectly with God's restorative program in creation.

As we have seen in this chapter, there are challenges that do not favor the realization of holism. But holism nevertheless can be realized. There should be deliberate efforts on the part of those concerned to see it happen. One such effort is to learn from the mistakes of the church in history, as exposed in this

---

42. Kato, *African Cultural Revolution*, 23.
43. Kato, 31.
44. John Goldingay, *Key Questions about Christian Faith: Old Testament Answers* (Grand Rapids: Baker Academic, 2010), 41.
45. Goldingay, *Key Questions*, 240.

chapter, and avoid making similar errors. When the church goes wrong in any area, it provides space for human beings to go their own way with alternative pursuits. When the church loses its integrity, spirituality, and dynamic influence in society, it will be relegated to the status of a nonessential by the world. Jesus taught that when salt has lost its saltiness, it becomes worthless except to be trodden underfoot by people (Matt 5:13). The saltiness of the church lies in its truthful and vibrant spirituality, sound integrity, and dynamic influence on society. Without this, other forces in society can take over humanity with their influence. Movements such as postmodernism, false religions, and materialistic worldviews can influence the world holistically, and perhaps irreversibly. The mission of advancing the kingdom of God on earth remains a significant calling and a practical concern for the church in Africa and worldwide.

Finally, one of the greatest advantages of holistic Christianity is that it involves the presence of God in everything. This attracts the blessings of God on those who uphold it. Holistic Christianity also lessens the evils that affect the welfare and true fulfillment of human beings. People experience peace, joy, and freedom in their lives. Furthermore, holistic Christianity improves people's relationships with one another, for God is seen and respected in all human dealings. People will also have a better understanding of themselves and their potential in life. This can lead to their better performance in life. This chapter suggests that every believer should submit to God in every area of his or her life and in every concern, and let God address them his way. All Christian leaders and ministers should endeavor to impart a holistic Christian worldview from their pulpits, podiums, pens, and personal lives. And they should lead the way in influencing every aspect of society with Christian truths and values. This can transform society for God both in Africa and throughout the rest of the world. To God be the glory!

Bibliography

Bray, Gerald. *The Doctrine of God*. Leicester: Inter-Varsity, 1993.
Buxton, Graham. *Celebrating Life*. Milton Keynes: Paternoster, 2007.
Cairns, Earle E. *Christianity through the Centuries: A History of the Christian Church*. Grand Rapids: Zondervan, 1981.
Corrie, John. "Kingdom of God." In *Dictionary of Mission Theology: Evangelical Foundations*, edited by John Corrie, 195–99. Nottingham: Inter-Varsity, 2007.
Erickson, Millard J. *Christian Theology*. Grand Rapids: Baker, 1985.
Goldingay, John. *Key Questions about Christian Faith: Old Testament Answers*. Grand Rapids: Baker Academic, 2010.

Grudem, Wayne. *Systematic Theology: An Introduction to Biblical Doctrine*. Grand Rapids: Zondervan, 1994.
Kasali, David M. "Romans." In *Africa Bible Commentary*, edited by Tokunboh Adeyemo, 1349–76. Nairobi: WordAlive, 2006.
Kato, Byang. *African Cultural Revolution and the Christian Faith*. Jos: Challenge, 1976.
———. *Theological Pitfalls in Africa*. Nairobi: Evangel, 1975.
Mbiti, John S. *African Religions and Philosophy*. Nairobi: East African Educational, 2015.
O'Donovan, Wilbur, Jr. *Biblical Christianity in Modern Africa*. Carlisle: Paternoster, 2000.
Packer, J. I. *A Quest for Godliness: The Puritan Vision of the Christian Life*. Wheaton: Crossway, 1990.
Pearcey, Nancy. *Total Truth: Liberating Christianity from Its Cultural Captivity*. Wheaton: Crossway, 2004.
Rankin, Jerry. *Empowering Kingdom Growth: To the Ends of the Earth*. Richmond: International Mission Board, 2005.
Renwick, A. M., and A. M. Harman. *The Story of the Church*. 3rd ed. Nottingham: Inter-Varsity, 2007.
Taliaferro, C. "The Enlightenment." In *New Dictionary of Christian Apologetics*, edited by Gavin McGrath and W. C. Campbell-Jack, 233–35. Leicester: Inter-Varsity, 2006.
Toussaint, Stanley D. "Acts." In *The Bible Knowledge Commentary: New Testament*, edited by John F. Walvoord and Roy B. Zuck, 349–432. Wheaton: Victor, 1983.

15

The Logical Implications of Trinitarian Exclusivism

Joseph B. Onyango Okello
*Professor of Philosophy of Religion and Ethics at
Asbury Theological Seminary, Orlando, Florida*

Abstract

In philosophy of religion, the claim of Christian exclusivism – that Jesus is the only salvific way to God the Father – generates a major challenge to the evangelistic enterprise within contemporary African contexts. Specifically, the challenge attacks the claims of exclusivism by observing how exclusivism so defined fails to account for the fate of the unevangelized. It fails to give reasons why the loving God of evangelicalism's Judeo-Christian tradition unjustly condemns individuals from unreached cultures without giving them the unique chance of hearing the gospel. This problem is not uniquely African, for the simple reason that many evangelistically unreached cultures exist outside Africa. Hence, while this presentation focuses uniquely on Africa, it can arguably be used as a philosophical model for responding to the challenge faced by exclusivism among unreached people groups outside the African continent. In the following presentation, I will argue that a certain robust and philosophical construal of exclusivism *does* give all humans a chance to hear and believe the salvific message of the gospel of Jesus Christ. Hence, God remains uniquely and divinely justified, by his own standards, to give those who reject this message the eternal state they deserve, as a consequence of their rejection of his message of salvation.

Key words: exclusivism, inclusivism, pluralism, salvation, unevangelized, revelation, Trinity

Introduction

The claim of Christian exclusivism – that Jesus is the only salvific way to God the Father – generates a major challenge to the evangelistic enterprise within contemporary African contexts. Specifically, the challenge attacks the claims of exclusivism by observing how exclusivism so defined fails to account for the fate of the unevangelized. It fails to give reasons why the loving God of evangelicalism's Judeo-Christian tradition unjustly condemns individuals from unreached cultures without giving them the unique chance of hearing the gospel.

This problem is not uniquely African. Many evangelistically unreached cultures exist outside Africa. Hence, while this presentation focuses uniquely on Africa, it can arguably be used as a model for responding to the challenge faced by exclusivism among unreached people groups outside the African continent. In the following presentation, I will argue that a certain robust construal of exclusivism *does* give all humans a chance to hear and believe the salvific message of the gospel of Jesus Christ. Hence, God remains uniquely and divinely justified, by his own standards, to give those who reject this message the eternal state they deserve, as a consequence of their rejection of his message of salvation.

Roughly speaking,[1] the main contours of this debate revolve around three views: exclusivism, pluralism, and inclusivism. Exclusivism holds that only one religion is salvifically valid,[2] hence that religion holds the privileged position of being the sole custodian of religious truth – especially salvific truth. Religious pluralism maintains that *all* religions are salvifically valid, hence adherents of all religious traditions will, indeed, be saved. Inclusivism, as adumbrated by the Catholic theologian Karl Rahner, holds that anonymous Christians exist in other religions because they maintain, within their belief systems, practices identical, or nearly identical, to those we find within the Judeo-Christian tradition. In other words, they are liberated because the

---

1. See Michael Peterson et al., *Reason and Religious Beliefs*, 5th ed. (New York: Oxford University Press, 2011), 319–43.
2. Jerry Walls, *Heaven: The Logic of Eternal Joy* (New York: Oxford University Press, 2002), 68–75.

specific conditions and requirements we find specified by the one true religion have obtained, have been fulfilled, or have been met in some way.[3]

In this chapter, I intend to address the challenge faced by exclusivism, specifically because it comes as a stumbling block to the proclamation of the gospel in Africa. More significantly, such a challenge arises from versions of religious pluralism dominating the African religious scene, and from humanist secular quarters characterized by institutions of learning within Africa itself. The contention, of course, faults exclusivistic Christianity for failing to account for the fate of the unreached people groups. The force of the argument stems from the reality that many Africans, or, for that matter, unreached global populations, have died without hearing the gospel of Jesus Christ. Assuming this fact obtains in many African settings, would God not be morally at fault for condemning individuals who never had the chance to hear the gospel?

In order to formulate a response to this question, I wish to begin with what we find in Scripture. Consider, for example, how, in recorded conversations with his disciples, Jesus makes several significant claims about his relationship with God the Father. In one of them he says, "I and the Father are one" (John 10:30); in another, he says, "No one comes to the Father except through me" (John 14:6). Equally significant is the following claim: "I am in the Father, and . . . the Father is in me" (John 14:10, 11). This last claim comes in response to a request from Philip asking Jesus to reveal the Father to his disciples: "Show us the Father and that will be enough for us." Christ's answer, seems importantly surprising. He says, "Don't you know me, Philip, even after I have been among you such a long time? Anyone who has seen me has seen the Father. How can you say 'Show us the Father'?" (John 14:8–9). From these words of Jesus, we get the impression that wherever Jesus has been revealed, God the Father has also been revealed. Theologians committed to belief in the deity of Christ find no problem with this contention.

Theologically suspect, however, is the converse of that statement, possibly stated as follows: Wherever God the Father has been revealed, Jesus has also been revealed. This contention is sustained in the following interesting way: Given that Christ and the Father are one, and that Christ is in the Father and the Father is in Christ, wherever the Father has revealed himself, Christ is, thereby, equally revealed. This statement seems quite logical. To be sure, a logical demonstration would render this contention logically valid. I attempt it below.

---

3. Karl Rahner, "Religious Inclusivism," in *Philosophy of Religion: Selected Readings*, eds. Michael Peterson et al., 5th ed. (New York: Oxford University Press, 2014), 613.

The Logic of Exclusivism

Let me begin with Christ's contention of his oneness with the Father. This relation suggests that Jesus is identical with the Father and, conversely, the Father is identical with Jesus. It seems consistent with the law of identity outlined by the German Christian philosopher and mathematician Gottfried Leibniz.[4] The law suggests for any sets A and B, if A remains identical with B, then every member of A must also be a member of B. This way of denoting seems quite consistent with the claims of Christ alluded to earlier. Just the same, in an important sense the denotation is, perhaps, mistaken, or unsound, as I will show in my response to the fourth objection later in this chapter.

Meanwhile, let us consider Christ's statement in John 14:6. The statement could be reworded as follows without losing its meaning: No one comes to the Father unless that person comes through Christ. Or, to follow the language of the logician, we can express it more formally as follows: For any person x, x does not come to the Father unless x comes through Christ.

The third contention captures the vital relationship existing between Christ and his Father. That contention could be recaptured as follows: Christ is in the Father and the Father is in Christ. Suppose we have all three statements as members of a set, A, as follows:

1. Jesus is identical to the Father.
2. A person x cannot come to the Father unless x comes to Jesus.
3. Jesus is in the Father and the Father is in Jesus.

Quite interestingly, we find that set A is a consistent set. In other words, the three members of set A are consistent with each other. If we deny any one of the three, the denial yields an instance of inconsistency with the rest of the members. Even more curious is the fact that the set itself can be restated as a theorem. Any logician will affirm that a theorem is a necessarily true statement.[5] A necessarily true statement cannot be false. To formulate this contention as a theorem, T, I state it as follows:

---

4. Frances Howard-Snyder et al., *The Power of Logic* (New York: McGraw-Hill, 2013), 492.

5. Geoffrey Hunter, *Metalogic: An Introduction to the Metatheory of Standard First Order Logic* (Los Angeles: University of California Press, 1996), 61.

T: If Jesus is identical to the Father, and Jesus is in the Father, and the Father is in Jesus, then a person x cannot come to the Father unless x comes through Jesus.[6]

Analogous to set *A*, a denial of *T* results in a contradiction. If we accept the antecedent that tries to capture the claim that Jesus and the Father are one, and that Christ is in the Father and the Father is in Christ, we must, of necessity, arrive at this consequent of *T*.

This finding concerning truth preservation is not the only interesting feature about *T*. Potentially more exciting about *T* is the possibility that *T* presents a more promising solution to the apparent problem of exclusivism presented by the claim of Christ located in John 14:6. If Jesus is indeed the only way to the Father, then those who die without hearing the gospel of Jesus remain eternally lost. Does *T* give us a possible way out of the pitfall presented by some pluralists and a variety of secular humanists, even if somewhat obscure? It seems to do just this very thing, but with a slight modification. Let me outline it below.

Recall my earlier contention that if Jesus is in the Father and the Father is in Jesus, then wherever Jesus is revealed, the Father is also revealed. The converse of the contention is that if the Father is revealed, then Jesus is also revealed. More accurately, if the Father reveals himself, then Jesus reveals himself simultaneously. To be sure, if we add a version of this claim to set *A*, we will still arrive at a consistent set, a theorem, which I will call T^R (my use of the letter *T* implies *T* is a theorem, and my introduction of the superscript ^{R} on *T* tries to capture the idea of God revealing himself), as follows:

T^R: If Jesus is identical with the Father and Jesus is in the Father and the Father is in Jesus and a person x cannot come to the Father unless x comes through Jesus, then where the Father has revealed himself, Jesus has revealed himself.

Admittedly, the theorem is rather long, but it remains a logically acceptable way of translating T^R. However, and more to the point, we find ourselves once again faced with a necessary truth, such that if we deny the claim, or one of its components, the denial will yield a contradiction.

As stated earlier, the implications for this contention are enormous. The enormity begins with the apostle Paul's words in Romans 1:18–21. According to that passage, Paul seems to indicate that God's self-revelation in nature remains

---

6. For the logically curious, the theorem could be restated in a more formal way as follows: $\{(j=f) \cdot (Ijf \cdot Ifj)\} \to (\sim Cxj \vee Cxf)$, where the dot represents a conjunction and the arrow represents the conditional.

sufficient to condemn those who neither glorified God nor gave thanks to him, but instead suppressed the truth by their wickedness. Basing our argument on the model defined by T^R we can fairly say that the suppression of God's truth on the part of the godless was not merely a rejection of God; it was a rejection of Christ as well. Specifically, because Christ and the Father are one, Christ remains in the Father and the Father is in Christ, and rejecting one entails rejecting the other.

Of course, T^R would also imply that the Father's (or Yahweh's) revelation of himself in the Old Testament is also Christ's revelation of himself. Hence, salvation in the Old Testament involves faith in Christ as much as it involves the Abrahamic faith that Paul discusses so eloquently in Romans 4, where Abraham believed God and that belief was credited to him as righteousness (Rom 4:3). Here, T^R would suggest that one would be just as correct if one said, "Abraham believed Christ and it was credited to him as righteousness." To be sure, Christ himself affirms this truth when he says, "Abraham rejoiced at the thought of seeing my day; he saw it and was glad" (John 8:56). If T^R is a sound theorem, T^R would seem to indicate that all the Old Testament saints were saved as much by faith in Christ as they were by faith in God, even though their faith anticipated Christ's death on the cross.

Scriptural Evidence for God's Universal Revelation

We do know, from Scripture, that God the Father revealed himself to non-Hebraic cultures. Roughly speaking, God the Father indirectly revealed himself in a dream to Pharaoh in Genesis 41. Hence, when Joseph was called to interpret Pharaoh's dream, Joseph said, "God has shown Pharaoh what he is about to do" (Gen 41:28). Similarly, God the Father revealed himself indirectly, in a dream, to Nebuchadnezzar in Daniel 2. When Daniel interpreted the dream to Nebuchadnezzar, he said at the end of his interpretation, "The great God has shown the king what will take place in the future" (Dan 2:45). More directly, God revealed himself to Balaam in Numbers 22:9. Anyone familiar with the postulates of Scripture knows that these are not the only times God the Father revealed himself to non-Hebraic cultures in the Old Testament. Hence, this fact remains biblically clear and uncontroversial.

However, would we be correct to suggest that God the Father has revealed himself outside the cultures mentioned in Scripture such that if he did, we could validly postulate that Christ revealed himself to those cultures as well? If we accept T^R and Romans 1:18–21, this supposition would, out of necessity, follow. Not only can God the Father reveal himself to those cultures not mentioned in Scripture; he *has* already done so. In other words, God has revealed himself to all human beings, and as a consequence, Christ has also revealed himself to all human beings. Perhaps this reason underscores why the apostle Paul points out our lack of excuse if we claim we have not perceived God's revelation (Rom 1:20). Hence, a rejection of God entails a rejection of Christ, and a rejection of Christ entails a rejection of God. Moreover, one would be in error to suppose that one can reject Christ and accept God, or for that matter, accept Christ and reject God. A rejection of one entails a rejection of the other. More accurately, a rejection of God the Son remains a sufficient and necessary condition for rejecting God the Father. Anyone well versed with the rules of logic will find the converse equally entailed in this statement.

This formulation, of course, implies that a person can arrive inferentially at a saving knowledge of the Trinitarian God through general revelation – in other words, through nature – without exposure to the special revelation of Scripture. However, error, which I read as sin, keeps us from making such an inference, as Thomas Aquinas argues.[7] If general revelation is sufficient to warrant the condemnation of the unbeliever, as implied by Romans 1:18–21, it should also be sufficient to lead one to ask questions about salvation, depending on how human beings respond to it, and to possibly find salvation. Bear in mind that this response is based on knowing and submitting to the Trinitarian God of Judeo-Christian theism. Thus, one can still be saved through God in Christ of Scripture without a cognitive awareness of the existence of Scripture. The supposition is based on the fact that where God the Father is revealed, God the Son is also revealed.

Let me explain. An individual completely unaware of the existence of the Bible can still know the Trinitarian God of the Bible without reading, or hearing the reading of, a page of holy writ. The apostle Paul makes this fact very clear in Romans 1:20 when he contends that God's "eternal power and divine nature have been clearly seen, being understood from what has been made." Besides simply observing the complex nature of our universe, one can cognize how the heavens are declaring the glory of God as stated by Psalm 19.

This fact holds because the message of salvation presented indirectly by nature or directly by word of mouth remains consistent with the contents of Scripture, even if it is not word-for-word identical with the pages of Scripture. Indeed, what preachers do from the pulpit every Sunday is provide an interpretation of the scriptural message, though they do so, admittedly,

---

7. Thomas Aquinas, *Summa Theologica*, trans. Fathers of the English Dominican Province (New York: Hanover, 1957), vol. 1, Q1., art. 1.

after reading the Scriptures to the congregation. They may use illustrations not found in Scripture to press certain points to the congregation. But one assumes those messages are still based upon Scripture, which, in turn, derives its ultimate origin from the Trinitarian God of Christian theism. The indirect message given by nature comes from two sources. Externally, it comes from the complexity of the designed world following Romans 1:18–20. Internally, it comes from the moral law within each person, following Romans 2:14–15.

Let me explain. According to the apostle Paul, no one has an excuse for not knowing God, whether one lives in the jungle or the city, in the Majority or Minority World, or among the "reached peoples" or the "unreached peoples." Humans capable of distinguishing right from wrong remain aware of God's laws as well as of God himself, the giver of those laws, though perhaps in a manner not as clearly articulated as those we find in Scripture. An awareness of God entails his divine revelation as the Trinitarian God. Thus, a rejection of any member of the Trinity is a rejection of God. This is the external message.

Internally, the Christian apologist could appeal to Romans 2:14–15. Paul writes:

> When Gentiles, who do not have the law, do by nature things required by the law, they are a law for themselves, even though they do not have the law. They show that the requirements of the law are written on their hearts, their consciences also bearing witness, and their thoughts sometimes accusing them and at other times even defending them.

The implication of this passage seems clear: God has written his law in the hearts of all humans. Hence, all humans have knowledge of God to the extent that they are aware of some form of right and wrong. They may not be morally mature. They may remain incapable of applying moral principles to their lives up to a certain stage in their development. However, they seem to arrive at the stage needed to make those applications later in their lives.

We conclude, then, that our evangelistic enterprise is an attempt to bring back the lost people groups or tribes or nations to the God whom they already knew and rejected or ignored. It is not about enlightening them, for the very first time, that a being called God exists and that they now need to believe in him. Only this understanding helps us make sense of the apostle Paul's assertion that these individuals are without excuse. They are without excuse because what can be known about God is plain to them by merely observing the intricate nature of creation and listening to the voice of conscience in their hearts.

Possible Objections to Trinitarian Exclusivism

Several objections can be raised against the argument hitherto advanced. First, one could argue that this way of looking at God's revelation renders evangelistic ministries quite irrelevant. If we all possess some cognitive awareness of God, the awareness renders the Great Commission unnecessary. Second, one could observe that this way of looking at the problem of exclusivism in Christianity says nothing about the salvific validity, or for that matter, invalidity, of other religions. Third, one could contend that this formulation fails to address the question of infants who die before hearing the gospel. Fourth, one could observe that a major component of T^R, which also appears in T and set A, rests on a false theological assumption, and that if the falsity of that theological assumption can be shown, then T^R, T, and A are no longer necessary truths. The false theological assumption can be summarized as follows: The formulation falsely assumes that God the Son and God the Father are identical persons. Whereas both are God, the objection would continue, we can locate at least one instance where God the Father and God the Son do not have identical properties and, therefore, cannot be identical persons in the Leibnizian sense. Fifth, one could complain that this model does not account for adults with malfunctioning cognitive faculties which severely limit them from making any significant moral choices or decisions. The sixth and final objection holds that the view I present is really some disguised form of religious pluralism. How could we overcome these objections and remain consistent with the thesis I am trying to defend?

Let me respond to these objections in the following way. I argue that the first objection can be answered easily. The evangelistic enterprise seems to be in place precisely because humans have rejected God's revelation, whether general or special, and not because humans have no factual knowledge of God. They may not have heard a formal proclamation of God such as the one described in Romans 10:14–15. However, they do remain in possession of some knowledge of God, however small. The aim of evangelism and discipleship, therefore, involves the attempt to clarify this knowledge and to call God-rejecters to a position of repentance and have them embrace the Holy Trinity they seem to have abandoned in the first place. If this consideration is correct, then the first objection seems to lose its force, because, according to Scripture, all humans possess some cognitive awareness of God – a sense of divinity, as Thomas Aquinas,[8] John Calvin,[9] and, most recently, Alvin Plantinga[10] have observed.

Let's examine the second objection. Consider that all religions (with the exception, perhaps, of Christianity) are understood as human attempts at reaching God. However, T^R, T, and set A represent models that try to capture ways in which God is understood as revealing himself to human beings. For that reason, the formulation I propose has nothing to do with validation of any one religion over another, though it answers religious concerns about God's revelation. More exactly, the formulation herein proposed tries to articulate the revelation of the Trinity to all people, Christian or not. Hence, the objection seems wrongheaded, for according to the apostle Paul's own words in Romans 1:18–21, God has revealed himself to all people.

The third objection is slightly more forceful. It notes that T^R seems to say little or nothing about stillborn children and infants who die before hearing the gospel. Seemingly, however, we get the impression, from the very words of Christ, that children have some kind of a "pass" into the kingdom of heaven (see Matt 18:1–5) and that anyone who adopts a childlike heart attitude will indeed be among the greatest in that kingdom. Of course, more needs to be said about this postulation, in light of the fact, for example, that the sorts of children being referred to here are those who die before reaching the age of accountability – where they seem unable to differentiate between right and wrong. The idea I wish to press, however, is that God, or for that matter, Christ, is gracious enough not to bypass the eternal destiny of such children. Also, Isaiah 7:14–15 assumes that children do, in fact, reach a point where they know the difference between right and wrong. Prior to this stage of their lives, they really do not have such knowledge. We also get the impression, from Deuteronomy 1:39 and from Jonah 4:11, that such a state of affairs exists in humans. To be sure, some of them remain in that state into adulthood, as postulated by Jonah 4:11, and God always reveals his concern for them. When God is concerned about them, he creates an opportunity for them to hear his message of redemption – specifically because, whether we reach the age of accountability or not, as humans we will all be judged – including children. We must bear in mind, however, that judgment need not imply condemnation.

---

8. Aquinas, *Summa Theologica*, vol. 1, Q2., art. 1.

9. John Calvin, *Institutes of the Christian Religion*, trans. Ford Lewis Battles (Philadelphia: Westminster, 1960), I.iii.1.

10. Alvin Plantinga, *Warranted Christian Belief* (New York: Oxford University Press, 2000), 170–72.

Some will be judged and ushered into eternal life, while others will be judged and punished eternally.

The fourth objection presents the deepest challenge to this postulation. Recall how, in my adumbration of the identity relation between God the Father and God the Son, I noted how my locution might possess some unsound features. The fourth objection places its finger on this very feature. The objection can be located in the nature of the relationship between the Father and the Son. Despite the fact that Jesus said that he and the Father are one, we can identify a logical property possessed by Jesus that the Father does not have, and vice versa, as follows: Jesus has the property of "being the Son of God the Father," and God the Father, of course, has the property of "being the Father of God the Son." This type of relationship between the Father and the Son is one of the key attributes distinguishing the Son from the Father. If this supposition is correct, then even if the Son is one with the Father, they cannot be logically identical, at least not in the sense envisioned by Leibniz's theory of identity. Of course, this supposition renders T^R inconsistent and, therefore, unsound. In what ways, then, can we overcome this challenge?

One possible way involves modifying T^R by dropping the first member of its set, namely that Jesus is identical with the Father. This leaves us with the other members: those suggesting that the Son is in the Father and the Father is in the Son, and that a revelation of the Father is simultaneously a revelation of the Son. This move helps us to overcome the challenge. However, it fails to capture the oneness that the Son shares with the Father. Moreover, we are no longer left with T^R as initially formulated; we are left with its subset, and whether or not this subset is a necessary truth remains unclear.

These difficulties, therefore, seem to warrant another way to try to overcome the challenge. A promising way entails replacing the identity relation with the notion of material equivalence. The notion would translate as follows: Christ being the Son of God the Father is a sufficient and necessary condition for Christ possessing the attributes simultaneously possessed by God the Father; and God the Father being the Father of Christ is a sufficient and necessary condition for God the Father possessing the attributes also possessed by Christ. Another postulate presents itself, based on the very words of Christ: Christ being in God the Father is a sufficient and necessary condition for Christ having the attributes of God the Father, and God the Father being in Christ is a sufficient and necessary condition for God the Father possessing the attributes of God.

Do these two postulates solve the worry of collapsing the attributes of deity? They do not, unless we include an additional qualifier warning the theological epistemologist about this error. The theological epistemologist needs to specify at least two things: first, he or she must specify the condition that the attributes alluded to in the two new postulates involve the attributes of *sameness of nature*. In other words, though the members of the Trinity have distinct identities in terms of their personhood, the substance of their nature remains identical. Thus, the expression "Jesus is identical to the Father" could perhaps be treated as one demonstrating equality between God the Father and God the Son without necessarily falling into the trap of "collapsing" at least one of their distinct properties alluded to earlier. In other words, when you behold the Son, you behold God, and when you behold the Father, you likewise behold God. In that sense they are one and the same entity with at least one distinct property the other does not have.

Whether or not this sort of understanding preserves the theological accuracy of T^R remains to be seen, but it seems to preserve its consistency. With regard to the theological accuracy, consider, for example, Christ's contention that the Father is greater than the Son. If the Father is indeed greater than the Son, we must look for ways in which the greatness can find some explanation in light of our contention that the two have identical properties. Perhaps the greatness of the Father over the Son is demonstrated by the nature of the earthly salvific role that Christ had to play, such as obedience to the Father's will by allowing himself to be sent into the world to save sinful humanity.

I now turn to the fifth objection. It complains that this model of exclusivism fails to account for individuals with malfunctioning cognitive faculties, which, in turn, severely limit those individuals from making any significant ethical decisions. For example, a blind person unfamiliar with braille can, at best, only hear a presentation of the gospel. A deaf person unfamiliar with sign language can, at best, only read the presentation of the gospel. But the situation becomes enormously difficult if the recipient of the gospel is both blind and deaf from birth. First, notice how the person in this predicament could, conceivably, fail to reach the age of accountability, that is, of knowing the difference between right and wrong, following the malfunction of his or her cognitive faculties. The person could still arrive at some knowledge of God in some way. I have already addressed this possibility. Recall, for example, that in cases of individuals who, for some reason, remain incapable of choosing right from wrong through no fault of their own, God seems to make it his responsibility to reveal himself in some way, as we saw in the case of Jonah proclaiming the gospel to the citizens of Nineveh. Scripture says that God has not left himself without a witness even to the most unreached person (Acts 14:17). The assumption is clear: even for this kind of blind and deaf person, God has not left him or her without a witness.

A final objection one could raise against this view could run as follows: one could complain that this presentation is really an attempt to sneak religious pluralism back into evangelicalism through the back door specifically because it contends that all humans have some knowledge of God. The objection is wrongheaded. Religious pluralism, as espoused and presented by John Hick and his cohorts, rejects the contention that only one religion is salvifically valid and insists, instead, that all religious are salvifically valid.[11] The view I present maintains that humans who reject Jesus Christ will be condemned because a rejection of God is a rejection of Jesus Christ and a rejection of Jesus Christ is also a rejection of God. This claim, I argue, is at the heart of exclusivism and quite contrary to religious pluralism.

Conclusion

If my contentions in these pages are correct, then we need to rethink our understanding of the doctrine of exclusivism. Moreover, we would also seem very close to absolving exclusivism from the charge of failing to give an account of those who seem to die without hearing the gospel. Indeed, exclusivism of the sort I am endorsing does offer such an account. According to this view, and according to Paul's view in the first chapter of Romans, all humans with properly functioning cognitive faculties demonstrate some form of awareness of God. If they do, then they necessarily have some awareness of Christ. If this reality is even remotely possible, the evangelistic enterprise of missions does not involve making people originally ignorant of God aware of God. They already seem aware of God. The evangelistic enterprise involves calling all people back to the One from whom they turned away in the first place and to believe in him. This goal, indeed, remains the crux of the Great Commission.

Bibliography

Aquinas, Thomas. *Summa Theologica*. Vols. 1–3. Translated by Fathers of the English Dominican Province. New York: Hanover, 1957.

Calvin, John. *Institutes of the Christian Religion*. Translated by Ford Lewis Battles. Philadelphia: Westminster, 1960.

Hick, John. *The Problem of Religious Pluralism*. London: Palgrave Macmillan, 1985.

---

11. John Hick, *The Problem of Religious Pluralism* (London: Palgrave Macmillan, 1985), 47.

Howard-Snyder, Frances, et al. *The Power of Logic*. New York: McGraw-Hill, 2013.
Hunter, Geoffrey. *Metalogic: An Introduction to the Metatheory of Standard First Order Logic*. Los Angeles: University of California Press, 1996.
Peterson, Michael, William Hasker, David Basinger, and Bruce Reichenbach. *Reason and Religious Belief*. 5th ed. New York: Oxford University Press, 2011.
Plantinga, Alvin. *Warranted Christian Belief*. New York: Oxford University Press, 2000.
Rahner, Karl. "Religious Inclusivism." In *Philosophy of Religion: Selected Readings*, edited by Michael Peterson et al., 606–13. 5th ed. New York: Oxford University Press, 2014.
Walls, Jerry. *Heaven: The Logic of Eternal Joy*. New York: Oxford University Press, 2002.

16

Emerging Soteriological Issues in African Christianity in the Light of Resurgent African Cultures

The Practice of Ancestral Debts

Kamau Thairu
Presbyterian Minister, Nairobi
Lecturer, Presbyterian University of East Africa

Abstract

Salvation is defined as redemption or deliverance from bondage or sin. It is a product of the work of Christ at the cross apportioned to a person by grace through faith. Salvation means that a person has been released from sin and all that "heavily entangles" him or her. However, in recent years, there have been practices in the Kenyan Christian community that demand that we revisit our understanding of salvation and the extent of its impact in our ordinary lives. This is especially important in light of the resurgent African cultures that now stir apathy toward missionary Christianity. This apathy is built on the premise that the missionaries introduced Christianity as a tool for colonization and demolition of African cultures. It has led to syncretism, through which some cultural practices are now held as orthodoxy in the Kenyan church. These practices are manifest in the teaching that a believer needs further deliverance and redemption after salvation. The argument is that a believer's lack of material and social progress in life results from ancestral curses, debts, and non-redemption in the case of the firstborn. Most of these practices are a product of a lack of vigorous theological reflection on sociological phenomena. This chapter examines the scope of the work of Christ, profiles a select heretical teaching – the practice of ancestral debts – and then reflects theologically on this practice.

Key words: redemption, ancestral debts, living dead, cultural revival, *ngomi*, *ngoma*

Introduction

Recently among the Agĩkũyũ community of Kenya there has been a campaign to abandon Christianity and return to "culture."[1] The call is built on the premise that Christianity is a fraud and should be abandoned in favor of African Traditional Religion. Christianity is seen as a white man's religion and the Bible as a tool for colonization and continued domination. To emancipate the African from these shackles, Christianity has to be abandoned in favor of African Traditional Religion. Ultimately, this has led to syncretic Christians who pledge allegiance to culture but also identify as Christians. This resurgence of culture has given rise to various teachings that endanger the Christian community's faith.

Among many heresies, one prevalent teaching among Christians in Central Kenya is the practice of *thiiri wa ngomi*, the payment of ancestral debts. In response to this, evangelical Christians on one side of the divide assert that Christ's redemptive work has satisfactorily paid all debts, including those of the ancestors,[2] while the syncretic Christians on the other side argue that his redemptive work did not pay ancestral debts, and therefore the families must pay them. They further assert that because of the unpaid debts, the ancestors visit the living with calamities such as diseases and failed businesses as a punishment.[3] Many Christians are lost in between.

---

1. Online resources such as Caroline, Kimeu. 'Restoring the River': Why Kenyans are Returning to Precolonial Spirituality. September 22, 2022. https://www.theguardian.com/global-development/2022/sep/22/kenyans-returning-to-precolonial-kikuyu-traditions-spirituality (accessed August 1, 2023).

2. See "Tutiri thiiri wa Ngomi," performed and directed by Isaiah Ndung'u, YouTube, February 2021, accessed 22 January 2022, https://www.youtube.com/watch?v=ldceg_XlrRI. This song summarizes the view that Christ's redemptive work has paid all debts.

3. See the following online resources for more insight: "Tutiri thiiri wa Ngomi" by Isaiah Ndung'u; and "Nderirwo Ngane Jesu Na Nduithio Nĩguo Ngomi Cindathime," Eliza wa Narumoro, interview by Wambui wa Mwangi, YouTube, accessed 28 April 2021,

This raises questions as to the extent of Christ's work. Does his work include redemption from these ancestral debts? In light of the Scriptures, do these ancestral debts exist? Are they also culturally existent? Can the ancestors cause havoc in people's lives, as proposed by the cultural revivalists? If the debts do exist, how are they to be paid?

The Scriptures can authoritatively answer these questions because culture belongs to general revelation. This is not to say that culture has nothing to offer in answering the questions; rather it is to point out the frailty and incompleteness of culture to communicate the things of God. Culture is a human effort to know God and his creation. It proceeds from the notion that God has left evidence of himself in the world he has created and a person has the capacity to deduce it.[4] It is imperfect and finite, and therefore cannot be relied upon to reveal knowledge of an infinite being authoritatively. Culture is an amalgamation of the experiences our forefathers have had of God. Their knowledge about where the dead go is built on superstition rather than concrete knowledge gained from God's self-disclosure. It was initially built on animism, in which God is seen in nature. Then, as communities advanced, it was rationalized in traditional religions.

This rationalization built the understanding of the afterlife on the present life; that is to say, their vision of the "world to come" was conceptualized along the patterns of the present world. The African "worldview of life as [a] continuum with dynamism of rhythm of cycles is the people's way of describing the dynamism of existence and its dependence on a higher order, which is beyond humankind's full comprehension."[5] For this reason, in many African communities, the dead would be buried with items that were thought to be useful in the spiritual world. Additionally, the afterlife is conceived in terms of communion, where the dead are in an active relationship with the living, the spirits themselves, and God. Activities such as paying ancestral debts are thus meant to maintain or rekindle lost relationships with the ancestors.

The Scriptures, however, contain the special revelation of God to humanity. This revelation is intertwined with the historical events and the divine speech in which God made himself known, and culminates with the incarnation. It is superior to general revelation (culture) since it overcame the "natural

---

https://www.youtube.com/watch?v=aiyPTjbAiPU. They are in Gĩkũyũ and therefore translation may be needed for non-Gĩkũyũ speakers.

4. Millard J. Erickson, *Christian Theology*, 3rd ed. (Grand Rapids: Baker, 1983), 129.

5. Francis Anekwe Oborji, *Towards a Christian Theology of African Religion* (Limuru: Gaba, 2005), 21.

limitations of human finiteness and the moral limitation of human sinfulness."[6] The knowledge revealed in the Scriptures is not just for the sake of knowing of God's existence, but is to lead a person to a redemptive relationship with God. Only special revelation, that revealed in the Scriptures, can help determine if the extent of the redemptive work of Christ includes the payment of debts to the ancestors.

The Practice of *Thiirĩ wa Ngomi*

In Agĩkũyũ[7] tradition, the family of the young man who intends to marry a young woman must give a dowry to the parents (by extension, the clan) of the young woman. This dowry is quantified and paid over the lifetime of the couple, until such time that the wife's family agree that enough has been paid. There are some families, however, who do not honor this tradition. They take the girl and do not pay the dowry; or in some cases they pay but not to the full extent agreed. In the event that the couple beget a daughter, the man is under obligation to complete the dowry owed to his wife's family first, before he receives his daughter's dowry. If the wife's parents die before they have received the entire dowry or agreed that it has been paid, then this creates a debt (*thiirĩ*). If this cycle continues so that the daughter of the man who had not cleared the dowry marries and she also has a daughter . . . eventually, according to this teaching, there will be a generation that must pay the debt. Otherwise calamities will befall them. In a nutshell, *thiirĩ* is an unpaid debt of dowry owed to previous generations.

Among the consequences of these unpaid debts is sickness (*ndwari*). This is distinguished from diseases (*mirimu*). *Ndwari* is an illness like cancer, diabetes, arthritis, and so on, while *mirimu* are like malaria, typhoid, and cholera. Diseases are those caused by negligence or inaction: for example, drinking contaminated water leads to contracting typhoid; if you do not use a mosquito net, you may contract malaria. In this there is a direct correlation between human negligence and the outcome. But *ndwari* are caused by *ngomi*.

The cultural revivalists[8] argue that people in the community suffer from *ndwari* because of the *thiirĩ wa ngomi* – debt of the dead (*ngomi* is the plural;

---

6. Erickson, *Christian Theology*, 144.

7. This is a Bantu community found in the central parts of Kenya. They occupy the area around Mount Kenya.

8. These are the proponents of a return to culture and an abandonment of missionary Christianity.

ngoma, the singular). For example, if for the dowry of a grandmother her father had asked for a cow and it had never been delivered, her descendants are likely to suffer from arthritis or joint pain because the great-grandfather did not enjoy the milk from that cow that should have provided calcium to prevent such joint pains.⁹ Further, it is argued that the rise in alcoholism, juvenile delinquency, and divorce can be attributed to the ancestors seeking vengeance for the debts owed to them. Other consequences include stunted businesses, children who never get employment, premature deaths, and lack of suitors in the case of young women.

Like many other African communities, the Agĩkũyũ divide human existence into four categories: the unborn who are still in their mothers' wombs; the living; the living dead; and the ancestors. *Ngomi* means the "spirits of the dead" but are rightly called the living dead.¹⁰ They go back five to six generations.¹¹

The "living dead" person is someone "who is physically dead but alive in the memory of those who knew him in this life as well as being alive in the world of the spirits."¹² Death is the process which removes a person from the present to the past. Further defining the living dead, Mbiti submits that

> after the physical death, the individual continues to exist in the *Sasa* period and does not immediately disappear from it. He is remembered by relatives and friends who knew him in this life and who have survived him. They recall his name, though not necessarily mentioning it; they remember his personality, character, words and incidents of his life.¹³

If the living dead appear, it is usually to the older members of the family who knew them for the longest time, and they are acknowledged by name (they rarely or never appear to the children). Their appearances may continue up to four or five generations, so long as someone who once knew them personally and by name is alive. So long as they are remembered, they are in a state

---

9. "'Rihai Thirî wa Ngomi, Tondu Mûndû Owothe Niarî Thirî wa Ngomi' Kiarie wa Ndung'u Kuga," interview by Wambui wa Mwangi, 25 March 2021, accessed 22 January 2022, https://www.youtube.com/watch?v=yrkTkTvL64M. This is one of many videos that teach this practice.
10. Ancestors are properly referred to as *agu*.
11. John S. Mbiti, *African Religions and Philosophy* (Nairobi: EAEP, 1992), 23.
12. Mbiti, *African Religions*, 25.
13. Mbiti, 25.

of "personal immortality," which is externalized through procreation, where children are named after them, and libations.

The living dead are multilingual: "they speak the language of men with whom they lived until 'recently'; and they speak the language of the spirits and of God."[14] These are the spirits that people are most concerned with for it is through them that the spirit world becomes real. The living dead return to the living from time to time to share meals and have interest in the ongoing lives of the living. They are the guardians of family and traditions. If they have been offended, or their instructions not properly fulfilled, or they were improperly buried, it is feared that they will come back for revenge by causing misfortunes or illness.

The libations and other acts of communion are the "mystical ties that bind the dead to their surviving relatives."[15] They allow a person to access the eschatological realm of existence through rituals by invoking the ancestors' power to renew and revitalize their potencies, and put right broken relationships.[16] The oldest-surviving family member, who also has the longest memory of the departed, performs or supervises the performance of these rituals. They are performed within the family. "When, however, the last person who knew the departed also dies, then the [latter] passes out of the horizon and in effect he now becomes completely dead as far as family ties are concerned."[17] They transition to ancestors. The debts are therefore owed to the living dead; those whom we still have memory of. Often the debts will be traced back to the furthest living memory possible.

With regard to the ancestors,

> the departed in this state become members of the family or community of the spirits and if they appear to human beings they are not recognized by human beings, especially in genealogies, but they are empty names which are more or less without personality or at best with only a mythological personality built around fact and fiction. . . . This point is reached when there is no longer anyone alive who remembers them personally by name. . . . Then the process of dying is completed.[18]

---

14. Mbiti, 83.

15. Mbiti, 26.

16. E. Ikenga-Metuh, *Comparative Studies of African Traditional Religions* (Onitsha: IMICO, 1987), 262.

17. Ikenga-Metuh, *African Traditional Religions*, 25.

18. Ikenga-Metuh, 26.

The living lose contact with them and they now enter into the state of "collective immortality." If they are "seen" it is

> through activities and many folk stories of spirits described in human form, activities and personalities, even though elements of exaggeration are an essential part of that description. Because they are invisible, they are thought to be ubiquitous, so that a person is never sure where they are or are not.[19]

They speak through mediums and become guardians of the clan. In some societies they become the intermediaries between God and humans.

The ancestors do not appear to the living as often as the living dead do. "They appear in people's dreams, especially to diviners, priests, medicine men and rainmakers to impart some information."[20] A person may become mentally disturbed if the ancestors or the living dead appear too frequently. When they possess a person, they are thought to cause forms of illness. Not all spirit possession is see negatively, however. There are occasions when it is desirable and people induce it through ritual dancing and rhythmic drumming. When a person is thus possessed he or she becomes a medium for the oracles, and what the person communicates is honored by the community. It is the unsolicited possession with catastrophic consequences that is to be feared. In African Traditional Religion, such possession was removed through exorcism, but in the cultural revival it is exorcised through paying the ancestral debts.

The rituals accompanying the payment of debts aim to restore broken relationships physically, psychologically, and spiritually. Healing in this case means a return to wholeness. It is a process that incorporates God, the ancestors, and the living.[21] These rituals include tracing the descendants of the family to whom the debt is owed and paying the balance of the debt to the surviving members of that family. An animal, usually a goat, is slaughtered to pay for the fellowship.

---

19. Ikenga-Metuh, 79.
20. Ikenga-Metuh, 81.
21. Joseph Healey and Donald Sybertz, *Towards an African Narrative Theology* (Nairobi: Paulines Publications, 1996), 298.

Response to the Practice: Is the Debt within the Scope of the Redemptive Work of Christ?

To resolve the questions whether the living can have debts to the living dead, whether the dead can demand payment of those debts and in the case of nonsettlement cause havoc on the living, and therefore whether the redemptive work of Christ has settled these debts, the following questions must be answered: What is the scope of Christ's work? And can the dead see us – that is, are they aware of what is going on in the physical world?

The Scope of Christ's Work

Christ's work can be summarized under three roles: revelatory, ruling, and reconciliatory.[22] He revealed the Father and the heavenly truths. By doing so, he was prophetic in his earthly ministry. He also introduced himself as a ruler who will sit on the "glorious throne."[23] But it is his work as a priest that is our focus. He reconciles God and humanity. He pays the debt accrued by human beings by offering his own life to God as a ransom so that they can be freed from sin.[24]

Christ's work at the cross secures

> the communication of the blessings of salvation to the sinner and his restoration to divine favor and to a life in intimate communion with God.... It deals with restoration, redemption, and renewal, [and] can only be understood properly in the light of the original condition of man as created in the image of God, and of the subsequent disturbance of the proper relationship between man and his God by the entrance of sin into the world.[25]

This redemption of the sinner involves the restoration of the personal relationship with God and the removal of the sinner's guilt.

Having determined the scope of the work of Christ, the question still stands as to whether Christ's work applies to the payment of ancestral debts. On the one hand, Christians have misappropriated their understanding of salvation to respond to the cultural revivalist demand for payment of the ancestral debts. This misunderstanding is caused by the Christians seeking to understand and

---

22. These roles are explained in detail in Erickson, *Christian Theology*, 697–703.
23. Matt 19:28; 13:41; Heb 1:8.
24. Rom 6:15–18.
25. Louis Berkhof, *Systematic Theology*, 2nd ed. (Grand Rapids: Eerdmans, 1949), 457.

appropriate the work of Christ from an existential, anthropological perspective rather than from a transcendent perspective first. Salvation is entirely the work of Christ to deal with the debt of sin owed to the Father. To therefore apply the work of Christ to the payment of ancestral debts is a misappropriation; Christ's work pays only the debts owed to God, not those to ancestors.

However, this misappropriation still persists. We must not therefore stop at the work of Christ, but we need to establish why the practice persists and answer consequent questions.

The Understanding of Salvation among the Agīkūyū

The Agīkūyū, like many other African communities, perceive "sin" as "faults" committed by the living. Aylward Shorter affirms this view that faults in African Traditional Religion are the equivalent of "sin" in Christianity when he argues that faults "are not transgressions of a 'law', but a factual contradiction of the established order. However a distinction can be observed between sins which offend and invite punishment from God and spiritual beings and faults which bring about a physical disorder by themselves."[26] These faults are neither morally good nor bad but they are dangerous because they upset the balance of life; they upset the relations between the living and the dead. They are antisocial in character and harm those who commit them rather than offending others. Committing those sins is a manifestation of a person's ill will to another or to the community.

From a biblical perspective, sin is ontological: it is a loss of relationship between God and humanity. In African Traditional Religion, sin is not only ontological but also social.

> The Agīkūyū saw sin as a social evil only noticeable when there was a tragedy in the community or broken relationships. God's love was experienced in rain, healthy families, large livestock herds and bountiful harvest. In many cases the social evils which were considered sin among the Agīkūyū were manifested in calamities like famine and diseases. The missionaries' Christian message, built upon the concept of "fallen man" and "merciful God," was a complete deviation from what was known by the community. It was an affront to their norm to insinuate that the original parents

---

26. Aylward Shorter, *African Culture and the Christian Church* (London: Geoffrey Chapman, 1974), 62.

had fallen out of favor while the oral tradition had all along insisted that progenitors had favor from God. They did not understand this new definition of sin whose consequences made God angry. It was a fallacy by the missionaries to claim that Agĩkũyũ had sinned against God yet they were already having bumper harvests and whole families. When the evidence of God's mercy was obvious through good harvests, how could these "foreigners" say that He was unhappy with the community?[27]

Upsetting established community order is not a sin in Christianity but it is a grave sin (fault) in African Traditional Religion. A person who lets down the community loses the respect of that community, which makes the person guilty.[28] It is not only an affront to the living but also to the dead. This social aspect of sin means that when a person or a family refuses to pay a debt, the consequences can be passed on to anyone in the community who shares that lineage, regardless of how remote the connection is.

"Ritual faults and omissions which are direct affronts to spiritual beings involve society also in the retribution which they bring. Faults which affect the relationship between men and spiritual beings are sins, and tend to be collective in their implications."[29] With specific reference to debts, therefore, it means that if the direct debtor does not pay, the ancestors will punish anyone who is of direct lineage because of the communal nature of the understanding of sin in African Traditional Religion.

This is not to say that the idea of direct individual offenses to God is alien, but rather the emphasis is mostly on offenses to the spirits and community. Sin is also thought to be a reality, a state, not merely a fear of punishment or an affront to the established order. Rites of purification and reconciliation are attempts to get rid of this state. It is also thought to be a violation of the covenant in which the two families agreed to give certain gifts in exchange for the girl.[30] This state is mostly defined by the type of the consequent disaster, whether death, sickness, bareness, or poverty. It is shown in the symbolism of purification rites in which blood is allowed to flow onto the ground, and when it is absorbed by the soil it is believed that the ancestors have "drunk" it and accepted it as a propitiation. Restoring the relationship involves an

---

27. Kamau Thairu, *Priest as an Elder: Inculturation of Ministerial Priesthood in Light of the Agikuyu Eldership* (Nairobi: Choices Graphics, 2022), 227.

28. Communal not strictly ontological – an affront to God, in Christianity.

29. Shorter, *African Culture*, 62.

30. Shorter, 66.

appeal to the ancestors for forgiveness of the nonpayment of the debt and imploring them to release the blessing and restore communion. In addition, acceptance of the payment of the outstanding debt to the surviving members of the family is thought to finally appease the angry ancestors, making the atonement complete.

To further illustrate the understanding of sin among the Agĩkũyũ, Teresia M. Hinga, profiling the concept of salvation among the Agĩkũyũ Christians – *ahonoki*[31] – in the 1980s, notes that there are several dimensions to how they understand salvation. They see salvation as a negative process in which one is saved from sin, death, and the anger of God. They define sin as the "willful transgression of what is forbidden by God. To answer the question of what is sin, one is given a list of what is forbidden like adultery, drunkenness, licentiousness and jealousy."[32] These sins are a manifestation of a deeper personal disorder and show how an individual is disoriented. Consequently, they understand salvation as moral transformation. One is "saved" not only from sin but also from sinfulness.[33] Salvation is also forgiveness of sins by God. Christ's death secured the atonement and reconciliation of the sinner to God.

The *ahonoki* see salvation "in terms of victorious living."[34] After salvation, one is expected to conquer Satan. Satan is seen in personal calamities, sickness, and temptations that may befall a Christian. Thus, on the one hand life is seen as a constant battle against Satan and his ways, while on the other they have confidence that since they have the Holy Spirit they will be victorious in every way. It is this understanding of salvation as a constant battle against Satan that exposes them to believe in *ngomi* when there is prolonged suffering or constant failure.

---

31. They do not only subscribe to the doctrine of salvation; they also claim to be saved. In their understanding, being saved starts from the conviction that one has sinned and God has done something about it by offering his Son to die for these sins, and of public confession of sin and water baptism as a sign of faith and of the Holy Spirit as the seal of salvation. See Teresia M. Hinga, "An African Understanding of Salvation: A Case Study of a Group of Christians Popularly Known among the Agikuyu as Ahonoki (Saved Ones), and an Evaluation of Their Understanding of Salvation, vis-à-vis a New Testament Interpretation" (Master's diss., University of Nairobi, 1980), 80–81.

32. Hinga, "African Understanding of Salvation," 81–83.

33. Hinga, 83.

34. Hinga, 87.

Can the Dead See Us?

Having established the nature of ancestral debts, the scope of the work of Christ, and the African understanding of salvation, we now need to establish if the ancestors have the capacity to demand those debts. For this, we first have to determine if the dead, whether in hell or in heaven, can see us – that is, are they aware of current affairs in the physical world?

According to Agĩkũyũ culture, two terms describe the dwelling place of the living dead: *ũkirinĩ* and *na Mũrungũ*. *Ũkirinĩ* is the most popular reference. It has its root in the word *kira*, meaning "be silent," and therefore *ũkirinĩ* becomes "the place of the silent." The second term is derived from one of the many names of God, *Mũrungũ*, which

> means literally the "Dweller of the underworld." In Gĩkũyũ mythology there dwells a people under the earth and they are the ones who gave the Gĩkũyũ [the patriarch of the community] fire. In this underworld which is somehow connected to the roots of the sacred fig tree, the *Mugumo*, dwell the spirits of the ancestors, *Ngomi*, and God, *Mũrungũ*, "Dweller of the underworld," visits it occasionally. The *Ngomi* then have an opportunity to intercede directly to *MweneNyaga* [another name for God] for their living relations.[35]

The title denotes that God dwells below and is connected to the roots of the *Mugumo* tree which is symbolic of his presence. The dead dwell among the people and may be incarnate in animals or plants, but they also live in the realm of *Mũrungũ*. They are the connection between the dead and the living.

The Bible, on the other hand, reveals that when death occurs, the soul returns to God[36] to face judgment.[37] At the judgment, Christ will sit on his throne and separate the "sheep" from the "goats."[38] The criterion will be not only whether people helped the poor but also whether they had a personal relationship with Christ. Those who believed in him while here on earth will live again. Those who confessed him while here on earth he will confess before the Father; but those who denied him he too will deny. That is, those who believed in him will die physically but will live again in the presence of the

---

35. Gikuyu Documentation Centre, "Gikuyu Names for God," 20 March 2011, accessed 2 February 2022, https://mukuyu.wordpress.com/tag/murungu/.
36. Eccl 12:6.
37. Heb 9:27.
38. Matt 25:31–41; John 5:28; 11:25.

Father in heaven. Those who did not believe will die physically and will die again spiritually and be separated from him to live forever in hell.

The Agĩkũyũ culture teaches that those who die are here with us, while the Scriptures teach that the dead are in heaven or hell. The Bible further reveals that the dead neither see nor know about current events. For example, Isaiah 63:16 is a text in praise of God who has redeemed the Israelites from exile. They beseech God to look at them with tenderness and compassion for he is their Father. The prophet then discloses that Abraham and Israel (Jacob) have no idea what is currently happening to the Israelites. They do not know if the Israelites are in exile or not.

Job 14:21 also reveals what happens to human beings when they die. Job discloses that if the children of the dead succeed or fail, the dead do not know it. In other words, the dead, whether in heaven or hell, simply have no idea of the current situation of their family. Keck et al. argue that, for Job, death "is the separation from the bond of kinship. He considers not what the living remember of the dead but what the dead can know of the living – which is nothing, neither their good fortune nor bad."[39] In addition, at a certain stage, the dying concentrate wholly on the dying process such that they become isolated from their kin. This is the beginning of the process of separation from the living. For Job, therefore, death becomes the symbol of separation from the physical world.

Luke 16:19–31 shows the rich man conversing with Lazarus and Abraham. It again reveals that there are two dwelling places in the afterlife: heaven and hell. It is evident that those in hell can see those in heaven and vice versa, but neither can see those on earth. Further, those in heaven and hell are separated by a "great chasm" so that no one can move from one to the other after judgment.

Ecclesiastes 9:10 shows that in death, there is no activity of the physical world that will be carried over. This is because the kind of body we will have then is an imperishable resurrection body which has transcended physical needs.[40] This text uses "Sheol," hell, to describe the final destination of the dead. This text neither describes the painful experiences of hell as does the New Testament, nor discloses the criteria for going to hell. Rather, "Sheol" is

---

39. Leander E. Keck et al., *The New Interpreter's Bible*, vol. 4, 12 vols. (Nashville: Abingdon, 2000), 443.

40. 1 Cor 15:53.

used to refer to the final destination of the dead where earthly experiences, activities, plans, and wisdom will come to an end.[41]

Since the dead cannot see the living, they cannot therefore ask for payment of debts. Also, since they do not need the things of the physical world to survive in the spiritual world, paying physical debts becomes irrelevant. They cannot influence the affairs of the physical world for they do not know what is going on in the world. As such, the argument that the dead can demand the payment of debts lacks merit.

Pastoral Concerns the Practice Seeks to Address

We must consider the pastoral concerns that this practice of ancestral debts seeks to address. Christians are convinced that the difficult experiences they have, such as their businesses not flourishing or their children not being successful, are due to the fact that they have "debts to the ancestors." Additionally, they argue that the reason women are more promiscuous now compared with earlier generations is because of the "debts to their grandmother," *thiirĩ wa cucu*;[42] and the reason why there are so many single mothers is because of *kuhata mururu*.[43]

This concept must be seen as a people trying to deal with constant failure in life or commercial enterprise. It is a cultural response to the question of where God is in the midst of pain. Christians are especially vulnerable because they may have tried prayer, fasting, pastoral prayers, "seed planting," and all manner of other things. When all else has "failed" they turn to culture for answers.

---

41. Michael A. Eaton, *Ecclesiastes: An Introduction and Commentary* (Leicester: Inter-Varsity, 1983), 129.

42. Translated "debts to the grandmother," this is a euphemism for female circumcision. In the Gĩkũyũ tradition, it was believed that when a girl was circumcised by an incision in her genitalia, the oozing blood that was allowed to drip onto the ground and be absorbed by the soil united the girl, now a woman, with the ancestors.

43. According to *Cottage of Revolutionary Rebels*, a blog that comments on Gikuyu culture, this was a goat offered by the family whose daughter got pregnant without marriage. Often the girl's father would find out who was responsible for the pregnancy and he would charge the man three fattened he-goats. The first was referred to as *mbũri ya kũhata mĩruru* – a goat to cleanse of the yolk – this "yolk" is borrowed imagery of the "egg yolk." This "yolk" is symbolic of the amniotic fluid which at birth is spilt in the father's house. Traditionally the girl should give birth in her husband's house. If she gives birth in her father's house, it is considered a taboo and therefore she desecrates her father's house. She causes uncleanliness when she spills the "yolk" in her father's house rather than her husband's house. In contemporary usage, it is argued that there are so many single parents because they have not offered this goat. As such they are cursed, and this cycle of lack of spouses will likely follow their children: they will not enter marriage, and if they do, their marriages will not last.

The question of pain and suffering must therefore be addressed if the propagation of this heresy is to be curtailed and corrected in the public theology of the Kenyan church. Although Christianity is being presented as irrelevant and impotent in addressing life's challenges, Jürgen Moltmann observes that Christian faith, compared with all other faiths and philosophies, is the only one that offers hope not only in the present life but also into the afterlife.[44] Other faiths have a future but no God in it, while Christianity has both the future and God in it. If Christians hold on to unwavering hope in God, they "begin to assume responsibility for the personal, social and political problems of the present."[45]

The Christian hope will then transform people from those who have lost hope and slipped into angst through being fatalistic, passive observers of the unfolding events of their lives, to those who actively pursue the fulfillment of God's will in their lives with undying hope in the face of personal calamity.[46] This hope brings transformation from the resignation brought about by constant failure in life, and it invites Christians to work and transform those failures. "So faith becomes action, which will in turn help bring the object of that faith."[47]

The practice of ancestor debt claims that wealth and good health are a sign of the ancestors' favor while prolonged illness and material poverty signify the ancestors' displeasure. Jean-Marc puts this challenge in perspective when discussing Jesus as a healer: illness is not "experienced as an objective fact; [rather it is] a scandal that belongs in the anthropological realm of evil and misfortune."[48]

> Illness is not simply the body malfunctioning but the external manifestation of broken relationships with the society, the ancestors or God. As such, illness is not only personal but also communal and religious. While the social contributors may easily be recognized, the spiritual aspects require someone versed in the "language of God and the ancestors."[49]

---

44. Jürgen Moltmann, "Politics and the Practice of Hope," *The Christian Century* (1970), 288.

45. Moltmann, "Politics," 370.

46. Moltmann, 371.

47. Erickson, *Christian Theology*, 1066.

48. Jean-Marc Ela, *My Faith as an African*, trans. Susan Perry and John Pairman Brown (Maryknoll: Orbis, 1988), 50.

49. Thairu, *Priest as an Elder*, 226.

The resurgence of the practice must also lead us to examine evangelization among communities. It seems that even after years of missionary activity in Central Kenya, the perception of the afterlife informed by African Traditional Religion has not changed. As the Scriptures teach, the idea of a continuum of the physical and eternal life and the distinct separation between the living and the dead is still alien. This challenge is not helped by the delivery of tributes to the departed during interment services. Often the kin will address the dead in the second person, as if the dead hear what they say.

Conclusion

From the above discussion, it is evident that the claim by Christians that Christ's work at the cross has paid ancestor debts is misinformed and a misappropriation of Christ's work, because the debts are nonexistent in the first place. The insistence by cultural revivalists, most of whom were born and raised as Christians, must be seen as a juxtaposition of the African understanding of "faults" with the Christian understanding of "sin." It must be seen as their struggle to explain pain and suffering.

Bibliography
Books, Journals, and Websites

Berkhof, Louis. *Systematic Theology*. 2nd ed. Grand Rapids: Eerdmans, 1949.

Cottage of Revolutionary Rebels. Blog. 25 October 2018. Accessed 22 January 2022. https://thingirawairegi.wordpress.com/2018/10/25/.

Eaton, Michael A. *Ecclesiastes: An Introduction and Commentary*. Leicester: Inter-Varsity, 1983.

Ela, Jean-Marc, *My Faith as an African*. Translated by Susan Perry and John Pairman Brown. Maryknoll: Orbis, 1988.

Erickson, Millard J. *Christian Theology*. 3rd ed. Grand Rapids: Baker, 1983.

Gikuyu Documentation Centre. "Gikuyu Names for God." 20 March 2011. Accessed 2 February 2022. https://mukuyu.wordpress.com/tag/murungu/.

Gordis, Robert. *Koheleth, the Man and His World: A Study of Ecclesiastes*. New York: Schocken, 1968.

Healey, Joseph, and Donald Sybertz. *Towards an African Narrative Theology*. Nairobi: Paulines Publications, 1996.

Hinga, Teresia M. "An African Understanding of Salvation: A Case Study of a Group of Christians Popularly Known among the Agikuyu as the Ahonoki (Saved Ones), and an Evaluation of Their Understanding of Salvation, vis-à-vis a New Testament Interpretation." Master's diss., University of Nairobi,

1980. Accessed 10 February 2022. http://erepository.uonbi.ac.ke/bitstream/handle/11295/95867/Hinga_An%20African%20Understanding%20of%20Salvation.pdf?sequence=4&isAllowed=y.

Ikenga-Metuh, E. *Comparative Studies of African Traditional Religions*. Onitsha: IMICO, 1987.

Keck, Leander E., et al. *The New Interpreter's Bible*. 12 vols. Nashville: Abingdon, 2000.

Kimeu, Caroline. *"Restoring the River": Why Kenyans are Returning to Precolonial Spirituality*. September 22, 2022. https://www.theguardian.com/global-development/2022/sep/22/kenyans-returning-to-precolonial-kikuyu-traditions-spirituality (Accessed August 1, 2023).

Kolie, Cece. "Jesus As Healer." In *Faces of Jesus in Africa*, edited by Robert J. Schreiter, 127–35. Maryknoll: Orbis, 1991.

Mbiti, John S. *African Religions and Philosophy*. Nairobi: EAEP, 1992.

Moltmann, Jürgen. "Hope and History." *Theology Today* 25, no. 3 (1968): 369–86.

———. "Politics and the Practice of Hope." *The Christian Century* (1970).

Oborji, Francis Anekwe. *Towards a Christian Theology of African Religion*. Limuru: Gaba, 2005.

Olowola, Cornelius. "The Person and Work of Christ." In *Issues in African Christian Theology*, edited by Samuel Ngewa, Mark Shaw, and Tite Tienou, 155–74. Nairobi: EAEP, 1998.

Shorter, Aylward. *African Culture and the Christian Church*. London: Geoffrey Chapman, 1974.

Thairu, Kamau. *Priest as an Elder: Inculturation of Ministerial Priesthood in Light of the Agikuyu Eldership*. Nairobi: Choices Graphics, 2022.

Online Videos

"Nderirwo Ngane Jesu Na Nduithio Nîguo Ngomi Cindathime." Eliza wa Narumoro, interview by Wambui wa Mwangi. YouTube. Accessed 28 April 2021. https://www.youtube.com/watch?v=aiyPTjbAiPU.

"'Rihai Thirî wa Ngomi, Tondu Mûndû Owothe Nîarî Thirî wa Ngomi.' Kiarie wa Ngung'u Kuga." Interview by Wambui wa Mwangi. YouTube. 25 March 2021. Accessed 22 January 2022. https://www.youtube.com/watch?v=yrkTkTvL64M.

"Tutiri thiiri wa Ngomi." Performed and directed by Isaiah Ndung'u. YouTube. February 2021. Accessed 22 January 2022. https://www.youtube.com/watch?v=ldceg_XlrRI.

17

Finding New "Alphabets" for Proclaiming Salvific Faith in Africa

Julius Kithinji
St. Paul's University

and

Pauline K. Mwaura
Minister, Presbyterian Church of East Africa

Abstract

In the many years since missionaries brought the good news of salvation to the African continent, the effects of that salvation have gradually been compromised by a monotonous retention of and obsession with old religious practices. As a result, many African Christians have remained such mainly by confession and not by practice. Statistics testify to the rising numbers of people in Africa who become Christians yet they have no positive Christian influence in society, as levels of crime, corruption, and other social evils escalate. In a recent tweet, Pope Francis stated: "Finding new 'alphabets,' or 'ABCs' for proclaiming the Gospel, without nostalgia for a bygone era, is the most urgent task for the churches among the peoples."[1] Talk of the "alphabet" in the proclamation of faith does not mean literal English or other linguistic

---

1. Pope Francis (@Pontifex), finding new alphabets, #Apostolicjourney, Twitter, 13 September 2021.

aspects, but symbolizes church practices that can over time become worn out, rendering Christianity ineffective. Pope Francis elaborated these alphabets according to his particular religious point of view, but this chapter is a response to the problem that the contemporary African church's "alphabet" is tired, worn out, and ineffective for the proclamation of salvation. The consequence of the church remaining fixated on the old "alphabet" is that expressed in the words frequently attributed to Kwame Bediako,[2] that Christianity in Africa is an ocean wide but only an inch deep. In the view of the authors of this chapter, this is the product of worn-out "alphabets." The task of this chapter, therefore, is through an evangelical framework to examine what can be termed "old" and "worn-out" faith proclamation alphabets in African church practices, so as to chart the way forward to find new "alphabets" for proclaiming the message of salvation in Africa.

Key words: alphabets, proclamation, faith, gospel, renewal, discipleship, Christianity, Africa, salvation

Introduction

In linguistic studies, alphabets are a part of language that make that language intelligible and understood. They are drivers of articulation and assist in decoding meaning. Alphabets depend on a particular linguistic arrangement in order to form parts of a whole. It is amazing how just a few letters – for example, twenty-six in English, twenty-four in *Koine* Greek, twenty-eight in Arabic – form thousands of words that are spoken daily. If Christianity is pictured as a language that is spoken, then necessarily it has its own distinctive ABCs or characters. If the meaning received is not the meaning intended, then one of the areas to check is if the alphabets are properly arranged so as to produce the required message. If, for example, poor notes are struck in a musical language, then a discordant or poor musical sound is produced.

The call for new alphabets for proclaiming the Christian faith in this chapter is motivated by a recent address by Pope Francis urging the Christian church, and not just Roman Catholics, to renew the proclamation of faith. In particular, the primate argued that "finding new 'alphabets,' or 'ABCs' for proclaiming the Gospel, without nostalgia for a bygone era, is the most urgent

---

2. No one seems to know who exactly made this statement or its variant of "a mile wide, an inch deep."

task for the churches among the peoples of Europe."³ Although his primary audience was the Roman Catholic Church, there is a need to consider the applicatory range of this clarion call because the church has always been in a state of self-renewal, replacing old proclamatory ways with newer ones. Throughout its history, the church has fallen into traps of poor proclamation, but that has not always been its fossilized posture.

The Contemporary Need for Renewal of Proclamation

The call for new and contemporary alphabets for the proclamation of faith is necessitated by the lack of depth in the state of growth of Christianity, as perceived not only on the world scene in general but in particular by Africa itself, which is currently seen as the center of global Christianity. Consideration of "how far you have fallen" (Rev 2:5) is a constant task for the church and, in the case of the contemporary African church, is more urgent now than at any other time. The need for proclamation renewal in Africa is first necessitated by the faint scholarly voices focused on this field. The available literature on proclamation resonates around several themes but scant literature is available on renewal. The few scholars who have written on the need for proclamation renewal have not gone ahead in proposing the type of pattern for approaching a proclamation renewal as is given in this chapter. Maribei and Mugambi lament the consumer model of proclamation that leaves members only as church attendees.⁴ They propose a connected model;⁵ however, their model does not propose a major paradigm shift in proclamation.

While acknowledging the proclamation problem posed by the spread of neo-Pentecostalism in Africa, Nicholas Moore⁶ insists on the development of a viable hermeneutics for Africa. He advocates a return to a Christocentric interpretation of the Bible in Africa. Therefore, for him, "the best way for the African Church to ensure growth and vitality while guarding against

---

3. Pope Francis (@Pontifex), finding new alphabets, #Apostolicjourney, Twitter, 13 September 2021.

4. Peter Maribei and Kyama Mugambi, "Contextualized Missions and Theological Education in the Global South: A Case Study from East Africa," in *Africa Bears Witness: Mission Theology and Praxis in the 21st Century*, ed. Harvey Kwiyani (Nairobi: ATNP, 2021), 126–40.

5. A connected model as advocated by Maribei and Mugambi creates a sense of community within a church community and not necessarily the Christian community.

6. Nicholas A. Moore, "Insist on Viable Hermeneutics: A Return to Christocentric Interpretation in Africa," in *The Abandoned Gospel: Confronting Neo-Pentecostalism and Prosperity Gospel in Sub-Saharan Africa*, eds. Philip Barnes et al. ([Africa]: AB316, 2021), 171–79.

counterfeits is for her to remain true to her roots – namely the Bible."[7] Moore's view is more defensive than offensive. As much as the African church needs to defend its spiritual and ecclesiastical heritage, however, it needs offensive alphabets with which to proclaim the gospel by weathering the assaults of secularism. In a recent volume, *African Public Theology*, Sunday Bobai Agang et al. have rallied several contributors who pursue this discipline from an African perspective. What is common among the contributors in the book is that the public issues facing Africa all have a theological bearing which points to inadequate proclamation.[8] Although this chapter does not front the concept of "proclamation alphabets" as a proposal for an academic discipline, it does raise an awareness of the scant scholarly writings on the need for constant renewal in proclamation strategies.

The second issue that raises the need for renewal is Africa's fixation with secondary proclamation issues. In many parts of Africa, for example, appeal to development has drowned the scene of proclamation, with "abundant life" being translated as "prosperous life." It is no wonder that theologies of development have taken center stage in African seminaries, with their graduates being promised that this is the key to the proclamation of faith. If left unchecked, curriculums of development-centered theologies can become very similar to prosperity gospel proclamations because they tend to focus on a basic equation between salvation and the pursuit of material goods. Undeveloped places like most parts of Africa count it good news when development is fronted for abundant life. However, if at its best development theology stops at only the improvement of livelihoods, then an essential aspect of the gospel (εὐαγγελίον) is left out, and the doctrine ends up usurping the core power of Christian proclamation. In fact, it cannot be differentiated from the prosperity gospel. No wonder that in *The Man God Uses*, Oswald J. Smith stated,

> If your mission is merely one of social service, education, political reform, you had better leave it to the social service expert, the school teacher, the doctor and the reformer. If it is to substitute Western civilization along with the Christian religion for

---

7. Moore, "Viable Hermeneutics," 176.

8. Sunday Bobai Agang, Dion A. Forster, and H. Jurgens Hendricks, eds., *African Public Theology* (Bukuru: HippoBooks, 2020).

heathenism, better leave it to government agencies with their systems of uplift and reform[9]

Not only does obsession with the ethic of winning souls to development without winning them to Christ undermine the Christian goal of reconciling humanity to God, it also undermines the goal of Christian development, which is to use development as a way of pointing a lost world to a God of development. It is no wonder that Christianity in so-called "developed" worlds has become the preference of the minority. As the old reformer John Wesley once said, "Where riches have increased, religion may have decreased in the same proportion."[10]

The third issue that propels the need for seeking new proclamation alphabets in Africa is the current state of preaching. What issues from many African pulpits hardly yields salvific grace. Much of the proclamation that comes from African pulpits today is redirected toward particular ideological nuances of congregations with their whimsical desires. Such preaching can no longer yield broken souls who come to God asking, "What shall we do?" (Acts 2:37). Transforming preaching by couching it in human inventions undermines the souls which proclamation is meant to transform. Much of this proclamation issues from African preachers who shun training in Bible colleges, seminaries, or theological schools. Paradoxically, such preachers sit for long periods in front of their TVs or YouTube and other websites, learning by copying (Jer 23:30) their pet preachers, some of whom have invested years in training and others who like them have no training. Alternately, some of those trained have passed through schools whose homiletical persuasions are not enriched by adequate curriculum. Mark Dever cites expository preaching as an indispensable mark of a healthy church.[11] Unlike other forms of preaching – for example, topical preaching – expository preaching centers on the Bible. It unfolds the Bible and leads to submission to the Bible's authority.

The fourth characteristic of worn-out proclamatory habits is ecclesiastically conditioned proclamation. In many churches today, congregation maintenance is regarded by those who maintain a housed flock as one of the most important aspects of ministry. In contrast, evangelists who proclaim the faith outside

---

9. Oswald J. Smith, *The Man God Uses*, edited by John Stahnke (New York: Christian Alliance Publishing, 2013),12. https://christiandiet.com.ng/wp-content/uploads/2021/06/The-Man-God-Uses-Oswald-Smith-Christiandiet.com_.ng_.pdf.

10. In Richard P. Heitzenrater, *An Exact Likeness: The Portraits of John Wesley* (Nashville: Abingdon, 2016), 69.

11. Mark Dever, *Nine Marks of a Healthy Church* (Wheaton: Crossway, 2013), 43.

buildings are regarded less highly. The reverend is viewed as greater than the evangelist because in the worn-out proclamation alphabet the hierarchy of proclaimers is humanly tilted in a manner contrary to the expectations of New Testament Christianity. In well-established churches in Africa, salvation is undermined when emphasis is laid on the differentiation of these offices purely motivated by sociological/political/administrative reasons and not divine reasons. A secular dimension in the patterning of ministerial offices has dogged Africa, with the result that proclamation is seriously undermined. It is not possible to retain these worn-out ways and still expect salvific results from African proclamation.

Another pertinent issue that calls for a unique proclamation alphabet is the many alien cultures that are competing for the African church's endorsement. Many churches in the West have advocated for the ordination of gay priests and the solemnization of gay marriages. The LGBTQ[12] dilemma in Africa is commonly seen as mainly a Western problem while Africa grapples with its traditional prevalent problem of polygamy. As James Beilby and Paul Rhodes have noted, while many within the LGBTQ movement are disenchanted with religion, "it is also true that a significant sector of this community takes religion – including Christianity – very seriously."[13] When it comes to polygamy, Emily Onyango has noted that the African church is currently almost overwhelmed by the resurgence of this culture, especially among churched people.[14] Faced with these subtle forces, the African church cannot just preach the gospel in a way that does not give Christian and biblical answers to the questions presented by these realities. It is not enough just to embrace and love people of different orientations without giving a decisive Christian voice regarding the emerging practices.

Other issues have also affected proclamation in Africa. Apart from sexual and gender orientation and polygamy, other retrogressive cultures have complicated the architecture of Christian proclamation in Africa. Although this is not the place to elaborate on all of them, particular notice should be

---

12. The abbreviation stands for lesbian, gay, bisexual, transexual, and queer.

13. James Beilby and Paul Rhodes, *Understanding the Transgender Identities: Four Views* (Grand Rapids: Baker Academic, 2019), 45.

14. Emily Awino Onyango, *Gender and Development: A History of Women's Education in Kenya* (Carlisle: Langham Monographs, 2018), 147.

taken of the emerging Agikuyu *mburi cia kiama*[15] and the Meru *njuri nceke*,[16] which advocate for oathing and their components that undermine the gains of Christianity on the African soil. There is also a rapid increase in deliberate single motherhood which is occasioned by *mipango ya kando*[17] on account of relaxed sexual morals. *Mipango ya kando* and deliberate single motherhood are now being almost openly advocated by "independent" women who feel that marriage is no longer necessary for the completion of a woman. These subtle institutions undermine the ideal Christian image of family and marriage, and in a deliberate manner.

These and many other emerging realities call for the church to be ready with new alphabets for the proclamation of the gospel. As has been stated, "new alphabets" refers to new imagination, intelligent approaches to the packaging and repackaging of the gospel to retain its relevance and efficacy on the African soil. It also means providing counter answers to realities and cultures, whether indigenous or borrowed, which from time to time undercut the reasoning of Christian proclamation.

Consequences of Sticking to Worn-Out Alphabets

We are living in highly dynamic times. Perspectives keep changing, and truth and reality keep begging for new ways to be conceived and understood. The truth and reality of Christianity is not isolated or shielded from the demands of our times. It is paramount that those who present the gospel message engage in seeking new ways of presenting the gospel of God to the ever-changing realities of the times. If the trend of sticking to worn-out ways of preaching the faith is uncritically upheld and retained, several dangers may be experienced. This section briefly considers two worn-out alphabets as examples of the dangers of remaining irrelevant.

First is the danger of maintaining the old alphabets that were introduced by the missionaries and which give preference to elders at the expense of the

---

15. There has been a recent push from the Gikuyu traditional council of elders to "return to our roots." Part of this return is the call to participate in rituals when giving away a goat or goats, called *mbūri cia kiama*, which is usually given to the council of elders as part of the progression of a man into the status of eldership. Many Christian churches have argued that the ritualistic underpinnings of the practice obfuscate the new covenant in Christ and should therefore be repudiated.

16. The Ameru *njuri nceke* vows and accent on eldership has similarities with the Gikuyu *mburi cia kiama* and involves one undergoing several rituals, some of which put at loggerheads belief in one's Christian sacramental vows and cultural ritualistic vows.

17. Side and unofficial marriages or secret marriages – sometimes several of them.

young. Ridden with colonial codes, these alphabets were initially captivating because they produced a Christianity that helped African Christians make the transition from the colonial world to spaces of self-propagation, self-sustenance, and self-governance in terms of indigenizing Christianity in Africa. However, since leadership in many parts of Africa is mainly an affair of the elders, many young people felt that they were being left out in the growth of the church and its methods of proclamation. As a consequence, young people have become disengaged from the Christian church in what is a predominantly youthful continent. Joseph Ola argues that there is a "disparity between the youthfulness of African Christianity (judging by its age distribution) and its leadership – a disparity which, left unchecked, has potential to undo the growth of African Christianity."[18] In his view, the youth are a neglected group by the elders who have a monopoly on leadership. In areas where the youth are not neglected, Ola argues that they are left to invent their own self-affirming proclamation alphabets and styles of worship, some of which may not be theologically sound. A proclamation alphabet that is intergenerational and theologically sound is therefore preferable.

The second worn-out alphabet concerns the note that was struck by the initial protagonists of Pentecostalism in Africa. Initially, Pentecostalism was a kind of reformation protesting against the institutionalization of the gospel and the loss of spiritual fervor mainly among the so-called mainline churches. One of the views of this movement was that mainline churches were preaching the gospel with a boring demeanor. Following the Pentecostal proclamation mode which housed many imported mannerisms, many churches, especially in Kenya, made it their aim to proclaim relevance and a more "exciting gospel," often at the expense of the gospel of Jesus Christ. Proclamation of relevance manifests in an overreliance on the coziness of the church and other means of making a congregation comfortable within the church precincts. The alphabet of coziness gained currency in the 1990s when the church was declared boring for young people. During this period, many churches relaxed the stringent moral requirements that were an effect of the East African Revival movement and *mutaratara*[19] (liturgical) churches, and instead encouraged unregulated dancing, dress, and so on. In terms of liturgy, spontaneous and unsystematized

---

18. Joseph Ola, "Missiology for a Youthful Continent," in *Africa Bears Witness: Mission Theology and Praxis in the 21st Century*, ed. Harvey Kwiyani (Nairobi: Africa Theological Network Press, 2021), 155.

19. A term sometimes employed derogatorily to mean that liturgical churches exhibit dry and mechanical worship.

forms of worship, with prolonged sessions of singing, prayers, and sermons were introduced, in order to make the gospel attractive, throwing theological caution to the wind of the "spirit" – the spirit of which was a socialized type of atmosphere; apparently it was *kuongozwa na roho* (being led by the Spirit), yet in practice it was sheer *kuongoza roho* (leading or controlling the Spirit). Mugambi points out that such a climate encouraged nonorthodox teaching and extravagant lifestyles which became commonplace among leaders.[20] This deviation from the norm of early proclamation in Africa bred opulence among preachers and pastors, drawing criticism and leading to a public outcry. One outcome of this lame alphabet, as Mugambi points out, was that the adoption of kinship language in the performance of ministry became common. Though kinship language is a biblical concept that is acceptable in reference to the children of faith, Mugambi exposes that in Pentecostal circles it was exploited as a basis not only for preaching the gospel but also for maintaining control and the power imbalance within the movement. Tat-Siong observes that infantilization is the worst form of control.[21]

These forms of gospel proclamation, whether they have worked in prior generations or not, have been exploited in our times, while other forms have been employed to make the gospel attractive but not so intelligible in Africa. The indictment often attributed to Kwame Bediako remains true: African Christianity is miles wide but only inches deep. The plea now is for newer and more relevant alphabets in which to couch the language of salvific proclamation in African Christianity.

Proclamation Renewal: Some Historical Examples

In pursuit of a new proclamation alphabet, Pope Francis referred to Cyril and Methodius, calling for the church to emulate "the example of a creative Church, much like the saints of these lands, Cyril and Methodius, who invented a new alphabet to communicate the faith to the people."[22] Throughout its history, the church has sought to retain the purity of the gospel of Christ. When the

---

20. Kyama M. Mugambi, *A Spirit of Revitalization: Urban Pentecostalism in Kenya* (Waco: Baylor University Press, 2020), 124.

21. Benny Liew Tat-Siong, "The Gospel of Mark," in *A Postcolonial Commentary on the New Testament*, eds. Fernando F. Segovia and R. S. Sugirtharajah (London: T&T Clark, 2009), 124.

22. Reported by Andrea Tornielli, "Secularization and the New 'ABCs' for Proclaiming the Faith," 13 September 2021, Vatican News, https://www.vaticannews.va/en/pope/news/2021-09/pope-francis-slovakia-editorial-secularization-proclaiming-faith.html.

gospel message has encountered times of pollution, moments of renewal have been available to purify it.

Christianity itself was a renewal movement within Judaism. Failure to recant their confession of Jesus as the Messiah led the early Christians to be expelled from the synagogues. Their insistence on the messiahship of Jesus left them with no option other than to imagine a new alphabet for their proclamation. The Reformation is another prime example. Because of the laxity and twisted proclamations of the sixteenth century, the Reformers followed Luther and others to protest against the heresies of the Roman Catholic Church, and reimagined new ways of proclaiming the faith. The Reformation in particular, with its five *solas*,[23] gave proclamation new alphabets that have remained to date.

The Wesleyan revival was also a time of new proclamation alphabets. Wesley decried the low state of the Church of England of his time and by God's grace championed a renewal movement within the church that led to the emergence of the Methodist movement. The Wesleyan movement added the open-air preaching alphabet into proclamation. Although this was not uniquely Wesleyan because Jesus and his followers also preached in the open spaces, Wesley revived this practice that had long been rejected in the catholicized church. Wesley and the revivalists of his day also left an unprecedented legacy in the pathway of holiness that has enabled many generations to proclaim the faith with ease.

Following the pattern of Wesley and other revivalists, the East African Revival movement was itself an alphabet. Unlike other revival movements that led to church schisms, the East African Revival was a renewal of the church from within. Although the movement slowly waned over time, for almost five decades it sustained a holiness within the church that helped Christian proclamation through some of the most difficult periods – especially the transition from the colonial church to the postcolonial church.

The Pentecostal movement that swept Africa in the 1970s was another alphabet that helped to proclaim the gospel. Initially, the movement was a powerful tool for proclaiming salvation. Many young people were born again and transformed during this wave. Salvific faith became a promising tool for cohesion and nation-building. However, due to its fluidity and lack of organizational dimensions occasioned by overreliance on "the spirit," the

---

23. The five *solas* of the Reformation, which distinguished the Reformers from the teachings of Rome, are as follows: *sola scriptura* (Scripture alone), *solus Christus* (Christ alone), *sola fide* (faith alone), *sola gratia* (grace alone), and *soli Deo gloria* (glory to God alone).

Pentecostal movement was highjacked by religious merchants and became the bedrock of schisms.[24]

In order to strike the note of a new proclamation alphabet, the African church needs to reimagine itself. Jacob Kimathi Samuel, pleading for a new approach to evangelization in Africa, decries the poor state of African morality and posits that the African church is based on the wrong social imagination.[25] This is blamed on the missionaries who disrupted Africans' former life. African resources should be used to reimagine new ground for evangelizing the continent. According to Katongole, daring to invent the future in Africa requires a different kind of church.[26]

Proposals for Proclamation Renewal in Africa: New Alphabets

Having noted that renewal is a constant call to every generation of Christian preachers for the continuity of genuine salvation, and the setbacks for genuine salvation in Africa, this section proposes ways in which salvation can be renewed in our times.

Creation of a Pentecost community becomes a pertinent issue in the new alphabet discourse. It should be noted that there is a difference between classical Pentecostalism and a Pentecost community. Classical Pentecostalism here refers to that wave of "spiritualism" and "pseudo charismaticism" that swept Africa from the 1970s and has mutated into several branches: most genuinely proclaiming faith, but others being almost cultic and heretical. Recovery of a Pentecost community as an alphabet for proclaiming salvific faith in Africa means reviving community based upon Pentecost. Pentecost, although celebrated as a particular point of time within Christendom, was meant to be an everyday experience. Pentecost is the moment of fusion between God the Holy Spirit and humanity, producing a new dimension of living and Christian witness. It is a moment of unity for believers with God, a moment of salvation, and a moment of proclaiming the good news. Church as a Pentecost community assures its catholicity and puts it in opposition only to a nonbelieving world and not itself. Pentecostalism, on the other hand, raised the danger of circularity, whereby Pentecostalism was presented as small

---

24. According to the 2019 national census, Kenya has more than four thousand registered churches and church ministries. The majority of these are Pentecostal church-based ministries.

25. Jacob Kimathi Samuel, *Re-Imagining Theology for Postcolonial Africa: A Case Study of the Kenyan Akurinu Church* (Phoenixville: Borderless Press, 2019), 19.

26. Emmanuel Katongole, *The Sacrifice of Africa: A Political Theology for Africa* (Nairobi: ATNP, 2011), 137.

Pentecostal communities competing against other more established Pentecostal and Christian communities instead of winning a fallen humanity back to God.

Craig Keener argues that circularity becomes a danger when a set of beliefs functions coherently within one community yet confronts serious challenges in dialogue with other communities.[27] In contrast, a Pentecost community ensures unity in Christendom in terms of salvific proclamation. A Pentecost "community of proclamation" does not proclaim for its own sake or benefit, but for the sake of Christ and a lost humanity. It is a community that does not leave proclamatory business to the proclaimers but in itself becomes a proclamation as collective witness becomes the salvific model and energy. When in Matthew 5:13–16 Jesus says "You [plural] are" (ὑμεῖς ἐστε) the salt or light of the world, it is not the individual but the community of proclamation that is meant. In this way, the community of proclamation becomes the new altar call drawing people to Christ. In Africa, a tweaking of the concept of *Ubuntu*, for example, could act as a starting point or an ingredient, but not the finality of imagining a Pentecost community of proclamation. Therefore, there is need to redefine Pentecostalism and neo-Pentecostalism in Africa and purify these frameworks within the framework of a Pentecost community of proclamation.

Another alphabet that is necessary for proclaiming salvation in Africa is one that speaks directly to religio-ethnicism which is prevalent in Africa. Religio-ethnicism here refers to the subtle ethnocentrism that is couched in church, Christian, or religious language. As long as ethnicity is subtly celebrated in the space offered by churches, then proclamation of the gospel in Africa will be undermined. This form of ethnocentrism is manifested in churches that are based on particular tribes and ethnic groups for their existence. In Kenya, ethnicity is exploited for many reasons, such as politics and marketing, and sometimes is celebrated for such. However, if the task of a community of proclamation is to compete for membership based on ethnic affiliations, then salvation in Africa becomes a mirage. For Africa to hear the words that Jesus said to Zacchaeus – "Today salvation has come to this house" – Africa has to sacrifice the sense of power and distance that is propelled by tribal identity.[28] Although many scholars have argued for the positive exploitation of the category of "tribe" for right living in Africa, this is a vulnerable category. It stands in the gateway of negative distance and it takes little to ignite the fire. An alphabet that dissolves ethnic identity through the mystical union with Christ

---

27. Craig S. Keener, *Spirit Hermeneutics: Reading Scripture in Light of Pentecost* (Grand Rapids: Eerdmans, 2016), 279.

28. Katongole, *Sacrifice of Africa*, 137.

relocates African Christians from their rootedness in tribalism to rootedness in the community of Christ.

Rethinking Discipleship

Mugambi has taken a great step forward in explaining how the African church needs to rethink its discipleship programs in the midst of the rising heresies of neo-Pentecostalism.[29] Mugambi's point is that there is much mediocrity around the whole area of preparing disciples for Christ. Dietrich Bonhoeffer once said that "confirmands today are like young soldiers marching to war, the war of Jesus Christ against the gods of this world. It is a war that demands the commitment of one's whole life. Is not God, our Lord, worthy of this struggle?"[30] Unfortunately, much proclamation in Africa does not see discipleship as a necessary step in the journey of salvation. There is great emphasis on producing a salvation decision among converts, but less emphasis on discipling those converts. Discipleship programs have become opportunities for teaching converts to be loyal to pastors and ministries which support them. And even when discipleship is emphasized, the content is often merely skewed to "churching content" (content that makes one more a follower of a church denominational) and not "christening content" (content that makes one more of a follower of Jesus. Very few discipleship programs in the contemporary church have the trajectory of the requirements of the Great Commission: "teaching them to obey everything I have commanded you." Discipleship is not a new alphabet per se, and it even looks odd being aligned as an alphabet for proclamation in Africa. However, its trail needs to be de-idealized, de-idolized, and revamped, such that its focus remains retaining every Christian daily on the pathway to ultimate salvation, even heaven.

Conclusion

More than ever before, African Christianity needs to be clothed in new garments. Even though Global South Christianity is the admiration of many scholars of Christianity, insiders disclose that its efficacy and vitality are fast giving way to secularization and counterfeit methods of proclamation. The case for new alphabets for proclaiming saving faith in Africa made in this

---

29. Mugambi, *Spirit of Revitalization*, 183.
30. See Eric Metaxas, *Bonhoeffer – Pastor, Martyr, Prophet, Spy: A Righteous Gentile vs. the Third Reich* (Nashville: Thomas Nelson, 2010), 303.

chapter demonstrates that no way of proclaiming faith can be sufficient for every generation. What has worked for one generation is always challenged and does not necessarily work for another generation. African Christianity is at a point when its faith proclamation tools need to be sharpened and polished. Although this chapter has made several tentative proposals for revamping methods of proclaiming salvation to ensure the maintenance of a legacy of salvation in Africa, it advocates the renewal of the church, for it is the church that is the ultimate alphabet for faith proclamation in Africa.

Bibliography

Agang, Sunday Bobai, Dion A. Forster, and H. Jurgens Hendriks, eds. *African Public Theology*. Bukuru: HippoBooks, 2020.

Barnes, Philip W., Brazil Bhasera, Matthews A. Ojo, Jack Rantho, Trevor Yaokum, and Misheck Zulu, eds. *The Abandoned Gospel: Confronting Neo-Pentecostalism and the Prosperity Gospel in Sub-Saharan Africa*. [Africa]: AB316, 2021.

Beilby, James, and Paul Rhodes. *Understanding the Transgender Identities: Four Views*. Grand Rapids: Baker Academic, 2019.

Black, Joseph William. *Raising up Good Servants: God's People Using God's Money for God's Glory*. [India]: Oasis International, 2021.

Dever, Mark. *Nine Marks of a Healthy Church*. Wheaton: Crossway, 2013.

Heitzenrater, Richard P. *An Exact Likeness: The Portraits of John Wesley*. Nashville: Abingdon, 2016.

Katongole, Emmanuel. *The Sacrifice of Africa: A Political Theology for Africa*. Nairobi: ATNP, 2011.

Keener, Craig S. *Spirit Hermeneutics: Reading Scripture in Light of Pentecost*. Grand Rapids: Eerdmans, 2016.

Kwiyani, Harvey, ed. *Africa Bears Witness: Mission Theology and Praxis in the 21st Century*. Nairobi: African Theological Network Press (ATNP), 2021.

Maribei, Peter, and Kyama Mugambi. "Contextualized Missions and Theological Education in the Global South: A Case Study from East Africa." In *Africa Bears Witness: Mission Theology and Praxis in the 21st Century*, ed. Harvey Kwiyani, 126–40. Nairobi: ATNP, 2021.

Metaxas, Eric. *Bonhoeffer – Pastor, Martyr, Prophet, Spy: A Righteous Gentile vs. the Third Reich*. Nashville: Thomas Nelson, 2010.

Moore, Nicholas A. "Insist on Viable Hermeneutics: A Return to Christocentric Interpretation in Africa." In *The Abandoned Gospel: Confronting Neo-Pentecostalism and Prosperity Gospel in Sub-Saharan Africa*, edited by Philip Barnes et al., 171–79. [Africa]: AB316, 2021.

Mugambi, Kyama M. *A Spirit of Revitalization: Urban Pentecostalism in Kenya*. Waco: Baylor University Press, 2020.

Ola, Joseph. "Missiology for a Youthful Continent." In *Africa Bears Witness: Mission Theology and Praxis in the 21st Century*, edited by Harvey Kwiyani, 155–69. Nairobi: Africa Theological Network Press, 2021.

Onyango, Emily Awino. *Gender and Development: A History of Women's Education in Kenya*. Carlisle: Langham Monographs, 2018.

Priest, Robert J., and Kirimi Barine, eds. *African Christian Leadership: Realities, Opportunities and Impact*. Carlisle: Langham Global Library, 2019.

Samuel, Jacob Kimathi. *Re-Imagining Theology for Postcolonial Africa: A Case Study of the Kenyan Akurinu Church*. Phoenixville: Borderless Press, 2019.

Smith, Oswald J. *The Man God Uses*, edited by John Stahnke. New York: Christian Alliance Publishing, 2013. https://christiandiet.com.ng/wp-content/uploads/2021/06/The-Man-God-Uses-Oswald-Smith-Christiandiet.com_.ng_.pdf

Tat-Siong, Benny Liew. "The Gospel of Mark." In *A Postcolonial Commentary on the New Testament*, edited by Fernando F. Segovia and R. S. Sugirtharajah, 105–32. London: T&T Clark, 2009.

Tornielli, Andrea. "Secularization and the New 'ABCs' for Proclaiming the Faith." 13 September 2021. Vatican News. https://www.vaticannews.va/en/pope/news/2021-09/pope-francis-slovakia-editorial-secularization-proclaiming-faith.html.

18

Salvation and the Problem of Negative Ethnicity and Schism in the Church in Kenya

Toward an *Ubuntu* Salvation Theology

Rev. Jackline Makena Mutuma and Rev. Dr. John M. Kiboi

St. Paul's University, Limuru, Kenya

Abstract

Although according to the 2019 Kenya Bureau of Statics census Kenya's population is 80 percent Christian, the country experiences serious negative ethnicity. This problem has been blamed on the missionary enterprise which divided the country into spheres of missionary influence along ethnic lines, enhancing negative ethnicity both in the nation and in the church. Negative ethnicity and divisions in the church undermine the very meaning of salvation in both the church's definition and the African understanding of salvation. The traditional African notion of salvation is wholeness of life, and salvation is communal not individual. The existence of negative ethnicity begs the question: Can the church be divided and saved? Whereas the African notion of salvation is communal, the missionary notion of salvation has been individual and spiritual, raising a question in the minds of African Christians: Is it possible to be saved spiritually even without physical wellness? Given that in African *ubuntu*, a person's humanity is irrevocably tied to that of other people, is it possible for a person to be saved when others around are experiencing the evil of discrimination? Individualism, negative ethnicity, and denominationalism undermine the very values Christianity and African *ubuntu* espouse. Therefore, this chapter proposes and develops an *ubuntu* salvation theology for the church in Africa. It argues that through the philosophy of *ubuntu* these evils can be mitigated. The research is literature-based.

Key words: African culture, *ubuntu*, salvation, missionaries, spheres of influence, denominationalism, negative ethnicity, schism

Introduction

Division within the church in Africa is rife. The church is divided into various denominations. As well as there being divisions between Catholics and Protestants, Protestants are further divided into evangelicals and Pentecostals. The Pentecostals are further divided into tiny movements sometimes simply known as ministries. Unfortunately, some of these divisions are along ethnic lines. In Kenya, the main focus of this chapter, denominational divisions have been blamed on the missionary movement which divided the mission field into spheres of influence to avoid conflict in the scramble for converts. Since then, those missionary spheres have defined the ethnic composition of the denominations and religious leadership. Both political and religious leadership are ethnically defined.

In Kenya, every five years the country conducts political elections. These elections are marred by negative ethnicity, with every ethnic community wanting to have one of its own in power. Since the churches have clear ethnic divisions and the politicians who belong to these churches are aware of those divisions, they take advantage of the divisions and exploit them. This has strengthened the divisions in the churches as members support their own people to ascend to power. This creates hatred between the denominations, and even within denominations between members of different ethnic groups. The majority ethnic group in the church, which assumes church leadership, punishes the minority if they appear not to support political contenders from the majority ethnic group. With such a context of power struggles, divisions, discrimination, and hatred within the church, one wonders whether the church can experience true salvation.

Ecumenical movements have made efforts to heal the rifts and reconcile denominations. However, these attempts have not been successful as the rifts are still evident. This chapter argues that a construction of an *ubuntu* salvation theology, based on *ubuntu* philosophy, will challenge members of the different denominations to see each other as a people of one God with one heritage – Africa. This will then achieve positive ethnicity and unity in the church.

Negative Ethnicity and Schism in the Church as a Challenge to Salvation

In the vast geographical terrain of Kenya, there are many ethnic groupings. While this fact is part of the country's valuable heritage, it has on many occasions been used as an opportunity to cause division in both social and religious spaces. The exalting of some ethnic groups over others results in a phenomenon called "negative ethnicity." "Negative ethnicity" refers to the manipulation of ethnic identities for personal interests. Negative ethnicity is used to injure, frustrate, ridicule, and demean other groups, resulting in untold pain. This may result in division in the community along ethnic lines. When these divisions find their way into the church, the church's unity is undermined. Although historically major schisms in the church have been on theological grounds, today many schisms are occasioned by leadership wrangles due to negative ethnicity.

Schisms in the history of the church occasioned by theological differences include the *filioque* controversy of AD 1054 which split the Western church from the Eastern church.[1] In the sixteenth century the Reformation resulted in the split of the church into two strands: the Roman Catholic and Protestant churches. The various denominations were birthed from these two strands of theological differences.

With the advent of missionary work in Africa, the missionary sending bodies back in Europe and the USA subscribed to different denominational persuasions. Africa became a recipient of the already existing doctrinal and denominational differences. In Kenya, this led to missionary spheres of influence, as we explain below.

Christianity was properly established in Kenya with the British conquest of East Africa in the 1880s. The establishment of churches in the Kenyan interior was necessitated by the development of the Imperial British East African Company (IBEACO 1880–95).[2] The European churches started developing mission centers that served as their bases for missionary work,

---

1. Philipp Hauser and Jessica Whittemore, "The Great Schism of 1054: Origins and Effects," Study.com, https://study.com/learn/lesson/great-schism-1054.html.
2. Sydney Herbert Fazan, *Colonial Kenya Observed: British Rule, Mau Mau and the Wind of Change* (London: I. B. Tauris, 2015), 98.

and these mission centers not only spearheaded the European endeavors, but also provided for the European settlements.[3]

The schism in the Kenyan church, just as in many other African churches, has its genesis in the schismatic history of the Western churches. The majority of the Western churches that came on the missionary quest of evangelizing Africa – and Kenya in particular – carried the baggage of their denominational emphases. The missionary centers were also denominational. To deal with what appeared to be conflict between the different missionary groups, missionaries established spheres of influence. The demarcation was made along ethnic lines. This meant that each particular missionary group reached a particular ethnic group in its area of jurisdiction.

The Church Missionary Society (CMS) and the Church of Scotland Mission (CSM) were among the earliest missionary societies to enter the interior of Kenya. There were also the Roman Catholic missions of Mill Hill and White Fathers from France.[4] From the American and Canadian churches came the African Inland Mission, Friends Africa Mission, and the Seventh Day Adventists (SDA), among others.[5] Their differences in terms of states of origin, denominations, and theological positions created interdenominational conflict. Each group had to defend its own interests. Observing the danger of this demarcation, Diedrich Westermann questions the missionaries' intention of preaching a unifying God.[6] He further notes that the variations led to the development of a zoning policy of the churches, a move that marked the birth of a regional division of churches.[7] It is evident that the spheres of influence largely contributed to the ethnic mapping of churches in Kenya.

Westermann states that missionary Christianity came to Africa in a confusing form through its appearance in a multitude of systems, denominations, and sects.[8] He argues that although the missionaries claimed to preach and spread the one kingdom of God, they worked in fierce competition and at times fought against each other,[9] contrary to the purpose and nature of the kingdom of God which is supposed to be unified. Westermann comments, "It

---

3. Fazan, *Colonial Kenya Observed*, 98.
4. Fazan, 98.
5. Fazan, 98.
6. Diedrich Westermann, *Africa and Christianity* (London: Oxford University Press, 1937), 174.
7. Westermann, *Africa and Christianity*, 174.
8. Westermann, 174.
9. Westermann, 174.

is deplorable that the discords which have caused so many disastrous ruptures in Western Christianity should be transferred to Africa and there cause new clefts among people to whom these battles of a European past are meaningless and remain incomprehensible."[10]

Agreeing with Westermann, Ekitala and Wosyanju affirm that Christian missionaries played a critical role in the growth and development of negative ethnicity and ethnic ideologies in Africa. They note that this occurred through the creation of ideologies of social division propagated through the schemes of the dictatorial colonial administrations that the missionaries supported.[11] They further recount that they extended these divisions through the creation of written languages and reaffirmation of cultural identities through writing "tribal histories" of communities' traditions and customs. In their mission schools they incorporated in their educational curricula elements which created ethnic identities in the minds of the pupils.[12]

The distribution of churches in Kenya along ethnic lines resulted in the establishment of tribal churches and denominations. For example, Stephen Mutuku Sesi notes that

> the Methodist church is dominant among the Meru, Legio Maria is dominant among the Luo, Africa Inland Churches among the Akamba and Kalenjin tribes. The Presbyterian Church of East Africa and the Kenya Assemblies of God are greatly associated with the Kikuyu community and Seventh Day Adventist are largely associated with the Kisii tribe.[13]

Today, church denominations are synonymous with specific ethnic communities. Church leadership also reflects the ethnic distribution in the region in which the church is situated.

---

10. Westermann, 174.

11. Ariko L. Ekitala and Mary Goretti Wosyanju, "The Role of the Church in Combating Negative Ethnicity in Kenya: A Survey of Mainline Churches in Eldoret, Kenya," 2013, https://www.researchgate.net/publication/311671416_The_Role_of_the_Church_in_Combating_Negative_Ethnicity_in_Kenya_A_Survey_of_Mainline_Churches_in_Eldoret_Kenya.

12. Ekitala and Wosyanju, "Role of the Church."

13. Stephen Mutuku Sesi, "Ethnic Realities and the Church in Kenya," in *African Missiology: Contribution of Contemporary Thought*, eds. Stephen Mutuku Sesi et al. (Nairobi: Uzima, 2009), 27.

Effects of Negative Ethnicity and Schism

This denominational profiling among ethnic communities has strengthened animosity between communities in Kenya. During campaigns for leadership positions both in church and in society, contestants draw their power from the numerical strength of their communities, commonly known as the "tyranny of numbers." The "tyranny of numbers" has often been used by communities with a numerical advantage to oppress minorities. Members of minority groups have suffered discrimination and exclusion by members of the dominant community. This leads us to pose a question: Can one be in a context of discrimination, experiencing the agony of being discriminated against, and be saved at the same time?

Divisions along ethnic lines have led to ethnic violence. Kenya has experienced indescribable pain and suffering, and deaths, because of ethnic violence. While we must use the term "ethnic cleansing" with caution, accounts show that events are often not far short of that reality. Xan Rice, a reporter of the British newspaper *The Guardian* online, covered Kenya's postelection violence in 2007–8 and gave a detailed account of a victim describing the atrocities committed to some internally displaced people (IDP) at a church in Eldoret.[14] The victim painted a vivid picture. The heinous act is believed to have been caused by the bigotry and hatred between two ethnic communities in the Rift Valley.

While the church was located in the Rift Valley, its worshippers came from a minority community which had settled in the region. It is speculated that the majority of those hiding in the church were probably members of the same denomination as they were of the same tribe. Xan Rice brings out clearly the relationship between the church and ethnicity in Kenya.[15] The fact that this violence occurred within church premises in a country that has 80 percent of its population professing the Christian faith raises many questions.

It is often the case that church politics mimic the secular politics in the country. For example, in the Anglican Church, it seems that the ethnic demographics of a diocese determine who becomes bishop: the bishop is usually affiliated to the majority ethnic group of that diocese. But what if someone in a minority ethnic group is better qualified? Such discrimination produces

---

14. Xan Rice, "'We Told Them to Come Out of the Church but They Locked the Door. . . . So We Burned Them,'" *The Guardian* online, 2 January 2008, https://www.theguardian.com/world/2008/jan/02/kenya1. See also Xan Rice, "Kenya on the Brink as More Than 100 Killed in Poll Riots," *The Guardian* online, 2 January 2008, https://www.theguardian.com/world/2008/jan/01/kenya.topstories32.

15. Rice, "'We Told Them.'"

pain among those who feel excluded. Are the victims of discrimination who experience the pain of exclusion really saved?

Disgruntled members of a church sometimes leave in order to form their own churches, or they stay, with the result that schisms form within the fellowship. Thus, there is not only secular political intolerance within the larger community, but also sadly a fragmentation among believers within the church.

The above examples highlight the extent to which Christianity in Kenya is often ethnocentric. Because of this, evangelization, and the true nature of Christianity which aims at bringing unity in diversity, is greatly injured. The ethnoreligiosity in Kenyan Christianity through the years has brought ethnocentric denominations into existence. Kwame Bediako says, "Unfortunately, vernacular scriptures, though written and published under the auspices of missionary agencies, created vernacular churches that failed to read the scriptures in the mother tongue from the standpoint of the traditional worldview and in the light of realities."[16] Due to the ethnic divisions in the church, the church has failed to contextualize the vernacular Bibles written through a missionary lens, resulting in vernacular churches. This is another cause of ethnic division in the church in Kenya, as even the Bible is viewed through the lens of negative ethnicity.

If the essence of Christianity is unity, how is this seen in the schism of the church? Jesus said that he came that we might know the truth, and that the truth would set us free. Have the members of the church in Kenya been set free? Do they experience fullness of life in the spirit of tribalism and denominationalism? If the greatest commandment Jesus gave to his disciples was that they should love one another, how does the church realize this in the context of schism? In John 17, Jesus prays that his disciples might remain united so that through such unity the world might know God the Father who sent him. The schism, denominationalism, and tribalism that are evident in the church do not demonstrate what the gospel of Christ is all about. Schism in the church overflowing into the community does not uphold either the teachings of the church of unity, nor African *ubuntu*.

Ecumenism as an Attempt at Unity of the Church

Unity of the church means both its physical and intrinsic unity. A church that is physically divided cannot be one in nature either. The inner nature of

---

16. Kwame Bediako, *Christianity in Africa: The Renewal of a Non-Western Religion* (Edinburgh: Edinburgh University Press, 1995), 45.

the church is manifested in its outward appearance. A divided church cannot possibly be one, holy, catholic, and apostolic. A true church manifests these four marks.

Ecumenical bodies have made attempts to bring unity to the divided church. Ecumenical movements in Kenya date back to the missionary era. For example, the joint missionary effort was a result of the ecumenical agreement between the Lutheran Church and the Anglican Church under the auspices of the Church Missionary Society (CMS).

Between 1890 and 1910 there was an influx of different missionary churches in the Kenyan interior. Because of the different denominations spread across different parts of the country, the churches saw the need to collaborate toward unity of purpose. Despite the history of establishing multidenominational churches, the role of the missionaries in fostering cooperation and unity among the different churches is also a vital part of the history of ecumenism in Kenya. As a strategy for uniting the churches to work together for a common cause, ecumenical conferences were convened: the Vihiga conference of 1907–8; the United Missionary Conference at Maseno in 1909; the Kijabe Conference of 1908; and the United Missionary Conference Nairobi of 1909. In attendance were the Africa Inland Mission (AIM), the Church Missionary Society (CMS), the Church of Scotland Missions (CSM), the Friends Africa Industrial Mission (FAIM, Kaimosi), the United Methodist Mission (UMM), the Lumbwa Industrial Mission (LIM), the Seventh Day Adventists (SDA), and the Friends Industrial Mission (FIM, Pemba). These conferences raised the common concerns that the churches had to address. They resolved to reach unity in the areas of education, translation of the Bible, collaboration in providing health services, cooperation and unity of the churches, and economic development.[17] Thus, "unity of the church" did not anticipate the dissolution of denominations into one physical denomination (church). Each denomination would remain as it was, but they would participate together in the life of the society.

The culmination of the ecumenical conferences of 1909, 1910, and 1911 was the development and formation of the Ecumenical Alliance in 1913. The Ecumenical Alliance sought to foster ecumenical cooperation in the coordination of education policies, among other fronts. This led to the establishment of the Alliance High School in 1926, the first higher education institution for Africans.[18] The other notable ecumenical effort by the churches

---

17. National Council of Churches of Kenya, "History of NCCK," 20 May 2020, accessed 8 February 2022, https://www.ncck.org/ourjourney/.

18. National Council of Churches of Kenya, "History of NCCK."

was the establishment of a joint theological education among the Protestant churches. This was marked by the founding of St. Paul's United Theological College in 1955 after five years of experimentation of joint efforts by the churches.[19]

The Ecumenical Alliance evolved into the National Council of Churches in Kenya (NCCK) in 1984. The NCCK and its member churches have played major roles in promoting unity, peace, civic education, fellowship, and dialogue, together with sociopolitical and socio-economic development at the grassroots in the regions in which they operate.[20]

Another ecumenical alliance in Kenya emerged in 1975 when the Evangelical Alliance of Kenya (EAK) was formed. The focus of EAK is evangelism coupled with "providing a national forum for partnership, networking, and fellowship among the members, [and] advocacy as well as leadership on issues."[21] But how successful have these ecumenical movements been in their efforts to unite the church and the Kenyan community?

Evaluation of Ecumenism's Success

Despite the fact that most Protestant churches – especially the mainline churches such as Anglican, Presbyterians, Methodist, Reformed Church, and the small denominations affiliated to the NCCK – train their clergy together at St. Paul's University (formerly St. Paul's United Theological College) in Limuru, divisions are still evident in the field. Recently, the Methodist Church started its own university at Kaaga – the Kenya Methodist University (KEMU) – to train its clergy. The Presbyterian Church of East Africa has also established its own university with the same objective at Thogoto – the Presbyterian University of East Africa (PUEA). Such rifts are occasioned by suspicion.

The unity in training together did not achieve theological accommodation and tolerance. For example, each denomination ordained its own clergy, and ordained ministers needed to go through the entire process of catechism and fresh ordination to be allowed to practice in the churches with which they had shared training.

---

19. Emily Onyango, *For God and Humanity: 100 Years of St. Paul's United Theological College* (Limuru: St. Paul's United Theological College, 2003), 27.

20. National Council of Churches of Kenya, "History of NCCK."

21. World Faiths Development Dialogue, *Faith and Development in Focus: Kenya* (Berkeley Center for Religion, Peace & World Affairs, 2017).

The churches still compete for converts in the field; this is evident at open-air crusades. Members often move from one denomination to another, not because of administrative reasons or theological/doctrinal differences, but because they have been persuaded to move by the evangelization of the members of the other denomination.

Members of minority communities are still openly discriminated against by the dominant community. This is seen in the way ordained ministers are received by the faithful in different regions; some are resisted when posted in regions where their ethnic community is absent.

Despite the efforts and achievements on various fronts, it is evident that negative ethnicity between and within denominations has not been eradicated. Minority communities in a given denomination are still discriminated against, and there are still negative attitudes between denominations, because the denominations mimic the dominant ethnic communities they are situated in. Thus, a denomination represents the views of the dominant ethnic community regarding other denominations which represent the views of "rival" ethnic communities. Thus, the ecumenical approach has not been able to mitigate negative ethnicity among its member churches.

Regarding political trends in Kenya, churches are divided over which political stands to advance. If Kenya is 80 percent Christian, then Christian values should inform their response to political divisions, yet that has never been the case. This again shows that efforts by the ecumenical bodies to unite the church and thereby the community have not achieved their objective. It is for this reason that we are proposing an *ubuntu* salvation based on *ubuntu* philosophy.

Ecumenical movements were efforts at reuniting the community in church denominations and society, but divisions have remained. We argue that if salvation is approached from the African philosophy of *ubuntu*, the church may realize its true salvation.

To be able to apply *ubuntu* philosophy in developing *ubuntu* salvation, it is imperative to study the notion of *ubuntu*. Are there positive elements or values the church can learn from *ubuntu* philosophy?

Ubuntu Salvation as a Panacea for Negative Ethnicity and Denominationalism

Ubuntu is a term that originated from the Nguni and Bantu languages of sub-Saharan Africa. It is derived from the word "ubuntu," which means "being." The word *ubuntu* represents a sense of humanity and togetherness, and it is expressed in different vocabulary across Africa. For instance, in Uganda, it is obuntu, while in Kenya, it is umundu.²² Rwandan scholar Alexis Kagamé classified a Bantu existential philosophy into four categories: muntu (human being), kintu (thing), hantu (place), and kuntu (modal time), which includes all human beings, regardless of their gender, age, or social class.²³

This study employs *ubuntu* as a public philosophy that promotes inclusivity, appreciates individual identities, and advocates life-giving values for the good of everyone in the society. The African value system upholds communalism and affirms human freedom and dignity. The notion of *ubuntu* has been used in African theological underpinnings with regard to peace and reconciliation, African spirituality, ecological theology, and economic justice.²⁴ *Ubuntu* philosophy promotes social bonding and peaceful and harmonious coexistence in society. This is the principle of communitarianism.

Conceptual Analysis of Ubuntu

The concept of *ubuntu* has its origins in Nguni and Bantu languages of sub-Saharan Africa, with the word *ubuntu* meaning "being" and expressing a sense of humanity and togetherness. The term is used in different forms in various African languages, such as *umunthu* in Chewa language in Zambia and *unhu* in Shona in Zimbabwe.²⁵ The idea of *ubuntu* has been utilized in recent African discourse in three main trajectories: showing the eminence of being human, ethical theory, and relational cosmology. The concept of *ubuntu* reflects an African communitarian philosophy where personhood is achieved rather than being given at birth. Such an understanding designates the person as a process of coming into existence in the reciprocal relatedness of individual and community. *Ubuntu* emphasizes communality, communion, and interrelatedness, sharing the connection with life associated with other notions in African thought, such as vital participation and vital force. The morality of an act is determined by its life-giving potential in African ethics, and *ubuntu* promotes human dignity. Despite debates over the contested nature

---

22. P. H. Coetzee and A. P. J. Roux, *Philosophy from Africa: A Text with Readings* (Cape Town: Oxford University Press, 2002), 56.

23. Alexis Kagamé, *La philosophie băntu-rwandaise de l'être* (Rwanda: Académie royale des sciences coloniales, 1956), 98.

24. Ernst M. Conradie, *South African Perspectives on Notions and Forms of Ecumenicity* ([n.p.]: African Sun Media, 2013), 257.

25. Teddy C. Sakupapa, "Ecumenical Ecclesiology in the African Context: Towards a View of the Church as Ubuntu," *Scriptura* 117, no. 1 (June 2018): 1–15.

of *ubuntu*, it remains a living tradition that continually appreciates cultural dynamism and further affirms its African roots.[26]

The African Concept of Salvation

What is the African concept of salvation? According to Tokunboh Adeyemo, to be saved is to be accepted in the society of both the living and the living dead.[27] Any state of rejection, especially in the society of the living, is a pointer to being rejected in future in the community of the living dead, and that means not being saved. Thus, in this case salvation is a movement from the state of rejection to the state of acceptance.

Another aspect of salvation is being saved from material poverty to material well-being. To be materially impoverished is to be denied salvation. Manas Buthelezi says that to be saved is to be given opportunity in education to realize one's potential: "The passport to the place of receiving God's gifts is opportunity in education, employment and general development. To deny a person these opportunities is to displace him from his God-given place; it is to alienate him from wholeness of life."[28]

Salvation also means to be safe from any life-threatening situation such as sickness, poverty, and accidents. Human beings, like all animals, want to perpetuate their species. Any condition that threatens their perpetuation is abhorred and thus resisted. In the context of negative ethnicity and divisions, a person who is discriminated against feels the threat of being annihilated and therefore feels unsafe. Physical attacks on any group of people because of their vulnerability as a result of discrimination threatens and undermines their state of salvation.

Therefore, the ability to multiply in wealth, in children, and in assurance of security is a form of salvation. Thus salvation encompasses harmonious relationships and healthy coexistence in society.

---

26. T. Sakupapa, (2018). "Ubuntu: A very brief conceptual analysis." *Scriptura*, 117(1), 1–9. doi: 10.7833/117-1-1301.

27. Tokunboh Adeyemo, *Salvation in African Tradition* (Nairobi: Evangelical Publishing House, 1997), 93.

28. Manas Buthelezi, "Salvation as Wholeness," in John Parratt, *A Reader in African Christian Theology* (London: SPCK, 1997), 97.

Salvation in the Light of *Ubuntu* Theology

Christ came so that we might have life, and have it in abundance. This teaching resonates with the African notion of salvation: that salvation is wholeness of life. As stated above, this is realized when one is sufficiently provided for materially and mentally; when one experiences good health and a sound mind; and when one finds social acceptance among the community of the living and the community of the dead.

To find acceptance in the two communities – the living and the dead – one must demonstrate concern for the members of the communities by supporting them. This is the communitarian life espoused by the *ubuntu* philosophy. Someone who lives an isolated life is considered evil. This is best expressed in a Kiswahili saying: "*Mkataawengi ni mchawi*" – "One who refuses the company of many [the community] is a witch." Such a person does not realize salvation both now and in the life to come.

Communitarian life is working to support the welfare of one another. Those with abilities to realize wholeness of life support any who are underprivileged to realize that wholeness too. Thus, to be saved is to be saved with others. In *ubuntu* salvation theology, no one is saved alone, since "I am because we are." I am only saved if others are also saved alongside me. One is not saved until others are also saved.

Ubuntu philosophy is replicated in many African philosophies and especially the nationalistic philosophies such as *Harambee* philosophy (Kenya), *Ujamaa* philosophy (Tanzania), and the Negritude of Léopold Sédar Senghor. In the *Harambee* philosophy, the basic principle is support for one another with resources to uplift their livelihood. The same is encapsulated in the *Ujamaa*, which emphasizes sharing of resources. In negritude, those who are African or black, who have been treated with discrimination, are encouraged to have a positive view of being black – this is the concept of humaneness. That is to say, we are all human, regardless of our color, language, race, or creed.

This chapter has endeavored to demonstrate how an *ubuntu* salvation theology can enhance Christian salvation in the context of existing denominationalism and negative ethnicity. An effort has to be made to see the *ntu*[29] in every human person as one who is also struggling to realize the salvation you have already experienced. Failure to see the *ntu* in other humans is a failure to appropriate true salvation as taught by Jesus Christ. Jesus challenges his

---

29. In the context of the word "ubuntu," "ntu" means "person" or "human being" in the Bantu language of southern Africa.

followers to love one another before they can claim that they love God: this is indeed *ubuntu* salvation.

Ubuntu salvation echoes the principles of negritude and Jesus's teachings in Luke 4:18. It aims at setting the captives of negative ethnicity and denominationalism free: to give them eyes to see the slavery in which they have lived during years of division caused by the spheres of influence. In this *ubuntu* salvation, both the oppressor and the oppressed are liberated; the oppressor, on embracing *ubuntu* salvation, realizes the *ntu* in the other person and seeks to have that person saved too. Thus, through the *ntu* people are able to transcend cultural biases and barriers that have denied them true salvation. True salvation is to be liberated from sociocultural biases and blindness that hinder one from seeing the *ntu* in other people.

Unity in the church will be realized only when every member of the church sees the *ntu* in other people, regardless of their ethnic origin. We can liken *ntu* to the *imago Dei*. God created all human beings in his own image and likeness. Beyond the human person, *muntu*, lies the *ntu*, which carries God's image. Can any person claim to be saved when he or she abuses the image of God in which all human persons have been created? Negative ethnicity is an abuse of the image of God in human beings. Understanding this through *ubuntu* salvation theology enhances respect for other human beings regardless of their ethnic origin. One cannot be saved as an individual while oppressing, discriminating against, and threatening the existence of other human beings. In other words, as much as salvation is individual, it is also communal, in which the individual *muntu* appreciates the other *ntu*.

Conclusion

Underlying our argument is the philosophy that God has revealed his will to African people through the principle of *ubuntu*. Through *ubuntu*, God has revealed his love and his requirement that human beings should be concerned about the welfare of other people. We can thus know God and his will through his revelation of *ubuntu*.

We have argued that it is only through acknowledgment of each other's humanness that wholesome salvation can be achieved. *Ntu* salvation theology embraces human dignity and fullness of life.

For the church to realize its mandate as an agent of change in people's lives and a means of grace for God's people, that grace has to reach everyone in the human race without discrimination. This is only possible when the church embraces *ubuntu* salvation. It is only when all Christians regard people of other ethnic origins and denominations as human beings that they will minister to them and enable them to realize wholeness of life. Negative ethnicity and denominationalism are a real hindrance to this realization, and therefore we advocate an *ubuntu* salvation.

Bibliography

Adeyemo, Tokunboh. *Salvation in African Tradition*. Nairobi: Evangelical Publishing House, 1997.

Bediako, Kwame. *Christianity in Africa: The Renewal of a Non-Western Religion*. Edinburgh: Edinburgh University Press, 1995.

Britannica Online. "Christianity from the 16th to the 21st Century." https://www.britannica.com/topic/Christianity/Christianity-from-the-16th-to-the-21st-century.

Bujo, Bénézet. *Foundations of an African Ethic: Beyond the Universal Claims of Western Morality*. Nairobi: Paulines Publications, 2003.

Coetzee, P. H., and A. P. J. Roux. *Philosophy from Africa: A Text with Readings*. Cape Town: Oxford University Press, 2002.

Conradie, Ernst M. *South African Perspectives on Notions and Forms of Ecumenicity*. [n.p.]: African Sun Media, 2013.

Ekitala, Ariko L., and Mary Goretti Wosyanju. "The Role of the Church in Combating Negative Ethnicity in Kenya: A Survey of Mainline Churches in Eldoret, Kenya." 2013. https://www.researchgate.net/publication/311671416_The_Role_of_the_Church_in_Combating_Negative_Ethnicity_in_Kenya_A_Survey_of_Mainline_Churches_in_Eldoret_Kenya.

Fazan, Sydney Herbert. *Colonial Kenya Observed: British Rule, Mau Mau and the Wind of Change*. London: I. B. Tauris, 2015.

Fenton, Steve. *Ethnicity: Racism, Class and Culture*. New York: Rowman & Littlefield, 1999.

Hauser, Philipp, and Jessica Whittemore. "The Great Schism of 1054: Origins and Effects." Study.com. https://study.com/learn/lesson/great-schism-1054.html.

Hjort, Mette, and Eva Jørholt, eds. *African Cinema and Human Rights*. Bloomington: Indiana University Press, 2019.

Kagamé, Alexis. *La philosophie bǎntu-rwandaise de l'ětre*. Rwanda: Académie royale des sciences coloniales, 1956.

Magesa, Laurenti. *What Is Not Sacred? African Spirituality*. Maryknoll: Orbis, 2014.

Mbiti, John S. *African Religions and Philosophy*. London: Anchor, 1969.

Meneses, Eloise Hiebert. "If You Belong to Christ: Ethnicity and the Global Church." Paper presented at IAMS 12th assembly, Budapest, Hungary, August 2008. http://ojs.globalmissiology.org/index.php/english/article/view/195/546.

National Council of Churches of Kenya. "History of NCCK." 20 May 2020. Accessed 8 February 2022. https://www.ncck.org/ourjourney/.
Onyango, Emily. *For God and Humanity: 100 Years of St. Paul's United Theological College*. Limuru: St. Paul's United Theological College, 2003.
Parrat, John. *A Reader in African Christian Theology*. London: SPCK, 1997.
Rice, Xan. "Kenya on the Brink as More Than 100 Killed in Poll Riots." *The Guardian* online. 2 January 2008. https://www.theguardian.com/world/2008/jan/01/kenya.topstories32.
———. "'We Told Them to Come Out of the Church but They Locked the Door.... So We Burned Them.'" *The Guardian* online. 2 January 2008. https://www.theguardian.com/world/2008/jan/02/kenya1.
Sakupapa, Teddy C. "Ecumenical Ecclesiology in the African Context: Towards a View of the Church as Ubuntu." *Scriptura* 117, no. 1 (June 2018): 1–15.
Sesi, Stephen Mutuku. "Ethnic Realities and the Church in Kenya." In *African Missiology: Contribution of Contemporary Thought*, edited by Stephen Mutuku Sesi et al., 25–39. Nairobi: Uzima, 2009.
Tarimo, A. "Ethnicity, Common Good and the Church in Contemporary Africa." *Africa Tomorrow* 1, no. 2 (July 2000): 153–80.
Westermann, Diedrich. *Africa and Christianity*. London: Oxford University Press, 1937.
World Faiths Development Dialogue. *Faith and Development in Focus: Kenya*. Berkeley Center for Religion, Peace & World Affairs, 2017.

19

An All-Embracing, Contextual, Challenging, Now-and Not-Yet Salvation for Ugandan Rural Communities

Timothy J. Monger
CEO Amigos Worldwide

Abstract

Rural communities in Uganda have a complex story comprising colonialism, civil war, HIV/AIDS, and the resultant poverty which is exacerbated now by climate change, food insecurity, social breakdown, domestic violence, and a young population with a median age of fifteen. What kind of salvation do these communities long for? And how can the Ugandan church respond appropriately? After presenting survey results from the communities and the possibilities offered by traditional indigenous religion, the Western gospel, and the prosperity gospel, all of which on cultural and theological reflection prove insufficient, this chapter turns to Jesus for insight and, specifically, his response to first-century Israel. Israel's story had begun in a remarkable way but tragically had run aground and was in desperate need of intervention. We consider the needs, longings, and expectations of the people of Israel and how Jesus connects his life and ministry to their story and situation with compassion, confrontation, and challenge. He offers a salvation that is contextual and all-embracing, and yet substantially reworks their expectations, particularly with a salvation that is both now and not yet and, surprisingly, is also held out to others. But to respond to the salvation Jesus offers is also to follow him in self-denial and to join a new community of the kingdom which extends this salvation to other peoples. With Jesus's salvific framework in mind, we finally return to consider, in light of the survey's findings, how the Ugandan church can offer to all a salvation centered in Jesus that is both biblical and relevant to the cries of its rural communities, and which heals their story as they are welcomed into God's larger story.

Key words: holistic salvation, inaugurated salvation, contextualized gospel, integral mission, conflict resolution, narrative of hope, Northern Uganda, Jesus, Israel's story

Introduction

The people of Northern Uganda have experienced a well-known troubled recent history that painfully affects their lives to this day. The insurgency waged by the Lord's Resistance Army (LRA) between 1987 and 2006 regularly hit the international news. The atrocities committed included theft of property and land, child abduction, rape, and murder against Acholi communities. An estimated 1.7 million people in the north fled to internally displaced persons (IDP) camps where conditions were brutal and they had to rely on water and food aid. When they eventually returned to their land, they were destitute, their land had remained untended, and farming skills had been lost. On top of that, Uganda has been in the grip of an HIV/AIDS epidemic, resulting in children becoming orphans, in addition to those who lost parents in the civil war.[1] Today Uganda has one of the youngest populations in the world, with a median age of fifteen.[2] All of this leaves broken and traumatized families and communities still struggling to cope with daily life and looking for "salvation."[3]

Where is the church as people cry for "salvation"? What kind of salvation should the church be offering to its community? How can the church, rooted in that same community and frequently having suffered along with them,

---

1. UNICEF estimates that in 2015 there were 2 million orphans in Uganda with 50 percent due to HIV/AIDS (Ministry of Gender, Labour and Social Development and UNICEF Uganda, *2015: Situation Analysis of Children in Uganda* (2015), https://www.unicef.org/uganda/media/1791/file).

2. World Population Review, "Uganda Population (Live)," accessed 5 February 2022, https://worldpopulationreview.com/countries/uganda-population.

3. In Amigos's work in the region, it is not uncommon for us to hear people say, "Thank you. You are my savior."

An All-Embracing, Contextual, Challenging, Now-and Not-Yet Salvation   359

imbibe and hold out a different narrative?[4] And in so doing, how can the church remain true to the gospel of Christ? In this chapter I seek to explore these questions through surveys and biblical-theological reflection to discover how local churches can offer an authentic, vibrant, and powerful salvation for Ugandan rural communities. First, though, I step back to consider the historical, cultural, and religious context of the northern and mid-western parts of Uganda.

Some Ugandan Rural Communities and Salvation
History, Culture, and Religion

Northern Uganda is home to about 7.2 million people[5] and includes the Gulu, Kitgum, and Lira districts of which the main tribes are Acholi and Langi. They have traditionally practiced a mixed economy of pastoralism and agriculture and were known as skillful hunters.[6] The Acholi and Langi both suffered in colonial times when the British favored the southern Buganda in terms of development, but especially used the Acholi for manual and unskilled labor and recruitment for the military, thus unwittingly sowing the seeds of later conflicts that ensued after independence in the Milton Obote and Idi Amin eras and which arose after Yoweri Museveni came to power when northerners sensed injustice with the political arrangement.[7] This grievance then led to the emergence of the LRA. Ironically, once called "The Lord's Salvation Army,"[8] the LRA were mainly Acholi, but turned on their people in the face of a lack of support, with theft, killings, raping, and child abductions, resulting in the terror and displacement of Acholi peoples. Lira, neighboring the troubled area, was to a lesser degree also affected, with some communities experiencing

---

4. It has become well accepted in recent years that as human beings, whether consciously or not, we live by our stories, which are influenced in part by the events we have experienced (e.g. see Dan P. McAdams, *The Stories We Live By: Personal Myths and the Making of the Self* [New York: Guildford Press, 1997]). This is true at both personal and communal levels.

5. According to the 2014 Ugandan census ("Uganda: Administrative Division," City Population, https://www.citypopulation.de/en/uganda/admin/).

6. Kevin Ward, "'The Armies of the Lord': Christianity, Rebels and the State of Northern Uganda, 1986–1999," *Journal of Religion in Africa* 31, no. 2 (2001): 191.

7. International Crisis Group (IGC), *Northern Uganda: Understanding and Solving the Conflict*, ICG Africa Report no. 77 (14 April 2004): 3.

8. Charles Muwunga Mwebe, "The Genesis and Nature of the LRA in Northern Uganda," *AFER* 45, no. 4 (Dec. 2003): 352.

displacement, while the district received those fleeing the war zone.[9] In recent years, although the majority of people have returned to their homes, the rebuilding of livelihoods has been hampered by poor farming techniques and low crop yields, climate change, disease and poor health, domestic abuse, and disenfranchised youth.

The Masindi district is in mid-western Uganda, where the Banyoro and the Bagungu are the predominant tribes, and is known for its agriculture, fishing, and national park, Murchison Falls. It has mostly enjoyed a peaceful existence both among its tribes and with those of neighboring districts. It largely escaped the LRA insurgency, though it was involved in the Luwero Triangle guerrilla war in the 1980s, resulting in loss of life and property. Despite its fertility, the district has lacked an impetus for development and business, and today suffers from idle youth and high crime and teenage pregnancy rates.

For all these tribes, their religion has undergirded them throughout this history. Traditionally, like many African peoples, they have a holistic view of life, with the physical and spiritual realms intertwined.[10] Although there is the belief in a Supreme Being who is responsible for everything, life is traditionally seen as influenced by benevolent and malevolent spirits.[11] Communal rituals and ceremonies focus on maintaining good relationships with the benevolent spirits (who include the ancestors) so as to ward off the malevolent spirits which seek to harm life and bring disease and misfortune. These tribes also emphasize the communal rather than the individual aspects of life and when adversity falls efforts concentrate on restoring life to the community. In this way, salvation is communal, holistic, and integrated with life.[12] But it is also anthropocentric[13] and lacking a strong future dimension.[14]

Christianity came to the region in the nineteenth century through European missionaries and quickly spread, despite Catholic and Protestant rivalries.[15] The later colonial period opened the way especially for the Anglican Church,

---

9. Deusdedit R. K. Nkurunziza, "Insurgency in Northern Uganda: A Challenge to the Church in AMECEA," *AFER* 45, no. 4 (Dec. 2003): 314.

10. Cf. David Tonghou Ngong, "Salvation and Materialism in African Theology," *Studies in World Christianity* 15, no. 1 (2009): 2–3.

11. Ward, "Armies of the Lord," 193; P. N. Wachege, "Inculturation and Salvation within the African Context," *AFER* 43, no. 1 (Feb.–April 2001): 37.

12. Wachege, "Inculturation and Salvation," 33.

13. Ngong, "Salvation and Materialism," 16.

14. John Mbiti, "God, Sin, and Salvation in African Religion," *The Journal of the Interdenominational Theological Center* 16, no. 1–2 (Fall–Spring 1988–89): 66–67.

15. Kevin Ward, "A History of Christianity in Uganda," Dictionary of African Christian Biography, accessed 18 January 2022, https://dacb.org/histories/uganda-history-christianity/.

now known as the Church of Uganda, to be effective in spreading the gospel and founding churches, and latterly Pentecostalism has been particularly active in these areas. Unfortunately, missionaries and churches have generally not been attentive to the local context, culture, and strengths of traditional life. Indeed, Christianity has had a mixed history in its involvement in this locality. The LRA, for example, is a Christian extremist cult, whose leader, Joseph Kony, blended his approach to the Old Testament with terrorism and the occult in his attempt to instigate a state based on the Ten Commandments.[16] The church has an opportunity therefore to rethink how Christianity can be an unmitigated force for good in rural Uganda.

Salvation Survey among Communities in Gulu, Kitgum, Lira, and Masindi

In the context of this background to the unfortunate story of this part of Uganda, research was conducted with sixty-seven people in rural communities in Gulu, Kitgum, Lira, and Masindi districts to explore concrete perspectives on how events had affected their lives, what their expectations were for the future, and how they desired God to act for them.[17] Participants were categorized by age, gender, and church commitment, as shown in the table.

30 years old or under	**Over 30 years old**
33	34
Male	**Female**
35	32
Active church member	**Non-active church member**
39	28

The survey sought to understand what events had shaped their lives, how those events had affected them, and what changes they were looking for. Questions focused on personal, family, and community impacts. Given that all the events listed by respondents were painful (war, famine, family breakdown) and with negative effects, the exploration into what changes they were looking for amounted to *what kind of salvation they desired*. They were also invited to reflect on how the church could respond in terms of their situation and the changes they desired.

---

16. Mwebe, "LRA in Northern Uganda," 353.
17. I am grateful to my colleague Joshua Kizito for the collection of data.

A summary of the findings revealed war to be the dominant event that shaped life for communities in Gulu (84%), Kitgum (100%), and Lira (73%), while famine, also recognized in Gulu and Lira, was predominant in Masindi (64%). While war was recognized more by the older group, the youth saw famine more as the primary event. In all districts disease/death was also significant. The consequence of these events was an overwhelming hopelessness felt by respondents (84%), especially the young (91%) and women (90%). Participants noted that the events affected the ability to live, pointing to a struggle for education and low literacy rates, a lack of basic needs at the family level (57%), some land grabbing (36% in Kitgum), and communities still struggling to rebuild livelihoods (49%). Respondents considered harmony to be generally good in the community, although only 43% of women saw relationships between men and women as good. Overall, 55% saw the problems holding back their community as a combination of laziness and alcoholism, a lack of knowledge, witchcraft and injustice, and a lack of infrastructure.

In terms of changes desired for the future, while respondents noted the desire to see the above challenges overcome, Gulu alone registered a significant desire for the community to become God-fearing (31%) – with nearly three times more women recognizing this than men. Overall, more than anything else, people wanted to be able to support their families (45%), with starting a business being seen as a means to that end. Of those under thirty, 45% saw the combination of the community becoming God-fearing, peaceable, and with good infrastructure as the needed change, compared with only 26% of those over thirty. When asked to rank what they wanted God to do for them, there was an overall balance among good opportunities, a good local ecosystem, a purposeful life, a good relationship with God, a successful business, good relationships with family and neighbors, acquiring knowledge and wisdom, personal freedom, and joy and wholeness in the community.[18] Of these, a good relationship with God was first, followed by acquiring knowledge and wisdom, with good relationships with family and neighbors coming third. Active church members generally preferred the relational aspects. When asked to categorize the relative importance of a changed present life to possessing eternal life, 4.5%

---

18. The nine options were grouped into three triads. Triad 1 (a good relationship with God, a purposeful life, knowledge and wisdom) concerned some inner aspects of salvation; triad 2 (good opportunities in life, personal freedom, a successful business) some physical aspects of salvation; and triad 3 (good relationships with family and neighbors, joy and wholeness in the community, a good local ecosystem) some wider/communal aspects of salvation.

saw only a changed present life as important, 35.8%[19] only possessing eternal life, but 59.7% saw a balance as important.

We turn now to consider how adequately the kinds of salvation held out by the church have connected to its community as a revitalizing story.

Common Christian Responses of Salvation

The church has held out a varied "salvation" in its understandings of the gospel. At one end of the spectrum is the traditional Western gospel brought by many Western missionaries in the nineteenth and twentieth centuries in their earnestness to see Africans converted.[20] This understanding of the gospel conveys the message that people are sinful and condemned but that Jesus has died in their place so that if they believe in him they can be saved and go to heaven when they die. It is a narrow gospel focusing only on an individual's spiritual state before God and is still preached in many Ugandan rural churches today. Being otherworldly, it pays no attention to people's contexts and their daily struggles, and offers only a hope of transformation in the life to come.[21] Ugandan theologian John Mary Waliggo, writing with the purpose of ending violence in mind, recognizes this weakness, saying,

> Every missionary should constantly be exposed to a critical analysis of the holistic context in which he or she lives and works. This is the only way our Christian evangelization can ever be relevant, with proper priorities which will include effective remedies to violence. The deeper we understand Christianity, the more involved we become in stopping violence in our world. The more we appreciate the social teaching of the Church, the more we become committed to peace and justice. Holistic Christianity leads to holistic liberation and development. The church becomes fully committed to social justice and the elimination of violence of whatever type in the world.[22]

---

19. This was 73% in Lira. Women were more focused on eternal life and men on a changed present life.

20. See Michael W. Goheen, *Introducing Christian Mission Today: Scripture, History and Issues* (Downers Grove: IVP Academic, 2014), 228, for how this arose.

21. Although missionaries did often also attend to establishing schools and hospitals and ministries of compassion, these were not usually integrated into their understanding of the gospel. This is still largely true of the church's ministries today.

22. John Mary Waliggo, "The Religious Leaders' Response to Violence," *AFER* 43, no. 4 (Aug.–Oct. 2001): 182–83.

What he says in relation to violence can be extended to other challenges, from hunger and poverty to illiteracy and hopelessness.

At the other end of the spectrum is the prosperity gospel which, although also originating from the West, has taken root in many Ugandan churches, especially Pentecostal churches, not least because it finds some connection with the traditional indigenous worldview.[23] It does not deny the traditional Western gospel but extends it to promulgate the belief that through the atonement God's blessings of physical health, material prosperity, and personal success are available and appropriated by individual faith. It is not hard to see why it is attractive to disadvantaged people in poor health and struggling to make ends meet. Unlike the otherworldly gospel above, this is very much a this-worldly gospel with an over-realized eschatology. Sadly, though, it frequently becomes entirely focused on self and the love of things, rather than on taking up one's cross, following Jesus, and being transformed to love one's neighbor. And while it engenders the hope of transformation, it tends to leave "the poor more impoverished than ever."[24]

Both these gospels are incomplete and fail to adequately address the challenges and expectations the respondents highlighted. The same can be said of the traditional indigenous religion outlined above. Emmanuel Katongole, a Ugandan-Rwandese theologian who has written poignantly on Northern Uganda, argues that Africa, and in our case rural Uganda, needs a new story,[25] a new metanarrative, focused toward new creation. He has highlighted in his insightful book *The Sacrifice of Africa* that many of Africa's leaders have in effect sadly continued the colonial story by ruling for themselves and not for their people.[26] According to Katongole, the focus of African leaders has tended to be on holding on to power rather than on equitable nation-building.[27] There has been "the sacrificing of Africa" through their greed, ambition, and oppressive regimes.[28] These leaders have often perpetuated tribalism and

---

23. Cf. Ngong, "Salvation and Materialism," 1–2.

24. J. Kwabena Asamoah-Gyadu, "Did Jesus Wear Designer Robes? The Gospel Preached in Africa's New Pentecostal Churches Ends up Leaving the Poor More Impoverished Than Ever," *Christianity Today* (Nov. 2009): 38–41.

25. Emmanuel Katongole, *The Sacrifice of Africa: A Political Theology for Africa* (Grand Rapids: Eerdmans, 2011), 123–24. A people's "story" is basic to their existence, providing identity, the way they see the world, and their hope, leading to their way-of-being-in-the-world (see N. T. Wright, *The New Testament and the People of God* [Minneapolis: Fortress, 1992], 122).

26. Katongole, *Sacrifice of Africa*, 73–74.

27. Katongole, 73.

28. Katongole, 15–17, 195.

the resultant violence and poverty, and offered a vision of "mere survival" to their peoples.[29] Who will interrupt this story and bring real salvation? These Ugandan rural communities are calling out for a new, liberating, and revitalizing story, connecting to and healing the pain of existing stories, and which points toward a new future in which they can live.

Since it is evident that the church has often failed to offer a contextualized and integrated response to these communities and/or to stay true to the gospel espoused in the New Testament, we turn now to Jesus for insight and, specifically, how in the gospels he responds to the struggles and hopes of first-century Israel.

Jesus's Response to First-Century Israel
Context: Israel in the First Century

Israel, at the time of Jesus, are a people in need of, and in the main longing for, dramatic intervention. Their story had begun so promisingly as the family of Abraham, called to be a blessing to the world, divinely delivered from tyrannical slavery in Egypt, and settled in the promised land, a new Eden, to live out before the Creator their calling to the world. After God gives Israel a king through which he will rule over them, King David is promised an everlasting dynasty with a son, like a new Adam, to rule the nations (2 Sam 7; cf. Gen 1:26–28; Ps 2; Dan 7:1–14). Though his son, Solomon, began well, building a temple which was filled with God's awesome presence, he later turned away from God, leading Israel to follow, eventually resulting in their tragic exile in Babylon. It is hard to overestimate this catastrophe for Israel, who as God's treasured possession had not expected such an outcome to their story. And although a return to the land did happen, those who could remember the former days could not help but be distressed at the comparison (Ezra 3:12).

Important for our purposes, in the first century the people are suffering under the harsh foreign rule of Rome, and their own leaders, including the high-priestly families, are compromised and corrupt, often complicit with Rome. Although the working classes enjoy a moderate lifestyle, most tenants and day laborers struggle against local exploitation and Roman taxes, with debt being widespread.[30] Furthermore, Israel as a whole have not returned

---

29. Katongole, 79.
30. See P. H. Davids, "Rich and Poor," in *Dictionary of Jesus and the Gospels*, eds. Joel B. Green, Scot McKnight, and I. Howard Marshall (Downers Grove: InterVarsity, 1993), 701–10.

home,[31] and God's presence has not come to the rebuilt temple. The glorious return, the New Exodus and restoration envisaged by the prophets (e.g. Isa 60; 65; Ezek 36), is therefore yet to happen.[32] They had spoken of God exerting his rule to restore the Davidic kingdom with Israel enjoying shalom and being a light to the nations who would come under his rule. Such restoration would be brought through their coming messianic king, who would fulfill Israel's longings for the real return from exile, the defeat of evil, and the Lord's return to Zion (Isa 9:6–7; 11:1–9; 61:1–11; Jer 23:5–8).[33] So the people called to bring God's salvation to the world (Isa 26:18) need a Savior themselves.

Jesus and the Kingdom of God: A Rightful End to Israel's Story

When Jesus commences his ministry in Galilee, having been revealed as the Son of God and Israel's true representative (Mark 1:1–11),[34] he proclaims "the good news of God," saying, "The time has come. . . . The kingdom of God has come near. Repent and believe the good news!" (Mark 1:14–15; cf. Matt 4:12–17, 23–25; Luke 4:16–21). In this summary of his ministry, he announces good news from God which comprises three parts. First, "the time has come," which speaks of fulfillment – what the prophets had foretold and the people have been waiting for. Second, "the kingdom of God has come near," which explains what the fulfillment is; namely, God exercising his reign, and remembering his people and his promises of a New Exodus,[35] restored peace, and his presence with them. (In Luke 4:18–21, Jesus, drawing from Isaiah 61, articulates the shape of the kingdom as a time of Jubilee with good news to the poor, freedom for the oppressed, and sight for the blind. And in Matt 4:12–17, Jesus's ministry is presented in terms of bringing light to those in darkness

---

31. Jonathan R. Adelman estimates that 60 percent of Jews lived outside Palestine in this period (*The Rise of Israel: A History of a Revolutionary State* [Abingdon: Routledge, 2008], 46).

32. Even the picture in Ezra and Nehemiah and the postexilic prophets of Haggai, Zechariah, and Malachi is not of the glorious return imagined.

33. N. T. Wright, *Jesus and the Victory of God* (Minneapolis: Fortress, 1996), 205. When the temple was destroyed in 587 BC God's glory departed, and there is no evidence of this glory coming to the second temple (cf. Mal 3:1–2 where God's return to the temple is still in the future). Nicholas G. Piotrowski argues that the concept of Israel's sense of ongoing exile is persuasive ("The Concept of Exile in Late Second Temple Judaism: A Review of Recent Scholarship," *Currents in Biblical Research* 15, no. 2 (Feb. 2017): 214–47).

34. Mark 1:11 is a powerful affirmation wrapping up several Old Testament scriptures (Gen 22:2; Exod 4:22; Isa 11:1–9; 42:1–9) to reveal who Jesus is – God's unique son, true Israel, and Messiah.

35. The buildup to Mark 1:14–15 in vv. 1–13 has a New Exodus backdrop, with Jesus going through the waters and being tempted in the wilderness, evoking Israel's exodus from Egypt.

as an Isaianic fulfillment [Isa 9:1–2; cf. 42:1–9; 49:5–6].)[36] What is clear in this part of Jesus's announcement is that it is a *contextual response* (unlike the Western gospel), as he connects his ministry to Israel's story, even if he will later redefine their understanding of the kingdom. Third, "repent and believe the good news" challenges Israel that appropriation of this good news of the coming kingdom is not automatic, but involves the need to align themselves, personally and corporately, to Jesus and his mission. Here we have the first hint that Jesus's ministry might not be quite what Israel are looking for.

Following this summary, we see Jesus as the authorized bringer of the kingdom with mighty deeds in various rural and town settings and powerful teaching in the synagogue and to the crowds (Mark 1:16 – 8:21 and par.). People are amazed at the authority and wisdom of his words. His mighty deeds include exorcizing unclean spirits, dramatic healings of the sick, forgiveness of sins, miraculous provisions of food, and his power over creation, demons, and death. In so doing, Jesus displays *the all-embracing nature of God's kingdom*, with his words and actions demonstrating that the exile is coming to an end and God's order is being put back into the world with Jesus as Son of God revealing what God is like. All this is not only in line with but surpasses the general Jewish expectation of the thoroughness of God's kingdom (as the onlookers' amazement shows; Mark 1:27; 2:12; 5:20; 7:37).

Furthermore, Jesus seamlessly conjoins the meeting of spiritual and physical needs (e.g. Mark 2:1–12; Luke 17:11–19). The gospel writers seem to use the word *sōzō* ("to save") in expansive ways. It is employed with notions of "to rescue" (Matt 8:25), "to heal" (Mark 3:4; 5:23, 28, 34; 6:56; 10:52), "to exorcize" (Luke 8:36), and "to deliver from ruin or being lost" (Matt 10:22; 24:13; Mark 8:35; Luke 8:12; 19:10). The last meaning often has the sense of "now being in right relationship with God." Jesus also understands the salvation he is bringing in terms of illumination (John 3:16–21; cf. Luke 2:30–32), opening the eyes of the physically and spiritually blind so they can share in life (John 8:12; 9:1–41). Interestingly, *sōzō* is used in Luke 17:19 when Jesus responds to the man he had healed from leprosy who returns to thank him. He had healed this man and nine others not only physically but also socially,

---

36. Jesus in Mark opens the eyes of the blind but Mark uses these episodes to show Jesus bringing illumination to the people on God's New Exodus way (cf. Isa 35:5). Israel had been spoken of as God's blind and deaf servant (Isa 42:19) and the Essenes envisaged "a community emerging from blindness to sight" (Suzanne Watts Henderson, "The Damascus Document and Mark 8:1–26: Blindness and Sight on 'The Way,'" in *Reading Mark in Context: Jesus and Second Temple Judaism*, eds. Ben C. Blackwell, John K. Goodrich, and Jason Maston (Grand Rapids: Zondervan, 2018), 125, in reference to the Damascus Document 16:2).

sending them to show themselves to the priest that they might be restored within the community.[37] As the man arrives back and falls at Jesus's feet to thank him, Jesus says (literally), "Rise and go; your faith has *saved* you" (v. 19). This is clearly intended to mean more than "to make well," as most English translations put it, and almost certainly includes the man's relationship with God.[38] Now his healing is complete – physically, socially, and spiritually. There is nothing partial about the salvation Jesus offers. Rather, salvation, in Jesus's ministry, has the sense of being brought into *wholeness*, the impartation of life in all its dimensions (cf. John 10:10).

It is evident that this understanding of salvation is drawn from Old Testament understandings, which gave rise to first-century expectations, even if, as we will see, it finally goes beyond them. There the fundamental understanding of salvation is drawn from the exodus where God delivers Israel *from* Egyptian bondage *to* a life of well-being, enjoying his favor in the promised land. People come to Jesus looking for deliverance from the things that restrict life so that they can have the freedom to enjoy life, even though he can give them more than they bargained for, such as fulfilling the paralyzed man's deeper need of forgiveness of sins (Mark 2:5).

This so far seems to at least connect with the people's expectations of God's powerful kingdom being inaugurated. Naturally questions arise as to who he is, his authority, and whether he is the expected (Davidic) Messiah (Mark 8:27; Luke 3:15; John 1:41). Jesus discloses himself as "the Son of Man" (Mark 2:10; Luke 5:24; 6:5; 7:34; 9:22). While scholars debate the meaning of this phrase, it likely is drawn from Daniel 7:13–14,[39] and for our purposes points to Jesus's humanity, which is representative as the New Adam (Luke 3:22, 38), *and* to him as the bringer of the ultimate dominion over evil and oppression (Luke 4:1–13; 24:46–47).[40] We see his solidarity with and compassion for the people who are suffering the effects of "beastly" leadership and regimes and desperately need salvation (Matt 9:36).

---

37. See Lev 13:9–17; 14:1–20; cf. Luke 5:14.

38. So Joel B. Green, *The Gospel of Luke*, NICNT (Grand Rapids: Eerdmans, 1997), 627. The same is likely also to be true with the woman with the issue of blood when Jesus says, "Daughter, your faith has healed [lit. 'saved'] you. Go in peace and be freed from your suffering" (Mark 5:34), not least because he addresses her as "Daughter," indicating her new status with God.

39. In Dan 7 "one like a son of man" is given authority to inflict total defeat on evil, will be vindicated, and thus will receive an everlasting kingdom.

40. Cf. Rom 5:12–21; 1 Cor 15:20–49.

Jesus As God's Son: God's Story Is Bigger Than Israel's Expectations and Demands Sacrifice and Costly Service to Share in True Salvation

But within this broad framework of his ministry as inaugurating God's all-embracing kingdom, which is welcomed by many, Jesus challenges Israel's attitudes and expectations to the core, and reveals how misaligned they are with God's own larger intentions. The following themes emerge:

First, Jesus clashes almost as soon as his ministry begins with the Jewish religious leaders, revealing *the root-and-branch nature of his transforming work*. They are indignant with him because he eats with "tax collectors and sinners," to which he replies, "It is not the healthy who need a doctor, but the sick. I have not come to call the righteous, but sinners" (Mark 2:17). In their striving to remain pure before God so that he would act, they are ignoring the people who most need salvation. It quickly becomes evident that the culture imbibed by them to gain God's favor is not so much like a garment requiring a patch or a wineskin requiring a refill; on the contrary, Jesus's brand-new approach is to be embraced if Israel is to be a fit partner in God's kingdom mission (Mark 2:21–22). The conflict over healing on the Sabbath shows that as far as Jesus is concerned God's work and intentions are people-centered, not system-centered (Mark 2:23 – 3:6). And their claim that he is doing these mighty deeds by Satan's power only reveals how unfit they are as leaders in God's work (Mark 3:22–29). Instead, to be part of Jesus's mission requires a thorough repentance expressing God's holiness and heart for sinners and the sick, and is achieved by being good soil for God's seed in accepting Jesus's words (Mark 4:1–20).

Second, Jesus shows that the coming of the kingdom is not as envisaged but *is present and yet still to come*. The kingdom is present, as he announces in Nazareth in Luke 4:21 ("Today this scripture is fulfilled in your hearing"), to the crowd in Luke 11:20 ("But if I drive out demons by the finger of God, then the kingdom of God has come upon you"), and to the Pharisees in Luke 17:20–21 ("The coming of the kingdom of God is not something that can be observed, nor will people say, 'Here it is,' or 'There it is,' because the kingdom of God is in your midst"). This last scripture highlights that the kingdom makes its appearance in the person and ministry of Jesus, who is in their midst as God's Son (Luke 1:35; cf. 1:32–33 where he is also David's son). In John's gospel Jesus is presented as the new temple filled with God's presence (John 1:14; 2:13–22). But at the same time the kingdom is yet to arrive. The parables of the growing seed and the mustard seed reveal that the kingdom grows over time rather than coming all at once (Mark 4:26–34). Jesus instills the need for watchfulness in people's expectations of the kingdom (Luke 12:35–48) and lays out its future dimension with such phrases as "when the Son of Man comes" (Matt 10:23;

25:31; Mark 8:38; Luke 9:26; 18:8) and "the end of the age" (Matt 13:49; 24:3). It is this revised understanding of the kingdom as already and not yet, over against its expected sudden and complete coming, that surprises many (e.g. Luke 7:18–23) and calls for a different orientation of ongoing trust in God.[41]

Third, Jesus further surprises his hearers by revealing that *God's salvation is not simply for the righteous in Israel but also for the sinners and outcasts and even for the Gentiles.* Right from the inception of his ministry there are hints that salvation and the good news of the kingdom will go to unexpected people. In his home synagogue, after reading Isaiah 61 and applying it to himself, only to be greeted with "Isn't this Joseph's son?" (Luke 4:22b), his reply reveals that his Jewish questioners want him to minister to them, his own people. He predicts their rejection of him, and informs them that, like Elijah and Elisha, his will be a ministry that includes those outside Israel at the expense of some within (Luke 4:24–27). We see Jesus "intentionally crossing ethnic, religious, and social boundaries for the sake of extending the blessings of God to gentiles"[42] (Mark 7:24–30; Luke 7:1–10) and sinners and tax collectors (Luke 19:1–10). Indeed, Jesus, in contrast to prevailing attitudes toward the Gentiles, intentionally sees his ministry as fulfilling end-time Old Testament prophecies about the ingathering of the nations (e.g. Zech 8:20–23; 9:10).[43] Furthermore, it becomes apparent that not all Israel will partake of God's salvation (Luke 13:22–35; cf. 2:34–35) and many of its leaders will miss out (Mark 12:1–12). Jesus, drawing from Isaiah and the whole Old Testament story, shows the task of God's people as being a light to the nations and taking the gospel to them (Matt 5:13–16; 28:19; Mark 11:17; 13:10; Luke 24:47).

Fourth, and most surprising of all, Jesus declares that *his is a suffering messiahship and his followers must also embrace this suffering* (Mark 8:31–38; 9:30–34; 10:32–45). As he starts his journey to Jerusalem and concurrent emphasis on discipleship, he begins "to teach them that the Son of Man must suffer many things and be rejected by the elders, the chief priests and the teachers of the law, and that he must be killed and after three days rise again" (Mark 8:31). Here Jesus reconfigures their understanding of him as Messiah,

---

41. This might suggest that Israel's longed-for deliverance from their political situation is being relativized.

42. Kelly R. Iverson, "Jubilees and Mark 7:24–37: Crossing Ethnic Boundaries," in Blackwell, Goodrich, and Maston, *Reading Mark in Context*, 118.

43. Iverson, "Jubilees and Mark 7:24–37," 118, observes, "If the portrayal of gentiles in the book of Jubilees is negative, the Gospel of Mark moves in an entirely different direction." Coming immediately after the discussion about "uncleanness" (Mark 7:1–23), this passage (7:24–37) depicts Jesus as not avoiding Gentiles.

presenting himself as one whose destiny it is to suffer unto death and then to rise again. Salvation can be achieved only through defeating the powers that oppress and ruin life, not only the powers of Rome or religious practice, but ultimately the power of Satan and his reign of sin and death. In this way, Jesus secures victory for the kingdom of God as God's suffering servant (Isa 52:13 – 53:12; cf. Mark 10:45; John 19:19–20, 28–30). But immediately he continues, explaining to his hearers, "Whoever wants to be my disciple must deny themselves and take up their cross and follow me. For whoever wants to save their life will lose it, but whoever loses their life for me and for the gospel will save it" (Mark 8:34–35). Thus, to be his disciple is to follow the suffering Messiah into the world. He wants to form a community of followers who as good disciples "see everything clearly," like the man he healed with two touches (Mark 8:22–25), and thus embody and extend the gospel to others. He elaborates that *the way of the cross*, of casting aside one's own ambitions, for his and the gospel's sake, is to *gain true salvation*, a salvation beyond this present life (in distinction to the prosperity gospel). Hence, Jesus continues unabated his journey to the cross to give his life for the world (John 12:23–30; 19:30).

Summing Up Jesus's Response

Jesus, as God's Son and true Israel, commits himself to fulfilling God's agenda; namely, inaugurating God's reign, which means a new day for all creation and salvation for the world. As such, he comes to where the people of Israel are, entering into the struggles of their daily life, understanding the oppression they are under, showing that God's saving promises to them are coming true by taking the injustice upon himself, and offering a striking deliverance to bring their story to its rightful and glorious end. In Jesus – his life, death, and resurrection – God has indeed returned to dwell as a new temple, defeat evil, end their exile from him, and reign justly, while at the same time inviting them to participate in his work his way, the way of the cross.

Jesus is not captive to their wishes and religious and nationalistic struggles, but, motivated by God's larger plan, is able to diagnose their plight better than they can, so as to extend a deeper and fuller salvation. The kingdom of God does not merge with or fulfill other agendas but supplants every unwholesome force and ambition that seeks to harm, kill, or destroy. In this way, a true salvation, a new holistic life, *centered in Jesus and flowing from him*, can be enjoyed now while awaiting the full reality. And so after his resurrection, Jesus instructs those who receive his salvation to go as his servants and share it with all peoples and nations.

Now, applying the framework we have seen in Jesus's ministry to Israel, we offer reflections for how Ugandan churches can offer a powerful salvation to their struggling rural communities.

How Ugandan Churches Can Offer a True and Relevant Salvation and Inaugurate a New Story for Their Communities

1. Living God's Story

Like Jesus with the Old Testament, Ugandan churches need to read the whole of Scripture as *a single story* from Genesis to Revelation, understanding God's purposes in creation and vision for new creation and the role of his people in participating in his story in bringing his intentions to fruition. Both the traditional Western and prosperity gospels are superficial and incomplete readings of Scripture. But Jesus read the Old Testament Scriptures carefully and at times differently from the religious experts, so as to embrace God's intentions of bringing about a thoroughgoing salvation for the world (e.g. Matt 22:29–32, 41–46; Mark 9:12; 11:17; 12:10–11; Luke 2:46–47; 4:21; John 10:34–36; 17:12; 19:28). *This biblical story frames the life and vocation of God's people, and provides the inspiration and imagination to improvise, weaving a relevant response to current situations within God's larger creational purposes.* When this story, God's story, becomes the church's controlling narrative, then the church is able to think through a contextual integrated response while remaining true to the gospel.[44] The alternative is to allow the wider cultural story to be dominant, which will subvert or contaminate our initiatives as Christians.

2. Our God Reigns Here

The Ugandan church needs to appreciate *the vibrant connection between salvation and the kingdom of God.* Jesus's ministry was to inaugurate in his person, words, and deeds the reign of God, and *the effect* was salvation.[45] He did not say, "God cannot reign here, so I have come to rescue you to another place" – a charge the Western gospel is open to – but announced the inbreaking kingdom of God "here and now." Many Ugandan communities have

---

44. This now answers the question posed at the beginning: How can the church, rooted in that same community and frequently having suffered along with them, imbibe and hold out a different narrative?

45. I. Howard Marshall, "Salvation," in Green, McKnight, and Marshall, *Dictionary of Jesus and the Gospels*, 719–24.

experienced the terror and devastating results of civil war and the impotence of their own government, and need instead to hear "God has come to reign here" and that he is entering into their stories of pain and hopelessness to bring about a tangible new life. The concept of a Supreme Being held by Africans opens the door for the church to express the rule of God, but then it must go beyond traditional categories to convey this rule in a deep, intimate, caring, and healing way, launching a narrative of hope among those who have given up. Hope for a new beginning comes by knowing who is truly in charge and that he cares. And to be *brought into relationship with him* activates the hope.

Jesus understood the gospel as a fulfillment of prophetic and hoped-for expectations of a life-brimming end to the story, encapsulated in "The kingdom of God is at hand," with the result being a day of salvation from what prevented the life God intended. In the same way, churches should hold out a *storied and contextualized* gospel of the kingdom – that God is here to reign – to broken and downtrodden rural communities, and that his intentions are for life in all its fullness. They can present a true homecoming to displaced peoples with God rebuilding the ruins into something beautiful (cf. Isa 54:11–15; 61:1–6).

3. Holistic Salvation

Ugandan churches need to hold out a *holistic salvation* as we saw in Jesus's ministry. If the reign of God and salvation are understood as intrinsically linked, then *the biblical and African views that God reigns over everything necessitate a salvation that affects the whole of life*. It is vital that Ugandans do not let this heritage go. With the African understanding of the interconnectedness of life, appropriate salvation embraces the spiritual and the physical, the personal and the communal, the creational and the economic. This is what the survey's respondents were calling for from the church. Just as we saw that Jesus nowhere attempts to limit the scope of his salvation, so churches need to follow him, or communities will conclude that God's salvation is limited and go to other perceived sources of power such as witchcraft or the secular approaches of others willing to help. The wide usage of *sōzō* as a description of Jesus's activities requires us not to restrict the understanding of salvation as the traditional Western gospel does to merely "eternal salvation." As one Lira resident said, "The church should help strengthen lives towards eternal life and drill boreholes for them." And generally, responses varied widely as to how the church could be involved in bringing personal and corporate change.

Speaking of Africa in general, Wachege and Ngong separately urge for a *contextual salvation*, which is how a holistic salvation is properly grounded.

"To an African, *Salvation* is lived, rather than talked about, practised, rather than discussed."[46] "Don't only talk about salvation. Show us! Show us now!"[47] People are after a lived salvation that can be seen and connects with daily life. Of course, daily life is complex with many aspects. These include the communal dimension of salvation that is traditionally valued in Uganda and was highlighted by many respondents but is usually missing from Western theology. Another aspect is how salvation renews creation since people depend on the land for their livelihood.[48] Churches would be wise to work with communities to show how these kinds of aspects dovetail with and reinforce each other to display an *integrated salvation*. For example, as people come into a good relationship with God through Christ, they can learn that part of their purpose in life is to know how, by participating with Christ the New Adam, to care for God's world through conservation agriculture (Gen 1:26–28; 2:15). In this way, they will gain a good harvest and supportive local ecosystem, and by sharing this knowledge with neighbors there will be increased joy and wholeness in the community as famine is ended, with Jesus once again seen as the feeder of multitudes and God's power over creation displayed. This also highlights that salvation is not just an event but also a process whereby people learn to live the saved life and enjoy its benefits and flourish. And as many have recognized that the painful effects of the war still linger, a salvation that changes attitudes to neighbors, bringing a resumption of peace in the community, declares the power of this salvation. It fits with the biblical understanding that salvation is *from* bondage, ruin, death, and wrath, and *to* freedom, renewal, life, and favor; indeed, *to* shalom. *It is however vital that churches keep a christological focus, showing a proper integral salvation, with all these blessings flowing from Jesus, the Savior, as the community increasingly aligns itself with him.*

4. Salvation Especially for the Downtrodden and Marginalized

Churches need *to be attentive to ensuring that salvation reaches the most disadvantaged*. When God reigns, he rights wrongs and brings salvation to those on the margins. Salvation and justice go hand in hand! Wherever Jesus went, people reached out to him for their basic needs. Many of those questioned

---

46. Wachege, "Inculturation and Salvation," 31.

47. David Tonghou Ngong, "God's Will Can Actually Be Done on Earth: Salvation in African Theology," *American Baptist Quarterly* 23, no. 4 (Dec. 2004): 373.

48. See Ben-Willie Kwaku Golo, "Redeemed from the Earth? Environmental Change and Salvation Theology in African Christianity," *Scriptura* 111 (2012): 348–61, for how salvation connects with creation faith in the light of the current ecological crisis.

in the survey highlighted that the past had robbed the community of basic needs (79% in Gulu). When asked how the church could bring good change, one Gulu woman naturally replied, "By providing basic needs to vulnerable groups." Churches should prayerfully ask, "What are the fundamental needs of these people, without which life and a future are impossible?" Churches should be open to the desperate and those passed over by others, as Jesus was with the woman subject to bleeding for twelve years. In this way, menstrual hygiene management projects reaching teenage girls and conducted holistically can save them in more ways than one! And training in household sanitation can contribute to show the community God's concern to rid them of the diseases and death which have plagued them. When God's people attend to the downtrodden and their basic needs, his salvation is unveiled, not as lightweight and abstract but as substantial and concrete, rebuilding life from the bottom up, and giving them a new song to sing.

5. Embracing the Cross and Leading Sacrificially

Christians and churches that are faithful to the gospel will be careful *to keep the cross of Christ at the center of salvation*. The prosperity gospel ultimately feeds off the selfish desires of people and removes the cross as an experienced reality. Rather, these words of Jesus need to be heard and reheard: "Whoever wants to be my disciple must deny themselves and take up their cross and follow me. For whoever wants to save their life will lose it, but whoever loses their life for me and for the gospel will save it" (Mark 8:34–35). Two points are worth making here. First, while the larger context of people's lives should be in view for a thorough salvation, communities should not simply set the agenda and define what kind of "salvation" the church should seek to give. The shape of salvation should come from God as he has revealed in the biblical narrative, in which to receive his salvation is always costly (Mark 10:21). The challenge of discipleship, of life reorientated from selfishness to follow Jesus, must always be heard. Several respondents mentioned that they wanted God to give them a successful business so they could become rich, but such an attitude needs to be challenged. If the church offers business training without training in preferring others, the business will bring shalom neither to the business owners nor to the community. Whereas salvation in Africa is usually anthropocentric, in the Bible it is theocentric.[49]

---

49. Ngong, "Salvation and Materialism," 16–17.

Second, the church and its leaders should appreciate that to be saved *entails living differently*, wanting to lose their lives and put themselves out for others, especially the marginalized, so they too receive salvation. As these leaders do this, they will in fact "save" their lives and come into the fullness of salvation. And as the church lives out self-sacrificial leadership, God and the light of his salvation will be clearly seen. It is this grasp of salvation as something not to be selfishly held on to but actively embraced as *good news to be shared to transform others* that lies at the heart of the church's commission.

6. Salvation for Those Different from Us

Another important issue for Ugandan churches to consider is that, as they embrace the cross and become servants of the gospel, *they will be motivated to extend salvation to those different from them*. Jesus saw himself as Isaiah's suffering servant, whose vocation as a new Israel was to be "a light for the Gentiles, that my salvation may reach to the ends of the earth" (Isa 49:6; cf. 42:6; 52:15). This was in contradistinction to the people of Israel who wanted to keep the gift of salvation for themselves, but God's intention has always been that salvation would reach all tribes, languages, peoples, and nations. This includes the Acholi tribe's neighbors, the Karamojong, with whom there have long been tension and animosity. But also in Northern Uganda, the UNHCR gives the number of refugees as approaching 1 million.[50] Most are South Sudanese who fled because of famine and brutality along ethnic lines. Generally, the Ugandan government allocates refugees plots of land and gives them materials to build basic homes,[51] but this frequently leads to tensions with the host community, not least due to the competition over scarce resources. Can the church work with God as a *world-embracing community* to bring about a larger communal salvation where different nations live in peace with one another as brothers and sisters in Christ?

---

50. UNHCR, "Uganda: Refugee Statistics May 2021," accessed 18 January 2022, https://data2.unhcr.org/en/documents/download/87081.

51. Cristiano D'Orsi, "Why Uganda Has Suspended Hundreds of Refugee Aid Agencies," ReliefWeb, 14 September 2020, accessed 18 January 2022, https://reliefweb.int/report/uganda/why-uganda-has-suspended-hundreds-refugee-aid-agencies.

7. Salvation As Beginning a New Chapter and the Hope of All Things Made New

Finally, these rural churches should acknowledge the *already/not yet* nature of salvation in Christ. As they participate in Christ, they will experience the beginning of a desperately needed new story, enjoying many of the wonderful interconnecting dimensions of salvation in Christ and being used by him to extend that salvation to others – including, as one respondent suggested, "constructing ministries for the hopeless." But they cannot expect to experience this salvation in fullness until Christ returns and finally puts everything to rights. If they can live in the healthy tension of the already/not yet and avoid the pitfalls of the traditional Western gospel and the prosperity gospel which end up at opposite extremes, they will be able to offer communities a salvation to enjoy today while looking forward to the full reality, which also far transcends that offered by traditional indigenous religion.

Almost 60 percent of respondents to the survey recognized that God's coming into the present *and* securing their eternal future were vital, with the weight of significance being on possessing eternal life. The church must wisely keep this balance and appreciate, with the brevity of this life, that the people's emphasis on looking forward to their eternal salvation is surely correct. *A salvation that opens a definite new chapter and instills an unbreakable hope for the best which is yet to come is undeniably a powerful salvation.*

Looking beyond the gospels through the rest of the New Testament, we see that the salvation we have just sketched out for Ugandan rural communities is indeed in keeping with the salvation pictured at the end of the biblical story. Paul envisages our full redemption amid the transformation of the created order (Rom 8:18–25; Eph 1:10; Col 1:19–20). And John sees a new heaven and a new earth, the worldwide restoration of Eden, where God will dwell with his peoples[52] (Rev 21:1–5; 22:1–5). *God's plan is not to take us to heaven, but to bring heaven to earth!* His salvation is a thorough salvation in which he will make us and everything new – a permanent and complete renovation. The church is called to participate with God to show signs of this salvation to communities now. *In this way, the rural Ugandan church will also demonstrate a striking approach to salvation that churches in other African countries can learn and suitably contextualize for their communities.*

---

52. The Greek, *laoi*, is plural, meaning "peoples," perhaps suggesting that the diversity of tribes and nations will not be obliterated in the new creation but somehow brought to a glorious and harmonious fulfillment.

Conclusion

This chapter has shown how Jesus's response in the gospels to Israel's expectations and longings for salvation, whereby he connects with their story in both compassion and confrontation, and calls them to follow him in self-sacrifice, provides the framework for Ugandan churches as by the Spirit they participate with Christ in his rule to offer their communities a *magnificent salvation* – contextual, holistic, and both present- and future-orientated. Communities will see displayed the reign of the Savior Jesus Christ who is inaugurating a new story for them, in which their troubled and painful stories find healing and wholeness, and in which God richly welcomes them into life with him.

Bibliography

Adelman, Jonathan R. *The Rise of Israel: A History of a Revolutionary State*. Abingdon: Routledge, 2008.

Asamoah-Gyadu, J. Kwabena. "Did Jesus Wear Designer Robes? The Gospel Preached in Africa's New Pentecostal Churches Ends up Leaving the Poor More Impoverished Than Ever." *Christianity Today* (Nov. 2009): 38–41.

Blackwell, Ben C., John K. Goodrich, and Jason Maston, eds. *Reading Mark in Context: Jesus and Second Temple Judaism*. Grand Rapids: Zondervan, 2018.

Davids, P. H. "Rich and Poor." In *Dictionary of Jesus and the Gospels*, edited by Joel B. Green, Scot McKnight, and I. Howard Marshall, 701–10. Downers Grove: InterVarsity 1993.

D'Orsi, Cristiano. "Why Uganda Has Suspended Hundreds of Refugee Aid Agencies." ReliefWeb. 14 September 2020. Accessed 18 January 2022. https://reliefweb.int/report/uganda/why-uganda-has-suspended-hundreds-refugee-aid-agencies.

Goheen, Michael W. *Introducing Christian Mission Today: Scripture, History and Issues*. Downers Grove: IVP Academic, 2014.

Green, Joel B. *The Gospel of Luke*. NICNT. Grand Rapids: Eerdmans, 1997.

International Crisis Group (IGC). *Northern Uganda: Understanding and Solving the Conflict*. ICG Africa Report no. 77 (14 April 2004): 1–33.

Katongole, Emmanuel. *The Sacrifice of Africa: A Political Theology for Africa*. Grand Rapids: Eerdmans, 2011.

Kwaku Golo, Ben-Willie. "Redeemed from the Earth? Environmental Change and Salvation Theology in African Christianity." *Scriptura* 111 (2012): 348–61.

Marshall, I. Howard. "Salvation." In *Dictionary of Jesus and the Gospels*, edited by Joel B. Green, Scot McKnight, and I. Howard Marshall, 719–24. Downers Grove: InterVarsity, 1993.

Mbiti, John. "God, Sin, and Salvation in African Religion." *The Journal of the Interdenominational Theological Center* 16, no. 1–2 (Fall–Spring 1988–89): 59–68.

McAdams, Dan P. *The Stories We Live By: Personal Myths and the Making of the Self.* New York: Guildford Press, 1997.

Ministry of Gender, Labour and Social Development and UNICEF Uganda. *2015: Situation Analysis of Children in Uganda.* 2015. https://www.unicef.org/uganda/media/1791/file.

Mwebe, Charles Muwunga. "The Genesis and Nature of the LRA in Northern Uganda." *AFER* 45, no. 4 (Dec. 2003): 349–72.

Ngong, David Tonghou. "God's Will Can Actually Be Done on Earth: Salvation in African Theology." *American Baptist Quarterly* 23, no. 4 (Dec. 2004): 362–77.

———. "Salvation and Materialism in African Theology." *Studies in World Christianity* 15, no. 1 (2009): 1–21.

Nkurunziza, Deusdedit R. K. "Insurgency in Northern Uganda: A Challenge to the Church in AMECEA." *AFER* 45, no. 4 (Dec. 2003): 314–28.

Piotrowski, Nicholas G. "The Concept of Exile in Late Second Temple Judaism: A Review of Recent Scholarship." *Currents in Biblical Research* 15, no. 2 (Feb. 2017): 214–47.

"Uganda: Administrative Division." City Population. https://www.citypopulation.de/en/uganda/admin/.

UNHCR. "Uganda: Refugee Statistics May 2021." Accessed 18 January 2022. https://data2.unhcr.org/en/documents/download/87081.

Wachege, P. N. "Inculturation and Salvation within the African Context." *AFER* 43, no. 1 (Feb.–April 2001): 28–40.

Waliggo, John Mary. "The Religious Leaders' Response to Violence." *AFER* 43, no. 4 (Aug.–Oct. 2001): 174–90.

Ward, Kevin. "'The Armies of the Lord': Christianity, Rebels and the State of Northern Uganda, 1986–1999." *Journal of Religion in Africa* 31, no. 2 (2001): 187–221.

———. "A History of Christianity in Uganda." *Dictionary of African Christian Biography.* Accessed 18 January 2022. https://dacb.org/histories/uganda-history-christianity/.

World Population Review. "Uganda Population (Live)." Accessed 5 February 2022. https://worldpopulationreview.com/countries/uganda-population.

Wright, N. T. *Jesus and the Victory of God.* Minneapolis: Fortress, 1996.

———. *The New Testament and the People of God.* Minneapolis: Fortress, 1992.

20

An Exploration of Pentecostal Theology and Praxis of Salvation in Kenya

Kevin Muriithi Ndereba

Lecturer, and HOD, Practical Theology, St. Paul's University and Research Fellow, Department of Practical Theology and Missiology, Stellenbosch University

Abstract

Appreciating the role of Pentecostalism in African Christianity, this chapter engages with scholars of Pentecostalism and African Christianity in order to explicate a Pentecostal theology and praxis of salvation within the Kenyan context. Grounded in practical theology, this chapter engages the "four theological voices" approach, which considers the lived realities of Christian practices as important sites for theological reflection. As a practical theological method, it seeks to engage in theological reflection not only by beginning with theological texts but also by considering Christian practices in theological reflection. This chapter outlines Pentecostal soteriology as dominion (creation mandate), empowerment (charismata in the Christian life), and present wholeness (over-realized eschatology). The chapter then analyzes these doctrines and practices from a Reformed perspective, so as to foster fruitful mutual dialogue. The chapter commends Pentecostalism for seeking to contextualize soteriology to engage African realities, while also critiquing its need for a holistic biblical theology.

Key words: African Christianity, African theology, Kenyan Christianity, lived theology, Pentecostalism, practical theology, salvation, soteriology

Pentecostalism in Kenya

Christianity in Africa has taken various stripes and shades. Missionary Christianity in the continent can be traced back to the fifteenth century, with a reintroduction in the eighteenth century. Rather than this being a monochromatic history that reads the direction of these missionary impulses as from West to South, Hanciles observes that there was a level of initiative, control, and negotiation on the part of African peoples.[1] This complexity of the nature of African Christianity remains evident in current Christianity on the continent. Whereas historic or missionary-founded churches such as Anglican, Methodist, Presbyterian, and Roman Catholic were doctrinally defined by their missionary agencies, they have gone through distinct phases of Africanization and, subsequently, charismatization as a result of the growth of Pentecostalism on the continent. Thus, Pentecostalism is a critical force and factor in African Christianity.

The scholarly consensus locates the beginning of the Pentecostal movement in the early 1900s, tracing it to the Azusa Street Revivals in Los Angeles, California, under the preaching of the African American William J. Seymour through a series of missions in 1906–9.[2] Allan Anderson traces the history of Pentecostalism within global Christian history by observing the Pentecostal emphases among the early church fathers, the Reformation movement, early modern revivals such as Methodism and Quakerism, as well as the twentieth-century revival movements.[3] Elsewhere, Anderson observes the contemporary development of Pentecostalism in world Christianity, noting the "charismatic wave" that was a renewal within mainline denominations in the 1960s and the "neo-charismatic wave" that has birthed a number of independent churches that eschew simplistic definition. He provides four helpful categories of the Pentecostal movement: classic Pentecostal churches (CPC),

---

1. Jecu Hanciles, "Back to Africa: White Abolitionists and Black Missionaries," in *African Christianity: An African Story*, ed. Ogbu Kalu (Trenton: Africa World Press, 2013), 192.

2. Mookgo Solomon Kgatle, "The Influence of Azusa Street Revival in the Early Developments of the Apostolic Faith Mission of South Africa," *Missionalia* 44, no. 3 (2016): 323.

3. Allan Heaton Anderson, *An Introduction to Pentecostalism: Global Charismatic Christianity* (Cambridge: Cambridge University Press, 2013), 39.

older church charismatics (OCC), older independent charismatics (OIC), and neo-Pentecostal or neo-charismatic churches (NCC).[4]

The CPC trace their heritage to the evangelical and missionary movements of the nineteenth century and can be further distinguished by their differences over sanctification (holiness Pentecostals, finished-work Pentecostals), their differences over the doctrine of the Trinity (oneness Pentecostals), and their different interpretation of the apostolic office (apostolic Pentecostals). The OCC trace their beginnings to the charismatic revivals in mainline church traditions, with a focus on the continuation[5] of the miraculous gifts as well as exuberance in liturgical worship, while remaining grounded within their distinct theologies. The IPC may be described as those who, rather than staying within the mainline churches, left to begin independent churches that have no distinct theology or liturgy, but which have similarities with the classic

---

4. Allan Heaton Anderson, *To the Ends of the Earth: Pentecostalism and the Transformation of World Christianity* (Oxford: Oxford University Press, 2013), 5–7.

5. In church practice and theological debate, the terms "continuationist" and "cessationist" are used to describe one's perspective on the gifts of the Spirit for the church today. The continuationist position argues that the spiritual gifts (especially the miraculous gifts such as healing, speaking in tongues, etc.) continue today, while the cessationist position argues that the miraculous gifts were necessary for the early church but "ceased" in the first century. Various arguments are made in support of both positions, with various sub-positions in each position. For instance, Sam Storms distinguishes between functional and practicing continuationists. According to Storms, functional continuationists believe the gifts continue for the church today, but they don't actively seek the gifts. Practicing continuationists regularly engage in and seek more manifestations of the spiritual gifts. Within the West, the cessationist position is supported by most Christians and theologians in the Reformed tradition, either explicitly or implicitly, while the continuationist position is supported in the broadly evangelical and Pentecostal tradition. However, in global Christianity, and in many of the churches in Africa, the boundaries are less clear. There are many Christians and theologians in the Reformed stream who are open to the gifts of the Spirit, while grounding this in a high view of Scripture. This however is a minority position. Engaging the specific arguments goes beyond the scope of this chapter; for more, see Sam Storms, *Understanding Spiritual Gifts: A Comprehensive Guide* (Grand Rapids: Zondervan, 2020). Another Reformed theologian considers the miraculous gifts in the modern church as "analogous to but not identical with the divinely authoritative gifts exercised by the apostles." In his paper, Poythress utilizes a triad in his understanding of the gifts. He sees Jesus as the one with the full manifestation of the Spirit, then the apostles as a second-level authority entrusted with the foundation of the early church, then special offices (e.g. elder or deacon), and finally ordinary believers. While church leaders and ordinary believers may express spiritual gifts, they function under the authority of the Bible – which is different for Jesus and the apostles, the latter being used for the foundation of the church and the inspiration of Scripture. See Vern Poythress, "Modern Spiritual Gifts as Analogous to Apostolic Gifts: Affirming Extraordinary Works of the Spirit within Cessationist Theology," *Journal of the Evangelical Theological Society* 39, no. 1 (1996): 71–101. Another African scholar views Pentecostalism at large, and continuationism in particular, as a "response to modernistic liberalism and Protestant fundamentalist cessationist orthodoxy." See Marius Nel, "A South African View of Pentecostalism as Another Response to Modernism," *In die Skriflig* 54, no. 1 (2020): 1–7.

Pentecostals in terms of their approach to the gifts. Lastly, the NCC are more recent churches with an emphasis on the "Word of Faith" and apostolic renewal churches. Anderson notes that, while this is a more nuanced way of defining the Pentecostal movement in global Christianity, the above categories have areas of overlap.[6]

Within the Kenyan religious landscape, Pentecostal churches or churches with a Pentecostal orientation include Full Gospel Churches, Assemblies of God, Mavuno Church, Nairobi Chapel, Deliverance Church, and a host of other AICs (African Initiated Churches) such as African Independence Pentecostal Church of Kenya and other Zionist churches. The East Africa Revival, which started in Rwanda and expanded to Uganda, Kenya, and Tanzania, is also seen as a spiritual revival in these countries, with many of their members worshipping in a number of the mainstream churches and having influenced the theologies of those churches – particularly in the Anglican, Presbyterian, and Methodist Churches.[7] Pentecostalism is also alive and well within the parachurch landscape, with Kenya Students Christian Fellowship (KSCF) as well as the Fellowship of Christian Unions in Kenya, an umbrella body made of Christian Unions in various universities, as representatives. Mugambi has offered a longer history on how Pentecostalism was a key contributor to the Student Movements of Kenya, and how young people were key participants, if not originators, of these revivals.[8]

Pentecostalism and the Role of New Media

The point is clear that while many have lauded the growth of Christianity on the continent, a key contributor to this quantitative advance has been Pentecostalism. The following statistics help to support this observation. In a 2003 study by Barret and Johnson, Pentecostals numbered about 500 million adherents, and were largely to be found in non-Western regions such as Africa, Latin America, Asia, and Oceania, according to Adogame.[9] In 2011, the

---

6. Anderson, *To the Ends of the Earth*, 7.
7. Bernard Gechiko Nyabwari and Dickson Nkonge Kagema, "Charismatic Pentecostal Churches in Kenya: Growth, Culture and Orality," *International Journal of Humanities, Social Sciences and Education (IJHSSE)* 1, no. 3 (2014): 27–33.
8. Kyama M. Mugambi, "Revivalists and Student Movements," in *A Spirit of Revitalization: Urban Pentecostalism in Kenya* (Waco: Baylor University Press, 2020), 55–88.
9. Afe Adogame, "Pentecostal and Charismatic Movements in a Global Perspective," in *The New Blackwell Companion to the Sociology of Religion*, ed. Bryan S. Turner (Chichester: Wiley-Blackwell, 2016), 498.

Pew Research Forum noted an increase to about 584 million adherents. If one collates the statistics of Pentecostals and charismatics, they constitute 26.7 percent of the total Christian population.[10] Another recent study from the Center for the Study of Global Christianity at Gordon-Conwell Theological Seminary traces the meteoric rise of Pentecostals from 58 million in 1970 to 656 million in 2021.[11]

To understand this growth, various proposals, largely sociological, have been made. The religious scholars Parsitau and Mwaura note that the flexibility offered by Pentecostalism grants it supreme adaptability in different sociocultural contexts, such as is a marker of the rapidly urbanizing and globalizing Kenyan context.[12] These scholars keenly observe the makeup, as well as the growth, of the Pentecostal movement in Kenya when they say:

> Pentecostal and charismatic churches, fellowships and ministries have proliferated throughout the country. Examples of Pentecostal and charismatic churches in Kenya are the Deliverance Churches, Neno Evangelism Ministries, Maximum Miracles Ministries, Jesus is Alive Ministries, The Happy Churches, Faith Evangelistic Ministries, Redeemed Gospel churches and the Winners Chapel International Ministries. These Pentecostal and charismatic movements in Kenya currently constitute a large Christian constituency that commands hundreds of thousands, if not millions, of followers.[13]

---

10. Joseph Liu, "Global Christianity: A Report on the Size and Distribution of the World's Christian Population," *Pew Research Center's Forum on Religion & Public Life* (2011): 69–70. The Pew report distinguishes Pentecostals as those belonging to distinct Pentecostal denominations, and charismatics as those in non-Pentecostal denominations but who are open to manifestations of the spiritual gifts. The report however acknowledges that the two terms are often used interchangeably, and views them within the larger description of "renewalist" movements. While distinguishing a third category of Christianity as evangelicals – those who believe in conversion, biblical authority, and evangelism – in many parts of the world, and in Africa especially, these three categories are not mutually exclusive. Thus, there are nondenominational churches that are charismatic, there are Pentecostals who would describe themselves as evangelical, and there are evangelicals who would describe themselves as charismatic, to offer just a few examples. Additionally, there are many Christians globally who would not describe themselves with any of these markers.

11. Gina A. Zurlo, Todd M. Johnson, and Peter F. Crossing, "World Christianity and Mission 2021: Questions about the Future," *International Bulletin of Mission Research* 45, no. 1 (2021): 18.

12. Damaris Seleina Parsitau and Philomena Njeri Mwaura, "God in the City: Pentecostalism as an Urban Phenomenon in Kenya," *Studia Historiae Ecclesiasticae* 36, no. 2 (2010): 95–112.

13. Parsitau and Njeri Mwaura, "God in the City," 4.

Here, Parsitau and Mwaura provide several factors for the growth of Pentecostalism in Kenya. These include language adaptability, a focus on Kenya's youth population, the charismatic leaders of these movements, as well as a theological orientation that is focused on upward mobility for Kenyans in the lower-to-middle classes. Within another Majority World context – that of El Salvador – Wadkins, observing participants in a nationwide gathering of evangelical leaders at the Mueso Nacional de Antropología, comments how the Pentecostal movement has been embraced among educated and upwardly mobile evangelicals, the economically poor, younger urbanites, and Catholic charismatics, revealing its permeability across race, class, worldviews, and liturgical orientations.[14] In addition to these factors, Asamoah-Gyadu has also explored the role of media in the expansion and absorption of the movement within various African countries. For instance, he notes that the theological language used by Pentecostal (and charismatic) preachers has a canny ability to reach wide Ghanaian audiences through televised media.[15] He contends that Pentecostal presence accounts for 90 percent of religious television.[16] In Kenya, televised media has led to the explosion of the Pentecostal movement. In 2006, Bishop T. D. Jakes pulled a crowd of 1 million people.[17]

Other prominent Pentecostal leaders who are iconic on Kenya's Christian television, and who have visited the country in the past, include Juanita Bynum, an African American televangelist and prophetess, Reinhardt Bonkke, Morris Cerullo, Loren Davis, Cecil Stewart, and Peter Youngren. Asamoah-Gyadu has also observed the influence of Oral Roberts, who through new media reached a wider audience beyond the West and visited Kenya, South Africa, Ghana, and Nigeria.[18] With the rise of social media, new Pentecostal preachers have gained prominence particularly among millennials and Generation Z, often referred to as the "digital generation."[19] Preachers such as Steven Furtick, Michael Todd, and David Oyedepo are well known among younger

---

14. Timothy Wadkins, *The Rise of Pentecostalism in Modern El Salvador* (Waco: Baylor University Press, 2017), 25–27.

15. J. Kwabena Asamoah-Gyadu, "Anointing through the Screen: Neo-Pentecostalism and Televised Christianity in Ghana," *Studies in World Christianity* 11, no. 1 (2005): 10.

16. Asamoah-Gyadu, "Anointing through the Screen," 11.

17. Damaris Seleina Parsitau and Philomena Njeri Mwaura, "Gospel without Borders: Gender Dynamics of Transnational Religious Movements in Kenya and the Kenyan Diaspora," in *Religion Crossing Boundaries*, eds. Afe Adogame and James V. Spickard (Leiden: Brill, 2010), 192.

18. J. Kwabena Asamoah-Gyadu, "'Your Miracle Is on the Way': Oral Roberts and Mediated Pentecostalism in Africa," *Spiritus: ORU Journal of Theology* 3, no. 1 (2018): 5, 12.

19. Kevin Muriithi Ndereba, "Apologetics in a Digital Age: Incarnating the Gospel for Africa's Next Gens," *Global Missiology* 18, no. 4 (2021): 24–32.

Christians – showing how the older and newer forms of media have led to the religious transformations, and vice versa.[20]

While the above sociological analysis has observed statistical trends and offered sociocultural analysis, the question remains: Is it possible to study the theology of Pentecostalism? And if so, what might be the contours of its doctrine of salvation, both in theoretical formulation and in practical Christian life? How may these offer prospects and challenges for African Christianity at large, and for historic mission churches specifically?

A Practical Theology of Pentecostal Soteriology

Within the Kenyan context, Mugambi has offered a careful analysis of the Pentecostal movement, while attending to some of its distinctive theological emphases. Mugambi observes that the foundational aspect of Pentecostal theology is its commitment to "personal transformation," which moves beyond conversion to the experiential engagement of one's life.[21] While noting that Pentecostal "excesses" have abounded, he seeks to demonstrate the positive contribution of the movement. Thus, Pentecostal soteriology is viewed within a wider theological lens, and given the Pentecostal teachings on subjects such as dominion, deliverance, and hope beyond material and spiritual poverty, the aspects discussed below emerge from the literature.

Understanding soteriology within Kenyan Christianity is problematic since Pentecostalism thrives on "informal liturgies" that may not be codified in a systematic manner as you would find within the historic Protestant traditions. For instance, Anglicans have codified their theology in the Thirty-Nine Articles and Presbyterian theology is systematized in the Westminster Confessions and catechisms. Pentecostal theology, in contrast, tends to be fluid and dynamic, with some of its expressions utilizing formal liturgies while others are more varied in their theological beliefs. Thus, a major way to understand Pentecostal soteriology is through examining particular songs, prayers, or mission and vision statements of churches within this varied tradition. Following this path, this chapter utilizes the "four theological voices" in practical theology so as to discern the themes that arise from Pentecostal theology and praxis of salvation.

The "four theological voices" approach has emerged through empirical studies within diverse Christian contexts, and is championed by Helen

---

20. Nimi Wariboko and L. William Oliverio, "The Society for Pentecostal Studies at 50 Years: Ways Forward for Global Pentecostalism," *Pneuma* 42, no. 3–4 (2020): 330.
21. Mugambi, *Spirit of Revitalization*, 8.

Cameron, Deborah Bhatti, Catherine Duce, James Sweeney, and Clare Watkins.[22] These distinct voices seek to discern how theology interrelates with the actions of communities of faith. They are summarized as operant theology, espoused theology, normative theology, and formal theology. Operant theology is the kind of theology that is understood from the practices of a faith community and, while usually not explicitly reflected upon, shows up in various aspects of the community's life. As an illustration, one could think of the software in a computer that runs in the background. Espoused theology then becomes voiced through songs and prayers, and these can contain helpful insights into a community's practices. Normative theology is what is codified into statements of belief or mission statements of the church as a way to seek coherence in a community of faith. Formal theology is the type of theological activity engaged by the academic community, which utilizes more technical tools in the theological task.

This chapter seeks to explore the concept of soteriology in Kenyan Pentecostalism by taking seriously the practices of Pentecostal Christians as a way of bringing to the foreground the operant and espoused theologies. Within practical theology, this is a way of theological research that seriously considers the lived realities of faith communities. This sensitive interplay of theory and praxis is what lends credence to practical theology as a methodology that can hold in tension the tools of theology (systematics, exegesis) with the textures of the everyday (formation, ministry).

A good place to start then, in the absence of formal Pentecostal soteriology, is the worship practices of Pentecostal churches, including the rituals, preaching, and songs, as Vondey argues.[23] In the following sections, I draw out various salvation themes that are salient among Pentecostal churches by looking at a few practices, such as prayers of dominion, and the mission statements of a sample of churches. As argued earlier, salvation in Pentecostal theology is not narrowed down to the conversion experience but is focused on personal transformation. Consequently, salvation in Pentecostal preaching and singing is often connected to the account of creation, particularly the doctrine of dominion, as well as to the future, in its over-realized eschatology in terms of Pentecostal expressions and concerns around deliverance and healing.

---

22. Peter Ward, *Introduction to Practical Theology: Mission, Ministry, and the Life of the Church* (Grand Rapids: Baker Academic, 2017), 60–61.

23. Wolfgang Vondey, "Soteriology at the Altar: Pentecostal Contributions to Salvation as Praxis," *Transformation* 34, no. 3 (2017): 223–38.

Salvation As Recovery of the Dominion Mandate (Creation)

Within the Pentecostal tradition in contemporary Kenyan Christianity, dominion teaching has taken the form of the "Seven Mountain Mandate" (SMM). This teaching is taught in various Pentecostal churches, such as Parklands Baptist Church (PBC), Deliverance Churches, and Dominion Centre International, Kamulu. For example, Dominion Centre International "has a Divine mandate to bring up believers to a place of Dominion and Success through teaching of the Word of God."[24] One of the associate pastors at Parklands Baptist Church views prayer as a tool of regaining dominion. Expounding on prayer from the story of Moses lifting up his hands in Rephidim during the Israelites' battle with the Amalekites (Exod 17:8–16), the pastor notes that

> prayer can bring you from a place of defeat or oppression to a place of victory. . . . Prayer is a game changer, whether it is business, and you want to rise to the next level, a place of dominion and a place of victory, whether it's family life, whether it's relationships, whatever it is, whether it's school work.[25]

Whereas such dominion teaching seeks to encourage those who find themselves in contexts of pain, it may be oversimplistic to read biblical dominion mainly through an anthropocentric way. To put it succinctly, prayers in the Bible can also be made for God's sustenance through difficult times, as we see in the prayers of Paul in Philippians 1. Jesus's high-priestly prayer is another example: "I do not ask that you take them out of the world, but that you keep them from the evil one. They are not of the world, just as I am not of the world. Sanctify them in the truth; your word is truth" (John 17:15–17).[26]

The SMM teaching is popular within the New Apostolic Reformation movement (NAR)[27] and argues that Christians are called to radically

---

24. "Dominion Centre Int'l: DCI Church Kamulu," Facebook, accessed 16 February 2022, https://web.facebook.com/dci.kenya/?_rdc=1&_rdr.

25. "Redemptive Dominion: Impact of Mandate, September 2020 Week 4," Sermon by Associate Pastor, Parklands Baptist Church, Facebook, https://web.facebook.com/watch/?v=1299884943713030.

26. Scripture quotations in this chapter are from the ESV.

27. The New Apostolic Reformation (NAR) traces its origins to the missiologist C. Peter Wagner (1930–2016) who served as missionary under the Society of International Missions (SIM) between 1956 and 1971, as a professor of Church Growth at Fuller Theological Seminary's School of World Missions from 1971 to 2001, and as the president of Global Harvest Ministries from 1993 to 2011. The NAR is a movement that seeks to re-establish the apostolic and prophetic office, based on a reading of Eph 4:11, as a distinct strand within global Christianity, and it has spread through international networks, prayer groups, and church ministries. For more, see

transform culture through influencing the seven spheres, namely religion, family, education, media, government (political and legal), business (trade unions), and entertainment.[28] Tanksley and Schaich explore the tensions between Christianity and culture through the works of influential theologians such as Augustine in his *City of God* and R. J. Rushdony, as well as Christian leaders such as Bill Bright (Campus Crusade for Christ) and Francis Schaeffer (apologist and missionary of L'Abri Fellowship). They reveal how their teachings have contributed to Christian influence in culture, driven by a cultural and nationalistic mandate. Further, they show the parallels between SMM teaching and Marxist philosophy.[29] In terms of biblical precedent, the SMM doctrine is founded upon an exegesis – a faulty one – of the creation mandate of Genesis 1:26–28, as is shown below. Largely tied to this text is the concept of stewardship, which is derived from creatureliness as compared with the sovereign Lord.

Westermann is helpful in unpacking the usage of the verb *radah*, which literally means "to tread the wine press," and explores its usage in Joel 4:13; Numbers 24:19; and Leviticus 26:17. In some translations of Genesis 1:26–28, it is rendered as "have dominion over." However, Westermann argues that in other Old Testament passages it refers to kingly dominion, as in 1 Kings 5:4; Psalms 8:6; 72:8; 110:2; Isaiah 14:6; Ezekiel 34:4; and that the usage of *radah* has similar parallels in ancient Near Eastern royal ideology, such as in Egyptian narrative.[30] Longman also compares how the biblical creation account reveals the dignity of humanity, in contrast to the Babylonian creation accounts found in *Enūma Eliš* – where humanity is created from dust and the spirit of rebellious demon gods – and the Akkadian epic *Atrahasis* – where humans are created to replace the lesser gods.[31] Both Westermann and Longman concede that the concept of dominion is given to living beings to rule creation, but state that this rule is only secondary to God's primary rule over creation: human dominion is commissioned by God. Thus, dominion is not a "take it all" nationalistic or individualistic approach, but a creative cultivation of the earth's resources for the extension of God's reign in light of his mission for the world.

Kelebogile Resane, "The New Apostolic Reformation: The Critical Reflections of the Ecclesiology of Charles Peter Wagner," *HTS Teologiese Studies/Theological Studies* 72, no. 3 (2016): a3240.

28. Richard Tanksley and Marlin Schaich, "Marxist Parallels with the Seven Mountain Mandate," *The Evangelical Review of Theology and Praxis* 6 (2018): 3–30.

29. Tanksley and Schaich, "Marxist Parallels," 3–30.

30. Claus Westermann, *Genesis 1–11: A Commentary* (Minneapolis: Augsburg, 1984), 158–60.

31. Tremper Longman III, *How to Read Genesis* (Downers Grove: InterVarsity 2005), 160.

Salvation As Empowerment and Deliverance (Sanctification)

Pentecostal theology also emphasizes wholeness in terms of the practical application of salvation. Mugambi paraphrases Asamoah-Gyadu to explain how Pentecostal soteriology emphasizes healing and deliverance as channels of coming to terms with and coming out of various obstacles "for their own personal advancement."[32] The doctrine of healing and deliverance speaks to the challenges – due to economic pressure, political chaos, as well as supernatural causes – that African Christians face. As a result, salvation is not only about "being born again," as is common within some evangelical circles, but, through the power of the Holy Spirit, as in the East African revivals, proffers a personal testimony of transformation from past sins.[33] At the same time, empowerment in the Christian life is lived out practically through the manifestation of the gifts of the Spirit. Within Pentecostal theology, the traditional offices of Christian ministry, such as ordained pastors and deacons, have been abrogated for the more public and power-display types of prophets and apostles. In addition, the Pentecostal movement, by and large, has vested a lot of responsibility in lay leaders through a more open church governance structure, leading to indigenous leadership development among Christian communities.[34] Salvation therefore is conceived as a doctrine that transforms the personal lives of believers and empowers them with gifts and offices of service within the body of Christ.

Salvation As Present Wholeness and Perfection (Over-Realized Eschatology)

Connected to this aspect of empowerment is an over-realized eschatology. Since Pentecostal soteriology focuses on the here and now, its conceptualization of healing and deliverance is not grounded within the future-oriented doctrine of glorification, which follows sanctification and the other doctrines of salvation (see, for example, 1 John 3:1).[35] Thus, in emphasizing deliverance and healing in the present, Pentecostal soteriology misunderstands all the benefits of

---

32. Mugambi, *Spirit of Revitalization*, 8–9.

33. Mugambi, 55.

34. Mugambi, 25, 239. Over time, however, Pentecostal churches have formed more ordered governance structures and even liturgies for the ordination of pastors, and adoption of ritualistic symbols such as collars and gowns, following the example of historic mission churches. Examples include Mamlaka Hill Chapel and Nairobi Chapel.

35. Christopher M. Tuckett, "Galatians 1:4: Present and Future Salvation in Galatians," in *Sōtēria: Salvation in Early Christianity and Antiquity*, eds. David du Toit, Christine Gerber, and Christiane Zimmermann (Leiden: Brill, 2019), 330–44.

salvation as being present experiences for the here and now. This is contrary to biblical precedent. For example, within the Abrahamic covenant, where God pledged land, people, and blessing to the nations, we see that these blessings came partially through a four-hundred-year sojourn through Egyptian slavery (Gen 12:1–3; 15:4–6; 17:1–10). The experience of Job is also illustrative, being an Old Testament character whose faith in God helped him to navigate pain and suffering in his life. The New Testament also records that Abraham did not see some of the blessings promised (Heb 11:8–19).

Perhaps this overemphasis is due to a lack of distinguishing what is normative and what is prescriptive in the book of Acts – a central book for the understanding of Pentecostalism, yet also a key missiological text in the New Testament. From reading Acts together with the gospels and the New Testament letters, we reach the following conclusions:

- Healing and deliverance are realities that can happen but they are not normative for all.
- Healing and deliverance serve to focus people on the lordship of Christ.
- Healing and deliverance have both physical and spiritual connotations.

Some aspects of the Pentecostal practice of deliverance have taken on a commercialized agenda that seeks to utilize fear as a way to keep adherents confined. Excessive practices that have accompanied deliverance services include using commercial workers to offer paid testimonies of miraculous transformation, sexual infidelity among pastors, and congregants doing bizarre things to receive miraculous interventions.[36] While one may argue that these excessive practices in Pentecostal churches are exceptions, the high number of such cases within the broadly Pentecostal tradition should arouse a critical approach toward those deliverance ministries that are used merely for financial gain.[37] Further, some forms of deliverance ministries focus more on the "man of God" than on the One who heals. Lastly, deliverance (from life's misfortunes) is not automatic, and sometimes people need to go through suffering in order for God to accomplish both his visible and mysterious purposes in the life of

---

36. Mookgo S. Kgatle, "The Unusual Practices within Some Neo-Pentecostal Churches in South Africa: Reflections and Recommendations," *HTS: Theological Studies* 73, no. 3 (2017): 1–8.

37. Julius Gathogo, "Infidelity among Afro-Pentecostal Leadership: The Kenyan Case," in *Genders, Sexualities, and Spiritualities in African Pentecostalism*, ed. Chama Kaunda (London: Palgrave Macmillan, 2020), 391–409.

the church. The experiences of the apostles and the Christian martyrs of the early church serve to illustrate this point.

Within the recent past, Pentecostal churches have offered the deliverance practice of "redeeming the firstborn sons" which, according to adherents, offers deliverance from generational curses that affect families. Within African religion, the firstborn son of a family is responsible for making sure that life is transmitted from one generation to another, for sustaining healthy bonds within the community, and, eventually through his own fatherhood, for connecting his own father into the status of ancestorhood.[38] Following this line of thinking, some African preachers connect misfortunes experienced in families and through generations as symptoms of a problem with the firstborn of those families.

For instance, during a church service Rev. Lucy Natasha suggested to her congregation, "Lift up your hands: I declare that for me and all the firstborns in my generations, we shall not make wrong choices regarding marriage, regarding career, regarding investments. . . . I erase that mark."[39] In many such services, followers of these teachers pay tithes in order to gain the benefits of "redeeming their firstborn." We will see below how this is due to a faulty exegesis of "primogeniture" in the Bible. It is clear that such teachings address the surface-level issues facing many Africans, such as poverty, sickness, and other forms of suffering, without focusing on the responsibility that people have to pursue more abundant life. Contrary to these prosperity preachers, the true gospel goes much deeper, transforming us from the inside out. In a richer sense, the gospel addresses issues of stewardship, health, and joy. Additionally, God's presence is with us even through the valley of the shadow of death, therefore offering a more grounded theology of suffering (Ps 23).

A Reformed Theological Analysis
Negotiating African Worldviews with Biblical and Systematic Theology

The concept of "primogeniture" or the firstborn, as mentioned in the case above, is important in biblical theology as it traces God's redemptive plan for the nations, beginning in the Old Testament. First, the priesthood was set

---

38. Laurenti Magesa, *African Religion: The Moral Traditions of Abundant Life* (Nairobi: Paulines Publications, 1997), 85–86.

39. Rev. Lucy Natasha, "Redeeming the Firstborn!," a three-hour service, Facebook, 19 November 2018, at 2:12:00, https://www.facebook.com/Revlucynatasha/videos/509453882908772/.

aside for the firstborn in a family. Second, laws were given concerning the redemption of firstborn humans and animals (Exod 13:12–15; Lev 12:2–4; Num 3:45; Deut 12:6). The teaching on redeeming the firstborn was based on a ritualistic understanding of the firstborn. This understanding parallels that of our African communities, which honor the firstborn with family introductions, family responsibilities, and family inheritances. In the New Testament, Jesus Christ is also described as "the firstborn among many brothers" (Rom 8:29). This interprets the Jewish understanding of the firstborn to show that Christ has preeminence in God's work of salvation. In the context of this verse, Jesus Christ is the centerpiece of all the realities and blessings of salvation. If salvation is a diamond, with calling, justification, regeneration, sanctification, adoption, and glorification representing different faces, then Jesus Christ is the entire jewel.

The preceding section begs the question: Is the Pentecostal theology of salvation underpinned by a biblical-theological framework, or is it anchored mainly on lived realities that are ubiquitous to an African worldview? The concept of the "man of God" as the mediator between the people of God and God himself has been abused in Kenyan ecclesiological practice, in that some leaders have vested more authority in their office than is mandated for an under-shepherd, bishop, or minister (Titus 1:5–9; 1 Tim 3:1–7). Through this overemphasis on the "man of God," some Pentecostal pastors take advantage of the power distance and culture of honor that is a marker of an African worldview. Second, while this author is sympathetic to a continuationist position when it comes to the charismata, the Pentecostal practice seems to either over- or underemphasize the broader theology and context of the gifts as outlined in Ephesians 4:7–16; 1 Corinthians 12–14; and Romans 12:3–8.

In summary, Pentecostal pneumatology is severed from God's sovereignty, a healthy ecclesiology, and a future-oriented eschatology. Lastly, in overemphasizing healing and deliverance today, some may be falling into the trap of the five hundred who wanted physical bread more than they wanted the Bread of Life, Jesus Christ (see John 6). The pattern in the New Testament is that God's miraculous interventions are always tied to his glory and his redemptive purposes for us in Christ. The healing of the paralyzed man in Matthew 9 is illustrative of this: here Jesus emphasizes both physical healing and spiritual healing, as a display of his divine sonship. Recovering biblical-theological underpinnings is critical for ensuring that Pentecostal soteriology does not serve its own ends – and thereby make an idol of a singular perspective of one doctrine. Otherwise, Pentecostal theology may thrive merely because it addresses the African worldview concerns of evil and malevolent spiritual forces, rather than because it focuses on the Lord who is victorious over all.[40]

Biblical theology is also critical in helping Christians of all stripes to view the Christian doctrines in unity rather than in isolation. This provides a more holistic doctrinal understanding as well as a coherent Christian life that is vibrant and stable in all seasons. Thus, our African worldviews and cosmologies must be subservient to the biblical revelation; as Kombo contends in his theological treatise on the Trinity, following Barth: whatever language we use to theologize will always be an inadequate expression of its object.[41] While we need to do contextualization, our starting points and our assumptions matter, even as we seek to explore what salvation means within the context of poverty, corruption, and sickness. As Kombo asserts, "the Trinitarian hermeneutic has what it takes to incarnate biblical cosmology into the African cosmology and to cast the entire theological discourse on a completely different plane."[42]

Viewing Pneumatology within the Broader Scope of Systematic Theology

A grounding in a coherent systematic theology of the Spirit would expand the categories of Pentecostal pneumatology and its implications for soteriology. While Pentecostal soteriology emphasizes an experiential outlook of salvation and the charismata of the Holy Spirit, this must not be severed from the other critical ministries of the Spirit, which are as follows:

- The Spirit in the work of effectual calling
- The Spirit in the work of regeneration
- The Spirit in the impartation of faith
- The Spirit in the work of justification
- The Spirit in the work of sanctification
- The Spirit in the work of glorification

These terms "effectual calling," "regeneration," "impartation of faith," "justification," "sanctification," and "glorification" are critical aspects of a Reformed perspective on the loci of salvation. The Reformed confessions – for example, the Westminster Confession of Faith – view each of these aspects through the agency of the Holy Spirit. So, for instance: *"Effectual calling*

---

40. Dale Coulter, "Delivered by the Power of God: Toward a Pentecostal Understanding of Salvation," *International Journal of Systematic Theology* 10, no. 4 (2008): 447–67.

41. James Henry Owino Kombo, *Theological Models of the Doctrine of the Trinity: The Trinity, Diversity and Theological Hermeneutics* (Carlisle: Langham, 2016), 11.

42. Kombo, *Theological Models*, 12.

is the work of God's Spirit, whereby, convincing us of our sin and misery, enlightening our minds in the knowledge of Christ, and renewing our wills, he [does] persuade and enable us to embrace Jesus Christ, freely offered to us in the gospel" (2 Tim 1:9; Acts 2:37; 26:18; Ezek 36:26; John 6:44).[43]

The Reformed view on these key doctrines connects them to the ministry of the Holy Spirit, with the attendant blessings of justification, adoption, and sanctification. Similarly, the Belgic Confession, another central document that outlines the theology of the Reformed churches, understands the critical ministry of the Holy Spirit in the work of sanctification and in ecclesiology. On the work of sanctification it states:

> We believe that this true faith, produced in us by the hearing of God's Word and by the work of the Holy Spirit, regenerates us and makes us new creatures, causing us to live a new life and freeing us from the slavery of sin. Therefore, far from making people cold toward living in a pious and holy way, this justifying faith, quite to the contrary, so works within them that apart from it they will never do a thing out of love for God but only out of love for themselves and fear of being condemned. So then, it is impossible for this holy faith to be unfruitful in a human being, seeing that we do not speak of an empty faith but of what Scripture calls "faith working through love," which moves people to do by themselves the works that God has commanded in the Word.[44]

What is clear is that a Reformed view of salvation is not by any way cold or passive. It is primarily through the ministry of the Holy Spirit that believers are transformed. Yet this work is both tied to Christology and grounded in the doctrine of Scripture, for the church's mission and well-being. Pentecostals are right to state that soteriology is not only about the objective work of Christ. Yet soteriology is centered on this objective work of Christ on the cross before it moves outward in its application of that cross-work in the lives of Christian believers. Thus, within the Reformed understanding of salvation, the Father plans salvation, the Son accomplishes salvation, and the Spirit applies salvation. As Michael Horton argues extensively, the ministry of the Holy Spirit is critical not only in the work of personal salvation (as particular camps of Christian faith emphasize), nor only in the work of the spiritual gifts (as

---

43. The Westminster Shorter Catechism, Question 35, in *The Westminster Confession* (Edinburgh: Banner of Truth Trust, 2018), 435.

44. Nicolaas Hendrik Gootjes, *The Belgic Confession: Its History and Sources* (Grand Rapids: Baker Academic, 2007).

Pentecostals would want to emphasize), but also in creation, providence, and even consummation.[45] Viewed this way, then, the charismata are seen as tied, not to denominational separation or spiritual pride, but to the redemptive work of God. Pentecostal soteriology, which is necessarily tied to its pneumatology, must be grounded within the wider scope of God's redemptive plan and agency, particularly through the various ministries as mentioned above.

Conclusion

This chapter has explored the understanding of salvation in Pentecostal theology and praxis. The strength of the Pentecostal view of salvation, as argued, is that it utilizes a holistic worldview approach that connects the doctrine of salvation to the doctrines of creation, pneumatology, sanctification, and eschatology, to name but a few. In this way, Pentecostal soteriology avoids a dualistic understanding of the Christian life that can be a weakness of dichotomous thinking. Thus, according to Pentecostal scholars, salvation is seen in the recovery of the mandate of humanity given at creation and in the possibility of well-being in this life. These are critical pointers to how salvation can be contextualized within African realities that are colored by corruption, poverty, and inadequate public health systems.

On the other hand, this chapter has also critiqued the theology and praxis of salvation in the Pentecostal tradition. This critique was stated in two ways. First, Pentecostal soteriology must maintain a dialogical engagement between the African worldview and biblical theology. The chapter critiqued Pentecostal soteriology for its overemphasis on African traditional worldviews, through its overbearing focus on African cosmologies, the spirit world, and the understanding of life. While it could be lauded that, contrary to other theological traditions, Pentecostalism has at least engaged African realities in a helpful way, this chapter proposes that the tradition can be enriched by allowing the biblical worldview and theology to inform its understanding and practices. For example, the chapter has demonstrated that in its reading of the creation mandate in Genesis 1:26–27, the practice of SMM severs the meaning of that passage from the wider context of the theology of the Pentateuch, such as in its understanding of humanity as stewards of God. Second, the chapter also proposes that Pentecostal soteriology can be enriched by expanding its

---

45. Michael Horton, "Let the Earth Bring Forth: The Spirit in Human Agency in Sanctification," in *Sanctification: Explorations in Theology and Practice*, ed. Kelly M. Kapic (Downers Grove: IVP Academic, 2014), 127–49.

doctrine of pneumatology. Utilizing the tools of systematic theology, Pentecostal soteriology can be enriched by viewing salvation within the broader scope of the Spirit's work in creation, sanctification, and consummation.

The benefits of this dialogical exploration of the Pentecostal and Reformed traditions are evident. It is evident that the Pentecostal tradition has provided freedom for Africans to theologize and live the Christian life in a genuinely "African" way, especially outside the grasp of a Euro-centric and denigrating imperialism as part of mission history. However, this chapter has also explored some of the Pentecostal tradition's shortcomings. Likewise, the Reformed tradition offers the global church today a serious engagement with biblical revelation and seeks to learn from the wisdom of the church through the church's confessions and creeds. If these emphases are lost, they may sever the church in Africa from its rich historical past as the body of Christ through the ages. Yet, on the other hand, the Reformed tradition can sometimes give more credence to traditionalism and pride, which prevent it from benefiting from the work of the Spirit in the world today. The greatest takeaway from this chapter is that in a dynamic African religious context, the better option lies in a conversation between the various Christian traditions. This way, the quality of Christianity remains rich while we remain attendant to God's salvific work on the continent, as we participate with him through the Spirit to bring his eschatological purposes to fruition.

Bibliography

Adogame, Afe. "Pentecostal and Charismatic Movements in a Global Perspective." In *The New Blackwell Companion to the Sociology of Religion*, edited by Bryan S. Turner, 498–518. Chichester: Wiley-Blackwell, 2016.

Anderson, Allan Heaton. *An Introduction to Pentecostalism: Global Charismatic Christianity*. Cambridge: Cambridge University Press, 2013.

———. *To the Ends of the Earth: Pentecostalism and the Transformation of World Christianity*. New York: Oxford University Press, 2013.

Asamoah-Gyadu, J. Kwabena. "Anointing through the Screen: Neo-Pentecostalism and Televised Christianity in Ghana." *Studies in World Christianity* 11, no. 1 (2005): 9–28.

———. "Pentecostalism and the Transformation of the African Christian Landscape." In *Pentecostalism in Africa: Presence and Impact of Pneumatic Christianity in Postcolonial Societies*, edited by Martin Lindhardt, 100–14. Leiden: Brill, 2014.

———. "'Your Miracle Is on the Way': Oral Roberts and Mediated Pentecostalism in Africa." *Spiritus: ORU Journal of Theology* 3, no. 1 (2018): 5–26.

Coulter, Dale. "Delivered by the Power of God: Toward a Pentecostal Understanding of Salvation." *International Journal of Systematic Theology* 10, no. 4 (2008): 447–67. https://doi.org/10.1111/j.1468-2400.2008.00380.x.

"Dominion Centre Int'l: DCI Church Kamulu." Facebook. Accessed 16 February 2022. https://web.facebook.com/dci.kenya/?_rdc=1&_rdr.

Gathogo, Julius. "Infidelity among Afro-Pentecostal Leadership: The Kenyan Case." In *Genders, Sexualities, and Spiritualities in African Pentecostalism*, edited by Chama Kaunda, 391–409. London: Palgrave Macmillan, 2020.

Gootjes, Nicolaas Hendrik. *The Belgic Confession: Its History and Sources*. Grand Rapids: Baker Academic, 2007.

Hanciles, Jecu. "Back to Africa: White Abolitionists and Black Missionaries." In *African Christianity: An African Story*, edited by Ogbu Kalu, 191–216. Trenton: Africa World Press, 2013.

Horton, Michael. "Let the Earth Bring Forth: The Spirit in Human Agency in Sanctification." In *Sanctification: Explorations in Theology and Practice*, edited by Kelly M. Kapic, 127–49. Downers Grove: IVP Academic, 2014.

Kalu, Ogbu. *African Pentecostalism: An Introduction*. Oxford: Oxford University Press, 2008.

Kgatle, Mookgo Solomon. "The Influence of Azusa Street Revival in the Early Developments of the Apostolic Faith Mission of South Africa." *Missionalia* 44, no. 3 (2016): 321–35.

———. "The Unusual Practices within Some Neo-Pentecostal Churches in South Africa: Reflections and Recommendations." *HTS: Theological Studies* 73, no. 3 (2017): 1–8.

Kombo, James Henry Owino. *Theological Models of the Doctrine of the Trinity: The Trinity, Diversity and Theological Hermeneutics*. Carlisle: Langham Global Library, 2016.

Liu, Joseph. "Global Christianity: A Report on the Size and Distribution of the World's Christian Population." *Pew Research Center's Forum on Religion & Public Life* (2011): 1–130.

Longman, Tremper, III. *How to Read Genesis*. Downers Grove: InterVarsity 2005.

Magesa, Laurenti. *African Religion: The Moral Traditions of Abundant Life*. Nairobi: Paulines Publications, 1997.

Maseno, Loreen. "Prayer for Rain: A Pentecostal Perspective from Kenya." *The Ecumenical Review* 69, no. 3 (2017): 336–47.

Mugambi, Kyama M. *A Spirit of Revitalization: Urban Pentecostalism in Kenya*. Waco: Baylor University Press, 2020.

Natasha, Rev. Lucy. "Redeeming the Firstborn!" A three-hour service. Facebook. 19 November 2018. https://www.facebook.com/Revlucynatasha/videos/509453882908772/.

Ndereba, Kevin Muriithi. "Apologetics in a Digital Age: Incarnating the Gospel for Africa's Next Gens." *Global Missiology* 18, no. 4 (2021): 24–32.

Nel, Marius. "A South African View of Pentecostalism as Another Response to Modernism." *In die Skriflig* 54, no. 1 (2020): 1–7.

Nyabwari, Bernard Gechiko, and Dickson Nkonge Kagema. "Charismatic Pentecostal Churches in Kenya: Growth, Culture and Orality." *International Journal of Humanities, Social Sciences and Education (IJHSSE)* 1, no. 3 (2014): 27–33.

Parsitau, Damaris Seleina, and Philomena Njeri Mwaura. "God in the City: Pentecostalism as an Urban Phenomenon in Kenya." *Studia Historiae Ecclesiasticae* 36, no. 2 (2010): 95–112.

———. "Gospel without Borders: Gender Dynamics of Transnational Religious Movements in Kenya and the Kenyan Diaspora." In *Religion Crossing Boundaries*, edited by Afe Adogame and James V. Spickard, 185–201. Leiden: Brill, 2010.

Poythress, Vern. "Modern Spiritual Gifts as Analogous to Apostolic Gifts: Affirming Extraordinary Works of the Spirit within Cessationist Theology." *Journal of the Evangelical Theological Society* 39, no. 1 (1996): 71–101.

"Redemptive Dominion: Impact of Mandate, September 2020 Week 4." Sermon by Associate Pastor, Parklands Baptist Church. Facebook. https://web.facebook.com/watch/?v=1299884943713030.

Resane, Kelebogile. "The New Apostolic Reformation: The Critical Reflections of the Ecclesiology of Charles Peter Wagner." *HTS Teologiese Studies/Theological Studies* 72, no. 3 (2016): a3240. http://dx.doi.org/10.4102/hts.v72i3.3240.

Storms, Sam. *Understanding Spiritual Gifts: A Comprehensive Guide*. Grand Rapids: Zondervan, 2020.

Tanksley, Richard, and Marlin Schaich. "Marxist Parallels with the Seven Mountain Mandate." *The Evangelical Review of Theology and Politics* 6 (2018): 3–30.

Tuckett, Christopher M. "Galatians 1:4: Present and Future Salvation in Galatians." In *Sōtēria: Salvation in Early Christianity and Antiquity*, edited by David du Toit, Christine Gerber, and Christiane Zimmermann, 330–44. Leiden: Brill, 2019. doi: https://doi.org/10.1163/9789004396883_018.

Vondey, Wolfgang. "Soteriology at the Altar: Pentecostal Contributions to Salvation as Praxis." *Transformation* 34, no. 3 (2017): 223–38.

Wadkins, Timothy. *The Rise of Pentecostalism in Modern El Salvador*. Waco: Baylor University Press, 2017.

Ward, Peter. *Introduction to Practical Theology: Mission, Ministry, and the Life of the Church*. Grand Rapids: Baker Academic, 2017.

Wariboko, Nimi, and L. William Oliverio. "The Society for Pentecostal Studies at 50 Years: Ways Forward for Global Pentecostalism." *Pneuma* 42, no. 3–4 (2020): 327–33.

Westermann, Claus. *Genesis 1–11: A Commentary*. Minneapolis: Augsburg, 1984.

The Westminster Confession. Edinburgh: Banner of Truth Trust, 2018.

Zurlo, Gina A., Todd M. Johnson, and Peter F. Crossing. "World Christianity and Mission 2021: Questions about the Future." *International Bulletin of Mission Research* 45, no. 1 (2021): 15–25.

Contributors

Isaac Ampong, originally from Ghana, currently serves as the pastor for youth and families at St. Paul's Anglican Church, Tervuren, Belgium. He holds an MDiv from Tyndale Theological Seminary, Netherlands.

Samuel K. Bussey is a doctoral student in intercultural theology at the Protestant Theological University in Groningen, Netherlands. His dissertation focuses on how African theological reflection on the concept of sacrifice can contribute to the atonement debate in Western evangelical theology. He is also the managing editor of the website, African Theology Worldwide, which aims to make African theology more accessible, both in Africa and around the globe.

Henry Marcus Garba is an ordained minister who serves with the Evangelical Church Winning All (ECWA) in Nigeria. He holds a masters degree in church history from Africa International University, Kenya. Currently, he is pursuing a PhD in theology (World Christianity) at Africa International University, Kenya.

John Michael Kiboi is an ordained priest in the Anglican Church of Kenya, serving as a senior lecturer in the Faculty of Theology at St. Paul's University Limuru, Kenya. He holds a PhD in dogmatic theology from the Catholic University of Eastern Africa. Previously he served as a parish priest in the diocese of Bungoma and Principal at Wycliffe Centre for Theology. Currently, he is the leader of PhD programs in the Faculty of Theology at St. Paul's University, Kenya.

Julius Kithinji is a senior lecturer and Dean of the Joshua and Timothy School of Theology at St. Paul's University, Kenya. He serves in various committees, including the Africa Society of Evangelical Theology and the Presbyterian University of East Africa. Dr. Kithinji is an expert in biblical studies and specializes in the New Testament. His interest in interpreting the Bible from a postcolonial perspective counts for many of his publications. He is an ordained minister serving with the Methodist Church in Kenya.

Edwin Mwangi Macharia is the National Government Administrative Officer currently serving as an Assistant Secretary in the Ministry of Defence. He holds a bachelors degree in Communication (Public Relations) from

Daystar University, Kenya. Currently pursuing a Master of Divinity at Africa International University.

Joseph Mutua Mavulu is an ordained minister in the Africa Inland Church, Kenya, serving as an adjunct faculty member in the Faculty of Theology and Ministry in the International Leadership University, Kenya. He holds a Master of Divinity from the International Leadership University, Kenya. He is currently a PhD candidate in theological studies at the International Leadership University, Kenya. Previously he served as the Director of Christian Education in Africa Inland Church and assistant lecturer in Scott Christian University and adjunct faculty in Pan Africa Christian University, Kenya.

Micah Moenga is an ordained minister and founder of Grace and Power of God (G.A.P) International Ministries, an affiliate ministry of Calvary Assemblies of Kenya. He is serving as a lecturer in the faculty of Pan Africa Christian University, Nairobi, Kenya. He holds a PhD in biblical studies from Africa International University, Kenya.

Kenosi Molato works as a researcher at SHINE Africa Project and also as a national director of Romans Project in Botswana, a position he has held since 2014. He is currently a PhD candidate in systematic theology at South African Theological Seminary.

Timothy J. Monger works with Amigos Worldwide which equips churches in Uganda and South Sudan for transformational mission. Previously he was a missionary in Tanzania serving from 2010 to 2020 with Emmanuel International, which equips churches in mission among marginalized communities, and was the Country Director from 2018 to 2020. He was also a part-time lecturer at St. Paul College, Mwanza, Tanzania. He received his BA from the University of Oxford, UK, and his Master of Christian Studies from Regent College, Vancouver, Canada.

Gift Mtukwa was born and raised in Harare, Zimbabwe, and currently lives in Nairobi, Kenya. He is an ordained minister with the Church of the Nazarene, teaches New Testament and Greek, and is Chair of Department in the School of Religion and Christian Ministries of Africa Nazarene University. He holds a bachelor's degree in theology, an MA in religion from Africa Nazarene University, Kenya, an MA in theology and a PhD in biblical studies from the University of Manchester, UK.

Kyama Mugambi is assistant professor of World Christianity at the Yale Divinity School, USA. He specializes in historical, ecclesial, social, cultural, theological, and epistemological themes within African urban Christianity. Prior to this he served in various academic and church planting roles in Africa. His PhD in World Christianity is from Africa International University.

Jackline Makena Mutuma is a minister in the Methodist Church in Kenya and a theologian. She holds a BD from St. Paul's University, Kenya, and a masters in theology, majoring in systematic theology and theology of culture from Yonsei University, South Korea. She is passionate about researching and writing on contemporary theological issues, especially on gender, religion, and social justice. Her specific focus area is providing theological perspectives on emerging issues and advocating for women, the needy, and the marginalized.

Daniel Mwailu lectures in theology and biblical studies at Africa Nazarene University since 2012. He is former superintendent minister and lay preachers' tutor in the Methodist Church of Great Britain. He holds a BA(Hons) and MA in theology and biblical studies from the London School of Theology, UK, and a PhD in theology from the University of Birmingham, UK.

Pauline Kanuthu Mwaura is an ordained minister with the Presbyterian Church of East Africa and is also a part-time lecturer at the Presbyterian Church of East Africa. She holds a masters degree in theology and is pursuing her PhD at St. Paul's University, Kenya. Her academic and pastoral interests are in the area of church and development.

Kevin Muriithi Ndereba is a lecturer and head of the Department of Practical Theology at St. Paul's University, Kenya. He has served in pastoral ministry with the Presbyterian Church of East Africa. He holds a PhD in theology from the University of South Africa and is also a postdoctoral research fellow in the Department of Practical Theology and Missiology, Stellenbosch University, South Africa. He serves on the executive boards of the International Association for the Study of Youth Ministry and the Africa Society of Evangelical Theology.

David K. Ngaruiya is an associate professor, former acting Deputy Vice Chancellor for Academic Affairs and Director of the PhD in Theological Studies program at International Leadership University. He holds a PhD in intercultural studies from Trinity Evangelical Divinity School, USA. He served as chair of the Africa Society of Evangelical Theology (2015–2016). He has published journal and book articles and served as co-editor and contributor to *Communities of Faith in Africa and African Diaspora* (Pickwick Publications,

2013) and was a director of the research study that produced *African Christian Leadership* (Langham Global Library, 2019).

Moses Iliya Ogidis is a minister with Evangelical Church Winning All (ECWA) in Nigeria. Currently he is a PhD in theology (New Testament) candidate at St. Paul's University, Limuru, Kenya.

Joseph B. Onyango Okello is a professor of philosophy and ethics at Asbury Theological Seminary's extension site in Orlando, Florida. He holds a PhD and a Master of Arts, both in philosophy from the University of Kentucky, USA. He also holds a Master of Divinity and a Master of Arts in Church Music, both from Asbury Theological Seminary, USA. He is also an ordained pastor in the Africa Inland Church, Kenya. He lives in Oviedo, Florida, with his wife, Sophie, and their son, Sean.

Philemon Ongole is a regional Overseer of Deliverance Churches in Eastern Uganda, a member of the governing council of JOY Theological College in Kampala and the leader of a Christian leadership training organization known as Field Bible School for You (FIBISU) based in Tororo. Currently he is a PhD student in theological studies at International Leadership University, Kenya.

Rodney L. Reed is a missionary educator who has been serving at Africa Nazarene University in Nairobi, Kenya, since 2001. Currently, he is the Deputy Vice-Chancellor of Academic Affairs, a position he has held since 2010. Prior to that, he served as the chair of the Department of Religion for nine years. He holds a PhD in theological ethics from Drew University and is an ordained minister in the Church of the Nazarene.

Kamau Thairu is a Presbyterian minister serving within Nairobi and also lectures at Presbyterian University of East Africa since 2017. He holds a PhD in systematic theology from Catholic University of Eastern Africa.

Jamie Viands serves as a lecturer in the Biblical Studies Department at Nairobi Evangelical Graduate School of Theology, Africa International University, Kenya. Previously, he served as the Dean of the School of Theology at Scott Christian University, Machakos, Kenya. He holds a PhD in Old Testament theology and exegesis from Wheaton College, USA.

Danson Ottawa Wafula is the National Coordinator for Africa Center for Apologetics Research (ACFAR), Kenya. He is currently pursuing a Master of Divinity in Biblical Studies. Danson is also a podcast host at The Christian

Life Podcast (TCLP). Danson is a pastoral assistant at Hope City Bible Church (HCBC), a Reformed Baptist congregation in Nairobi.

Subject Index

A
Adeyemo, Tokunboh 25
African Christian 116, 242
African Christian theology 112
African Christianity 22–23, 35–36, 40, 338
African church 208, 238, 257, 330
African church fathers 184
African context 114
African tradition 315
African Traditional Religion 30–31, 108, 112, 242, 253, 257, 322
African women's theologies 135
Agĩkũyũ 308, 311, 315
Agĩkũyũ culture 319
Alexandrian Christian theology 164
ancestral debts 315
Annang 244
Artemis 140, 146–147
Athanasius of Alexandria 157
ATR. *See* African Traditional Religion

B
Baker, Mark and Green, Joel 188
Belgic Confession 396
biblical idea of salvation 23
biblical salvation 254

C
Catholicism 25
Christian exclusivism 294
Christian faith 321
Christology 119
church in Africa 150
circumcised 97
circumcision 97
communal 69
community 34, 60–69, 107, 200–201, 213–15, 217–18, 315–16, 335–37, 347, 350–53, 358, 362, 374–76, 388
contemporary African Christian 226
contemporary African Christianity 233
contemporary Christians 16
conversion 58–59, 61–69, 75–77, 79–80, 82–84, 86–89, 98, 114–18, 173, 278–280, 387–88
Council of Nicaea 163
Culture 309

D
deification 164
doctrine of adoption 209
doctrine of salvation 43, 55, 171, 174–75, 277, 387

E
East African Revival 334, 384
Ekem, John 192
evangelical Christians 58
evangelical models 69
evangelical perspective 59, 61
exclusivism in Christianity 301

F
faith 15–16, 62, 65–69, 78–80, 85–88, 99–103, 106–108, 114–16, 128, 158–59, 163, 166, 193, 235–37, 278–79, 287–89, 298, 321, 333–35, 395–96
faith in Jesus Christ 101
false prophets 17
firstfruits 126

G
gnostics 142
God's people 12
God's present plans 12
gospel 251

Gospel of Mark 234
grace 16, 26
Greco-Roman culture 218
group conversions 84

H
holism 274
hopeful future 11, 13, 19
household 81, 83
household conversion 77, 86, 89
huiothesia 218, 220
humanism 276
hypocrisy 97

I
"I am because we are" 34, 107, 126
incarnation 166, 169
infertility 134, 137

J
"Jesus is the answer" 23
justification 108, 115

K
Kalengyo, Edison 195
kingdom worldview 286

L
LGBTQ 330
LRA 361

M
"man of God" syndrome 108
man of God 394
marriage in West African countries 138
Mbiti, John 27, 30
Mbuvi, Andrew 208, 212

N
negative ethnicity 343
new alphabets 331
new covenant 14
new covenant believers 18
nominal faith 278

Northern Uganda 359, 376

O
Oduyoye, Mercy, A. 199
old covenant 13

P
paterfamilias 85, 87
Pauline theology 24
Pentecostalism 31, 41, 332, 382
  African 42
  Classical 335
  movement 382, 391
  soteriology 387, 391, 395, 397
  theology 387, 391, 394
  tradition 398
personal salvation 69, 79
personal soteriology 68
plans for welfare 8
poor 52, 249
poverty 40, 129, 352, 364–65
prayers 389
primogeniture 393
proclamation in Africa 337
prophets in Africa 18
prophets of prosperity 19
prosperity gospel 232, 377
prosperity gospel preachers 55

R
rejection of Christ 299
rejection of God 300
religio-ethnicism 336
repentance 15, 22, 24, 30, 34, 36, 76, 166–7, 279–280
Rice, Xan 346
ruponeso 113

S
sacrifice 190, 251
saltiness of the church 290
salvation 2, 23, 44, 69, 226, 229, 277
  in Africa 114, 172, 375
  in ATR 244
salvific process 61

saving faith 279
schism in the church 347
Sheol 319
Siamese quadruplets 23
Son-Logos 167
sōtēria 227, 252–53, 271
sōzō 367, 373
"suffering now, glory later" 13

T
The Pilgrim's Progress 58
T^R 297, 302
traditional Western gospel 363–64, 377
Trinitarian hermeneutic 395
tyranny of numbers 346

U
ubuntu 350–351, 354
    philosophy 342, 350–51, 353
    salvation 350, 354–55
    salvation theology 342, 353–54
unbalanced concept of salvation 234
unbelievers 124–25, 128

W
Western model of adoption 216
Western theology 216
works of the law 103
World Council of Churches 243
wrath 121, 123

Y
Yasha 23

Scripture Index

OLD TESTAMENT

Genesis
1:26–28 .... 286, 365, 390
1:28 137
2:22 50
2:7 50
3 .... 142, 145
5:2 50
12:1–3 392
15:1–4 209
15:4–6 392
17:1–10 392
17:1–14 97
17:11–13 98
17:14 98
41:28 298
49:1 46
49:18 46

Exodus
1 50
3 50
12 98
12:44–49 98
13:12–15 394
14:13 .... 2, 46
14:19–21 46
17:8–16 389
20:2 51
20:2–3 51
34:6–7 10
34:7 10

Leviticus
12:2–4 394
26:17 390

Numbers
3:45 394

22:9 298
24:19 390

Deuteronomy
1:39 302
5:6 51
10:12–13 13
12:6 394
13:1–5 17
18:15 50
18:15–22 .... 17–18, 51
28 .... 45, 51
28:1–14 13–14
30:1–10 8

Joshua
5:4–8 98

1 Samuel
11 48
13:14 48

2 Samuel
3:18 45
7 365
7:14 209

1 Kings
5:4 390

Ezra
3:12 365

Job
14:21 319

Psalms
2 365

2:7 209
8:6 390
18:36 .... 45, 229
44:7 .... 45, 229
51 48–49
51:10 49
66:12 .... 45, 229
72:8 390
89:27 209
95:1–2 49
107 45
110:2 390

Ecclesiastes
9:10 319

Isaiah
7:14–15 302
9:1–2 367
9:6–7 366
11:1–9 366
14:6 390
26:18 366
37:14–20 230
38:9 45
42:1–9 367
49:5–6 367
52:13 – 53:12 371
53:4–6 13
54:11–15 373
58:6 249
60 366
61 .... 366, 370
61:1–2 249
61:1–6 373
61:1–11 366
61:2 248
65 366

Jeremiah 5, 117
1:10 11
2:27–28 2
3:23 2
4:6 7
4:14 2
5:1 9
6:13–14 17
6:19 7
7:16 9
8:3 10
8:10–11 17
8:20 2
10:10 117
10:21 9
11:11 7
11:12 2
11:14 8
11:23 7
14:11 9
15:20 2
16:15 10
18:11 7–8
19:3 7
21:10 7
23:3 10
23:3–8 .... 2, 7
23:5–6 2
23:5–8 366
23:8 10
23:21–22 17
24:4–7 7
24:8–10 3
24:9 10
25:8–14 3
25:11–12 7
26:3 8
27:6–8 3
27:12–22 3
27:22 7
28:2–4 3
28:11 3
28:15 3
29:4–14 16
29:4–23 3–4
29:5–6 17
29:5–9 11
29:7 .... 12, 17
29:8–9 17
29:9 18
29:10 17
29:10–11 7
29:10–14 .... 2, 6, 13, 15–16
29:11 .... 2, 11–15, 17–18
29:12–13 .... 8, 15
29:13 15
29:14 .... 10, 17
29:15–23 15
29:26 6
29:27 6
29:28 6
29:29–32 6
29:31 6
29:32 6
30:7 45
30:10–11 2
30:18–21 8
31:3 7
31:4–14 8
31:7–9 2
31:8 10
31:9 7
31:16–17 8
31:20 7
31:23–28 8
32:37 10
32:40–41 7
33:14 7
33:14–16 2
36:3 8
46:27–28 2

Ezekiel
34:4 390
36 366

Daniel
2:45 298
7:1–14 365
7:13–14 368
9:1–2 9
9:3 10
9:4–19 10

Hosea
1:7 230

Joel
2:32 15
4:13 390

Jonah
4:11 302

Zechariah
8:20–23 370
9:10 370

NEW TESTAMENT

Matthew
1:21 .... 51, 119, 230, 250
1:23 52
4:12–17 366
4:18–22 65
4:19 65
4:23–25 366
5 50
5:13 290
5:13–16 .... 282, 284, 370
5:28 229
6:19–21 13
6:25–34 14
7:15–20 17
8:25 .... 229, 250, 367
9 394
9:21 250
9:22 234

9:36 368
10:22 367
10:23 369
10:28 15
12:22 234
13:49 370
13:54–58 247
14:30 250
18:1–5 302
18:11 250
22:29–32 372
22:41–46 372
24:3 370
24:13 367
25:31 370
28:19 370

Mark
1:1–11 366
1:14–15 366
1:15 .... 15, 52
1:19–20 65
1:27 367
2:1–12 367
2:10 368
2:12 367
2:17 369
2:21–22 369
2:23 – 3:6 369
3:22–29 369
3:4 367
4:1–20 369
4:26–34 369
5:20 367
5:21–43 235
5:21 – 6:6 235
5:22–23 235
5:23 367
5:25 235
5:27–28 235
5:28 367
5:29 235
5:32 236
5:34 .... 234–235, 237, 367
6:1–6 247

6:56 367
7:24–30 370
7:37 367
8:22–25 371
8:27 368
8:31 370
8:31–38 370
8:34–35 371
8:35 367
8:38 370
9:12 372
9:22 234
9:30–34 370
10:32–45 370
10:45 .... 189, 235, 371
10:52 .... 234, 237, 367
11:17 .... 370, 372
12:1–12 370
12:10–11 372
13:10 370
15:29–31 144
15:30 230
16:16 .... 78, 278

Luke 248
1:1–4 .... 75, 247, 279
1:32–33 369
1:35 369
2:10–11 49
2:10–12 51
2:34–35 370
2:46–47 372
23:29 144
24:26 13
24:46–47 .... 280, 368
24:47 370
3:15 368
3:22 .... 248, 368
3:38 368
4:1 248
4:1–13 368
4:14 248
4:14–30 248
4:14–44 247
4:16–21 .... 36, 366

4:18 248–249
4:18–19 52
4:18–21 366
4:19–30 247
4:21 .... 369, 372
4:22b 370
4:24–27 370
4:38–40 65
4:40 228
4:43–44 247
5:1–11 65
5:17 248
5:24 368
6:5 368
7:1–10 370
7:18–23 370
7:34 368
7:50 234
8:12 367
8:36 .... 250, 367
8:42 235
8:48 234
9:22 368
9:26 370
10:21 248
11:20 369
12:35–48 369
13:3 15
13:22–35 370
15:7 49
16:19–31 319
17:11–19 367
17:19 234
17:20–21 369
18:8 370
19:1–10 370
19:9 228
19:10 .... 52, 250, 367

John
1:14 369
1:29 52
1:35–42 65
1:41 368
2:13–22 369

3:16 .... 146, 278	10:28 96	5:8 ....17, 61
3:16–17 60–61	10:44 87	5:9 ....14, 250
3:16–21 367	11:14 80–81	5:17 287
3:36 78	11:18 15	6:1–2 104
4:53 86	11:19–21 87	7:14–25 105
5:25–29 15	11:3 ....80, 96	8:15 .... 208, 218
6 394	12:12 234	8:16–23 12
8:12 367	12:25 234	8:17 14
8:24 15	13:22 48	8:18 13
8:56 298	14:3 87	8:18–25 377
10:10 368	14:17 304	8:21 286
10:30 295	14:22 12	8:23 .... 125, 208, 218
10:34–36 372	15 ....99, 234	8:28 .... 12, 15–16
12:23–30 371	16:9–10 82	8:29 .... 12, 280, 394
14:10 295	16:11–15 ....77, 82	8:30 14
14:11 295	16:13–15 82	10:8–15 61
14:6 295–296	16:14 82	10:9 .... 15, 78, 278
14:8–9 295	16:15 82–83	10:9–10 228
17 347	16:19–24 77	10:12 100
17:12 372	16:25–34 77	10:13 59
17:15–17 389	16:31 .... 15, 87, 278	10:14–15 301
19:19–20 371	16:40 82	11:16 125
19:28 372	17:6 282	12:1 198
19:30 371	18:4 83	12:3–8 394
	18:6 83	13:11 250
Acts	18:8 ....77, 83	14:7–8 289
1:1–5 279	20:27 238	14:18 118
2:16 99	27:20 .... 144, 230	15:5 125
2:21 ....15, 230	27:31 .... 144, 230	16:18 118
2:37–38 87	27:34 144	
2:38 ....15, 280		**1 Corinthians**
2:40 250	**Romans**	1:14 84
2:42–47 69	1:16 228	5:5 .... 144, 250
4:3 87	1:18–20 300	7:16 66
4:11–12 78	1:18–21 ......297–299, 302	9:5 65
4:12 230	1:20 299	10:14 117
4:33 87	2:14–15 300	12–14 394
8:1–4 12	3:22 101	15 144
9:32–34 87	3:22–23 100	15:19 13
9:36–43 87	3:23–24 60	15:20 125
10 69	3:25a 194	15:23 125
10:1 – 11:18 ......77, 80	3:26 101	15:42–57 14
10:1–2 80	4:3 298	16:15 125
10:2 80	5:1–5 238	
10:24 81	5:3–5 12	

Scripture Index   415

2 Corinthians
4:17 13
5:11–21 59
5:15 280
6:14–18 284

Galatians
1:6–7 97
2 94
2:1 94
2:1–5 98
2:1–10 97
2:3–6 94
2:7 95
2:7–8 .... 94, 96
2:9 95
2:11 96
2:11–14 97
2:11–21 .... 93, 95
2:14 98
2:15–16 99
2:15–21 .... 93, 96
2:17–18 103
2:17–20 105
2:19 104
2:19–20 105
2:20 61
2:20–21 105
3:1 104
3:6–7 101
3:13 .... 13, 105
3:22 101
3:24 105
3:28 104
4:29 53
4:5 .... 208, 218
5:13 104
5:16–25 61
5:22–23 49

Ephesians
1:3 .... 14, 17
1:3–14 14
1:5 .... 17, 67
1:6 17

1:7 .... 14, 17
1:9–10 286
1:10 377
1:11 14
1:13 14
2:1–10 60
2:4–5 17
2:5 87
2:7 13
2:8 .... 15, 78
2:8–10 24
2:12 99
2:19 67
4:7–16 394
4:15 67
4:22–24 280
5:8–9 282

Philippians
1:21 280
2:5–11 13
3:9 101
3:20 13
3:20–21 14
4:11–13 14

Colossians
1:19–20 377
1:20 286
3:1–2 13
3:5–11 280
3:24 118
4:10 234
4:10–11 247
4:14 247

1 Thessalonians
1:8 114
1:9b–10 114
1:10 .... 14, 121
2:13 125
2:14 .... 116, 127
2:16 111
3:13 118
4:3 14

4:4 118
4:7 118
4:15 122
5:1 120
5:2 120
5:2–3 121
5:5 120
5:8 111
5:8–10 120
5:9 111
5:9–10 230
5:23 118

2 Thessalonians
2:1 123
2:3 123
2:4 123
2:8–10 123
2:10 .... 111, 119, 124–125
2:10–14 123
2:11 124
2:12 124
2:13 .... 111, 124–125
2:13–14 124

1 Timothy
1:2 141
1:3–11 141
1:5 142
1:15 230
1:20 141
2 146
2:6 146
2:15 .... 133, 135, 142
3:1–7 394
4:3 148
5:8 66
5:15 141
5:20 141
6:3–10 141
6:6 14
6:6–8 14
6:20–21 141

2 Timothy
1:2–3 67
1:5 .... 67, 141
2:25 15
3:16 11
4:18 .... 146, 250

Titus
1:5–9 394
2:11–14 230
3:5 278

Hebrews
5:8 238
11:1–40 13
11:8–19 392
11:13 13
11:13–16 15
12:18–24 15

James
1:2–4 12
1:2–8 238
2:18–26 278

1 Peter
1:1 13
1:4 14
1:5 250
1:10–11 13
2:11 13
2:21 13
2:24 13
4:12–13 12
5:13 234

2 Peter
2:1–22 17

1 John
1:5–7 282
2:15–17 284
3:1 391
5:13 278

Revelation
3:20 60–61
5:10 14
20:15 15
21:1 14
21:1–5 377
21:3 14
22:1–5 377
22:5 14

Langham Literature and its imprints are a ministry of Langham Partnership.

Langham Partnership is a global fellowship working in pursuit of the vision God entrusted to its founder John Stott –

> *to facilitate the growth of the church in maturity and Christ-likeness through raising the standards of biblical preaching and teaching.*

Our vision is to see churches in the Majority World equipped for mission and growing to maturity in Christ through the ministry of pastors and leaders who believe, teach and live by the word of God.

Our mission is to strengthen the ministry of the word of God through:
- nurturing national movements for biblical preaching
- fostering the creation and distribution of evangelical literature
- enhancing evangelical theological education

especially in countries where churches are under-resourced.

Our ministry

Langham Preaching partners with national leaders to nurture indigenous biblical preaching movements for pastors and lay preachers all around the world. With the support of a team of trainers from many countries, a multi-level programme of seminars provides practical training, and is followed by a programme for training local facilitators. Local preachers' groups and national and regional networks ensure continuity and ongoing development, seeking to build vigorous movements committed to Bible exposition.

Langham Literature provides Majority World preachers, scholars and seminary libraries with evangelical books and electronic resources through publishing and distribution, grants and discounts. The programme also fosters the creation of indigenous evangelical books in many languages, through writer's grants, strengthening local evangelical publishing houses, and investment in major regional literature projects, such as one volume Bible commentaries like *The Africa Bible Commentary* and *The South Asia Bible Commentary*.

Langham Scholars provides financial support for evangelical doctoral students from the Majority World so that, when they return home, they may train pastors and other Christian leaders with sound, biblical and theological teaching. This programme equips those who equip others. Langham Scholars also works in partnership with Majority World seminaries in strengthening evangelical theological education. A growing number of Langham Scholars study in high quality doctoral programmes in the Majority World itself. As well as teaching the next generation of pastors, graduated Langham Scholars exercise significant influence through their writing and leadership.

To learn more about Langham Partnership and the work we do visit **langham.org**

www.ingramcontent.com/pod-product-compliance
Lightning Source LLC
Chambersburg PA
CBHW050133240426
43673CB00043B/1655